丛书主编 周江

海洋·极地·自然资源法研究丛书 国别海洋法系列

澳大利亚海洋法律体系研究

刘畅 著

知识产权出版社
全国百佳图书出版单位
—北京—

图书在版编目(CIP)数据

澳大利亚海洋法律体系研究/刘畅著.—北京：知识产权出版社,2025.1.—(海洋·极地·自然资源法研究丛书/周江主编).—ISBN 978–7–5130–9572–3

Ⅰ.D951.226

中国国家版本馆 CIP 数据核字第 2024RF2657 号

策划编辑：庞从容　　　　　　　　责任校对：谷　洋
责任编辑：张琪惠　　　　　　　　责任印制：孙婷婷
封面设计：黄慧君

澳大利亚海洋法律体系研究
刘　畅 ◎ 著

出版发行：	知识产权出版社 有限责任公司	网　　址：	http://www.ipph.cn
社　　址：	北京市海淀区气象路 50 号院	邮　　编：	100081
责编电话：	010-82000860 转 8782	责编邮箱：	963810650@qq.com
发行电话：	010-82000860 转 8101/8102	发行传真：	010-82000893/82005070/82000270
印　　刷：	北京建宏印刷有限公司	经　　销：	新华书店、各大网上书店及相关专业书店
开　　本：	710mm×1000mm　1/16	印　　张：	19.25
版　　次：	2025 年 1 月第 1 版	印　　次：	2025 年 1 月第 1 次印刷
字　　数：	356 千字	定　　价：	98.00 元
ISBN 978–7–5130–9572–3			

出版权专有　侵权必究
如有印装质量问题，本社负责调换。

重庆市高校哲学社会科学协同创新团队
"海洋与自然资源法研究团队"阶段性成果

总 序

中国是陆海兼备的海洋大国，海洋开发历史悠久，曾创造了举世瞩目的海洋文明。"鱼盐之利，舟楫之便"是先人认识和利用海洋之精炼概括，仍不悖于当今海洋之时势。然数百年前，泰西诸国携坚船利炮由海而至，先祖眼中的天然屏障竟成列强鱼肉九州之通道。海洋强国兴衰，殷鉴不远。

吾辈身处百年未有之变局，加快建设海洋强国已成为中华民族伟大复兴的重要组成。扎实的海洋工业、尖端的海洋科技及强大的海军战力，无疑为海洋强国之必需。此外，完备的海洋治理体系和卓越的海洋治理能力等软实力亦不可或缺。海洋治理体系之完备，海洋治理能力之卓越，皆与海洋法治息息相关。经由法律的治理以造福生民，为古今中外人类实践之最佳路径。

海洋法治之达致，需赖全体国人之努力，应无沿海内陆之别。西南政法大学虽处内陆，一向以"心系天下"为精神导引。作为中国法学教育研究的重镇，西南政法大学独具光荣的历史传承、深厚的学术底蕴和完备的人才积累。她以党的基本理论、基本路线、基本方略和国家的重大战略需求为学术研究之出发点和归宿。

西南政法大学海洋与自然资源法研究所之成立，正是虑及吾辈应为建设海洋强国贡献绵薄。其国际法学院、经济法学院（生态法学院）、国家安全学院相关研究团队，合众为一，同心勠力，与中国海洋法学会合作共建而成。我所将持续系统地研究涉海法律问题，现以"海洋·极地·自然资源法研究丛书"之名，推出首批公开出版成果。

本丛书拟设四大系列：国别海洋法系列、海洋治理系列、极地治理系列及自然资源法系列。系列之间既各有侧重又相互呼应，其共同的目标在于助力中国海洋治理体系与治理能力的现代化。

本丛书推崇创作之包容性，对当下及今后各作者的学术观点，都将予以最大程度的尊重；本丛书亦秉持研究之开放性，诚挚欢迎同人惠赐契合丛书主题及各系列议题的佳作；本丛书更倡导学术的批判性，愿广纳学友对同一问题的补正、商榷甚或质疑。若经由上述努力与坚持，可将本丛书打造为学界交流与争鸣的平台，则是我们莫大的荣幸。

本丛书能由构想变为现实，离不开诸多前辈、领导及同人的关心、指导与支持，我相信，丛书的付梓是对他们玉成此事最好的感谢！

是为序！

周江

2020 年 3 月 31 日

目　录

一、澳大利亚海洋基本情况 / 001
　　（一）海洋地理概况 / 001
　　（二）政治和外交概况 / 002
　　（三）海洋经济及海洋资源利用概况 / 003

二、海洋事务主管部门及其职能 / 007
　　（一）基本政治结构 / 007
　　（二）海洋管理相关的行政机构 / 008
　　（三）海上武装执法机构 / 021

三、国内海洋立法 / 027
　　（一）划定管辖海域的法 / 028
　　（二）海上安全相关立法 / 058
　　（三）海洋渔业相关立法 / 065
　　（四）海洋能源相关立法 / 068
　　（五）海上运输相关立法 / 072
　　（六）海洋环境保护立法 / 079

四、缔结和加入的国际海洋法条约 / 093
　　（一）联合国框架下的海洋法公约 / 093
　　（二）南极条约体系下的相关公约 / 096
　　（三）国际海事组织框架下的相关条约 / 098

五、海洋争端解决 / 102
　　（一）与葡萄牙、东帝汶之间的帝汶海相关争端 / 102
　　（二）通过协议解决的其他海洋划界争端 / 122
　　（三）通过法律方法解决的海洋渔业相关争端 / 151

六、国际海洋合作 / 166

  （一）海洋防务合作 / 166

  （二）海洋油气资源合作 / 181

  （三）海洋渔业合作 / 184

  （四）海洋研究合作 / 186

  （五）区域性国际合作 / 189

  （六）全球性国际组织框架下的合作 / 195

七、对中国海洋法主张的态度 / 199

  （一）对"南海仲裁案"的态度 / 199

  （二）对《南海各方行为宣言》及"南海行为准则"的态度 / 210

  （三）在"一带一路"框架下与中国合作的态度 / 213

结　语 / 220

参考文献 / 223

附　录 / 228

  附录 1　1973 年《海洋与水下土地法》 / 228

  附录 2　《海洋与水下土地（领海基线）2016 年公告》 / 237

  附录 3　《海洋与水下土地 2005 年 1 号修订公告》 / 256

  附录 4　《海洋与水下土地（大陆架界限）2012 年公告》 / 260

  附录 5　《海洋与水下土地（历史性海湾）2016 年公告》 / 264

  附录 6　1933 年《澳大利亚南极领地接纳法》 / 267

  附录 7　1954 年《澳大利亚南极领地法》 / 268

  附录 8　2018 年《澳大利亚与东帝汶民主共和国确立在
帝汶海海洋边界的条约》 / 275

  附录 9　澳大利亚缔结和加入的国际海洋法条约 / 297

一、澳大利亚海洋基本情况

澳大利亚是南半球最大的国家，也是世界上唯一一个独占一个大陆的国家，其由澳大利亚大陆、塔斯马尼亚岛（Tasmania）等岛屿和海外领地组成，国土面积居世界第6位。[1] 在澳大利亚768.82万平方公里的领土中，有约70%处于干旱或半干旱地带，大部分地区不适宜人类居住，该国主要依靠沿海地带，特别是东南沿海的一片环绕大陆的"绿带"区域支撑其人口养育与经济发展。[2]

1770年，英国航海家詹姆斯·库克（James Cook）抵达澳大利亚东海岸，宣布英国将占有这片土著人居住的土地。1788年1月26日，英国流放到澳大利亚的第一批犯人抵达悉尼湾，英国开始在澳大利亚建立殖民地，后来这一天被定为澳大利亚国庆日。1901年，澳大利亚各殖民区改为州，成立澳大利亚联邦。1931年，澳大利亚成为英联邦内的独立国家，并于1986年获得完全立法权和司法终审权。[3]

（一）海洋地理概况

澳大利亚位于南太平洋和印度洋之间，四面临海，没有陆地邻国，东濒太平洋，北、西、南三面临印度洋及其边缘海，海岸线长36735公里。在太平洋水域，澳大利亚向东与新西兰隔海相望，其大陆东南岸与新西兰的北岛（North Island）之间是水域宽广的塔斯曼海（Tasman Sea）；在印度洋水域，澳大利亚向北临帝汶海（Timor Sea）、阿拉弗拉海（Arafura Sea）及珊瑚海（Coral Sea），与印度尼西亚、巴布亚新几内亚隔海相望。[4] 澳大利亚的海岸线总体平缓，大陆周围分布着诸多海峡、海湾和半岛。其主要海峡包括：位于昆士兰州约克角半岛（Cape York Peninsula）与新几内亚岛（New Guinea Island）之间的托雷斯海峡（Torres Strait），位于维多利亚州与塔斯马尼亚岛之间的巴斯海峡

---

[1] 沈永兴、张秋生、高国荣编著：《列国志·澳大利亚》，社会科学文献出版社2010年版，第1页。
[2] 薛桂芳：《澳大利亚海洋战略研究》，时事出版社2016年版，第12页。
[3] 《澳大利亚国家概况》，载中华人民共和国外交部网站，https://www.mfa.gov.cn/web/gjhdq_676201/gj_676203/dyz_681240/1206_681242/1206x0_681244/，最后访问日期：2022年3月21日。
[4] 沈永兴、张秋生、高国荣编著：《列国志·澳大利亚》，社会科学文献出版社2010年版，第2页。

(Bass Strait)。其主要海湾包括：位于澳大利亚大陆北部的卡奔塔利亚湾（Gulf of Carpentaria），以及该海湾以西面积较小的范迪门湾（Van Diemen Gulf）、比格尔湾（Beagle Bay）、约瑟夫·波拿巴湾（Joseph Bonaparte Gulf）；位于澳大利亚大陆以南的宽广开阔、宛如弓形的大澳大利亚湾（Great Australian Bight），以及在该海湾东侧的斯宾塞湾（Spencer Gulf）、圣文森特湾（Saint Vincent Gulf）和恩康特湾（Encounter Bay）。其主要半岛包括：坐落于北部海湾的约克角半岛，以及散布于南部海湾的艾尔半岛（Eyre Peninsula）、约克半岛（Yorke Peninsula）。位于澳大利亚东北部与巴布亚新几内亚之间的珊瑚海因生长着众多珊瑚礁群而闻名。其中，澳大利亚大堡礁（The Great Barrier Reef）由南向北绵延2000多公里，最宽处161公里，被联合国教科文组织列为世界遗产。[1]

（二）政治和外交概况

澳大利亚定都堪培拉（Canberra），全国划分为6个州和2个地区。其中，6个州分别是新南威尔士州（New South Wales）、维多利亚州（Victoria）、昆士兰州（Queensland）、南澳大利亚州（South Australia）、西澳大利亚州（West Australia）、塔斯马尼亚州；2个地区分别是北方领地地区（Northern Territory）和首都领地地区（Australian Capital Territory）。[2]

在外交方面，澳大利亚的外交政策以亚太地区为首要关注对象，围绕地缘政治与战略安全的利益、经济与贸易的利益、国际成员的责任等考量因素，将自己定位为本区域的负责任大国，并长期将"印太地区"（The Indo-Pacific）的安全、开放和繁荣视为国家利益关注的重心。据澳大利亚政府相关文件，澳大利亚所称印太地区是指从印度洋东部至邻接东南亚之太平洋的区域，印度、北亚（North Asia）及美国均被涵盖其中。近年来，澳大利亚观察发现，全球化所带来的经济增长正反过来改变着该区域的权力平衡。为保障国家的安全与繁荣，澳大利亚政府制定了对外交往的五大目标：第一，促进印太地区的开放、包容与繁盛富足，尊重域内所有国家的权利；第二，在全球范围内提供更多商业机遇，并坚定反对保护主义；第三，保障澳大利亚人民在恐怖主义等的威胁下持续的安全、安定与自由；第四，倡行并维护支持稳定与繁荣的国际规则，并推进合作以应对全球挑战；第五，采取行动以

---

[1] 高京：《澳大利亚》，世界知识出版社1997年版，第3页；沈永兴、张秋生、高国荣编著：《列国志·澳大利亚》，社会科学文献出版社2010年版，第2页。

[2] 《澳大利亚国家概况》，载中华人民共和国外交部网站，https://www.mfa.gov.cn/web/gjhdq_676201/gj_676203/dyz_681240/1206_681242/1206x0_681244/，最后访问日期：2022年3月21日。

支持太平洋与东帝汶的发展。[1] 当前，澳大利亚"在坚持巩固澳美同盟、发挥联合国作用以及拓展与亚洲联系三大传统外交政策的基础上，通过积极参与全球和地区热点问题提升国际影响力，着力推进'积极的有创造力的中等大国外交'"[2]。

在上述外交基调与目标定位之下，澳大利亚表现出对海洋安全保障的极高重视。其指出，当前印太地区各国都在加强军事及民事海洋能力建设，一则域内海洋边界摩擦不断，二则海上恐怖主义及犯罪威胁不断增加，因此澳大利亚将着力加大对东南亚海洋安保能力建设的投入，推动在东亚峰会（East Asia Summit）、环印度洋联盟（The Indian Ocean Rim Association）等区域性论坛中对海洋问题的关注，强化对海洋领域意识的相关培训，保护海洋环境，维护国际法。

与此同时，南极及其周边海域问题则成为澳大利亚外交战略规划中的特色聚焦点。一方面，澳大利亚自视为《南极条约》（Antarctic Treaty）最具影响力的缔约方之一，一直忠实维护该条约的效力与执行，贯彻其环境保护与非军事化的原则，以确保南极成为有益于和平与科学之地，并减少澳大利亚以南潜在的战略竞争。另一方面，澳大利亚并不避讳其对南极的"勃勃雄心"，坚称对42%以上的南极大陆及其邻近海域享有主权，通过制订"澳大利亚南极战略及20年行动计划"（Australian Antarctic Strategy & 20 Year Action Plan，以下简称"战略及行动计划"）将具体行动提上日程，并有意加强对塔斯马尼亚岛的开发建设。[3]

（三）海洋经济及海洋资源利用概况

澳大利亚属工业化、高收入国家。2023年，澳大利亚国内生产总值达1.69万亿美元。[4] 澳大利亚既有发达的农牧业，自然资源丰富，盛产羊、牛、小麦和蔗糖，又有支柱性的采矿业，是世界重要的矿产品生产和出口国。在产业结构上，农牧业、采矿业为澳大利亚的传统产业，制造业和高科

---

[1] "2017 Foreign Policy White Paper", The Australian Department of Foreign Affairs and Trade, https://www.dfat.gov.au/publications/minisite/2017-foreign-policy-white-paper/fpwhitepaper/pdf/2017-foreign-policy-w-hite-paper.pdf, pp. 1-3, June 5, 2022.

[2] 《澳大利亚国家概况》，载中华人民共和国外交部网站，https://www.mfa.gov.cn/web/gjhdq_676201/gj_676203/dyz_681240/1206_681242/1206x0_681244/，最后访问日期：2022年3月21日。

[3] "2017 Foreign Policy White Paper", The Australian Department of Foreign Affairs and Trade, https://www.dfat.gov.au/publications/minisite/2017-foreign-policy-white-paper/fpwhitepaper/pdf/2017-foreign-policy-white-paper.pdf, pp. 47, 85, June 5, 2022.

[4] 《澳大利亚国家概况》，载中华人民共和国外交部网站，https://www.mfa.gov.cn/web/gjhdq_676201/gj_676203/dyz_681240/1206_681242/1206x0_681244/，最后访问日期：2024年9月10日。

技产业发展迅速，服务业也已成为国民经济主导产业。1991—2019年，澳大利亚连续28年经济保持正增长。不过，受新冠疫情和山火灾害影响，其2019—2020财年经济出现负增长。[1]

澳大利亚将近1400万平方公里海域纳入其海洋管辖及海洋经济的覆盖范围，所主张区域包括专属经济区、大陆架及毗邻澳大利亚所谓"南极领土"的海洋区域，为世界第三大沿海国管辖海域，占全球海洋面积的4%。[2] 澳大利亚宣称其国家领土的70%都在海水之下，而其人口的近85%都集中生活在距海岸线不足50公里的临海地带。2017—2018年，澳大利亚蓝色经济的产出价值为812亿美元，在过去20年里增长了4倍，其海洋产业涵盖了4大类，涉及14个海洋产业部门。第一类为海洋资源型产业，涉及与海洋资源利用直接相关的产业及其下游加工业，包括海洋油气业、渔业（商业捕鱼和休闲捕鱼）、海水养殖业、海底采矿业、依托海洋景观的国内和国际旅游业；第二类为海洋系统设计与建造业，包括船舶设计、建造和维修、近海工程和海岸工程；第三类为海上作业与航运业，包括海上运输系统、漂浮和固定海洋结构物的安装、潜水作业、疏浚和倾废等；第四类为与海洋有关的设备和服务业，包括海洋电子和仪器仪表制造、海上设施工程建造及咨询、海上通信及导航系统、海上设施设备专用软件及决策支持工具、海洋科考相关勘测服务等。[3] 据澳大利亚官方公布的相关数据，海洋经济为该国的繁荣作出了巨大贡献，2019年以前每年创造超过740亿美元的价值；即使受新冠疫情影响澳大利亚的国际旅游业出现下滑，2020年后海洋产业对澳大利亚国内生产总值的贡献仍增长至每年1000亿美元以上。[4]

在海洋渔业资源方面，澳大利亚的海洋渔业被划分为商业性捕捞、休闲性捕捞与土著人捕捞三大类。早在被欧洲国家殖民之前，渔业活动便是澳大

---

[1]《澳大利亚国家概况》，载中华人民共和国外交部网站，https://www.mfa.gov.cn/web/gjhdq_676201/gj_676203/dyz_681240/1206_681242/1206x0_681244/，最后访问日期：2022年3月21日。

[2] "Geoscience Australia's Marine Strategy 2018-2023", Geoscience Australia, https://ecat.ga.gov.au/geonetw-ork/srv/eng/catalog.search#/metadata/145244, March 22, 2022.

[3] 薛桂芳：《澳大利亚海洋战略研究》，时事出版社2016年版，第182页。

[4] See "Australian Institute of Marine Science Strategy 2025", The Australian Institute of Marine Science, https://www.aims.gov.au/sites/default/files/AIMS_Strategy-2025-Web.pdf, March 22, 2022; "Australian Institute of Marine Science Strategy 2030", The Australian Institute of Marine Science, https://www.aims.gov.au/sites/default/files/2023-07/AIMS751_Strategy30-Report_July2023web.pdf#:~:text=Strategy%202030%20provides%20a%20concise%2C%20clear%20and%20compact%20part%20of%20our%20mandated%20reporting%20requirements%20to%20government, July 12, 2023.

利亚土著人文化和信仰的体现。[1] 澳大利亚土著人是澳大利亚大陆及其附近岛屿族群的后代，他们傍海而生，捕鱼既是其生存手段，也能为其带来贸易机遇及就业机会，因此海洋渔业对于沿海土著居民和托雷斯海峡岛民的经济生活和可持续发展都至关重要。[2] 当前，澳大利亚是南半球最发达的海洋国家，所主张管辖的海域面积远超陆地领土面积，渔业资源丰富，有3000多种海水和淡水鱼以及3000多种甲壳及软体类水产品，其中已进行商业捕捞的约为600种。最主要的水产品有对虾、龙虾、鲍鱼、金枪鱼、扇贝、牡蛎等。[3] 2017—2018年，澳大利亚野生捕捞渔业的经济产出约为18亿美元。作为最有价值的野生捕捞物种，岩龙虾、对虾和鲍鱼共占野生捕捞渔业经济产出的64%。而水产养殖业的经济产出为14亿美元，其中鲑鱼、金枪鱼和牡蛎养殖贡献最大。海洋休闲性捕捞所产出的经济价值约为5.26亿美元。

在海洋油气资源方面，离岸油气资源的勘探和开发是澳大利亚近年来蓝色经济产出的最大贡献源。离岸油气产业产值在2017—2018年出现明显增长，这既受国内及出口销售价格上升的影响，也离不开海上油气勘探、输送管道等基础设施建设与维持运转等实质生产活动的带动。澳大利亚的油气开采生产主要依赖于分属联邦下不同州及领地地区的几大油气盆地。其中，西澳大利亚无论是海上石油、海上液化石油气还是海上天然气的开采都在各州中居于首位，其在2017—2018年度的产出值分别为：石油逾42亿美元、液化石油气逾5亿美元、天然气逾250亿美元。[4]

在海上运输方面，澳大利亚是世界航运大国之一，货运的相当一部分都依靠沿海航运，其原材料出口等出口货运更有99%均依赖海上运输。除传统运输业的维持与激活外，澳大利亚还致力于在海上航运新技术（无人驾驶船舶）研究与人才培养中争取领先地位。同时，通过与国际海事组织（International Maritime Organization）合作，积极推行国际海洋减排措施，提出至2030

---

[1] "Aboriginal Australians", National Geographic, https：//www.nationalgeographic.com/culture/article/aborigin-al-australians, April 4, 2022.

[2] "Fishing", Australian Institute of Aboriginal and Torres Strait Islander Studies, https：//aiatsis.gov.au/expl-ore/fishing#：~：text=Today%2C%20Aboriginal%20and%20Torres%20Strait%20Islander%20peoples%20primarily, on%20the%20South%20Coast%20of%20New%20South%20Wales, April 4, 2022.

[3]《澳大利亚国家概况》，载中华人民共和国外交部网站，https：//www.mfa.gov.cn/web/gjhdq_676201/gj_676203/dyz_681240/1206_681242/1206x0_681244/，最后访问日期：2022年3月21日。

[4] "The AIMS Index of Marine Industry 2020", The Australian Institute of Marine Science, https：//www.a-ims.gov.au/sites/default/files/2021-07/The%20AIMS%20Index%20of%20Marine%20Industry_final_21Jan2021_web.pdf, April 2, 2022.

年将国际航运的碳排放强度降至 2008 年的 40%，以巩固并维护其在国际海洋环境保护中的标杆国形象。[1]

在海上旅游方面，澳大利亚的旅游业与其海洋资源密切关联，被视为海洋经济能力的重要指标，也为其带来了重大的产业价值。例如，2017—2018 年，澳大利亚的国内海洋旅游消费约为 240 亿美元，国际海洋旅游消费约为 67 亿美元，其国内及国际海洋旅游业产出最高的 3 个州均为昆士兰州、新南威尔士州和维多利亚州。[2] 在遭受疫情重创之后，澳大利亚从联邦、各地区及各社区多层面采取措施，包括为其量身定做的"一揽子"经济计划、与多个太平洋岛国合作等，以促进海上旅游业复苏，重建相关海洋经济产业群。

---

[1] "Annual Report 2021-22", The Australian Department of Infrastructure, Transport, Regional Development, Communications and the Arts, https：//www.infrastructure.gov.au/sites/default/files/documents/ditrdc-annual-report-2021-22.pdf, January 2, 2023.

[2] "The AIMS Index of Marine Industry 2020", The Australian Institute of Marine Science, https：//www.a-ims.gov.au/sites/default/files/2021-07/The% 20AIMS% 20Index% 20of% 20Marine% 20Industry_final_21Jan2021_web.pdf, April 2, 2022.

二、海洋事务主管部门及其职能

（一）基本政治结构

澳大利亚为联邦制君主立宪制国家，与英国共戴一君，国家元首为英国国王。总督为国王代表，任期5年。现任总督戴维·赫尔利（David Hurley），于2019年7月1日宣誓就职。在政治体制上，澳大利亚沿袭英国式的议会制度，依照英国威斯敏斯特体制组建立法机关、行政机关和司法机关。

1. 立法机关

澳大利亚联邦议会是澳大利亚主要的立法机关。澳大利亚联邦议会成立于1901年，由国王（澳总督为其代表）、众议院和参议院组成。议会实行普选。众议院由151名议员组成，按人口比例选举产生，任期3年。参议院由76名议员组成，其中6个州每州占12个名额，2个地区各占2个名额。各州参议员任期6年，每3年改选一半，各地区参议员任期3年。[1]

为履行立法职能，除宪法第53条规定的特定事项外，联邦议会中的参议院与众议院对相关立法案具有同等的权限。联邦议会主要围绕下列事项行使立法权：（1）对外贸易和州际贸易；（2）征税，但各州间和各州的各地区间不得差别对待；（3）货物生产和出口的津贴，但整个联邦内的津贴应一致；（4）以联邦的信用举债；（5）邮政、电报、电话及其他类似事业；（6）联邦和各州的海军防卫、陆军防卫，以及管控武装部队以执行和维护联邦法律；（7）灯塔、灯船、信标和浮标；（8）天文和气象观测；（9）防疫；（10）领土范围外的澳大利亚管辖海域的渔业；（11）人口普查和统计；（12）通货、铸币和合法货币；（13）不属于州的银行业和本州以外的他州银行业，包括银行的设立和货币的发行；（14）不属于州的保险业和本州以外的他州保险业；（15）度量衡；（16）票据；（17）破产和无能力清偿债务；（18）版权、发明和设计专利权、商标；（19）入籍和外国人；（20）外国公司，在联邦境内设立的贸易公司和金融公司；（21）婚姻；（22）离婚和婚姻诉讼以及与此有关的亲权、未成年人的保育与监护；（23）残疾人和老年人的养老金，产妇津贴，儿童基金、失业、

---

[1] 《澳大利亚国家概况》，载中华人民共和国外交部官网，https://www.mfa.gov.cn/web/gjhdq_676201/gj_676203/dyz_681240/1206_681242/1206x0_681244/，最后访问日期：2022年4月4日。

药物、疾病和住院救济金，医科和牙科免费医疗，学生补助金和家庭津贴，等等。此外，对于下列事项，联邦议会在各州议会外享有单独立法权：（1）联邦政府所在地的相关事项及因公共利益而归属于联邦的各地方的相关事项；（2）关于根据宪法已移交给联邦政府任何部门的公共事业管理权的事项；（3）其他经宪法宣布为完全属于联邦议会权力范围的事项。[1]

2. 行政机关

澳大利亚联邦的行政机关由代表国王的总督、总理及各部部长组成。联邦行政权名义上属于国王，由总督以国王代表的名义行使，总督依据联邦行政会议（Federal Executive Council，以下称"内阁"）的建议任命联邦各部部长，并在内阁的建议下行使行政权。政府实权由总理领导的内阁掌握，总督无权代表政府进行决策，但在各议会及政府中均有独特地位。为构建负责任的政府（responsible government），澳大利亚联邦政府由众议院多数党或政党联盟组成，由该党领袖任总理，一般任期3年，向联邦议会负责。

3. 司法机关

1963年之前，英国国会上议院所作判决在澳大利亚均具有法律强制力。直至1978年，澳大利亚高等法院宣布英国枢密院司法委员会的判决对澳大利亚不再具有强制适用性，并且分别于1975年和1986年最终废除了由澳大利亚高等法院和州法院向英国枢密院上诉的机制。[2] 现今，联邦高等法院是澳大利亚最高司法机构，由1名首席大法官和6名大法官组成，对其他各级法院具有上诉管辖权，并可对涉及宪法解释的案件作出决定。各州设最高法院、区法院和地方法院，首都领地地区和北方领地地区只设最高法院和地方法院。[3]

（二）海洋管理相关的行政机构

1. 澳大利亚基础设施、交通、区域发展、通信和艺术部

澳大利亚基础设施、交通、区域发展、通信和艺术部（Department of In-

---

[1] "The Australian Constitution", article 51, 52, Parliament of Australia, https://www.aph.gov.au/About_Parliament/Senate/Po-wers_practice_n_procedures/Constitution/chapter2, June 16, 2022; "Separation of powers: Parliament, Executive and Judiciary", Parliamentary Education Office, https://peo.gov.au/understand-our-parliament/how-parliam-ent-works/syste-m-of-government/separation-of-powers/, June 16, 2022.

[2]《澳大利亚》，载中华人民共和国商务部全球法规网站，http://poli-cy.mofcom.gov.cn/page/nation/Australia.html，最后访问日期：2022年4月5日。

[3]《澳大利亚国家概况》，载中华人民共和国外交部网站，https://www.mfa.gov.cn/web/gjhdq_676201/gj_676203/dyz_681240/1206_681242/1206x0_681244/，最后访问日期：2022年4月3日。

frastructure, Transport, Regional Development, Communications and the Arts, 以下简称"澳基建运输部")于2022年7月改组,是澳大利亚政府整合了原基础设施、区域发展及城市、通信和艺术各职能部门后的主要部门之一,由7名部长级官员领导,下设1名秘书长及分管不同具体事务的6名助理秘书长。该重组部门的主要职能为:第一,地区开发建设,持续提升各城市及地区的生活水平,并助力其经济发展;第二,加强交通运输的覆盖连接,为更高效、可持续、安全及便利的交通系统提供支持,并通过相关基础设施投资提供工作岗位;第三,提升通信连接品质,使澳大利亚人民得以接入有效、安全的通信服务网,增加在通信技术领域的投资,以促进兼容且可持续的经济发展;第四,为北方领地地区和首都领地地区提供治理架构及相关服务以支持其社区发展;第五,支持可持续且具有包容性的文创事业,以保护和推广澳大利亚及其文化;第六,建设水资源相关基础设施,为区域发展及经济韧性提供支撑,提高农业及工业用水的可及性、连通性、可靠性及安全性。[1]

作为澳大利亚政府主要的海上航运监督和管理机构,澳基建运输部为发展澳大利亚经济和维护澳大利亚的海上利益作出了重要贡献,其通过极具效率的航运监管框架以及相关环境、安全法规,保证了澳大利亚航运系统的高效、安全运转。依澳基建运输部当前的职能分工,其在海洋管理方面的职能主要由其下设的澳大利亚海事安全局(Australian Maritime Safety Authority,以下简称"海安局")负责,并通过对澳大利亚国家海洋博物馆(Australian National Maritime Museum)的管理建设有效传扬了国家海洋文化。[2]

(1) 澳大利亚海事安全局。

澳大利亚海安局是根据1990年《澳大利亚海事安全局法》(Australian Maritime Safety Authority Act 1990)的规定设立,为联邦政府的部管局,是澳大利亚负责海洋管理的专门机构,其在海事航行安全、海洋环境保护、航空航海搜救等方面承担重要职能。根据上述法案,海安局的职能主要包括:第一,防治海洋环境污染(侧重于海上航行造成的污染);第二,提供海事搜索救援服务;第三,有条件地依据联邦政府、州政府、首都领地地区政府、北方领地地区政府及其下属机构的要求提供海事方面的服务;第四,与澳大利亚运输安全机构合作,依据2003年《运输安全调查法》(Transport Safety

---

[1] "About us", The Australian Department of Infrastructure, Transport, Regional Development, Communications and the Arts, https://www.infrastructure.gov.au/about-us, June 16, 2022.

[2] "Maritime", The Australian Department of Infrastructure, Transport, Regional Development, Communications and the Arts, https://www.infrastructure.gov.au/infrastructure-transport-vehicles/maritime, April 3, 2022.

Investigation Act 2003）进行航空和海洋航行调查；第五，其他与其职能、宗旨相关的工作及其他法案规定的工作；第六，履行澳大利亚签署的国际条约中规定的义务。在履行职能的过程中，由澳基建运输部部长向海安局提供具体的指引及关联文件和信息，海安局则每年向澳基建运输部部长提交年度报告。

海安局下设董事会、首席执行官。董事会由澳基建运输部领导，其由主席、副主席、执行官、5名成员和1名投资部门派驻的官员组成，主要职能是为海安局制定目标及政策，并保证海安局以高效、合适的方式履行职能。[1] 首席执行官在董事会的领导下具体负责监管四大职能的运行，包括：政策与规章（Policy and Regulation）职能，制定维护澳大利亚水域内所有船舶的海上航行安全和海洋环境保护相关的监管制度框架和标准；运营（Operations）职能，确保澳大利亚国内和国际航运按照监管制度框架安全运营，同时负责所涉船务登记、港务管理、许可证发放等常规业务；应急响应（Emergency Response）职能，通过下设的应急反应中心、联合行动小组、设备管理与评估小组、国家搜索救助理事会，负责为海事和航空部门提供全国搜救服务、海洋污染防治服务，并为海上航行安全提供设备和相关技术支持；企业服务（Corporate Services）职能，为海安局相关合作单位提供商务及技术的支持和协调，包括金融财务、人力资源、信息技术、公司治理等多项服务。[2]

近年来，海安局尤其在以下工作推进中卓有成效：第一，改善澳大利亚的海洋安全环境，提高海洋应急反应能力，包括通过建立健全各种标准、指南以及加强执行能力以提高海事管理法规的运行效率，同时增强应对复杂海洋环境问题的应急能力和海洋搜救能力；第二，加强对海洋环境的保护以应对气候变化带来的影响和挑战，通过国际海事组织就温室气体排放标准的发展与全球应对发挥其影响力，同时提升能力以高效应对各种海洋意外污染事件；第三，有效利用和积极创新相关应急救援技术，包括加大对相应信息技术系统的研发投入以充分利用多渠道海洋信息。

（2）澳大利亚国家海洋博物馆。

澳大利亚国家海洋博物馆于1990年依《澳大利亚国家海洋博物馆法》（Australian National Maritime Museum Act 1990）而设立，是隶属于澳基建运输

---

[1] "AMSA Board", Australian Maritime Safety Authority, https：//www.amsa.gov.au/about/who-we-are/amsa-b-oard, April 3, 2022.

[2] "Our structure", Australian Maritime Safety Authority, https：//www.amsa.gov.au/sites/default/files/2024-10/amsa-org-chart-oct2024.pdf, April 3, 2022.

部的事业单位公司实体。[1] 该博物馆位于悉尼的达令港（Darling Harbor），目前由一个十余人的董事会管理，其主要的职能有：第一，在澳大利亚国内外展示或供他人展示博物馆收藏的或博物馆以其他方式拥有的海事历史材料；第二，其他机构（无论是公共机构还是私人机构）合作展示或提供展示此类收藏品；第三，根据相关法律开发、保存和维护国家海洋收藏品；第四，传播与澳大利亚航海历史有关以及与博物馆职能有关的资料信息；第五，安排、开展和协助开展与澳大利亚海洋历史研究有关的事项；第六，开展服务于博物馆工作目标与功能实现相关的营销等商业活动。[2]

2. 澳大利亚农业、渔业与林业部

澳大利亚农业、渔业与林业部（Department of Agriculture, Fisheries and Forestry，以下简称"澳农渔林部"）于2022年7月由原来的农业与水资源部分立组建，是澳大利亚政府的主要职能部门之一。该部由1名部长领导，下设4个分管各部分职能的小组办公室以及多个承担具体职能的部管局。澳农渔林部的主要目标为：巩固和发展澳大利亚的农业、渔业和林业产业，创造和维持农业出口机会，为澳大利亚农业提供收益；防范国家生物安全风险，以保护澳大利亚的农业产业和人民的生活方式。[3]

在海洋管理方面，澳农渔林部的主要职能为：监管1999年《环境保护与生物多样性养护法》（Environment Protection and Biodiversity Conservation Act 1999）的施行，维护海洋生物多样性并防止外来海洋生物的入侵与威胁；保护澳大利亚海洋环境，管理澳大利亚海洋渔业，养护澳大利亚海洋资源，提高其产出；等等。在该部门的主导下，澳大利亚参与了多个区域渔业管理组织，包括：南方蓝鳍金枪鱼养护委员会（The Commission for the Conservation of Southern Bluefin Tuna，CCSBT）、印度洋金枪鱼委员会（Indian Ocean Tuna Commission，IOTC）、南太平洋区域渔业管理组织（South Pacific Regional Fisheries Management Organization，SPRFMO）、中西太平洋渔业委员会（The Western and Central Pacific Fisheries Commission，WCPFC）。同时，澳大利亚也在该部门的组织协调下参与了关于渔业问题的系列多边和区域论坛。如，南极海洋生物资源养护委员会（Commission for the Conservation of Antarctic Marine Living Resources，CCAMLR）、联合国粮农组织渔业委员会（United

---

[1] "About the museum", Australian National Maritime Museum, https://www.sea.museum/about/about-the-mu-seum, July 2, 2022.

[2] See "Australian National Maritime Museum Act 1990" section 6.

[3] "Science and research", The Australian Department of Agriculture, Fisheries and Forestry, https://www.agr-iculture.gov.au/about/who-we-are, July 3, 2022.

Nations Food and Agriculture Organization Committee on Fisheries，COFI），以及包括太平洋岛国论坛渔业局（The Pacific Islands Forum Fisheries Agency，FFA）、太平洋共同体秘书处（Secretariat of the Pacific Community）在内的太平洋区域论坛机构。[1] 而在该部门中，承担上述海洋管理方面职能的主要下设机关为澳大利亚渔业管理局（Australian Fisheries Management Authority，AFMA）和国家渔业咨询委员会（National Fishing Advisory Council）。

（1）澳大利亚渔业管理局。

澳大利亚渔业管理局于1991年在《渔政法》（Fisheries Administration Act 1991）和《渔业管理法》（Fisheries Management Act 1991）的授权下成立，是澳农渔林部下属的专门负责高效管理海洋渔业资源和保证渔业资源可持续发展利用的政府机构。当前，澳大利亚渔业管理局由渔业管理局委员会与1名首席执行官共同负责，该首席执行官同时也是该委员会的唯一全职成员。在责任分配上，渔业管理局委员会主要负责国内渔业的监管，而首席执行官则负责保证在澳大利亚管辖水域作业的外国相关从业方遵守澳方法律法规，同时协助委员会工作，并执行委员会作出的决定。首席执行官根据其主管部长的指示，对渔业管理局下设职能部门负责。这些职能部门主要有3个：渔业管理处（Fisheries Management Branch）、渔业行动处（Fisheries Operations Branch）和企业服务处（Corporate Services Branch）。

据1991年《渔政法》第7部分的授权，渔业管理局主要行使以下职权：第一，制定澳大利亚的渔业管理制度；第二，制定并执行相关管理制度，以监管澳大利亚在相关国际协定下负有义务的鱼群的捕捞，并使相关制度与所涉国际义务相一致；第三，协助履行澳大利亚在国际法及各类国际条约下的相关国际义务。对于悬挂澳大利亚国旗的船只在公海上的捕捞行为，渔业管理局主要围绕以下各项内容实施监管：第一，为1984年《托雷斯海峡渔业法》（Torres Strait Fisheries Act 1984）下的相关权力行使提供建议，并协助其履行职责；第二，制订渔业调整方案及渔业重组方案，并管理、推进此类方案的实施；第三，依据国内法及国际法下的相关义务，与国内外的其他机构开展合作，并提供所管理区域内的渔业信息；第四，除在行使职权时所收集的信息外，还可在获授权时收集并公开包括个人信息在内的相关事项，包括对澳大利亚法或其他外国法的可能违反，对澳大利亚边境的控制与保护，对渔业或海洋环境的管理、监测及研究；第五，在澳大利亚作为成员的区域或次区域渔业管

---

[1] "International fisheries", The Australian Department of Agriculture, Fisheries and Forestry, https://www.agr-iculture.gov.au/agriculture-land/fisheries/international, July 14, 2022.

理组织框架下,或在澳大利亚作为缔约方的区域或次区域渔业管理条约框架下,依据相关国际法采取行动以阻止船只在公海上实施危及鱼类养护与管理措施有效性的行为;第六,其他关联立法授权渔业管理局实施的行为。[1] 当前,澳大利亚渔业管理局在堪培拉和达尔文(Darwin)等地设有办事处,管理澳大利亚领海内的商业性渔区,为澳大利亚联邦政府和各州政府提供渔业管理服务,同时与国内外组织合作共同打击在澳大利亚渔区范围内的非法捕鱼活动。[2]

(2) 国家渔业咨询委员会。

国家渔业咨询委员会于2018年由改组前的澳大利亚农业与水资源部组建,其就澳大利亚商业性、娱乐性和土著人捕捞等各渔业部门面临的新兴问题向主管部委的部长提供咨询。作为澳大利亚的官方机构,国家渔业咨询委员会旨在围绕渔业与水产养殖问题、相关国家立法与政策等,向澳大利亚渔业部门负责人提供信息和建议。国家渔业咨询委员会并非与政府就渔业和水产养殖事务进行接触和磋商的唯一机制,但通过跨多个部门收集有关海鲜产业从业者的信息,该委员会得以围绕传统捕捞、野生捕捞、水产养殖、娱乐性捕捞及采收后续等多环节,为澳大利亚渔业及海产品部门应对当前问题提供有价值的参考。

国家渔业咨询委员会由澳农渔林部部长任命的15名成员组成。其中,主席为由部长决定的与渔业水产各部门均有利益关联的独立人员,其他14名成员则要求具有渔业和水产养殖的专业知识、具有地域代表性以及具备实现行业长期利益的能力。该委员会日常工作及会议由澳农渔林部提供秘书支持。

当前,国家渔业咨询委员会工作的优先事项有:第一,建立商业性、娱乐性及传统渔业部门间的联系;第二,促进资源获取及资源分享;第三,通过吸引劳动者进入渔业部门等来保障行业的未来发展;第四,协助制定国家渔业政策及管理办法;第五,探寻评估渔业各部门的一致路径;第六,提高管理决策所使用信息的可及性与透明度。[3]

3. 澳大利亚气候变化、能源、环境和水资源部

澳大利亚气候变化、能源、环境和水资源部(Department of Climate

---

[1] "Objectives and functions", Australian Fisheries Management Authority, https://www.afma.gov.au/about/obj-ectives-functions-powers, April 4, 2022.

[2] "Who We Are", Australian Fisheries Management Authority, https://www.afma.gov.au/about/about-afma, April 4, 2022.

[3] "National Fishing Advisory Council", The Australian Department of Agriculture, Fisheries and Forestry, https://www.agriculture.gov.au/agriculture-land/fisheries/national-fishing-advisory-council, December 12, 2022.

Change, Energy, the Environment and Water）于2022年7月改组成立，旨在保护澳大利亚的自然环境和遗产地，帮助澳大利亚应对气候变化并谨慎管理澳大利亚的水资源和能源资源。该部门的基本任务是：帮助应对气候变化并建立更具创新性、面向未来的能源系统；保护澳大利亚独特的环境、生物多样性和遗产；为工业和区域社区管理澳大利亚的水资源；保障澳大利亚在南极和南大洋的利益。[1] 由此，该部门就以下事项负有职责：环境保护和生物多样性保护、空气质量、土地污染、废弃物计划、工业化学品管理、气象、自然及人造的文化遗产、环境信息和研究、水资源及其政策、国家水利基础设施投资、气候变化适应战略与协调、气候变化科学活动的协调等。[2] 当前，该部门由3名部长级官员领导下的6个承担不同职能的分支构成，其海洋相关职能主要由该部门下设的澳大利亚气象局（Bureau of Meteorology）、大堡礁海洋公园管理局（Great Barrier Reef Marine Park Authority，以下简称"大堡礁管理局"）、澳大利亚南极司（Australian Antarctic Division，以下简称"南极司"）履行。[3]

（1）澳大利亚气象局。

早在1906年，澳大利亚气象局即已通过《气象法》（Meteorology Act 1906）整合原殖民领地及各州的气象服务机构而成立。1908年起，气象局开始作为英联邦机构开展工作。随着1955年《气象法》（Meteorology Act 1955）的颁布，上述1906年《气象法》被废止，气象局也随之正式重组。2002年7月1日，澳大利亚气象局根据1999年《公共服务法》（Public Service Act 1999）成为联邦政府的行政执行部门。2014年7月1日，气象局根据2013年《公共治理、执行和问责法》（Public Governance, Performance and Accountability Act 2013）改为非公司联邦实体。当前，气象局在1955年《气象法》和2007年《水法》（Water Act 2007）的授权下运行，同时积极履行澳大利亚在《世界气象组织公约》（Convention of the World Meteorological Organization）及相关国际气象条约和协定下的国际义务。[4]

作为澳大利亚国家气象、气候和水文监测机构，澳大利亚气象局致力于以其专业的知识和服务帮助澳大利亚人应对自然环境中包括干旱、洪水、火

---

[1] "What we do", DCCEEW, https://www.dcceew.gov.au/about/what-we-do, July 14, 2022.

[2] "Our responsibilities and legislation", DCCEEW, https://www.dcceew.gov.au/about/what-we-do/legislation, July 14, 2022.

[3] "Our portfolio", DCCEEW, https://www.dcceew.gov.au/about/who-we-are/portfolio, July 14, 2022.

[4] "Our Rich Past", Bureau of Meteorology, http://www.bom.gov.au/inside/rich_past.shtml, April 3, 2022; "About Us", Bureau of Meteorology, http://www.bom.gov.au/inside/, April 3, 2022.

二、海洋事务主管部门及其职能

灾、风暴、海啸和热带气旋在内的灾害。通过对澳大利亚地区和南极地区的气象、水文状况进行预报、预警、监测及海洋科考，气象局可以为澳大利亚政府提供覆盖领域广泛的基础性及专业性服务，并通过开展科学和环境相关问题的研究，为实现国家的社会、经济、文化和环境目标作出贡献。[1]

澳大利亚气象局设有专门的海事及海洋预报版块，定期在海洋电台广播有关风力、洋流及潮汐的预报，并就特定地区的资料形成描述和报告。据气象局所公开的数据，其每年都会对覆盖澳大利亚36735公里海岸线的78个沿海水域发布18000多份海洋预报，分别涉及：第一，海湾、港口及内陆水等本地水域预报；第二，距海岸60海里以内的沿岸水域预报；第三，澳大利亚周边的公海水域预报。[2] 气象局还设有专门的海洋气象知识中心（Marine Weather Knowledge Centre），为船员提供气象相关的预报信息，主要为澳大利亚周边公海海域及沿岸海域的船舶航行、捕捞活动等提供天气预报、风险预警及观测数据。[3]

(2) 大堡礁海洋公园管理局。

大堡礁是世界上最大的珊瑚礁生态系统，其面积超过意大利，在澳大利亚东北海岸绵延2300公里，有着近3000个单独礁体，全世界约10%的珊瑚礁都汇集于此。[4] 作为早在1981年即成为首个被列入《世界遗产名录》的珊瑚礁生态系统，大堡礁已经成为自然之美的全球符号，被视为澳大利亚民族认同中不可分割的组成部分，也是澳大利亚重要的经济引擎。

澳大利亚气候变化、能源、环境和水资源部下属的大堡礁海洋公园管理局是大堡礁的主要管理机构。自1975年成立以来，该机构就为澳大利亚这一标志性的自然奇观提供世界领先的海洋公园管理服务。依据1975年《大堡礁海洋公园法》（The Great Barrier Reef Marine Park Act 1975），大堡礁管理局成为澳大利亚政府授权成立的自然资源管理机构，在上述1975年法的指导下灵活运用现有科技手段来管理和保护大堡礁，维护区域价值，减少外来威胁，同时积极与土著居民土地所有者以及澳大利亚其他地区尤其是昆士兰州的政府机构、社区组织和个人开展合作，推动大堡礁及关联社区的即期与远

---

[1] "About Us", Bureau of Meteorology, http：//www.bom.gov.au/inside/, April 3, 2022.

[2] "Marine forecasts", Bureau of Meteorology, http：//www.bom.gov.au/marine/knowledge-centre/forecasts.shtml, April 3, 2022.

[3] "Marine Weather Knowledge Centre", Bureau of Meteorology, http：//www.bom.gov.au/marine/knowledge-ce-ntre/index.shtml, April 3, 2022.

[4] "Our story", Great Barrier Reef Marine Park Authority, https：//www.gbrmpa.gov.au/about-us/about-us, April 3, 2022.

景目标的实现。大堡礁管理局的总部设在汤斯维尔（Townsville），同时在凯恩斯（Cairns）、麦凯（Mackay）、耶蓬（Yeppoon）和布里斯班（Brisbane）设有地区办事处，以保持与地方行业群体的密切联系。[1]

在组织结构上，大堡礁管理局由董事会进行领导和日常管理，董事会由包括昆士兰州政府代表、当地土著居民和旅游行业代表在内的7名成员组成，这7名成员由澳大利亚气候变化、能源、环境和水资源部部长任命。董事会下设"珊瑚礁保护""企业服务""战略政策与伙伴关系"三大分支部门各司其职。[2] 当前，董事会的职责主要包括：第一，制定和实施相关计划和政策，保证以生态可持续性的方式利用大堡礁区域；第二，鼓励大堡礁区域的使用者们更好地参与对珊瑚礁的管理；第三，协助澳大利亚履行在《保护世界文化和自然遗产公约》（Convention Concerning the Protection of the World Cultural and Natural Heritage）下的相关国际义务。[3]

（3）澳大利亚南极司。

一如前述，"战略及行动计划"是澳大利亚在南极的国家利益以及澳大利亚未来参与南极洲活动愿景的集中体现与官方宣示。澳大利亚南极司正是在这一战略下成立的，其隶属于澳大利亚气候变化、能源、环境和水资源部，是负责领导、协调和实施澳大利亚南极计划（Australian Antarctic Program）的主要职能部门。该部门设立在塔斯马尼亚州的金斯顿（Kingston），约有300名全职员工在其中承担与南极有关的行政、医疗、科学及辅助支持等职能。澳大利亚在南极洲的活动，从物流运输到科学研究，都要通过澳大利亚南极计划进行协调。通过这一计划，澳大利亚政府和150多个国家及国际研究机构建立了伙伴关系，共同推进南极项目合作，协同为相关项目研究提供保障服务。[4]

立足"战略及行动计划"，澳大利亚南极科学委员会（Australian Antarctic Science Council）提出了"澳大利亚南极科学战略规划"（Australian Antarctic Science Strategic Plan）。以该战略规划为依据，南极司统筹领导澳大利亚政府所有的南极科研项目，主要涉及领域有：第一，环境保护与监管，在

---

[1] "Our story", Great Barrier Reef Marine Park Authority, https：//www.gbrmpa.gov.au/about-us/about-us, April 3, 2022.

[2] "About Us", Great Barrier Reef Marine Park Authority, https：//www.gbrmpa.gov.au/about-us, April 3, 2022.

[3] "Our Board", Great Barrier Reef Marine Park Authority, https：//www.gbrmpa.gov.au/about-us/our-bo-ard, April 3, 2022.

[4] "About Us", Australian Antarctic Program, https：//www.antarctica.gov.au/about-us/, July 2, 2022.

南极洲和南大洋有针对性地进行研究和监测,包括气候变化影响、生态系统养护、渔业管理、环境影响评估与环境救济等;第二,冰层、海洋、大气和地球系统监测,了解南极洲和南大洋对澳大利亚及世界的作用,包括高纬度气象科学、南极东部冰盖在全球海平面上升中的作用、南大洋环流及升温与酸化等;第三,人类在南极的存在与活动观测,为应对社会面问题提供实践建议,包括极地医学和人体生物学、极地政策与法律、污染监测、空间与天文学、人类影响等;第四,数据整合,推动数据收集与分析的创新,包括技术创新及远程系统、南极数字模型构建等。[1] 南极司在上述领域的科学研究成果也成为澳大利亚参与众多南极相关国际条约机制的重要支撑,如《南极条约》环境保护委员会(The Committee for Environmental Protection of the Antarctic Treaty)、国际捕鲸委员会(International Whaling Commission)、《南极海洋生物资源养护公约》(Convention for the Conservation of Antarctic Marine Living Resources)、《信天翁和海燕保护协定》(Agreement on the Conservation of Albatrosses and Petrels)等。[2]

在南极行动的支持与服务方面,所有澳大利亚的南极探险者在前往南极或近南极的麦夸里岛(Macquarie Island)之前都需在该司接受技能训练。对于将启程前往南极科考站工作或野外探险的人来说,南极司的引导信息和辅助服务是极为重要的。这些保障服务工作包括:南极相关工作培训、南极科考站点的指引、南极旅行线路及后勤服务站点规划、南极探险者中心服务、科考站外南极野外调查指导等。[3]

(4)悉尼港联邦信托。

为修复并保护悉尼港周边领地的自然和人造遗产,澳大利亚于1998年9月宣布成立悉尼港联邦信托(Sydney Harbour Federation Trust),授权其为法定机构负责悉尼港遗产地的维护。依据相关授权法案,该机构由8名成员组成,并向澳大利亚气候变化、能源、环境和水资源部部长报告工作。[4]

该机构的工作目标为:第一,确保对信托土地的管理有助于提高悉尼港

---

[1] "Australian Antarctic Science Strategic Plan", Australian Antarctic Program, https://www.antarctica.gov.au/science/information-for-scientists/australian-antarctic-science-strategic-plan/, January 5, 2023.

[2] "Scientific Research", Australian Antarctic Program, https://www.antarctica.gov.au/science/, January 5, 2023.

[3] "Antarctic Operations", Australian Antarctic Program, https://www.antarctica.gov.au/antarctic-operations/, January 5, 2023.

[4] "Our organisation", Sydney Harbour Federation Trust, https://www.harbourtrust.gov.au/en/corporate/our-peo-ple/, July 2, 2022.

地区的舒适度；第二，养护信托管理土地的环境，培育并推广相关土地的文化遗产价值；第三，最大限度地提高公众对信托管理土地的使用权限和使用效能；第四，与其他该港口土地的利益关联方合作管理信托，并合作推进上述目标的实现。该信托目前管理的土地包括夏沃德湾（Chowder Bay）、鹦鹉岛（Cockatoo Island）、沃森湾前海洋生物站（Former Marine Biological Station, Watsons Bay）、莫斯曼岬角公园乔治高地（Georges Heights, Headland Park, Mosman）、麦夸里灯塔（Macquarie Lightstation）、曼利北角保护区（North Head Sanctuary, Manly）、北悉尼鸭嘴兽潜艇观光基地（Sub Base Platypus, North Sydney）、伍尔维奇码头及公园（Woolwich Dock and Parklands）等。[1]

4. 澳大利亚工业、科学与资源部

澳大利亚工业、科学与资源部（Department of Industry, Science and Resource）原为澳大利亚工业、科学、能源与资源部（Department of Industry, Science, Energy and Resource），于2022年7月正式重组。[2]尽管"能源"职能分支在重组后被移出，但其组织机构仍较为庞杂。由3位部长级官员组成的委员会对该部门进行领导，这3位部长级官员分别是：工业与科学事务部部长、资源与北澳大利亚事务部部长、制造业与贸易事务部部长。委员会下设1名秘书长及3名助理秘书长，分别就澳大利亚工业增长、国家技术安全、制造业发展、科学与商业化、知识产权、空间活动、气候变化、核心矿产与开采项目、清洁及可再生能源等事务负责相关职能部门的日常运转。当前，澳大利亚工业、科学与资源部的主要职能在于，促进澳大利亚的经济复苏与产业发展，促进国内就业，鼓励科技发展与科学研发，管理自然资源勘探及开采，并为实现澳大利亚低排放的国家前景与国际承诺提供支持。在海洋管理方面，其职能主要集中于：其一，海洋科考的促进与管理；其二，海洋矿藏、油气资源的探明、开采和管理。由该部门下设或管理的澳大利亚海洋科学研究所（The Australian Institute of Marine Science，以下简称"澳海科所"）和国家海洋石油安全与环境管理局（The National Offshore Petroleum Safety and Environmental Management Authority，以下简称"澳海油安环局"）是上述海洋管理相关职能的具体履行单位。[3]

---

[1] "Our Story", Sydney Harbour Federation Trust, https：//www.harbourtrust.gov.au/en/our-story/, January 5, 2023.

[2] "Organisation chart", The Australian Department of Industry, Science and Resources, https：//www.industry.gov.au/about-us/organisation-chart, July 14, 2022.

[3] "About Us", The Australian Department of Industry, Science and Resources, https：//www.industry.gov.au/topic/about-us, April 3, 2022.

（1）澳大利亚海洋科学研究所。

澳大利亚海洋科学研究所于1972年根据《澳大利亚海洋科学研究所法》（Australian Institute of Marine Science Act 1972）设立，是澳大利亚的联邦法定机构之一。作为澳大利亚专门从事热带海洋科学研究的机构，澳海科所致力于为政府、各行业及更广泛的社会群体提供大规模的、长期的、世界一流的研究成果，以便相关机构能够就澳大利亚的海洋产业作出精准决策，并为生活或工作于澳大利亚水域的民众提供应对关键挑战的科学解决方案。澳海科所由60名以上的海洋科学家组成，他们的日常工作包括：第一，围绕从微生物到整个生态系统的海洋生物及其繁育体系，进行策略性及应用性研究；第二，监测海洋环境健康状况和趋势；第三，通过建立模型和编制算法，提供相应决策支持工具，以协助解释所收集的各类数据；第四，参与从分子科学到海洋科技等跨度巨大的各项技术研发。

澳海科所成立之初的主要任务是探索澳大利亚周边的海洋环境，了解大堡礁及其周边的生物多样性，让更多的澳大利亚人去认识和发掘澳大利亚北部的海洋生态系统。过去的20年里，该机构的工作重点已经转变为对澳大利亚周边海洋生态演化的监测和研究，从西澳大利亚的斯科特礁（Scott Reef）至北澳大利亚的达尔文市沿岸水域及大堡礁，均在被监测范围之内。[1] 2018年，澳海科所发布了"2025年战略目标"（AIMS Strategy 2025），意在对澳大利亚海洋环境的快速变化作出应对，以充分反映国内利益相关方的需求，符合国家及国际治理的优先规划，并帮助实现联合国可持续性发展目标。2022年，澳海科所庆祝成立50周年，并承诺下一个10年将是"行动"的10年，澳海科所将以维持和修复澳大利亚周边的海洋生态系统以应对气候变化等挑战为主要行动目标。同时，澳海科所将通过升级各种仪器和设备，为保护和促进热带海洋内外的能源、矿产、旅游业和粮食资源的可持续发展提供最佳的规划和决策。[2]

（2）国家海洋石油安全与环境管理局。

国家海洋石油安全与环境管理局原为2005年成立的国家海洋石油安全局（The National Offshore Petroleum Safety Authority）。随着2005—2010年一系列油气事故的发生，改革或重组原机关架构的呼声日渐高涨。2012年，开采设

---

[1] "About AIMS", The Australian Institute of Marine Science, https：//www.aims.gov.au/docs/about/about.html, April 3, 2022.

[2] "About Us", The Australian Institute of Marine Science, https：//www.aims.gov.au/docs/about/about.html, April 3, 2022; "AIMS Strategy 2025", The Australian Institute of Marine Science, https：//www.aims.gov.au/abo-ut/aims-strategy-2025, April 3, 2022.

施安全及环境管理事务被先后纳入机构职责范围，原安全局被正式改组，并更名为国家海洋石油安全与环境管理局。2019年及2021年，碳捕集与封存（carbon capture and storage，CCS）、海上可再生能源也分别被纳入澳海油安环局的授权监管范围。[1]

改组后的澳海油安环局是澳大利亚联邦下独立进行海上能源监管的专业机构，其主要职责是依据授权监督和管理澳大利亚管辖水域内的各种海洋资源开采活动。其监管范围包括：第一，海洋油气资源开采安全作业与健康生态；第二，海上油气井等开采设施的安全性与结构完整性；第三，各类油气作业的环境管理；第四，海上可再生能源的基础设施建设；第五，温室气体的储存活动。通过制订风险评估管理计划、检查监测执行情况、调查违规行为、采取行动纠正或阻止违规行为、提供咨询以促进相关行业持续改进，澳海油安环局能够较好地履行其法定职能，提高海洋资源开采行业的安全性和效率。[2]

澳海油安环局下设5大分支部门，分别为：首席执行官办公室；总法律顾问办公室；企业和财务担保部；环境、可再生能源和停运部；钻井安全和结构完整部。所有部门都应向首席执行官（CEO）报告工作。其中，首席执行官办公室负责提供外联、立法和监管事务服务，并监管各个部门的运行以就其工作提出改进建议。总法律顾问办公室主要为澳海油安环局业务运营的事项提供法律建议，确保其履行所有法定义务。企业和财务担保部提供各项法人支持服务，包括资金、计算机服务和人力资源支持。环境、可再生能源和停运部负责监管海上石油钻探活动和温室气体储存活动对环境造成的风险和影响，并规范相关风险管理方案的执行与措施的运用。钻井安全和结构完整部则负责保障海上石油开采设施的安全和结构完整性，保证作业人员的健康和安全。[3]

5. 澳大利亚就业和劳资关系部

就业和劳资关系部（Department of Employment and Workplace Relations）是2022年7月澳大利亚政府新组建的部门，其整合了原教育、技能与就业部（Department of Education, Skills and Employment）中的部分职能，旨在为澳大利亚人提供高质量的技能以及培训和就业机会，支持澳大利亚人在公平、高

---

[1] "Our history", NOPSEMA, https://www.nopsema.gov.au/about/what-we-do/our-history, April 3, 2022.

[2] "About Us", NOPSEMA, https://www.nopsema.gov.au/about, April 4, 2022.

[3] "Our structure", NOPSEMA, https://www.nopsema.gov.au/about/our-approach/our-structure, April 4, 2022.

效和安全的工作场所找到有保障的工作，从而为澳大利亚的经济繁荣和社会福祉作出贡献。对于海洋相关行业的劳工问题，就业和劳资关系部下设了船员安全、康复和赔偿局（Seafarers Safety, Rehabilitation and Compensation Authority），专门就船员雇佣管理、工作环境及相关福利与保障问题履行相应职责。[1]

根据1992年《船员康复和赔偿法》（Seafarers Rehabilitation and Compensation Act 1992）的规定，船员安全、康复和赔偿局负责监督国家职业健康和安全计划的实施，并针对特定船员的劳工赔偿作出安排。该机构成员共7人，包括主席与副主席各1人、雇员与雇主代表各2人及海安局首席执行官，皆由就业和劳资关系部部长任命。根据1992年《船员康复和赔偿法》和1993年《职业健康和安全（海运业）法》[Occupational Health and Safety (Maritime Industry) Act 1993]，该机构的职责范围主要为：（1）监督《船员康复和赔偿法》的实施，确保《职业健康和安全（海运业）法》下相关义务的履行；（2）促进船员雇主对有关索赔处理和有效康复程序的高标准执行；（3）与其他机构和人员合作以减少船员受伤概率；（4）就职业健康和安全事宜向经营者、雇主和承包商提供建议；（5）收集、解释和报告与职业健康和安全有关的信息；（6）制定与船员职业健康和安全相关的政策和策略；（7）根据相关法律授权认证职业健康和安全相关培训课程；（8）与其他职业健康和安全相关机构联络；（9）就本机构职能、权力以及与员工赔偿和康复有关的其他事项向相关部长提出建议。[2]

（三）海上武装执法机构

1. 澳大利亚皇家海军

澳大利亚皇家海军（Royal Australian Navy，以下简称"皇家海军"）隶属于澳大利亚国防军（Australian Defence Force）。1901年，澳大利亚联邦成立，其整合原殖民地海军的船只和资源成立联邦海军部队。1911年，作为本土重要防卫力量，联邦海军被授予"澳大利亚皇家海军"的称号。皇家海军作为地区重要的海上力量有助于保卫澳大利亚，促进地区安全，维护澳大利亚在全球的利益，并营造有利于其国家利益的战略环境。为实现其职责，皇家海军的行动主要包括：（1）海上巡逻和应急响应；（2）海岸封锁与战略打

---

[1] "Home", The Australian Department of Employment and Workplace Relations, https://www.dewr.gov.au/, July 14, 2022.

[2] "About the Seacare Authority", Australian Seafarers Safety, Rehabilitation and Compensation Authority, https://www.seacare.gov.au/about-us/about-the-seacare-authority, June 30, 2022.

击；(3) 保护海上航运，保护海上领地与自然资源；(4) 海事情报的收集和分析；(5) 海上护航；等等。除此之外，皇家海军还在和平时期对澳大利亚管辖海域进行海上监视和响应，采取行动为水文、海洋科学和气象研究提供支持，参与海上人道主义行动及灾难救助，进行海事搜索和救援。

  皇家海军由澳大利亚海军司令指挥，海军司令为皇家海军整体的培养、训练和持续发展负责。澳大利亚海军司令领导 2 个主要司令部：海军总部（Navy Headquarters）和舰队司令部（Fleet Command）。其中，海军总部由人员培训及物资负责人（副司令兼任）、海军军队能力建设负责人、海军工程监管及认证负责人、海军士官长 4 名官员分工负责；舰队司令部则由舰队司令领导各作战部队，舰队司令同时负责对各岸上设施、辅助机构及协同单位的指挥管理，如各岸上海军基地、潜艇部队、水下清障小队、海军航空兵部队等。皇家海军现设有 17 个基地或岸上设施，包括海军总部所在地、一东一西两大主舰队基地、海军舰队航空兵驻地及多个分舰队驻地与人员培训基地。当前，澳大利亚海军有 16000 余名士兵与其他人员，50 余艘在役舰艇，包括 12 艘"阿米代尔级"（Armidale Class）巡逻舰、8 艘"澳新军团级"（Anzac Class）直升机护卫舰、1 艘"海湾级"（Bay Class）登陆船坞舰、2 艘"堪培拉级"（Canberra Class）两栖攻击舰、6 艘"柯林斯级"（Collins Class）导弹潜艇、3 艘"霍巴特级"（Hobart Class）导弹驱逐舰、4 艘"胡恩级"（Huon Class）沿海扫雷舰、2 艘"卢因级"（Leeuwin Class）航道测量船、1 艘"天狼星级"（Sirius Class）舰队补给油船、1 艘多用途航空训练船"梧桐号"（MV Sycamore）、5 个海军航空兵中队的 9 架飞行器以及其他辅助型舰艇。[1]

  参与海洋环境治理是皇家海军较具特色的重要职能。据称早在 20 世纪 20 年代，皇家海军就已经开始在悉尼港基地发布指令参与海洋环境监管。当前，澳大利亚国防军发布了环境政策愿景声明，制订了详细的"2016—2036 年国防环境战略计划"（Defence Environmental Strategic Plan 2016 – 2036），其中提出：皇家海军必须适应政府和社会在环保领域日益严格的责任要求和合规审查，应将海上环境的可持续性视为皇家海军进入重要近海地区进行关键训练和演习活动的通道保障，应重视所有海军活动的潜在环境影响。为保护

---

[1] "About the Royal Australian Navy", Royal Australian Navy, https：//www.navy.gov.au/about-royal-australian-navy, April 4, 2022; "Organisation", Royal Australian Navy, https：//www.navy.gov.au/organisation, April 4, 2022; "Bases and Establishments", Royal Australian Navy, https：//www.navy.gov.au/establishments, April 4, 2022; "The Fleet", Royal Australian Navy, https：//www.navy.gov.au/fleet, April 4, 2022.

海洋环境与资源，捍卫澳大利亚人的未来，皇家海军采取的行动主要包括：阻止非法捕捞；支持建立海上检疫检验屏障，以阻止有威胁的非本土动植物从海上入侵本国；探测和清除在澳大利亚管辖水域被废弃的"幽灵渔网"，以避免对生物物种的持续威胁和伤害；保护沿岸土著居民地区的自然及人文遗产；等等。[1]

2. 澳大利亚边境行动队

2015年7月，澳大利亚海关与边境保护局经过整合成立了澳大利亚移民与海关事务部，同时建立了澳大利亚边境行动队（Australia Border Force，以下简称"边境行动队"）作为该部门下属的执法机关。2017年，澳大利亚边境行动队与国土事务部一样被归入国土事务综合职能系统内，成为担负起澳大利亚国土安全护卫职能的又一重要机关。[2]

作为澳大利亚的一线边境执法机构和海关服务机构，边境行动队的使命主要在于：第一，通过国内及国际行动，保证澳大利亚在空中、海上和陆地领域的安全，并在相应威胁到达澳大利亚边境前进行识别，以减轻和消除威胁；第二，保护跨越澳大利亚边境的合法贸易和旅行，通过简化贸易和旅客流程来促进经济增长，为国家繁荣作出贡献；第三，通过贸易执法活动保障政府收入，确保澳大利亚海关法律被遵守，在促进合法贸易的同时保护澳大利亚免受毒品、武器和假冒产品等非法货物的侵害。

尽管在部门预算、人事雇佣等事项上受国土事务部管理，但边境行动队仍具有独立的执法权。当前，边境行动队有近6000名成员，下设4大工作组，分别是：（1）国家行动组，负责包括旅客、货物、海事安全、移民扣留等在内的一切边界周边执行行动；（2）行动策略及协调组，负责提供行动计划，进行员工管理，并为实现行动目标提供海事、技术及监视层面的能力保障；（3）产业与边境系统组，负责引导边境行动队涉足相关产业，从而通过技术进步、行动计划调整和系统改革，推动边境管理的现代化；（4）海关组，通过相关政策管理及监管框架，促进旅客和货物的跨境流通，为澳大利亚的经济和安全提供支持。[3]

---

[1] "Environment", Royal Australian Navy, https：//www.navy.gov.au/environment, April 4, 2022.

[2] "Our history", The Australian Department of Home Affairs, https：//www.homeaffairs.gov.au/about-us/who-we-are/our-history, April 4, 2022.

[3] "Who We Are", Australian Border Force, https：//www.abf.gov.au/about-us/who-we-are, April 4, 2022; "The Department of Home Affairs 2020-21 Annual Report", The Australian Department of Home Affairs, https：//www.homeaffairs.gov.au/reports-and-pubs/Annualreports/home-affairs-annual-report-2020-21.pdf, pp.19-21, April 4, 2022.

拥有约37000公里海岸线、超过60个国际海港、将逾1000万平方公里海域纳入管辖范围的澳大利亚，其海上边界安全面临着极大挑战。为保障国家海上边境安全，边境行动队与澳大利亚国防军组建了海上边境指挥部（Maritime Border Command）作为其海上执法职能的主要承担者。该海上边境指挥部的作战、情报、监视及响应等活动均由位于堪培拉的边境行动队总部协调部署。海上边境指挥部致力于防范和阻截在澳大利亚管辖海域的非法活动，可以调用所配置的海上及空中设备作出响应，采取非军事化的海洋安保行动。海上边境指挥部由一位来自澳大利亚皇家海军的将军领导，该将军也是边境行动队的军官，能够同时调用边境行动队与国防军双方所授权的设备设施。

海上边境指挥部的主要使命在于：（1）侦测、阻止、应对或防范非军事性的海洋安全威胁；（2）参与边境主权保卫行动；（3）与澳大利亚联邦、各州及各领地地区政府的伙伴机构及国际相关利益方协同工作。在有关非军事性的海洋安全威胁方面，海上边境指挥部的主要行动目标在于应对8种被澳大利亚政府认定为危及国家利益的海洋安全威胁活动，即非法开发自然资源、在保护区内的非法活动、海洋污染、海上偷渡入境、违禁品进出口活动、危及海洋生态安全、海上恐怖主义、海盗与海上抢劫或其他海上暴力。海上边境指挥部的情报中心通过收集、整合、计算、分析各种情报以识别在澳大利亚管辖海域内的各种威胁，通过与其他政府部门合作对海上风险进行评估，并就政府的风险缓解策略进行确认。通过澳大利亚海事识别系统等定制系统，海上边境指挥部能够探测、评估和跟踪在澳大利亚海域内作业或接近澳大利亚海域的船只，并在有需要时大规模调用边境行动队和国防军的舰船和飞机参与行动、响应执法。在边境主权保卫行动方面，海上边境指挥部旨在通过参与具有军事导向的多机构联合行动，守卫澳大利亚边境，打击海上人口贩卖活动，并防止海上人员伤亡。而在国际、国内合作方面，海上边境指挥部除与澳大利亚各级政府、国际合作伙伴、非政府组织开展合作外，在执法中也多与海岸警卫队、海军相关单位、其他执法机关、全球各情报机构等协同配合、共同行动。[1]

除上述职权范围之外，海上边境指挥部还与澳大利亚海军、空军相关单位共同就保护海上基础设施进行定期巡逻。在必要时，巡逻队可以对处于海上设施5海里范围内的任何未授权船舶进行盘查。巡逻队在相关权限下可采取一切合理措施判定未授权船舶的意图，通过登临、搜查、扣押、逮捕、疏

---

[1] "Maritime Border Command", Australian Border Force, https://www.abf.gov.au/about-us/what-we-do/border-protection/maritime, April 4, 2022.

散在船人员等多种措施应对可能存在的威胁。[1]

3. 其他辅助性海上执法组织

在澳大利亚，传统的海岸警卫队职能事实上已由前述的海上边境指挥部承担。除政府直属的海上执法机构之外，澳大利亚尚有多个民间海上安全志愿者组织，在海上搜救、海洋安全教育等方面积极承担辅助性职能。其中，最具代表性的组织为皇家志愿海岸巡逻队（Royal Volunteer Coastal Patrol）及澳大利亚志愿海岸警卫队（Australian Volunteer Coast Guard）。

（1）皇家志愿海岸巡逻队。

皇家志愿海岸巡逻队是澳大利亚历史最悠久的海上救援志愿组织。早在20世纪初，英国首先提出让经验丰富的商船船员和游艇船员为海军和政府海事当局提供辅助服务的建议。基于这一思路，澳海军情报局局长于1936年与部分退役的高级船员进行了正式商讨，并在澳大利亚联邦海军委员会的支持下于1937年3月组建了最初的志愿海岸巡逻队。

自1937年以来，海岸巡逻队一直沿拜伦湾（Byron Bay）到南澳大利亚约克半岛的海岸线开展活动。二战期间，海岸巡逻队成员承担起特别治安官职责，巡逻护卫商业码头、桥梁和石油设施。至二战结束，海岸巡逻队完成了对约20.6万公里海岸线上港口和沿海水域的巡逻，为战争胜利贡献了39.3万个小时的支援服务。1974年，海岸巡逻队被授予"皇家"称号，以表彰它多年来的贡献。1984年，该组织开始正式使用皇家志愿海岸巡逻队的名称。[2]

当前，皇家志愿海岸巡逻队已成为新南威尔士州最大的海上救援志愿组织，从伊甸镇（Eden）到拜伦湾共有25个基地，可提供46艘救生艇。

除进行海上紧急搜索和救援行动外，皇家志愿海岸巡逻队还制订和执行了内容广泛的公共教育计划，以丰富新南威尔士州水域内航海爱好者的知识和技能。如船舶证书研讨、船用无线电使用、拖船操作、海岸导航及海洋气象等课程都包含在该教育计划之中。同时，皇家志愿海岸巡逻队也与地区政府、社区管理方及多个大型海事活动组织者建立了密切的工作联系。通过为悉尼港的澳大利亚国庆日庆祝活动、游艇俱乐部的游艇比赛等提供安全巡游、活动人群控制和协调、强制无线电检查、无线电转播等服务，扩展其工

---

[1] "Offshore facility security patrols", Australian Border Force, https://www.abf.gov.au/about-us/what-we-do/border-protection/maritime/offshore-facility-security-patrols, April 4, 2022.

[2] "Coast Guards in Australia Royal Volunteer Coastal Patrol", LiquiSearch, https://www.liquisearch.com/c-oast_guards_in_australia/royal_volunteer_coastal_patrol, January 6, 2023.

作范围，提升其工作成效。[1]

（2）澳大利亚志愿海岸警卫队。

澳大利亚志愿海岸警卫队是一个完全由志愿者组成的非营利性的海上搜救组织。其宗旨在于，为澳大利亚人的海上航行提供安全保障，为船舶使用者提供安全培训，并实施或协助实施海上搜救行动。该组织要求其成员为极具敬业精神与专业能力的志愿者，利用个人空闲时间来为组织及民众提供服务。

澳大利亚志愿海岸警卫队的成立源于1960年在维多利亚州某摩托艇爱好者俱乐部的船只安全讨论会议。经该会议推动，最终由5名成员组成了摩托艇中队，为本俱乐部活动提供安全巡逻保障。1961年，该摩托艇中队成员致信美国海岸警卫队，希望能得到相关技术及信息方面的帮助。这一请求得到了美国海岸警卫队的积极回复，以通信方式为这一志愿者小队提供了大量必要的信息，并向他们提供了相应指导。该小队的服务范围随之从俱乐部会员活动区域向所在州全境及澳大利亚全境扩展，并于1961年年底成立了第一个全国委员会，正式成立澳大利亚志愿海岸警卫队，此后逐渐发展成由一个全国性委员会领导、下设各地方中队的大型组织。随着组织规模的逐步扩大，其服务内容也从单纯的巡逻搜救扩展至海上安全教学等领域。当前，澳大利亚志愿海岸警卫队的主要职能有：海上搜救；海上船舶追踪；通过特定手机应用对游艇等娱乐性船只进行监控追踪；海上协助员资格认定；海上无线电监控；进行有关海事及海事无线电执照、沿岸航行等的公共培训与教育；协助解决相关海上社区事件；从事海上殡葬服务；等等。[2]

---

［1］ "Part 11 Royal Volunteer Coastal Patrol", Parliament of New South Wales, https：//www. parliament. nsw. gov. au/tp/files/47370/SES% 2007% 20-% 2011% 20Royal% 20Volunteer% 20Coastal% 20Patrol. pdf, January 6, 2023.

［2］ "About Us", Australian Volunteer Coast Guard, https：//coastguard. com. au/about-us/, April 4, 2022.

三、国内海洋立法

从1770年英国航海家詹姆斯·库克登上澳洲大陆之后，澳大利亚便逐渐沦为英国的殖民地。尽管在这里生活的土著居民早已形成了自己的社会规则和法律体系，但在澳洲大陆被认定为"无主土地"的情形下，原有的土著法律长期被殖民者无视，直到今日仍只在有限范围内得以适用。[1] 1900年，英国议会通过《澳大利亚联邦宪法》（Australian Federal Constitution）和《不列颠自治领条例》（British Dominion Ordinance），澳大利亚正式成为联邦制君主立宪制国家。作为英联邦成员国之一，澳大利亚法律体系的建立及其法律传统均很大程度上承袭了英国的普通法法律传统及法律原则，其正式法律渊源包括宪法、制定法、判例法。

依据2003年《立法法》（Legislation Act 2003），澳大利亚成文法（制定法）当前主要体现为三类：法案（acts）、立法文书（legislative instruments）和通报文书（notifiable instruments）。其中，法案是由议会两院通过并获得御准的法令或法律，即所谓"主法"（primary legislation）。立法文书是由获得授权的个人或机构就相关细节事项制定的法律文件，包括在"主法"中被描述或声明为立法文书的文件，在联邦立法登记处（Federal Register of Legislation）被登记为立法文书的文件，在议会授权下认定或修改相关法律规定的文件，以及《立法法》明确承认为立法文书的文件。如，"法规"（regulations）、"规则"（rules）、"条例"（ordinances）、"决定"（determinations）及部分公告（proclamation）都属立法文书。而通报文书则主要为"主法"或其下法规所描述或声明为此类文书的文件，或旨在宣告某项已颁布的法律自此生效、废止或修订的文件。如，对于澳大利亚缔结或加入的国际条约在本国的生效日期，即需经通报文书进行正式宣告。[2]

在判例法方面，1963年之前，英国国会上议院所作判决在澳大利亚均具有法律强制力。直至1978年，澳大利亚高等法院首次宣布英国枢密院司法委员会的判决对澳大利亚不再具有强制适用性，并且分别于1975年和1986年

---

[1] Barnes, Thompson & Brown, "Australia Legal System", https：//legal-translations.com.au/australian-legal-s-ystem/#：~：text=The%20Australian%20legal%20system%20is%20a%20combination%20of, the%20various%20sta-tes%20and%20federal%20government%20since%20federation, January 6, 2023.

[2] "Legislation Act 2003", Australia Federal Register of Legislation, https：//www.legislation.gov.au/Details/C2019C00084, January 7, 2023.

最终废除了由澳大利亚高等法院和州法院向英国枢密院上诉的机制，最终结束了澳大利亚对英国长期的法律依赖。[1]

（一）划定管辖海域的法

除就原殖民地纳入联邦各州后的领土范围及边界进行说明外，澳大利亚宪法[2]中并无对国家领土范围的明确规定，更未就其海洋边界与海洋主权有所伸张或澄清。有关其海洋主张或管辖海域的宣示或划定，主要由1973年的《海洋与水下土地法》（Seas and Submerged Lands Act 1973）及其附随的各时期公告予以认定、具化和明晰。

1. 1973年《海洋与水下土地法》

澳大利亚于1973年颁布了《海洋与水下土地法》，旨在：（1）对邻接澳大利亚的领海及其上空、海床和底土宣示主权；（2）强调对毗连区的控制与管辖权，以防止在澳大利亚领土范围内发生违反海关、财政、移民或卫生法的行为，并对已发生的违法行为予以惩处；（3）宣示对专属经济区的主权权利，确保澳大利亚得以探索该区域，开发、保护和管理该区域的自然资源，获取水能、风能和潮汐能等能源，获得对人工岛屿等设施和结构的管辖权，获得对海洋科学研究和海洋环境养护的管辖权，行使《联合国海洋法公约》（United Nations Convention on the Law of the Sea，以下简称《公约》）下有关专属经济区的其他权利并履行义务；（4）宣示对大陆架拥有主权，确保澳大利亚对此区域海床及底土上自然资源的勘探和开发。

除前言外，该法分两大部分，共16个条款。第1部分共4条，主要就时间、空间适用范围及关键术语进行解释说明。第2部分共分6节，分别就领海、专属经济区、大陆架、巨日升特别管理区（Greater Sunrise Special Regime Area）及部分例外事项作出规定。自1973年颁布以来，《海洋与水下土地法》已经被1980年《海洋与水下土地修正法》（Seas and Submerged Lands Amendment Act 1980）、1994年《海事立法修正法》（Maritime Legislation Amendment Act 1994）、2008年《制定法修订法》（Statute Law Revision Act 2008）、2019年《帝汶海海洋边界条约相应修正法》（Timor Sea Maritime Boundaries Treaty Consequential Amendments Act 2019）进行了多次修订更新。修订后的《海洋与水下土地法》管辖海域分区及划定原则上已调整至与《公

---

[1]《澳大利亚国家概况》，载中华人民共和国外交部网站，https://www.mfa.gov.cn/web/gjhdq_676201/gj_676203/dyz_681240/1206_681242/1206x0_681244/，最后访问日期：2022年8月29日。

[2] 即《澳大利亚联邦宪法法案》，自1901年颁布以来，历经多次修订，最近一次修订为1977年。

约》完全一致。如，该法第3条明确本法中的"领海""毗连区""专属经济区""大陆架"用语都为《公约》第3条、第4条、第33条、第55条、第57条、第76条下的相同含义；该法第7条、第10B条、第12条、第13B条也分别规定澳大利亚的领海、毗连区、专属经济区、大陆架的宽度及界限应以同《公约》第2部分第2节、第2部分第4节、第55条、第57条、第76条不相抵触的方式确定；该法附表1更直接将《公约》第2、5、6部分条款援引于后。该法第2AA节则反映了在经过艰难历程后澳大利亚与东帝汶在帝汶海上的划界成果，并通过附件2明确了巨日升特别管理区的边界坐标及示意图。[1]

值得一提的是：第一，该法第8条专门就历史性海湾和历史性水域作出了规定，明确可以由澳大利亚总督认定、宣告历史性海湾或历史性水域的存在，并就历史性海湾的海洋界限进行划定；第二，该法为包括领海、毗连区、专属经济区、大陆架的海域宽度都留下余地，允许其行使主权或主权权利的范围有随历史阶段延伸的可能；第三，该法并未明确其领海基线位置、走向及各管辖海域的宽度与外部界限，而是赋权总督在适当的时候通过公告的方式确定或修正基线位置、海域界限及范围，并授权澳大利亚总理负责相关区域海图的绘制与公布。[2]

2. 关于领海基线与领海宽度

1983年2月，澳大利亚总督依授权颁布了《内部界限（基线）公告》(Proclamation of 4 February 1983 [Proclamation of the Inner Limits (The Baseline)]) 和《外部界限（托雷斯海峡）公告》(Proclamation of 4 February 1983 [Proclamation of Outer Limits (Torres Strait)])，据《海洋与水下土地法》第7条就澳大利亚领海基线走向及领海宽度予以明确。

除对基线划定的相关术语及技术规则作出说明外，《内部界限（基线）公告》分别就澳大利亚大陆、塔斯马尼亚州大陆、包括北方领地地区在内的其他州和地区的基线划法、特殊及例外情况作出安排，并通过专门附表列明三者直线基线部分的基点坐标。《外部界限（托雷斯海峡）公告》则主要就在《内部界限（基线）公告》中被排除在外的昆士兰州下辖各岛作出规定，

---

[1] 有关澳大利亚在帝汶海上的海洋边界走向以及巨日升特别管理体制和巨日升特别管理区的具体规定，详见本书"五、海洋争端解决"下"（一）与葡萄牙、东帝汶之间的帝汶海相关争端"部分。

[2] "Seas and Submerged Lands Act 1973", Australia Federal Register of Legislation, https://www.legislation.gov.au/Details/C2019C00259, January 8, 2023.

分别通过附表1至附表8对15个岛屿、岩礁的领海外部界限进行了划定。[1]

1983年的《内部界限（基线）公告》并未对领海宽度作出规定，《外部界限（托雷斯海峡）公告》仅明确其8个附表中所涉各岛屿、岩礁的领海宽度为3海里。1990年，澳大利亚颁布《依据1973年〈海洋与水下土地法〉第7条的1990年11月9日公告》（Proclamation of 9 November 1990, pursuant to section 7 of the Seas and Submerged Lands Act 1973），将澳大利亚的领海宽度扩展至12海里。但由于澳大利亚与巴布亚新几内亚间的海洋划界协定已于1985年正式生效，该划界协定所涉的昆士兰州下辖各岛被排除在前述1990年公告的适用范围之外。[2] 2000年颁布的新公告（Proclamation under the Seas and Submerged Lands Act 1973, 29 August 2000）允许将卡奔塔利亚湾南部海域的外部界限延伸至上述1990年公告的范围之外，从而将昆士兰州卡兰巴港（Port of Karumba）附近的锚地纳入领海范围，但1983年《外部界限（托雷斯海峡）公告》附表中的昆士兰州其他岛礁至今仍维持着3海里的领海宽度。[3]

2006年，澳大利亚颁布《海洋与水下土地（领海基线）2006年公告》[Seas and Submerged Lands (Territorial Sea Baseline) Proclamation 2006]，基于澳大利亚地球科学局（Geoscience Australia）、澳大利亚水文局（Australian Hydrographic Office）以及各州和各领地地区测绘当局共同完成的有关领海基点和基线的数据调查，对澳大利亚领海基线的地理坐标进行全面修订和更新。澳大利亚的领海基点自此采用澳大利亚地心基准系统（Geocentric Datum of Australia），取代了之前各公告中使用的澳大利亚大地基准系统（Australian Geodetic Datum）。1983年《内部界限（基线）公告》由此废止。[4] 2016

---

[1] "Proclamation of 4 February 1983 [Proclamation of the Inner Limits (The Baseline)]", UN, https://www. un. org/Depts/los/LEGISLATIONANDTREATIES/PDFFILES/AUS_1983_Proclamation. pdf, January 9, 2023; "Proclamation of 4 February 1983 [Proclamation of Outer Limits (Torres Strait)]", UN, https://www. un. o-rg/Depts/los/LEGISLATIONANDTREATIES/PDFFILES/aus_1983_proclamation_torres. pdf, January 9, 2023.

[2] 有关澳大利亚与巴布亚新几内亚间海洋划界协定的具体情况详见本书"五、海洋争端解决"下"（二）通过协议解决的其他海洋划界争端"部分。

[3] "Seas and Submerged Lands Act 1973-Proclamation under section 7 (09/11/1990)", Australia Federal Register of Legislation, https://www. legislation. gov. au/Details/F2007B00736, January 9, 2023; "Seas and Submerged Lands Act 1973-Proclamation under section 7 (29/08/2000)", Australia Federal Register of Legislation, https://www. legislation. gov. au/Details/F2007B00629, January 9, 2023.

[4] "Seas and Submerged Lands (Territorial Sea Baseline) Proclamation 2006", Australia Federal Register of Legislation, https://www. legislation. gov. au/Details/F2006L00525, January 9, 2023.

年，澳大利亚再颁布《海洋与水下土地（领海基线）2016年公告》［Seas and Submerged Lands（Territorial Sea Baseline）Proclamation 2016，以下简称《2016年公告》］以取代上述2006年公告，但该公告的出台更多只是在2003年《立法法》规定下的定期更新[1]，其基本承袭了2006年公告的实质性内容，且无意对原公告所划定的领海基线作出实质性改变。

自1983年《内部界限（基线）公告》颁布后，澳大利亚的领海基线即采用混合基线方法，原则上以沿岸低潮线为基线，但为将部分海湾及河口包围其中，也在《公约》允许下对海岸线极为曲折或者存在紧邻海岸的系列岛屿区域采用直线基线。现行的《2016年公告》以第6条至第13条分别规定了不同海洋地形或区域的界定及基线划定规则，包括海湾的认定、澳大利亚大陆的基线划定、塔斯马尼亚州大陆的基线划定、北方领地地区及其他州的沿海岛屿的基线划定、低潮高地及其地位、自然地形低潮线与直线基线的交会、岛屿低潮线与直线基线的交会、不适用本法的岛屿与群岛等。其附表1对澳大利亚在基线划定中使用的地心基准及测地基站进行了说明，附表2则将澳大利亚划定的各区域直线基线的基点坐标逐一列明。澳大利亚大陆海岸基点坐标、塔斯马尼亚州大陆海岸基点坐标、北方领地地区及其他州的沿海岛屿基点坐标如表1、表2、表3所示：

表1　澳大利亚大陆海岸基点坐标[2]

序号	位置描述
1001	从32°44′27.0″S、152°11′09.5″E至32°44′23.9″S、152°11′30.6″E
1002	从32°44′23.9″S、152°11′41.1″E至32°44′24.3″S、152°11′56.5″E
1003	从32°44′24.4″S、152°11′58.2″E至32°44′31.5″S、152°12′18.3″E
1004	从32°44′31.8″S、152°12′19.6″E至32°44′32.2″S、152°12′20.9″E
1005	从32°44′32.5″S、152°12′21.6″E至32°44′33.5″S、152°12′22.4″E
1006	从32°44′33.7″S、152°12′22.6″E至32°44′40.1″S、152°12′27.0″E
1007	从32°44′41.0″S、152°12′27.1″E至32°44′51.4″S、152°12′21.7″E
1008	从32°44′53.1″S、152°12′21.0″E至32°44′59.9″S、152°12′18.1″E
1009	从32°45′00.9″S、152°12′16.7″E至32°45′01.3″S、152°12′15.0″E
1010	从32°45′02.0″S、152°12′12.7″E至32°45′13.2″S、152°11′18.6″E

---

[1] "Part 4 Sunsetting of legislative instruments, Chapter 3, Legislation Act 2003", Australia Federal Register of Legislation, https：//www.legislation.gov.au/Details/C2019C00084, January 9, 2023.

[2] "Seas and Submerged Lands（Territorial Sea Baseline）Proclamation 2016", Australia Federal Register of Legislation, https：//www.legislation.gov.au/Details/F2016L00302, January 9, 2023.

续表

序号	位置描述
1011	从 32°45′13.2″S、152°11′18.6″E 至 32°45′22.9″S、152°10′46.4″E
1012	从 32°45′22.9″S、152°10′46.4″E 至 32°45′45.4″S、152°10′24.0″E
1013	从 32°45′46.5″S、152°10′21.4″E 至 32°45′55.2″S、152°09′42.0″E
1014	从 32°45′55.2″S、152°09′42.0″E 至 32°46′05.5″S、152°09′11.7″E
1015	从 32°46′06.3″S、152°09′06.8″E 至 32°46′07.2″S、152°08′42.7″E
1016	从 32°46′07.2″S、152°08′42.7″E 至 32°47′05.1″S、152°07′28.1″E
1017	从 36°43′31.9″S、149°59′30.2″E 至 36°43′47.6″S、149°59′27.4″E
1018	从 36°43′49.4″S、149°59′26.9″E 至 36°45′14.2″S、149°59′02.3″E
1019	从 36°45′14.2″S、149°59′02.3″E 至 36°45′24.0″S、149°58′58.2″E
1020	从 36°45′25.4″S、149°58′57.8″E 至 36°46′04.4″S、149°58′44.7″E
1021	从 36°46′04.4″S、149°58′44.7″E 至 36°46′42.6″S、149°58′24.9″E
1022	从 36°46′44.8″S、149°58′23.4″E 至 36°47′08.7″S、149°58′11.8″E
1023	从 36°47′13.1″S、149°58′09.8″E 至 36°47′27.8″S、149°57′46.3″E
1024	从 36°47′28.6″S、149°57′45.8″E 至 36°47′28.6″S、149°57′44.4″E
1025	从 39°08′12.3″S、146°22′25.7″E 至 39°08′23.9″S、146°22′05.2″E
1026	从 39°08′24.9″S、146°22′01.1″E 至 39°09′29.6″S、146°18′52.3″E
1027	从 39°09′30.9″S、146°18′41.9″E 至 39°09′32.2″S、146°17′42.1″E
1028	从 39°09′30.1″S、146°17′33.2″E 至 39°07′03.9″S、146°14′13.7″E
1029	从 39°06′53.4″S、146°14′02.0″E 至 39°05′07.5″S、146°13′30.7″E
1030	从 39°04′16.8″S、146°13′19.8″E 至 39°01′20.4″S、146°14′11.1″E
1031	从 39°01′16.4″S、146°14′12.6″E 至 38°59′41.7″S、146°14′47.4″E
1032	从 38°59′39.8″S、146°14′48.8″E 至 38°59′37.8″S、146°14′54.0″E
1033	从 35°38′35.0″S、138°31′23.1″E 至 35°45′32.6″S、138°18′13.2″E
1034	从 35°45′32.6″S、138°18′13.2″E 至 35°46′33.9″S、138°17′35.8″E
1035	从 35°46′41.6″S、138°17′30.7″E 至 35°46′57.7″S、138°17′24.2″E
1036	从 35°47′07.0″S、138°17′16.1″E 至 35°50′38.3″S、138°08′03.0″E
1037	从 35°53′11.3″S、136°32′03.8″E 至 34°57′06.2″S、135°37′29.7″E
1038	从 34°56′57.9″S、135°37′29.5″E 至 34°56′48.3″S、135°37′27.1″E
1039	从 32°54′22.8″S、134°03′32.7″E 至 32°43′30.7″S、133°57′50.3″E
1040	从 32°43′30.7″S、133°57′50.3″E 至 32°35′19.6″S、133°16′52.8″E
1041	从 32°34′59.3″S、133°16′36.0″E 至 32°33′55.3″S、133°16′31.3″E
1042	从 32°33′55.3″S、133°16′31.3″E 至 32°30′49.4″S、133°15′04.9″E

续表

序号	位置描述
1043	从 32°30′20.7″S、133°14′55.8″E 至 32°13′27.9″S、133°06′38.3″E
1044	从 32°13′27.9″S、133°06′38.3″E 至 32°08′40.6″S、132°59′25.0″E
1045	从 32°08′35.4″S、132°59′21.9″E 至 32°07′34.0″S、132°58′49.0″E
1046	从 32°07′34.0″S、132°58′49.0″E 至 32°01′48.3″S、132°28′23.6″E
1047	从 33°58′47.4″S、123°17′15.3″E 至 34°00′53.9″S、123°17′38.5″E
1048	从 34°01′27.4″S、123°17′29.6″E 至 34°03′07.4″S、123°15′36.5″E
1049	从 34°03′11.1″S、123°15′32.4″E 至 34°04′17.2″S、123°14′15.7″E
1050	从 34°04′17.2″S、123°14′15.7″E 至 34°06′23.8″S、123°12′57.0″E
1051	从 34°07′09.0″S、123°12′26.3″E 至 34°09′57.0″S、123°08′51.4″E
1052	从 34°09′53.4″S、123°08′06.7″E 至 34°07′48.6″S、122°50′49.8″E
1053	从 34°07′48.6″S、122°50′49.8″E 至 34°11′51.3″S、122°29′49.7″E
1054	从 34°11′51.3″S、122°29′49.7″E 至 34°12′36.3″S、122°20′56.2″E
1055	从 34°12′36.4″S、122°20′55.1″E 至 34°13′27.5″S、122°08′58.6″E
1056	从 34°13′27.8″S、122°08′55.1″E 至 34°13′53.7″S、122°03′59.5″E
1057	从 34°13′53.8″S、122°03′55.7″E 至 34°10′46.7″S、121°56′38.6″E
1058	从 34°10′46.5″S、121°56′38.1″E 至 34°02′35.8″S、121°36′14.2″E
1059	从 34°02′35.2″S、121°36′13.9″E 至 33°52′22.3″S、121°20′44.0″E
1060	从 33°52′22.3″S、121°20′44.0″E 至 33°51′03.3″S、121°16′05.6″E
1061	从 32°22′15.1″S、115°42′50.8″E 至 32°21′17.0″S、115°41′21.7″E
1062	从 32°21′08.8″S、115°41′17.5″E 至 32°19′50.0″S、115°41′29.8″E
1063	从 32°19′50.0″S、115°41′29.8″E 至 32°19′22.8″S、115°41′26.5″E
1064	从 32°19′15.3″S、115°41′26.3″E 至 32°18′10.6″S、115°41′14.3″E
1065	从 32°18′05.1″S、115°41′14.3″E 至 32°16′16.3″S、115°41′08.9″E
1066	从 32°15′52.2″S、115°41′09.0″E 至 32°14′39.5″S、115°40′50.7″E
1067	从 32°09′21.9″S、115°39′38.9″E 至 32°07′14.9″S、115°39′28.3″E
1068	从 32°07′14.9″S、115°39′28.3″E 至 32°03′58.9″S、115°38′07.0″E
1069	从 32°03′58.9″S、115°38′07.0″E 至 32°01′38.8″S、115°31′44.1″E
1070	从 31°59′13.2″S、115°32′19.5″E 至 31°56′19.6″S、115°45′13.0″E
1071	从 26°08′35.1″S、113°09′32.7″E 至 26°07′22.7″S、113°10′51.5″E
1072	从 25°28′46.3″S、112°58′15.6″E 至 25°16′27.4″S、113°04′27.4″E
1073	从 24°59′31.5″S、113°07′00.8″E 至 24°59′11.2″S、113°07′05.2″E
1074	从 24°45′26.9″S、113°09′14.8″E 至 24°45′00.7″S、113°09′36.1″E

续表

序号	位置描述
1075	从 24°44′53.5″S、113°09′39.8″E 至 24°29′20.1″S、113°24′28.0″E
1076	从 21°46′53.3″S、114°09′44.1″E 至 21°43′03.6″S、114°18′01.3″E
1077	从 21°39′27.3″S、114°20′56.6″E 至 21°38′59.8″S、114°21′23.0″E
1078	从 21°37′19.5″S、114°23′33.6″E 至 21°35′52.2″S、114°30′10.7″E
1079	从 21°35′50.5″S、114°30′28.5″E 至 21°31′33.6″S、114°45′24.9″E
1080	从 21°31′06.7″S、114°45′52.2″E 至 21°15′42.7″S、115°01′24.8″E
1081	从 21°15′42.7″S、115°01′24.8″E 至 20°58′19.9″S、115°19′25.1″E
1082	从 20°56′49.4″S、115°18′28.2″E 至 20°56′22.1″S、115°18′34.8″E
1083	从 20°53′45.8″S、115°19′01.5″E 至 20°53′32.6″S、115°19′00.5″E
1084	从 20°39′58.9″S、115°25′57.8″E 至 20°26′00.6″S、115°30′01.8″E
1085	从 20°26′00.6″S、115°30′01.8″E 至 20°21′50.7″S、115°30′45.7″E
1086	从 20°22′01.3″S、115°32′21.8″E 至 20°22′37.4″S、115°33′32.3″E
1087	从 20°24′10.6″S、115°35′09.5″E 至 20°28′35.5″S、116°32′18.6″E
1088	从 20°28′35.5″S、116°32′18.6″E 至 20°26′24.6″S、116°36′47.4″E
1089	从 20°26′18.4″S、116°37′07.1″E 至 20°21′12.3″S、116°49′55.5″E
1090	从 20°25′16.2″S、116°57′37.5″E 至 20°25′46.3″S、117°04′09.7″E
1091	从 20°26′17.8″S、117°06′12.9″E 至 20°32′49.0″S、117°10′36.3″E
1092	从 20°32′57.2″S、117°10′43.9″E 至 20°34′32.9″S、117°12′10.8″E
1093	从 20°34′33.2″S、117°12′11.1″E 至 20°37′36.8″S、117°12′13.0″E
1094	从 16°23′58.1″S、122°55′24.4″E 至 16°23′18.0″S、122°55′04.1″E
1095	从 16°23′02.3″S、122°55′25.1″E 至 16°16′32.7″S、123°03′25.9″E
1096	从 16°16′24.7″S、123°03′36.3″E 至 16°02′27.6″S、123°16′13.9″E
1097	从 16°01′55.8″S、123°18′41.0″E 至 15°52′26.9″S、123°37′58.8″E
1098	从 15°51′42.3″S、123°38′24.4″E 至 15°50′52.4″S、123°40′19.7″E
1099	从 15°50′52.4″S、123°40′19.7″E 至 15°20′14.4″S、124°10′58.5″E
1100	从 15°20′14.4″S、124°10′58.5″E 至 15°12′43.1″S、124°15′31.6″E
1101	从 15°12′36.4″S、124°15′34.4″E 至 15°03′33.7″S、124°19′08.9″E
1102	从 15°02′43.4″S、124°19′34.8″E 至 14°59′08.7″S、124°32′03.7″E
1103	从 14°59′08.7″S、124°32′03.7″E 至 14°51′37.6″S、124°42′28.4″E
1104	从 14°51′37.6″S、124°42′28.4″E 至 14°30′36.9″S、124°55′09.1″E
1105	从 14°30′34.6″S、124°55′10.3″E 至 14°24′16.6″S、124°57′17.3″E
1106	从 14°22′59.5″S、124°58′24.4″E 至 14°16′57.8″S、125°13′18.0″E

续表

序号	位置描述
1107	从 14°16′57.8″S、125°13′18.0″E 至 14°14′22.5″S、125°19′11.7″E
1108	从 14°14′22.5″S、125°19′11.7″E 至 14°05′56.0″S、125°33′14.8″E
1109	从 14°05′56.0″S、125°33′14.8″E 至 13°55′51.9″S、125°37′08.6″E
1110	从 13°55′02.6″S、125°37′35.8″E 至 13°47′45.3″S、125°48′19.8″E
1111	从 13°47′45.3″S、125°48′19.8″E 至 13°44′23.5″S、126°08′29.1″E
1112	从 13°44′18.6″S、126°09′23.1″E 至 13°44′38.8″S、126°20′53.5″E
1113	从 13°45′00.5″S、126°22′38.7″E 至 13°43′48.3″S、126°46′32.8″E
1114	从 14°50′43.9″S、129°02′30.8″E 至 14°25′51.3″S、129°20′55.1″E
1115	从 12°38′51.8″S、130°19′47.6″E 至 11°49′32.8″S、130°02′54.9″E
1116	从 11°20′20.7″S、130°14′45.8″E 至 11°06′04.1″S、130°18′55.3″E
1117	从 11°11′14.2″S、131°16′51.2″E 至 11°09′21.8″S、131°51′49.8″E
1118	从 11°09′21.8″S、131°51′49.8″E 至 11°07′11.9″S、131°58′10.2″E
1119	从 11°07′17.2″S、132°08′14.3″E 至 11°06′39.6″S、132°11′23.7″E
1120	从 11°06′39.8″S、132°11′26.3″E 至 11°05′52.0″S、132°17′12.6″E
1121	从 11°05′49.7″S、132°17′31.7″E 至 11°01′11.3″S、132°27′23.0″E
1122	从 10°57′57.6″S、132°35′39.0″E 至 10°57′53.5″S、132°49′14.8″E
1123	从 10°57′56.6″S、132°49′57.2″E 至 11°01′51.1″S、132°58′18.3″E
1124	从 11°05′29.1″S、132°59′59.8″E 至 11°10′03.3″S、132°55′41.6″E
1125	从 11°10′09.4″S、132°55′39.7″E 至 11°19′54.2″S、132°55′05.5″E
1126	从 11°56′50.2″S、134°44′54.8″E 至 11°54′20.9″S、135°01′47.1″E
1127	从 11°55′06.1″S、135°07′22.6″E 至 11°54′47.5″S、135°07′54.5″E
1128	从 11°54′18.0″S、135°09′14.7″E 至 11°56′54.7″S、135°35′36.8″E
1129	从 11°44′35.6″S、135°52′18.8″E 至 11°41′35.7″S、135°56′24.9″E
1130	从 11°37′53.3″S、136°01′22.0″E 至 11°37′20.0″S、136°01′34.2″E
1131	从 11°36′02.7″S、136°03′26.8″E 至 11°35′01.0″S、136°04′07.7″E
1132	从 11°34′14.9″S、136°05′32.3″E 至 11°33′35.7″S、136°06′11.2″E
1133	从 11°32′26.6″S、136°07′24.8″E 至 11°28′24.1″S、136°25′42.7″E
1134	从 11°28′22.8″S、136°25′46.0″E 至 11°24′52.0″S、136°28′56.1″E
1135	从 11°24′47.2″S、136°28′59.4″E 至 11°23′33.9″S、136°29′47.6″E
1136	从 11°02′20.1″S、136°43′28.9″E 至 11°01′56.2″S、136°43′44.1″E
1137	从 11°01′35.0″S、136°43′50.6″E 至 11°00′18.6″S、136°44′04.7″E
1138	从 11°00′21.4″S、136°45′48.4″E 至 11°01′24.3″S、136°46′02.1″E

续表

序号	位置描述
1139	从 11°01′26.0″S、136°46′02.2″E 至 11°01′39.6″S、136°46′01.7″E
1140	从 11°02′08.9″S、136°46′01.7″E 至 11°39′13.8″S、136°50′18.1″E
1141	从 11°39′13.8″S、136°50′18.1″E 至 12°01′50.7″S、136°53′03.3″E
1142	从 12°01′50.7″S、136°53′03.3″E 至 12°20′31.0″S、136°58′45.6″E
1143	从 12°30′20.8″S、136°48′20.1″E 至 12°30′26.1″S、136°48′26.3″E
1144	从 12°30′34.8″S、136°48′31.2″E 至 12°30′51.3″S、136°48′44.8″E
1145	从 12°30′59.5″S、136°48′46.3″E 至 12°34′54.3″S、136°46′42.0″E
1146	从 12°35′06.6″S、136°46′24.3″E 至 12°35′11.3″S、136°46′17.5″E
1147	从 12°35′25.2″S、136°46′01.4″E 至 12°43′02.6″S、136°43′59.0″E
1148	从 12°43′06.6″S、136°43′58.3″E 至 12°44′42.4″S、136°43′33.0″E
1149	从 12°44′42.4″S、136°43′33.0″E 至 12°46′43.8″S、136°43′27.2″E
1150	从 12°46′43.8″S、136°43′27.2″E 至 12°52′56.2″S、136°43′53.0″E
1151	从 12°53′17.9″S、136°43′51.9″E 至 13°00′15.8″S、136°40′08.2″E
1152	从 13°00′15.8″S、136°40′08.2″E 至 13°37′28.4″S、136°57′39.1″E
1153	从 13°37′37.7″S、136°57′47.2″E 至 13°37′38.7″S、136°57′48.2″E
1154	从 13°37′42.0″S、136°57′49.2″E 至 13°48′21.8″S、136°55′31.3″E
1155	从 13°48′21.8″S、136°55′31.3″E 至 14°10′14.2″S、136°59′06.9″E
1156	从 14°10′18.3″S、136°59′07.4″E 至 14°13′02.7″S、136°58′52.4″E
1157	从 14°13′06.6″S、136°58′52.3″E 至 14°15′25.4″S、136°59′07.3″E
1158	从 14°15′44.9″S、136°59′05.6″E 至 14°18′04.5″S、136°57′53.6″E
1159	从 14°18′04.5″S、136°57′53.6″E 至 14°20′56.0″S、136°57′15.6″E
1160	从 14°21′10.8″S、136°56′55.3″E 至 14°21′06.3″S、136°56′35.4″E
1161	从 14°21′12.2″S、136°55′40.0″E 至 14°20′53.6″S、136°50′10.7″E
1162	从 14°20′53.5″S、136°50′10.5″E 至 14°18′46.7″S、136°39′39.3″E
1163	从 14°18′28.7″S、136°39′24.2″E 至 14°17′49.5″S、136°38′56.1″E
1164	从 14°14′46.9″S、136°19′32.1″E 至 14°11′46.8″S、135°53′50.2″E
1165	从 15°24′03.4″S、136°15′25.9″E 至 15°29′36.3″S、136°34′45.2″E
1166	从 15°29′36.3″S、136°34′45.2″E 至 15°30′12.7″S、136°52′10.2″E
1167	从 15°29′55.7″S、136°53′19.2″E 至 15°29′31.5″S、136°55′09.4″E
1168	从 15°29′32.9″S、136°55′16.0″E 至 15°29′56.7″S、136°57′14.4″E
1169	从 15°29′56.9″S、136°57′28.9″E 至 15°36′59.2″S、137°05′46.4″E
1170	从 15°37′12.1″S、137°05′47.3″E 至 15°44′51.4″S、137°06′26.0″E

续表

序号	位置描述
1171	从15°45′15.5″S、137°06′25.4″E 至15°46′12.4″S、137°06′29.9″E
1172	从15°51′11.0″S、137°04′44.4″E 至15°51′21.2″S、137°04′31.8″E
1173	从15°52′00.3″S、137°04′10.3″E 至15°57′58.7″S、137°09′38.6″E
1174	从16°53′03.9″S、139°00′58.2″E 至16°52′44.6″S、139°02′26.7″E
1175	从16°51′27.0″S、139°02′58.4″E 至16°48′41.6″S、139°05′27.6″E
1176	从16°48′37.4″S、139°05′31.5″E 至16°45′08.8″S、139°08′15.0″E
1177	从16°40′34.5″S、139°09′34.0″E 至16°39′57.0″S、139°09′36.4″E
1178	从16°30′17.4″S、139°14′27.8″E 至16°13′52.0″S、139°15′02.2″E
1179	从16°13′44.8″S、139°15′14.4″E 至16°23′21.1″S、139°33′05.0″E
1180	从16°27′02.8″S、139°40′37.0″E 至16°26′42.6″S、139°43′33.1″E
1181	从16°26′42.6″S、139°43′33.1″E 至16°26′24.6″S、139°46′12.1″E
1182	从16°26′26.6″S、139°46′25.1″E 至16°29′25.0″S、139°48′52.7″E
1183	从16°29′46.0″S、139°49′05.4″E 至16°38′36.6″S、139°53′57.6″E
1184	从16°38′43.1″S、139°53′57.4″E 至16°39′12.4″S、139°53′47.5″E
1185	从16°39′36.8″S、139°53′34.1″E 至16°42′24.9″S、139°50′37.8″E
1186	从16°42′36.2″S、139°50′30.2″E 至17°04′29.0″S、139°38′23.0″E
1187	从17°08′36.7″S、139°37′01.2″E 至17°24′34.4″S、139°30′07.5″E
1188	从11°04′09.7″S、142°07′46.7″E 至10°59′49.7″S、142°06′10.5″E
1189	从10°58′40.0″S、142°05′16.2″E 至10°53′11.1″S、142°01′24.5″E
1190	从10°52′53.7″S、142°01′26.2″E 至10°51′06.6″S、142°01′15.9″E
1191	从10°50′59.5″S、142°01′14.7″E 至10°36′26.4″S、141°54′34.3″E
1192	从10°36′14.5″S、141°54′29.0″E 至10°21′23.1″S、142°02′33.3″E
1193	从10°21′23.1″S、142°02′33.3″E 至10°15′30.8″S、142°02′14.5″E
1194	从10°15′27.9″S、142°02′14.4″E 至10°15′01.8″S、142°02′13.0″E
1195	从10°14′59.9″S、142°02′12.3″E 至10°13′08.9″S、142°03′05.3″E
1196	从10°12′58.6″S、142°03′06.9″E 至10°07′19.6″S、142°03′06.0″E
1197	从10°07′19.6″S、142°03′06.0″E 至10°02′41.1″S、142°03′34.5″E
1198	从10°02′32.6″S、142°03′39.8″E 至09°57′53.2″S、142°04′40.0″E
1199	从09°57′51.4″S、142°04′42.2″E 至09°56′54.0″S、142°05′00.5″E
1200	从09°55′52.3″S、142°10′09.6″E 至09°56′08.9″S、142°10′41.9″E
1201	从09°56′09.7″S、142°10′44.7″E 至09°56′31.3″S、142°12′10.7″E
1202	从09°56′53.4″S、142°12′48.6″E 至09°58′29.4″S、142°14′14.2″E

续表

序号	位置描述
1203	从 09°58′38.1″S、142°14′26.0″E 至 10°04′45.7″S、142°19′37.7″E
1204	从 10°04′54.5″S、142°19′47.9″E 至 10°09′12.1″S、142°30′14.6″E
1205	从 10°09′45.9″S、142°31′02.0″E 至 10°10′46.9″S、142°31′17.0″E
1206	从 10°10′52.7″S、142°31′16.6″E 至 10°11′09.5″S、142°31′19.5″E
1207	从 10°11′51.8″S、142°31′03.2″E 至 10°14′46.3″S、142°29′36.0″E
1208	从 10°15′39.4″S、142°29′10.4″E 至 10°27′44.9″S、142°27′04.7″E
1209	从 10°27′44.9″S、142°27′04.7″E 至 10°35′46.3″S、142°38′34.5″E
1210	从 10°35′48.2″S、142°38′37.7″E 至 10°39′17.5″S、142°45′16.1″E
1211	从 10°39′42.4″S、142°45′42.6″E 至 10°42′46.4″S、142°46′29.9″E
1212	从 10°43′37.3″S、142°46′46.7″E 至 10°50′14.4″S、142°47′01.2″E
1213	从 10°50′14.4″S、142°47′01.2″E 至 11°00′07.7″S、142°59′25.1″E
1214	从 11°00′32.8″S、142°59′50.1″E 至 11°09′13.9″S、143°04′45.5″E
1215	从 11°11′29.5″S、143°07′21.4″E 至 11°23′48.2″S、143°04′59.7″E
1216	从 11°23′48.2″S、143°04′59.7″E 至 11°42′01.5″S、143°11′44.3″E
1217	从 11°42′01.5″S、143°11′44.3″E 至 11°49′01.3″S、143°29′17.4″E
1218	从 11°49′55.0″S、143°29′48.6″E 至 11°55′59.5″S、143°29′25.8″E
1219	从 11°56′03.8″S、143°29′25.6″E 至 12°17′42.1″S、143°25′11.8″E
1220	从 12°17′42.1″S、143°25′11.8″E 至 12°24′09.4″S、143°29′22.4″E
1221	从 12°24′21.2″S、143°29′23.9″E 至 12°48′36.0″S、143°36′45.0″E
1222	从 12°48′41.0″S、143°36′44.9″E 至 12°53′11.6″S、143°36′21.0″E
1223	从 12°53′11.6″S、143°36′21.0″E 至 12°59′02.2″S、143°37′01.5″E
1224	从 12°59′32.9″S、143°37′04.7″E 至 13°01′55.1″S、143°38′24.4″E
1225	从 13°02′09.7″S、143°38′27.3″E 至 13°18′29.3″S、143°40′25.4″E
1226	从 13°18′29.3″S、143°40′25.4″E 至 13°27′54.8″S、143°45′35.3″E
1227	从 13°27′54.8″S、143°45′35.3″E 至 13°38′21.8″S、143°56′02.3″E
1228	从 13°38′24.8″S、143°56′06.6″E 至 13°46′53.3″S、144°00′12.2″E
1229	从 13°46′53.3″S、144°00′12.2″E 至 14°02′53.1″S、144°15′32.9″E
1230	从 14°03′05.4″S、144°16′09.9″E 至 14°05′04.4″S、144°20′04.5″E
1231	从 14°05′08.4″S、144°20′21.1″E 至 14°06′39.5″S、144°31′30.8″E
1232	从 14°06′59.3″S、144°31′57.4″E 至 14°18′32.0″S、144°51′50.1″E
1233	从 14°18′42.8″S、144°52′06.3″E 至 14°23′55.1″S、144°58′50.9″E
1234	从 14°24′05.7″S、144°59′08.5″E 至 14°38′41.0″S、145°27′14.9″E

续表

序号	位置描述
1235	从 14°40′14.7″S、145°28′42.3″E 至 14°44′46.8″S、145°31′00.0″E
1236	从 14°44′50.3″S、145°31′01.0″E 至 14°49′18.6″S、145°33′18.2″E
1237	从 14°49′28.5″S、145°33′15.7″E 至 15°01′30.2″S、145°26′57.5″E
1238	从 15°01′30.2″S、145°26′57.5″E 至 15°06′49.0″S、145°25′46.2″E
1239	从 15°07′14.1″S、145°25′39.8″E 至 15°16′29.2″S、145°21′27.0″E
1240	从 17°38′55.0″S、146°08′57.1″E 至 17°39′08.2″S、146°09′25.4″E
1241	从 17°39′23.1″S、146°09′38.0″E 至 17°40′27.7″S、146°10′48.8″E
1242	从 17°40′40.8″S、146°10′55.2″E 至 17°44′17.0″S、146°09′49.8″E
1243	从 17°44′17.0″S、146°09′49.8″E 至 17°58′03.0″S、146°10′50.5″E
1244	从 17°58′06.6″S、146°10′51.2″E 至 18°02′14.4″S、146°12′06.8″E
1245	从 18°02′14.4″S、146°12′06.8″E 至 18°09′14.6″S、146°18′20.7″E
1246	从 18°09′27.2″S、146°18′29.3″E 至 18°14′07.2″S、146°19′38.1″E
1247	从 18°14′07.8″S、146°19′38.5″E 至 18°25′06.2″S、146°21′26.7″E
1248	从 18°25′08.5″S、146°21′27.6″E 至 18°32′16.2″S、146°29′43.7″E
1249	从 18°32′34.2″S、146°30′08.3″E 至 18°44′15.8″S、146°41′06.9″E
1250	从 18°44′34.9″S、146°41′23.0″E 至 18°46′18.1″S、146°43′03.7″E
1251	从 18°46′20.3″S、146°43′06.4″E 至 19°06′30.2″S、146°52′52.6″E
1252	从 19°06′30.2″S、146°52′52.6″E 至 19°10′53.3″S、147°00′49.1″E
1253	从 19°57′14.8″S、148°13′24.1″E 至 19°58′18.7″S、148°26′53.0″E
1254	从 19°58′21.7″S、148°27′23.4″E 至 19°59′18.9″S、148°33′36.2″E
1255	从 19°59′19.0″S、148°33′36.7″E 至 20°00′49.1″S、148°37′31.7″E
1256	从 20°00′49.1″S、148°37′31.7″E 至 20°02′11.4″S、148°52′53.9″E
1257	从 20°02′14.6″S、148°53′13.6″E 至 20°03′34.7″S、148°57′54.9″E
1258	从 20°03′34.9″S、148°57′55.7″E 至 20°14′25.7″S、149°10′27.6″E
1259	从 20°14′34.8″S、149°10′31.7″E 至 20°15′10.5″S、149°11′07.4″E
1260	从 20°15′14.2″S、149°11′08.5″E 至 20°28′49.5″S、149°08′02.6″E
1261	从 20°28′49.5″S、149°08′02.6″E 至 20°36′03.3″S、149°11′15.3″E
1262	从 20°36′03.3″S、149°11′15.3″E 至 20°43′37.5″S、149°28′00.8″E
1263	从 20°43′37.5″S、149°28′00.8″E 至 20°45′38.9″S、149°37′23.3″E
1264	从 20°46′23.1″S、149°37′39.6″E 至 20°56′37.8″S、149°44′27.6″E
1265	从 20°56′37.8″S、149°44′27.6″E 至 20°59′14.6″S、149°48′07.3″E
1266	从 20°59′14.6″S、149°48′07.3″E 至 21°00′03.0″S、149°53′41.4″E

续表

序号	位置描述
1267	从 21°00′03.4″S、149°53′43.2″E 至 21°00′08.1″S、149°53′52.5″E
1268	从 21°01′24.8″S、149°54′57.2″E 至 21°06′28.0″S、149°58′00.0″E
1269	从 21°06′28.0″S、149°58′00.0″E 至 21°27′59.6″S、150°18′33.3″E
1270	从 21°28′08.0″S、150°18′38.6″E 至 21°40′22.4″S、150°21′24.7″E
1271	从 21°40′22.4″S、150°21′24.7″E 至 21°45′45.8″S、150°26′28.0″E
1272	从 21°45′45.8″S、150°26′28.0″E 至 21°56′15.1″S、150°41′31.0″E
1273	从 21°56′15.1″S、150°41′31.0″E 至 21°57′02.6″S、150°42′08.5″E
1274	从 21°57′02.6″S、150°42′08.5″E 至 21°57′07.3″S、150°42′10.6″E
1275	从 21°57′14.0″S、150°42′09.0″E 至 22°05′24.5″S、150°40′37.0″E
1276	从 22°05′24.5″S、150°40′37.0″E 至 22°20′12.0″S、150°43′18.3″E
1277	从 22°20′12.0″S、150°43′18.3″E 至 22°24′40.5″S、150°44′58.2″E
1278	从 22°24′40.5″S、150°44′58.2″E 至 22°26′50.9″S、150°45′54.3″E
1279	从 22°26′54.1″S、150°45′56.6″E 至 22°28′36.8″S、150°46′26.9″E
1280	从 22°28′36.8″S、150°46′26.9″E 至 22°39′14.9″S、150°57′41.7″E
1281	从 22°39′16.6″S、150°57′43.2″E 至 22°43′32.7″S、150°59′28.8″E
1282	从 22°44′05.2″S、150°59′53.5″E 至 23°09′13.9″S、151°05′10.6″E
1283	从 23°09′13.9″S、151°05′10.6″E 至 23°11′52.1″S、151°06′08.7″E
1284	从 23°11′52.1″S、151°06′08.7″E 至 23°24′31.3″S、151°11′05.6″E
1285	从 23°24′31.3″S、151°11′05.6″E 至 23°28′54.9″S、151°14′01.6″E
1286	从 23°29′14.1″S、151°14′18.8″E 至 23°31′43.9″S、151°16′33.3″E
1287	从 23°31′55.2″S、151°16′41.8″E 至 23°45′11.6″S、151°20′06.6″E
1288	从 23°48′18.5″S、151°22′06.6″E 至 23°48′48.6″S、151°23′16.3″E
1289	从 23°48′50.8″S、151°23′19.7″E 至 23°57′05.2″S、151°29′26.3″E
1290	从 23°57′05.2″S、151°29′26.3″E 至 23°58′24.5″S、151°37′33.9″E
1291	从 23°58′24.5″S、151°37′33.9″E 至 23°58′34.0″S、151°46′31.2″E
1292	从 23°58′35.4″S、151°46′34.3″E 至 24°08′52.3″S、151°53′08.8″E
1293	从 24°45′10.7″S、152°24′26.0″E 至 24°41′53.6″S、153°14′50.4″E
1294	从 25°47′37.4″S、153°04′38.3″E 至 25°48′38.1″S、153°04′22.4″E
1295	从 26°48′06.4″S、153°09′07.0″E 至 27°01′39.3″S、153°28′05.3″E
1296	从 27°01′42.8″S、153°28′07.2″E 至 27°23′27.8″S、153°33′11.3″E
1297	从 27°23′28.6″S、153°33′11.4″E 至 27°25′06.8″S、153°33′19.4″E
1298	从 27°25′07.4″S、153°33′19.3″E 至 27°26′11.1″S、153°32′48.2″E

续表

序号	位置描述
1299	从 27°43′36.5″S、153°27′10.3″E 至 27°44′39.1″S、153°26′48.1″E
1300	从 27°55′58.5″S、153°25′52.1″E 至 27°56′06.0″S、153°26′00.0″E

表2 塔斯马尼亚州大陆海岸基点坐标[1]

序号	位置描述
3001	从 41°51′12.9″S、148°16′39.8″E 至 41°51′22.2″S、148°17′24.0″E
3002	从 41°51′23.4″S、148°17′28.3″E 至 41°52′12.4″S、148°18′56.3″E
3003	从 41°52′12.9″S、148°18′57.1″E 至 41°52′35.7″S、148°18′58.3″E
3004	从 41°52′37.0″S、148°18′58.1″E 至 41°53′18.8″S、148°18′36.4″E
3005	从 41°53′19.7″S、148°18′35.7″E 至 41°53′40.5″S、148°18′33.0″E
3006	从 42°13′21.3″S、148°20′48.6″E 至 42°20′27.0″S、148°20′45.3″E
3007	从 42°20′30.9″S、148°20′44.7″E 至 42°38′58.6″S、148°10′09.1″E
3008	从 42°38′58.6″S、148°10′09.1″E 至 43°07′21.7″S、148°03′25.1″E
3009	从 43°07′22.0″S、148°03′25.0″E 至 43°13′18.0″S、148°00′41.5″E
3010	从 43°13′18.0″S、148°00′41.5″E 至 43°14′10.1″S、148°00′34.1″E
3011	从 43°14′37.6″S、148°00′26.2″E 至 43°14′45.8″S、148°00′19.2″E
3012	从 43°14′46.0″S、148°00′18.7″E 至 43°31′58.0″S、147°17′59.5″E
3013	从 43°31′58.6″S、147°17′57.5″E 至 43°38′18.8″S、146°52′16.2″E
3014	从 43°38′34.4″S、146°49′32.5″E 至 43°39′50.4″S、146°15′40.3″E
3015	从 43°39′50.4″S、146°15′38.9″E 至 43°39′49.9″S、146°14′57.0″E
3016	从 43°39′48.9″S、146°14′51.7″E 至 43°39′44.8″S、146°14′35.3″E
3017	从 43°39′44.6″S、146°14′34.9″E 至 43°34′20.6″S、146°01′50.4″E
3018	从 43°29′16.3″S、146°01′38.3″E 至 43°29′01.2″S、146°01′32.9″E
3019	从 43°29′01.2″S、146°01′32.9″E 至 43°28′10.2″S、146°00′30.1″E
3020	从 43°28′00.7″S、146°00′22.6″E 至 43°27′59.7″S、146°00′22.0″E
3021	从 43°27′57.9″S、146°00′20.6″E 至 43°26′02.9″S、145°59′50.8″E
3022	从 43°26′02.9″S、145°59′50.8″E 至 43°25′41.9″S、145°58′01.8″E
3023	从 43°25′41.1″S、145°57′59.6″E 至 43°25′41.1″S、145°57′58.7″E
3024	从 43°25′41.1″S、145°57′57.6″E 至 43°25′17.6″S、145°55′58.6″E
3025	从 43°25′17.6″S、145°55′58.3″E 至 43°25′12.2″S、145°55′21.1″E

[1] "Seas and Submerged Lands (Territorial Sea Baseline) Proclamation 2016", Australia Federal Register of Legislation, https://www.legislation.gov.au/Details/F2016L00302, January 9, 2023.

续表

序号	位置描述
3026	从 43°25′12.1″S、145°55′20.2″E 至 43°25′09.7″S、145°55′14.8″E
3027	从 43°25′04.4″S、145°55′13.3″E 至 43°22′56.0″S、145°55′09.2″E
3028	从 43°22′54.2″S、145°55′08.6″E 至 43°19′21.4″S、145°52′14.0″E
3029	从 40°50′09.7″S、144°42′39.6″E 至 40°50′00.3″S、144°42′19.0″E
3030	从 40°49′59.1″S、144°42′17.6″E 至 40°49′39.0″S、144°41′59.7″E
3031	从 40°49′36.8″S、144°41′59.2″E 至 40°49′17.4″S、144°41′50.9″E
3032	从 40°49′14.9″S、144°41′50.6″E 至 40°48′46.0″S、144°41′43.3″E
3033	从 40°48′43.3″S、144°41′43.4″E 至 40°48′14.3″S、144°41′46.2″E
3034	从 40°48′13.8″S、144°41′46.3″E 至 40°48′06.3″S、144°41′48.1″E
3035	从 40°48′06.3″S、144°41′48.1″E 至 40°48′00.6″S、144°41′48.8″E
3036	从 40°47′59.9″S、144°41′49.9″E 至 40°47′52.3″S、144°42′07.0″E
3037	从 40°44′06.9″S、144°41′03.2″E 至 40°43′32.3″S、144°40′39.8″E
3038	从 40°43′27.6″S、144°40′36.7″E 至 40°43′05.3″S、144°40′31.6″E
3039	从 40°43′03.9″S、144°40′31.1″E 至 40°40′16.0″S、144°40′10.1″E
3040	从 40°40′14.8″S、144°40′10.2″E 至 40°37′33.8″S、144°40′41.5″E
3041	从 40°37′33.1″S、144°40′41.7″E 至 40°36′29.2″S、144°40′57.7″E
3042	从 40°36′29.2″S、144°40′57.7″E 至 40°35′00.8″S、144°40′45.1″E
3043	从 40°34′59.5″S、144°40′45.2″E 至 40°33′55.0″S、144°40′39.3″E
3044	从 40°33′53.5″S、144°40′38.8″E 至 40°33′45.5″S、144°40′42.4″E
3045	从 40°33′45.4″S、144°40′42.5″E 至 40°30′21.1″S、144°42′14.2″E
3046	从 40°30′21.1″S、144°42′14.2″E 至 40°30′15.8″S、144°42′13.4″E
3047	从 40°30′14.7″S、144°42′13.1″E 至 40°29′36.8″S、144°42′07.5″E
3048	从 40°29′36.4″S、144°42′07.7″E 至 40°29′09.2″S、144°42′29.1″E
3049	从 40°23′57.7″S、144°47′05.8″E 至 40°23′19.0″S、144°53′04.4″E
3050	从 40°25′35.2″S、144°58′14.0″E 至 40°42′37.4″S、145°16′27.2″E

表3　北方领地地区及其他州的沿海岛屿基点坐标[1]

序号	位置描述
4001	从 40°12′34.1″S、148°20′03.7″E 至 40°17′30.6″S、148°20′00.5″E
4002	从 40°29′22.3″S、148°23′52.8″E 至 40°31′07.9″S、148°20′58.9″E

---

[1] "Seas and Submerged Lands (Territorial Sea Baseline) Proclamation 2016", Australia Federal Register of Legislation, https://www.legislation.gov.au/Details/F2016L00302, January 9, 2023.

续表

序号	位置描述
4003	从40°31′22.3″S、148°20′48.8″E 至40°33′44.6″S、148°14′50.1″E
4004	从40°33′44.6″S、148°14′50.1″E 至40°35′25.1″S、148°11′56.4″E
4005	从40°33′55.0″S、148°06′47.6″E 至40°33′24.3″S、148°05′53.3″E
4006	从40°33′22.6″S、148°05′49.6″E 至40°29′49.0″S、148°01′08.2″E
4007	从40°29′48.2″S、148°01′07.0″E 至40°22′48.3″S、147°53′31.0″E
4008	从40°22′48.3″S、147°53′31.0″E 至40°18′57.1″S、147°48′07.6″E
4009	从40°17′52.1″S、147°47′05.4″E 至40°17′47.8″S、147°47′00.0″E
4010	从40°17′37.9″S、147°46′49.5″E 至40°07′48.0″S、147°43′11.2″E
4011	从40°07′46.5″S、147°43′11.4″E 至40°06′13.3″S、147°43′32.4″E
4012	从40°05′29.3″S、147°43′21.8″E 至39°52′28.5″S、147°44′50.2″E
4013	从54°46′40.4″S、158°50′14.9″E 至54°46′49.6″S、158°48′57.1″E
4014	从54°46′49.7″S、158°48′54.7″E 至54°46′50.9″S、158°48′13.2″E
4015	从54°46′51.9″S、158°48′04.0″E 至54°46′29.3″S、158°46′30.5″E
4016	从54°46′28.3″S、158°46′27.9″E 至54°45′59.2″S、158°46′30.7″E
4017	从54°45′59.2″S、158°46′30.7″E 至54°45′30.0″S、158°46′31.8″E
4018	从54°45′29.3″S、158°46′32.0″E 至54°44′33.1″S、158°46′58.0″E
4019	从54°44′32.4″S、158°46′58.3″E 至54°43′49.9″S、158°47′21.5″E
4020	从54°43′49.9″S、158°47′21.5″E 至54°41′19.8″S、158°47′53.7″E
4021	从54°41′13.2″S、158°47′55.6″E 至54°38′15.1″S、158°48′51.7″E
4022	从54°38′11.6″S、158°48′52.6″E 至54°36′25.0″S、158°49′11.9″E
4023	从54°36′22.7″S、158°49′13.6″E 至54°35′28.8″S、158°49′50.4″E
4024	从54°35′28.8″S、158°49′50.4″E 至54°35′03.0″S、158°50′06.2″E
4025	从54°35′02.3″S、158°50′06.6″E 至54°34′16.7″S、158°50′34.8″E
4026	从54°34′16.7″S、158°50′34.8″E 至54°31′51.8″S、158°50′49.8″E
4027	从54°31′48.3″S、158°50′51.4″E 至54°31′10.6″S、158°51′04.4″E
4028	从54°31′04.7″S、158°51′08.7″E 至54°30′56.3″S、158°51′16.1″E
4029	从54°30′51.3″S、158°51′20.5″E 至54°29′47.2″S、158°52′30.8″E
4030	从54°29′46.4″S、158°54′29.5″E 至54°29′50.7″S、158°55′44.4″E
4031	从54°29′50.7″S、158°55′44.4″E 至54°29′13.3″S、158°55′53.9″E
4032	从54°29′13.0″S、158°55′53.9″E 至54°28′38.8″S、158°55′50.2″E
4033	从54°28′36.9″S、158°55′51.9″E 至54°28′11.5″S、158°56′08.1″E
4034	从54°28′11.6″S、158°56′10.3″E 至54°28′17.9″S、158°56′23.7″E

续表

序号	位置描述
4035	从 54°28′18.6″S、158°56′24.9″E 至 54°28′22.2″S、158°56′27.0″E
4036	从 54°28′23.0″S、158°56′27.9″E 至 54°29′27.5″S、158°57′09.7″E
4037	从 54°29′29.3″S、158°57′09.8″E 至 54°29′56.7″S、158°56′46.9″E
4038	从 54°29′56.7″S、158°56′46.9″E 至 54°30′01.8″S、158°56′42.7″E
4039	从 54°30′01.6″S、158°56′42.2″E 至 54°29′59.9″S、158°56′36.0″E
4040	从 28°52′36.2″S、113°48′33.8″E 至 28°47′36.8″S、113°44′33.8″E
4041	从 28°43′43.2″S、113°42′19.8″E 至 28°28′44.7″S、113°39′38.4″E
4042	从 28°28′44.7″S、113°39′38.4″E 至 28°20′20.3″S、113°35′26.4″E
4043	从 28°17′52.3″S、113°36′26.6″E 至 28°25′33.2″S、113°44′46.4″E
4044	从 28°25′33.2″S、113°44′46.4″E 至 28°27′26.7″S、113°48′41.8″E
4045	从 28°27′46.1″S、113°49′01.2″E 至 28°37′38.7″S、113°53′14.0″E
4046	从 28°37′38.7″S、113°53′14.0″E 至 28°47′55.9″S、114°02′31.8″E
4047	从 28°48′05.2″S、114°02′33.8″E 至 28°53′39.8″S、114°00′42.1″E

3. 关于毗连区与专属经济区

据《海洋与水下土地法》第13B条的授权，澳大利亚于1999年颁布《海洋与水下土地（毗连区界限）公告》[Seas and Submerged Lands (Limits of Contiguous Zone) Proclamation 1999]，其中规定：对于澳大利亚本土，其毗连区外部界限为从1973年《海洋与水下土地法》第7条所规定的领海基线量起24海里的线段；对于澳大利亚的海外领地，其毗连区外部界限为从基于国际法所确立的领海基线量起24海里的线段。但由于1985年澳大利亚与巴布亚新几内亚的海洋划界协定生效，该协定所及海床管辖界限以北区域，即东经141度子午线以东及东经145度子午线以西的海域，不属于澳大利亚毗连区范围。[1]

澳大利亚于1994年颁布了划定其专属经济区的首份公告，即《基于1973年〈海洋与水下土地法〉第10B条及1901年〈法律解释法〉第4条的1994年7月26日公告》（Proclamation of 26 July 1994, under section 10B of the Seas and Submerged Lands Act 1973 and section 4 of the Acts Interpretation Act 1901，以下简称《1994年公告》）。随着2004年澳大利亚与新西兰之间海洋划界协定的签署，澳大利亚于当年12月颁布了《海洋与水下土地2004年1

---

[1] "Seas and Submerged Lands (Limits of Contiguous Zone) Proclamation 1999", Australian Federal Register of Legislation, https://www.legislation.gov.au/Details/F2007B00589, January 10, 2023.

号修订公告》［Seas and Submerged Lands Amendment Proclamation 2004（No. 1），以下简称《2004年公告》］[1]，其修订了《1994年公告》所划定的相关专属经济区外部界限，确保与上述海洋划界条约中涉新西兰的专属经济区分界线相符。但澳大利亚随后发现其签署的条约文本中，靠近南极的麦夸里岛所邻接的专属经济区部分存在5个错误坐标点。为更正错误，澳大利亚迅速颁布《海洋与水下土地2005年1号修订公告》［Seas and Submerged Lands Amendment Proclamation 2005（No.1）］，受条约错误影响的《2004年公告》由此被撤销。[2]

除对部分措辞及地理测绘系统相关技术问题的修改外，《海洋与水下土地2005年1号修订公告》主要对诺福克岛（Norfolk Island）与新西兰间的专属经济区分界线、麦夸里岛专属经济区外部界限进行更新，并增加了豪勋爵岛（Lord Howe Island）专属经济区的外部界限坐标。澳大利亚公布的专属经济区外部界限如表4—表11所示：

表4　圣诞岛（Christmas Island）专属经济区外部界限[3]

线段序号	位置描述
a	从8°52′21″S、102°34′09″E开始
b	然后沿测地线向东北方向延伸至8°48′28″S、103°22′50″E
c	然后沿测地线向东北方向延伸至8°44′41″S、104°09′11″E
d	然后沿测地线向东北方向延伸至8°44′05″S、104°16′22″E
e	然后沿测地线向东北方向延伸至8°43′45″S、105°13′36″E
f	然后沿测地线向东北方向延伸至8°43′34″S、105°18′01″E
g	然后沿测地线向东南方向延伸至8°44′54″S、105°23′36″E
h	然后沿测地线向东南方向延伸至8°47′34″S、105°34′41″E
i	然后沿测地线向东南方向延伸至8°49′15″S、105°41′56″E
j	然后沿测地线向东南方向延伸至8°49′16″S、105°42′01″E
k	然后沿测地线向东南方向延伸至8°55′54″S、106°10′50″E
l	然后沿测地线向东南方向延伸至8°58′44″S、106°20′52″E

---

[1] 有关澳大利亚与新西兰间海洋划界协定的具体情况详见本书"五、海洋争端解决"下"（二）通过协议解决的其他海洋划界争端"部分。

[2] "Seas and Submerged Lands Amendment Proclamation 2005（No.1）", Australian Federal Register of Legislation, https：//www.legislation.gov.au/Details/F2005L01989, January 10, 2023.

[3] "Seas and Submerged Lands Act 1973-Proclamation under section 10B（26/07/1994）", Australia Federal Register of Legislation, https：//www.legislation.gov.au/Details/F2008B00721, January 10, 2023.

续表

线段序号	位置描述
m	然后沿测地线向东南方向延伸至8°59′23″S、106°23′10″E
n	然后沿测地线向东南方向延伸至9°02′18″S、106°33′31″E
o	然后沿测地线向东南方向延伸至9°07′57″S、106°49′22″E
p	然后沿测地线向东南方向延伸至9°09′04″S、106°50′55″E
q	然后沿测地线向东南方向延伸至9°10′20″S、106°52′42″E
r	然后沿测地线向东南方向延伸至9°18′39″S、107°04′21″E
s	然后沿测地线向东南方向延伸至9°24′39″S、107°11′58″E
t	然后沿测地线向东南方向延伸至9°42′32″S、107°34′41″E
u	然后沿测地线向东南方向延伸至9°49′34″S、107°43′34″E
v	然后沿测地线向东南方向延伸至9°49′47″S、107°43′47″E
w	然后沿测地线向东南方向延伸至10°00′04″S、107°54′18″E
x	然后沿测地线向东南方向延伸至10°04′37″S、107°59′01″E
y	然后沿测地线向东南方向延伸至10°08′26″S、108°03′00″E
z	然后沿测地线向东南方向延伸至10°24′42″S、108°19′46″E
za	然后沿测地线向东南方向延伸至10°34′22″S、108°29′24″E
zb	然后沿测地线向东南方向延伸至11°07′08″S、109°02′06″E

表5　帝汶海和阿拉弗拉海专属经济区外部界限[1]

线段序号	位置描述
a	从13°15′S、118°27′E开始
b	然后沿测地线向东北方向延伸至12°50′S、119°24′E
c	然后沿测地线向东北方向延伸至12°38′S、119°51′E
d	然后沿测地线向东北方向延伸至12°35′S、120°16′E
e	然后沿测地线向东北方向延伸至12°24′S、121°20′E
f	然后沿测地线向东北方向延伸至11°43′S、121°56′E
g	然后沿测地线向东北方向延伸至11°40′S、122°00′E
h	然后沿11°40′S线向东至与122°02′E子午线交会处
i	然后沿测地线向东北方向延伸至11°38′S、122°27′E
j	然后沿测地线向东北方向延伸至11°37′S、122°43′E

---

[1] "Seas and Submerged Lands Act 1973-Proclamation under section 10B (26/07/1994)", Australia Federal Register of Legislation, https://www.legislation.gov.au/Details/F2008B00721, January 10, 2023.

三、国内海洋立法

续表

线段序号	位置描述
k	然后沿测地线向东北方向延伸至11°33′S、123°14′E
l	然后沿测地线向东北方向延伸至11°32′S、123°18′E
m	然后沿测地线向东北方向延伸至11°31′S、123°22′E
n	然后沿测地线向东南方向延伸至11°33′S、123°56′E
o	然后沿测地线向东南方向延伸至11°34′S、123°58′E
p	然后沿测地线向东南方向延伸至11°31′S、124°26′E
q	然后沿11°31′S线向东至与124°27′E子午线交会处
r	然后沿测地线向东南方向延伸至11°34′S、124°34′E
s	然后沿测地线向东南方向延伸至11°40′S、124°57′E
t	然后沿测地线向东南方向延伸至11°47′S、125°20′E
u	然后沿测地线向东北方向延伸至11°45′S、125°25′E
v	然后沿测地线向东北方向延伸至11°37′S、125°45′E
w	然后沿测地线向东北方向延伸至11°31′S、126°00′E
x	然后沿测地线向东北方向延伸至11°26′S、126°12′E
y	然后沿测地线向东北方向延伸至11°21′S、126°28′E
z	然后沿测地线向东北方向延伸至11°20′S、126°31′E
za	然后沿测地线向东北方向延伸至11°19′S、126°48′E
zb	然后沿测地线向东北方向延伸至11°17′S、126°57′E
zc	然后沿测地线向东北方向延伸至11°14′S、127°31′E
zd	然后沿测地线向东北方向延伸至10°55′S、127°47′E
ze	然后沿测地线向东北方向延伸至10°45′S、127°58′E
zf	然后沿测地线向东北方向延伸至10°28′S、128°12′E
zg	然后沿测地线向东北方向延伸至10°26′S、128°18′E
zh	然后沿测地线向东北方向延伸至9°59′S、129°01′E
zi	然后沿测地线向东北方向延伸至9°45′S、129°30′E
zj	然后沿测地线向东北方向延伸至9°39′S、130°06′E
zk	然后沿测地线向东南方向延伸至9°45′S、130°43′E
zl	然后沿测地线向东南方向延伸至9°47′S、130°55′E
zm	然后沿测地线向东北方向延伸至9°42′S、131°28′E
zn	然后沿测地线向东北方向延伸至9°40′S、131°31′E
zo	然后沿测地线向东北方向延伸至9°36′S、131°43′E
zp	然后沿测地线向东北方向延伸至9°33′S、131°52′E

续表

线段序号	位置描述
zq	然后沿测地线向东北方向延伸至9°31′S、131°57′E
zr	然后沿测地线向东北方向延伸至9°23′S、132°12′E
zs	然后沿测地线向东北方向延伸至9°20′S、132°20′E
zt	然后沿测地线向东北方向延伸至9°16′S、132°30′E
zu	然后沿测地线向东北方向延伸至9°14′S、132°33′E
zv	然后沿测地线向东北方向延伸至9°06′S、132°46′E
zw	然后沿测地线向东北方向延伸至8°53′S、133°23′E
zx	然后沿测地线向东南方向延伸至9°25′S、134°50′E
zy	然后沿测地线向东北方向延伸至9°22′S、135°03′E
zz	然后沿测地线向东北方向延伸至9°17′S、135°13′E
zza	然后沿测地线向东北方向延伸至9°08′S、135°29′E
zzb	然后沿测地线向东南方向延伸至9°57′S、137°45′E
zzc	然后沿测地线向东南方向延伸至10°09′S、138°13′E
zzd	然后沿测地线向东南方向延伸至10°22′S、138°35′E
zze	然后沿测地线向东南方向延伸至10°24′S、138°38′E
zzf	然后沿测地线向东南方向延伸至10°50′S、139°12′E

表6　托雷斯海峡专属经济区外部界限[1]

线段序号	位置描述
a	从10°50′00″S、139°12′00″E开始
b	然后沿测地线向东南方向延伸至11°09′00″S、139°23′00″E
c	然后沿测地线向东北方向延伸至10°59′00″S、140°00′00″E
d	然后沿测地线向东北方向延伸至9°46′00″S、142°00′00″E
e	然后沿测地线向东北方向延伸至9°45′24″S、142°03′30″E
f	然后沿121°56′E子午线向北至9°15′43″S线交会处
g	然后沿测地线向东北方向延伸至9°12′50″S、142°06′25″E
h	然后沿测地线向东北方向延伸至9°11′51″S、142°08′33″E
i	然后沿测地线向东南方向延伸至9°11′58″S、142°10′18″E
j	然后沿测地线向东北方向延伸至9°11′22″S、142°12′54″E

[1] "Seas and Submerged Lands Act 1973-Proclamation under section 10B (26/07/1994)", Australia Federal Register of Legislation, https：//www.legislation.gov.au/Details/F2008B00721, January 10, 2023.

三、国内海洋立法

续表

线段序号	位置描述
k	然后沿测地线向东南方向延伸至9°11′34″S、142°14′08″E
l	然后沿测地线向东南方向延伸至9°13′53″S、142°16′26″E
m	然后沿测地线向东南方向延伸至9°16′04″S、142°20′41″E
n	然后沿测地线向东南方向延伸至9°22′04″S、142°29′41″E
o	然后沿测地线向东北方向延伸至9°21′48″S、142°31′29″E
p	然后沿测地线向东南方向延伸至9°22′33″S、142°33′28″E
q	然后沿测地线向东北方向延伸至9°21′25″S、142°35′29″E
r	然后沿测地线向东北方向延伸至9°20′21″S、142°41′43″E
s	然后沿测地线向东北方向延伸至9°20′16″S、142°43′53″E
t	然后沿测地线向东北方向延伸至9°19′26″S、142°48′18″E，与赛巴伊岛（Saibai Island）3海里领海的外部界限相接
u	然后沿上述外部界限穿过赛巴伊岛以东至9°23′40″S、142°51′00″E
v	然后沿142°51′00″E子午线向南至9°40′30″S线交会处
w	然后沿测地线向东北方向延伸至9°33′00″S、143°05′00″E
x	然后沿测地线向东北方向延伸至11°26′S、126°12′E
y	然后沿9°33′00″S线向东至与143°20′00″E子午线交会处
z	然后沿测地线向东北方向延伸至9°24′00″S、143°30′00″E
za	然后沿测地线向东北方向延伸至9°22′00″S、143°48′00″E
zb	然后沿测地线向东南方向延伸至9°30′00″S、144°15′00″E
zc	然后沿测地线向东南方向延伸至9°51′00″S、144°44′00″E
zd	然后沿测地线向东南方向延伸至12°20′00″S、146°30′00″E
ze	然后沿测地线向东南方向延伸至12°38′30″S、147°08′30″E
zf	然后沿测地线向东南方向延伸至13°10′30″S、148°05′00″E
zg	然后沿测地线向东南方向延伸至14°38′00″S、152°07′00″E
zh	然后沿测地线向东南方向延伸至14°45′00″S、154°15′00″E
zi	然后沿测地线向东北方向延伸至14°05′00″S、156°37′00″E

表7　珊瑚海专属经济区外部界限[1]

线段序号	位置描述
a	从14°04′00″S、157°00′00″E开始
b	然后沿测地线向东南方向延伸至14°41′00″S、157°43′00″E
c	然后沿测地线向东南方向延伸至15°44′07″S、158°45′39″E
d	然后沿测地线向西南方向延伸至16°25′28″S、158°22′49″E
e	然后沿测地线向西南方向延伸至16°34′51″S、158°16′26″E
f	然后沿测地线向西南方向延伸至17°30′28″S、157°38′31″E
g	然后沿测地线向西南方向延伸至17°54′40″S、157°21′59″E
h	然后沿测地线向西南方向延伸至18°32′25″S、156°56′44″E
i	然后沿测地线向西南方向延伸至18°55′54″S、156°37′29″E
j	然后沿测地线向西南方向延伸至19°17′12″S、156°15′20″E
k	然后沿测地线向东南方向延伸至20°08′28″S、156°49′34″E
l	然后沿测地线向东南方向延伸至20°32′28″S、157°03′09″E
m	然后沿测地线向东南方向延伸至20°42′52″S、157°04′34″E
n	然后沿测地线向东南方向延伸至20°53′33″S、157°06′25″E
o	然后沿测地线向东南方向延伸至21°12′57″S、157°10′17″E
p	然后沿测地线向东南方向延伸至21°47′21″S、157°14′36″E
q	然后沿测地线向东南方向延伸至22°10′31″S、157°13′04″E
r	然后沿测地线向东南方向延伸至22°31′38″S、157°18′43″E
s	然后沿测地线向东南方向延伸至23°14′54″S、157°48′04″E
t	然后沿测地线向东南方向延伸至25°08′48″S、158°36′39″E
u	然后沿测地线向东南方向延伸至26°26′30″S、163°43′30″E
v	然后沿测地线向东北方向延伸至26°12′04″S、165°51′37″E
w	然后沿测地线向东北方向延伸至25°50′42″S、168°44′18″E
x	然后沿测地线向东南方向延伸至25°55′51″S、169°25′54″E

[1] "Seas and Submerged Lands Act 1973-Proclamation under section 10B (26/07/1994)", Australia Federal Register of Legislation, https://www.legislation.gov.au/Details/F2008B00721, January 10, 2023.

表8 诺福克岛与新西兰间专属经济区分界线[1]

线段序号	位置描述
a	从30°53′11.23″S、171°13′28.85″E开始
b	然后沿测地线向西南方向延伸至31°16′01.68″S、170°37′06.34″E
c	然后沿测地线向西南方向延伸至31°19′31.67″S、170°31′15.10″E
d	然后沿测地线向西南方向延伸至31°40′26.30″S、169°56′12.27″E
e	然后沿测地线向西南方向延伸至31°47′23.99″S、169°44′25.06″E
f	然后沿测地线向西南方向延伸至32°04′50.57″S、169°14′37.00″E
g	然后沿测地线向西南方向延伸至32°06′52.74″S、169°11′06.79″E
h	然后沿测地线向西南方向延伸至32°25′18.55″S、168°39′03.72″E
i	然后沿半径200海里的测地弧向西依顺时针方向至32°22′18.95″S、166°58′54.37″E处凹向诺福克岛
j	然后沿半径200海里的测地弧向西依顺时针方向至32°09′22.23″S、166°17′34.30″E处凹向诺福克岛
k	然后沿半径200海里的测地弧向西北依顺时针方向至31°53′49.17″S、165°46′20.73″E处凹向诺福克岛
l	然后沿半径200海里的测地弧向西北依顺时针方向至31°30′S、165°13′27.08″E处凹向诺福克岛

表9 麦夸里岛专属经济区外部界限[2]

线段序号	位置描述
a	从51°04′48.96″S、158°01′25.98″E开始
b	然后沿半径200海里的测地弧向东依顺时针方向至51°01′S、158°59′53.57″E处凹向麦夸里岛
c	然后沿半径200海里的测地弧向东依顺时针方向至51°10′36.30″S、160°37′30.11″E处凹向麦夸里岛
d	然后沿半径200海里的测地弧向东南依顺时针方向至51°01′S、158°59′53.57″E处凹向麦夸里岛
e	然后沿测地线向东南方向延伸至52°11′26.54″S、161°57′11.15″E
f	然后沿测地线向东南方向延伸至52°15′53.24″S、162°03′07.43″E

---

[1] "Seas and Submerged Lands Amendment Proclamation 2005 (No. 1)", Australia Federal Register of Legislation, https://www.legislation.gov.au/Details/F2005L01989, January 11, 2023.

[2] "Seas and Submerged Lands Amendment Proclamation 2005 (No. 1)", Australia Federal Register of Legislation, https://www.legislation.gov.au/Details/F2005L01989, January 11, 2023.

续表

线段序号	位置描述
g	然后沿测地线向东南方向延伸至52°27′43.12″S、162°18′59.49″E
h	然后沿测地线向东南方向延伸至52°40′46.86″S、162°36′30.28″E
i	然后沿测地线向东南方向延伸至52°46′50.62″S、162°44′42.77″E
j	然后沿测地线向东南方向延伸至52°47′42.61″S、162°45′53.41″E
k	然后沿测地线向东南方向延伸至53°42′58.16″S、164°03′13.39″E
l	然后沿测地线向东南方向延伸至53°50′59.84″S、164°14′42.04″E
m	然后沿测地线向东南方向延伸至54°13′58.99″S、164°26′41.46″E
n	然后沿测地线向东南方向延伸至54°40′13.65″S、164°40′40.22″E
o	然后沿测地线向东南方向延伸至54°41′43.03″S、164°41′28.44″E
p	然后沿半径200海里的测地弧向西南依顺时针方向至54°56′14.18″S、164°39′00.39″E处凹向麦夸里岛
q	然后沿半径200海里的测地弧向西南依顺时针方向至55°00′11.94″S、164°38′17.35″E处凹向麦夸里岛
r	然后沿半径200海里的测地弧向西南依顺时针方向至55°10′06.11″S、164°36′21.26″E处凹向麦夸里岛
s	然后沿半径200海里的测地弧向西南依顺时针方向至55°14′12.61″S、164°35′21.12″E处凹向麦夸里岛
t	然后沿半径200海里的测地弧向西南依顺时针方向至164°35′21.12″S、164°26′46.41″E处凹向麦夸里岛
u	然后沿半径200海里的测地弧向西南依顺时针方向至55°52′23.70″S、164°23′57.71″E处凹向麦夸里岛
v	然后沿半径200海里的测地弧向西南依顺时针方向至56°38′56.15″S、163°56′44.86″E处凹向麦夸里岛
w	然后沿半径200海里的测地弧向西南依顺时针方向至56°52′19.72″S、163°44′04.71″E处凹向麦夸里岛
x	然后沿半径200海里的测地弧向西南依顺时针方向至57°09′53.30″S、163°23′17.53″E处凹向麦夸里岛

表 10 赫德岛和麦克唐纳群岛（Heard Island and McDonld Island）专属经济区外部界限[1]

线段序号	位置描述
a	从 53°14′07″S、67°03′20″E 开始
b	然后沿测地线向东北方向延伸至 52°42′28″S、68°05′31″E
c	然后沿测地线向东北方向延伸至 51°58′18″S、69°44′02″E
d	然后沿测地线向东北方向延伸至 51°24′32″S、71°12′29″E
e	然后沿测地线向东北方向延伸至 51°03′09″S、72°28′28″E
f	然后沿测地线向东北方向延伸至 50°54′23″S、72°49′21″E
g	然后沿测地线向东北方向延伸至 49°49′34″S、75°36′08″E
h	然后沿测地线向东北方向延伸至 49°24′07″S、76°42′17″E

表 11 豪勋爵岛专属经济区外部界限[2]

线段序号	位置描述
a	从 32°30′S、163°06′58.81″E 开始
b	然后沿半径 200 海里的测地弧向南依顺时针方向至 33°52′40.25″S、162°21′59.44″E 处凹向豪勋爵岛

4. 关于大陆架的主张及宣示

大陆架是澳大利亚最早通过立法明确宣示的管辖海域之一。早在 1953 年，澳大利亚即颁布相关公告宣布对邻接其海岸的大陆架的海床、底土及其上的自然资源拥有主权权利。[3] 1994 年 2 月，澳大利亚在《海事立法修正法》中抛弃了对 1958 年《大陆架公约》（Convention on the Continental Shelf）的适用，修改其大陆架外部界限的划定方式从而与 1994 年年底生效的《公约》相符。[4] 2004 年 12 月，依 1973 年《海洋与水下土地法》第 12 条的授权，澳大利亚颁布《海洋与水下土地（在塔斯曼海与南太平洋的大陆架界限）2004 年公告》[Seas and Submerged Lands（Limits of Continental Shelf in the Tas-

---

[1] "Seas and Submerged Lands Act 1973-Proclamation under section 10B（26/07/1994）", Australia Federal Register of Legislation, https：//www. legislation. gov. au/Details/F2008B00721, January 10, 2023.

[2] "Seas and Submerged Lands Amendment Proclamation 2005（No. 1）", Australia Federal Register of Legislation, https：//www. legislation. gov. au/Details/F2005L01989, January 11, 2023.

[3] "Commonwealth of Australia Gazette, No. 56, 11 September 1953", Australia Federal Register of Legislation, https：//www. legislation. gov. au/content/HistoricGazettes1953, January 12, 2023.

[4] "Maritime Legislation Amendment Act 1994", Australia Federal Register of Legislation, https：//www. le-gislation. gov. au/Details/C2004A04696, January 12, 2023.

man Sea and South Pacific Ocean) Proclamation 2004，以下简称《2004年大陆架公告》]。和前述划定专属经济区的《2004年公告》一样，该《2004年大陆架公告》也因澳大利亚与新西兰间条约文本的影响而存在坐标点错误，从而于2005年8月被《海洋与水下土地（在塔斯曼海与南太平洋的大陆架界限）2005年公告》［Seas and Submerged Lands (Limits of Continental Shelf in the Tasman Sea and South Pacific Ocean) Proclamation 2005］所取代。[1]

随着与新西兰间大陆架划界谈判的结束，澳大利亚在《2004年大陆架公告》颁布前即已依据《公约》第76条第8款向联合国大陆架界限委员会（Commission on the Limits of the Continental Shelf）提交了其200海里外大陆架划界案，就包括阿尔戈（Argo）、澳大利亚南极领地（Australian Antarctic Territory）、大澳大利亚湾、凯尔盖朗深海高原（Kerguelen Plateau）、豪勋爵海隆（Lord Howe Rise）、麦夸里海岭（Macquarie Ridge）、博物学家深海高原（Naturaliste Plateau）、南塔斯曼海隆（South Tasman Rise）、三王海岭（Three Kings Ridge）、沃勒比和埃克斯茅斯深海高原（Wallaby and Exmouth Plateaus）在内的10个海洋区域的大陆架外部界限提出审议申请。

针对澳大利亚划界案中有关南极的大陆架划界主张，美国、俄罗斯、日本、荷兰、德国、印度6国致信联合国秘书长表达了本国质疑或关切。上述各国一致表示：（1）依据《南极条约》第4条，不承认任何国家在南极的领土主张，也不承认任何国家对南极大陆延伸出的海床及底土的权利主张；（2）对于澳大利亚请求大陆架界限委员会就南极部分划界案暂不采取行动的做法，表示支持或赞赏。其中，美国、日本、德国、印度均重申了《公约》与《南极条约》的共同宗旨与原则，强调南极条约体系与《公约》的协调运作对确保南极地区的持续和平、安全、稳定至关重要；荷兰提出，澳大利亚在南极的主张关系到未决的领土争端，大陆架界限委员会应依其议事规则附件2拒绝审议；日本则进一步表示，澳大利亚向大陆架界限委员会所提交的大陆架界限信息，在任何情况下都不得影响《南极条约》下权利与义务的平衡。综合申请国澳大利亚及以上各国照会的请求及回应，大陆架界限委员会最终决定对划界案涉及的所谓"澳大利亚南极领地"部分不予审议。

针对澳大利亚划界案涉及的帝汶海部分，东帝汶于2005年致信联合国秘

---

[1] "Seas and Submerged Lands (Limits of Continental Shelf in the Tasman Sea and South Pacific Ocean) Proclamation 2005", Australia Federal Register of Legislation, https://www.legislation.gov.au/Details/F2005L01990, January 12, 2023.

三、国内海洋立法

书长表示，无论是澳大利亚向大陆架界限委员会提交的外大陆架信息，还是大陆架界限委员会就此通过的任何建议，都不得影响东帝汶与澳大利亚间海洋边界的划定。而针对澳大利亚划界案涉及的凯尔盖朗深海高原、三王海岭及新喀里多尼亚（New Caledonia）区域，法国于同年致信联合国秘书长表示，法国注意到其与澳大利亚在上述区域中的大陆架主张可能存在重叠，澳大利亚也已明确该申请不会影响两国后续的海洋划界，只要确保大陆架界限委员会的建议亦不影响两国间的海洋划界，法国就无意反对有关澳大利亚划界案中上述区域的审议与建议。[1]

2008年4月，经大陆架界限委员会第15届至第20届会议审议，澳大利亚2004年提交的200海里外大陆架划界案的有关建议最终获得通过。2012年5月，澳大利亚颁布了《海洋与水下土地（大陆架界限）2012年公告》［Seas and Submerged Lands（Limits of Continental Shelf）Proclamation 2012，以下简称《2012年大陆架公告》］，意在将新确立的外大陆架界限纳入正式立法，并将整合后的澳大利亚大陆架权利范围公诸于世。同年12月，澳大利亚将永久标明其大陆架外部界限的海图和有关情报交存联合国秘书长，其在相关立法中划定的大陆架界限由此应具有国际法下的确定性和拘束力。[2]

《2012年大陆架公告》共有11条正文及6个附表，除对本法生效、与前法关系、地理坐标系统的技术规则等的说明外，主要通过文字及详细列表确认了澳大利亚对9个独立区域约256万平方公里大陆架的管辖权利。这9个区域的大陆架外部界限分别通过5个附表列明其位置及走向，包括：附表1"邻接澳大利亚大陆、豪勋爵岛及诺福克岛沿岸的部分大陆架外部界限"、附表2"邻接麦夸里岛沿岸的大陆架外部界限"、附表3"邻接赫德岛和麦克唐纳群岛沿岸的大陆架外部界限"、附表4"邻接科科斯群岛（Cocos Islands）沿岸的大陆架外部界限"、附表5"邻接圣诞岛沿岸的大陆架外部界限"。[3] 同时，由于澳大利亚在该公告颁布前已与周边多个国家签订了海洋划界条约[4]，该公告

---

[1] "Reaction of States to the submission made by Australia to the Commission on the Limits of the Continental Shelf", UN, https://www.un.org/Depts/los/clcs_new/submissions_files/submission_aus.htm, January 12, 2023.

[2] "Submissions to the Commission: Submission by Australia", UN, https://www.un.org/Depts/los/clcs_new/submissions_files/submission_aus.htm, January 12, 2023.

[3] 各附表详见附录4《海洋与水下土地（大陆架界限）2012年公告》。

[4] 该公告涉及与巴布亚新几内亚、法国、新西兰、所罗门群岛等多国间的海洋划界条约。有关上述条约的具体规定详见本书"五、海洋争端解决"下"（二）通过协议解决的其他海洋划界争端"部分。

也就其中同时受到相关划界条约影响的坐标点作出相应说明。[1]

5. 关于历史性海湾的认定

为实现本国对历史性海湾的法律宣示，依 1973 年《海洋与水下土地法》第 8 条相关原则及授权，澳大利亚于 1987 年 3 月同时颁布了《依 1973 年海洋与水下土地法第 7 条的 1987 年 3 月 19 日公告》（Proclamation of 19 March 1987, pursuant to section 7 of the Seas and Submerged Lands Act 1973）与《依 1973 年海洋与水下土地法第 8 条的 1987 年 3 月 19 日公告》（Proclamation of 19 March 1987, pursuant to section 8 of the Seas and Submerged Lands Act 1973）。前者特别就 1983 年《内部界限（基线）公告》作出修订，从而在相关条款中加入"历史性海湾"的表述或就"历史性海湾"作出例外规定，并在原基线列表后补充了已认定的历史性海湾的基线坐标。后者则认定了安克舍斯湾（Anxious Bay）、恩康特湾、雷斯匹德湾（Lacepede Bay）、里沃利湾（Rivoli Bay）为澳大利亚的四大历史性海湾，说明了划定历史性海湾外部界限的技术性规则，并列明了四大海湾向海一侧界限的坐标点。[2]

2006 年，随着澳大利亚领海基线体系的全盘更新，调整其历史性海湾基线及外部界限的《海洋与水下土地（历史性海湾）2006 年公告》[Seas and Submerged Lands (Historic Bays) Proclamation 2006, 以下简称《2006 年历史性海湾公告》]也顺势颁布，上述 1987 年 3 月的两公告由此失效。

《2006 年历史性海湾公告》再次确认了安克舍斯湾等四海湾的历史性海湾地位，并依与《海洋与水下土地（领海基线）2006 年公告》一致的地理坐标体系对各海湾的基线及向海一侧界限的坐标点进行替换和更新。澳大利亚政府在《2006 年历史性海湾公告》附随的解释性声明中述称：其一，《公约》第 10 条并不能适用于历史性海湾；其二，在相当长的时间内持续地行使主权并为其他国家所容忍或默许，是习惯国际法下对相关水域提出历史性主张的要件；其三，随着澳大利亚领海基线的划定，斯宾塞湾、圣文森特湾、调查者号海峡（Investigator Strait）、柯芬湾（Coffin Bay）、斯特里基湾（Streaky Bay）及佛勒斯湾（Fowlers Bay）等都已被纳入澳大利亚内水；其

---

[1] "Seas and Submerged Lands (Limits of Continental Shelf) Proclamation 2012", Australia Federal Register of Legislation, https：//www.legislation.gov.au/Details/F2012L01081, January 12, 2023.

[2] "Proclamation of 19 March 1987, pursuant to section 7 of the Seas and Submerged Lands Act 1973", UN, https：//www.un.org/Depts/los/LEGISLATIONANDTREATIES/PDFFILES/aus_1987_proclamation_sec7.pdf, January 13, 2023; "Proclamation of 19 March 1987, pursuant to section 8 of the Seas and Submerged Lands Act 1973", UN, https：//www.un.org/Depts/los/LEGISLATIONANDTREATIES/PDFFILES/aus_1987_proclamation_sec8.pdf, January 13, 2023.

四,由澳大利亚联邦与南澳大利亚州共同组建委员会对相关海湾进行调查核验,最终认定安克舍斯湾等为历史性海湾。[1]

与《海洋与水下土地(领海基线)2006年公告》相同,《2006年历史性海湾公告》也在2003年《立法法》的要求下经历了十年一轮的阶段更新,于2016年3月被《海洋与水下土地(历史性海湾)2016年公告》[Seas and Submerged Lands (Historic Bays) Proclamation 2016]所替代。该2016年公告同样复刻了《2006年历史性海湾公告》的实质性内容,也明确无意于改变对历史性海湾的已有认定及界限划定。

依据该2016年公告第7条至第10条,各历史性海湾向海一侧的界限应由连接沿岸低潮线上的两点或相关条款中所列两个坐标点间的直线段构成。而依第11条,若是上述各条所指直线段连接了同一岛屿低潮线上的不同两点,则该两点间的线段应依此岛屿向海一面的低潮线划定。

由此,除第11条情形下的低潮线外,安克舍斯湾向海一侧的界限由连接沿岸低潮线上的两点或第7条第2款中坐标点间的直线段构成。安克舍斯湾向海一侧界限如表12所示:

表12　安克舍斯湾向海一侧界限[2]

线段序号	位置描述
a	从33°11′58.9″S、134°19′43.1″E到33°35′35.9″S、134°45′08.0″E
b	从33°35′45.2″S、134°46′00.3″E到33°35′53.9″S、134°46′35.0″E
c	从33°36′37.9″S、134°48′25.0″E到33°37′22.9″S、134°49′45.0″E

除第11条情形下的低潮线外,恩康特湾向海一侧的界限由连接沿岸低潮线上的两点或第8条第2款中坐标点间的直线段从南纬35度35分42.6秒、东经138度36分9.4秒到南纬35度35分42.8秒、东经138度57分29.0秒构成。

除第11条情形下的低潮线外,雷斯匹德湾向海一侧的界限由连接沿岸低潮线上的两点或第9条第2款中坐标点间的直线段从南纬36度35分47.4秒、东经139度50分2.8秒到南纬36度56分32.5秒、东经139度40分30.4秒构成。

除第11条情形下的低潮线外,里沃利湾向海一侧的界限由连接沿岸低

---

[1] "Seas and Submerged Lands (Historic Bays) Proclamation 2006", Australia Federal Register of Legislation, https://www.legislation.gov.au/Details/F2006L00526, January 13, 2023.

[2] "Seas and Submerged Lands (Historic Bays) Proclamation 2006", Australia Federal Register of Legislation, https://www.legislation.gov.au/Details/F2006L00526, January 13, 2023.

潮线上的两点或第 10 条第 2 款中坐标点间的直线段构成。里沃利湾向海一侧界限如表 13 所示：

表 13　里沃利湾向海一侧界限[1]

线段序号	位置描述
a	从 37°29′59.1″S、140°00′53.4″E 到 37°33′54.9″S、140°06′24.4″E
b	从 37°29′46.8″S、140°00′43.0″E 到 37°29′51.8″S、140°00′46.0″E

（二）海上安全相关立法

1. 海域安全的综合性立法

（1）1918 年《海军水域管控法》。

为在澳大利亚沿岸一定范围海域划定特殊军事区域并保障相关军事活动及设施安全，合理引导民用船舶及相关人员在特定海域内的行为，澳大利亚于 1918 年颁布了《海军水域管控法》（Control of Naval Waters Act 1918）。在经过 1966 年、1973 年、1978 年、1991 年、2001 年、2003 年、2016 年各关联立法的多次修订后，该法仍有效适用于包括海外领地在内的澳大利亚全境。

《海军水域管控法》共 15 条，除标题、生效时间、适用范围、术语解释等前导性内容外，相关条款主要涉及：海军水域的认定；豁免船舶的认定；海军水域监察官的任命；制定配套法规的权力；禁止修建某些建筑物；监察官在海军水域内及水域前滩对船舶、飞行器及其他交通工具给予指令的权力；对触犯本法的刑事责任认定及澳大利亚《刑法典》（Criminal Code）的适用；等等。

依据该法第 3B 条的规定，本法中的"海军水域"是指距某特定设施或该设施边界 5 海里以内的全部海域，或在无特定设施时，距军事用地边界 2 海里以内的全部海域。据其第 2 条的术语解释，相关特定"设施"包括：澳大利亚联邦所有或使用的海军设备、码头、船坞、船台、装载场、武器库、停靠或系泊处；澳大利亚联邦为海军防务目的所使用的固定结构、装置或设备。而为国家防务目的使用的"军事用地"包括：总督依 1989 年《土地收购法》第 122 条为联邦防务目的所保留或拨用的土地；依据某领土地区法律为联邦防务目的所保留的土地。

依据该法第 4 条，澳大利亚总督有权依据该法就该海域内的相关事项制

---

[1] "Seas and Submerged Lands (Historic Bays) Proclamation 2016", Australia Federal Register of Legislation, https：//www.legislation.gov.au/Details/F2016L00301, January 13, 2023.

定法规，包括：就船舶在海军水域内的系泊或下锚进行规范，以免影响出入该海域的航行活动；在海军水域内划定部分空间，专用于豁免船舶的停靠或锚泊；限制或禁止载有爆炸物、弹药、焦油、燃油或其他可燃物质的船舶进入海军水域的特定范围，并就爆炸物及弹药在该海域的装卸进行规范；限制或禁止在海军水域释放爆炸物或弹药；限制船舶在海军水域特定范围内使用明火和灯光；规范船舶在海军水域特定范围内的航速；要求超过特定吨位的船舶在该海域系泊、下锚或放置时应有至少 1 人全天候在船；禁止在该海域烘烤船底、倾斜船身或清洗船舶，或对上述行为进行规范；为军舰及其他船舶在该海域的航行指定可使用的灯光、信号及避碰措施；规范、限制或禁止相关人员、船舶在该海域的进出及相关行为在该海域的发生，并对指定管理人员进行授权；等等。[1]

(2) 2000 年《海上犯罪法》。

澳大利亚于 2000 年颁布《海上犯罪法》(Crimes at Sea Act 2000)，旨在实现联邦与各州间的刑事司法合作，从而使各州刑法能够在本州以外的澳大利亚沿岸水域得以适用，并就澳大利亚刑法适用于某些案件作出安排。1973 年《海上犯罪法》随该法的生效而废止。

经 2003 年、2006 年、2008 年、2011 年、2014 年修订，该法当前共有 4 部分 12 条正文、2 个附表，其主要内容包括：第一，法律生效、术语界定等说明性条款；第二，联邦与各州间合作方案的批准与法律地位；第三，澳大利亚刑法在本法"邻近海域"外的适用；第四，澳大利亚与东帝汶间海洋划界条约签署后，对在巨日升特别管理区适用刑法、移交犯罪嫌疑人等协议事项的执行；第五，与其他已有立法间的关系以及进一步制定相关法规的权力；等等。有关联邦与各州间刑法适用与刑事司法合作的范围划定、责任分配及限制例外等，均在该法附表 1 中得以具体体现。

根据该法，各州刑法可适用于以下"邻近海域"：从本州现行法律所划定的基线量起的 12 海里范围；在 12 海里以外，从本州现行法律所划定的基线量起至 200 海里范围，或至联邦法律所划定的大陆架外部界限范围。而在"邻近海域"外，澳大利亚刑法也可在一定条件下适用于特定区域，如：杰维斯湾领地 (Jervis Bay Territory) 的刑事实体法可在"邻近海域"外对澳大利亚船舶、澳大利亚公民、某些外国船舶及公民适用；在与他国管辖权竞合的情形下，澳大利亚司法部长需要依国际法相关规则将他国对本案管辖的意

---

[1] "Control of Naval Waters Act 1918", Australia Federal Register of Legislation, https://www.legislation.gov.au/Details/C2016C01077, January 14, 2023.

见纳入考量，以便决定是否同意相关案件进入聆讯或审判程序；是否获得司法部长的同意，不影响对犯罪嫌疑人的逮捕、指挥、引渡、遣送；诺福克岛领海以及圣诞岛、科科斯群岛、澳大利亚南极领地、赫德岛和麦克唐纳群岛、阿什莫尔和卡捷群岛（Ashmore and Cartier Islands）、珊瑚海群岛领地（Coral Sea Islands Territory）的沿岸海域，不适用本法有关"邻近海域"外的规定。[1]

(3) 2013年《海上权力法》。

为保证澳大利亚法在其海洋区域的落实和执行，澳大利亚于2013年颁布了《海上权力法》（Maritime Powers Act 2013），就可以行使于各海域或涉及各海域的执行权及其执行机关作出统一规定，并确保获授权的海事官员可依澳大利亚法、相关国际协定及国际裁决有效行使其职权。除为航空器识别及确保人身安全而行使相关权力外，包括海关官员、澳大利亚国防军成员、澳大利亚联邦警察及其他由总理所任命人员在内的海事官员，均需在得到相关授权的情形下方可对船舶、设施、航空器、保护区及被隔离人员行使其职权。

该法分7部分，共133条，除第1部分的解释说明性内容及第7部分的杂项规定外，其中：第2部分主要就国际协定及国际裁决所规定或明确的海洋权力行使予以确认和细化；第3部分就依第2部分可以行使的海洋权力进行逐一规范，包括登船和进入的权力、收集信息的权力、搜查权、扣留相关记录资料的权力、扣留船舶及航空器的权力、安置或扣留或移动或逮捕人员的权力、要求相关人员停止违犯澳大利亚法律的权力；第4部分规范执法过程中所涉记录、文件及船舶、航空器的处理程序，对于被扣留的文件，须书面通知其所有者、占有者或控制者，同时除后续司法程序要求、依澳大利亚法被处理、澳大利亚联邦获得所有权外，被扣留文件须在使用后归还其所有者；第5部分针对在执行过程中被逮捕或扣留的人员作出规定，要求必须尊重被逮捕或扣留人员的人格尊严，不得对其进行超出必要及合理范畴的侮辱或使其遭受残酷、非人道或有辱人格的对待；第6部分以列表形式说明了违反本法相关条款或规则要求的个人应受到的惩罚。

依据该法第8条，该法所指的地理意义上的"澳大利亚"包括：澳大利亚海外领地，澳大利亚及其海外领地的领海，附着于澳大利亚及其海外领地的大陆架上或其专属经济区海床上的设施、相关设施周围的安全区（safety zone），包括其海外领地及安全区在内的澳大利亚的上空。该法中使用的"领海"、"毗连区"、"专属经济区"、"大陆架"及"安全区"的含义与

---

[1] "Crimes at Sea Act 2000", Australia Federal Register of Legislation, https://www.legislation.gov.au/Det-ails/C2019C00248, January 14, 2023.

《公约》完全一致。行使本法规定的海上权力应遵守的监管性法律（monitoring law）则是指1901年《关税法》（Customs Act 1901）、1991年《渔业管理法》、1958年《移民法》（Migration Act 1958）、1984年《托雷斯海峡渔业法》、《刑法典》第73节等或1999年《环境保护与生物多样性养护法》附表1第8条以及其他获授权颁布的法规。

值得一提的是，据该法第41条，除了明确规定的例外情形，原则上该法并未授权执行机关对在澳大利亚与他国之间某海域的外国船舶行使国家海洋权力。而被视为例外情形之一的包括：以未曾中断的方式追赶的外国船舶。依据该法第42条，在海事官员可行使与某船舶有关的权力而尚未追赶该船舶的某地点，若海事官员要求负责该船的人员停船或协助登船而未被遵行，则可从该地点追赶该船，且该追赶不应中断。该法同时规定，不得仅因以下原因而认定追赶中断：由其他海事官员继续追赶；在相关要求作出时，追赶由包括外国船舶及航空器在内的其他船舶或航空器进行；当追赶由外国船舶或航空器继续时，无相应海事官员在船；被追赶的船舶已经离开所有海事官员或介入追赶的他国官员的视野；船舶无法被以包括无线电、雷达、卫星或声纳在内的远程手段追踪。作为体现国际协定及国际裁决的第2部分的内容之一，可以认为，上述第41条、第42条的规定是澳大利亚行使《公约》及习惯国际法中紧追权的细化规定。尽管使用"追赶"（chase）一词取代了《公约》第111条的"追逐"（pursuit），但其仍在遵行《公约》有关紧追权要件（如"未曾中断"）的框架下为本国在周边广阔海域中有力维护海洋权益提供有可操作性的行为规范。[1]

2. 海上设施安全相关立法

（1）1963年《海底电缆与管道保护法》。

一如澳大利亚对大陆架主权权利的较早关注，包括公海海底在内的海床和底土的安全利用等问题也早在20世纪60年代即被纳入了澳大利亚的立法考量。1963年10月，澳大利亚颁布《海底电缆与管道保护法》（Submarine Cables and Pipelines Protection Act 1963），专门就专属经济区及公海水下覆的电缆和管道的保护作出安排。该法颁布后，经1963年、1966年、1973年、2001年、2005年、2008年、2011年、2015年、2016年多次修订，除第1条、第2条外的所有法条都已经修改或更新。

当前，《海底电缆与管道保护法》共有12条，除该法本身的生效适用等

---

[1] "Maritime Powers Act 2013", Australia Federal Register of Legislation, https：//www. legislation. gov. au/ Details/C2017C00123, January 14, 2023.

说明外，主要就《刑法典》对违反本法行为的适用、对破坏或损害海底电缆或管道人员的惩处、对电缆或管道所有人的责任认定、对保护电缆或管道而受伤害的补偿、对相关罪行的认定及量刑以及国内管辖权分配等作出规定。依该法第7条，凡在澳大利亚登记的船舶上的人员的行为导致海底电报或电话缆线、海底管道、海底高压缆线被损毁的，将据其为故意或疏忽分别处以不同刑罚；但若相关电缆、管道的破损完全源于行为人挽救其生命或船舶的行为，且行为人已经采取了一切必要的预防措施都无法避免电缆或管道受损，则前述刑罚不予以适用。依该法第9条，若在采取了一切合理预防措施后，某一船舶为避免伤及海底电缆或管道而仍不得不牺牲其船锚、船网或其他捕捞设备时，船东有权请求电缆或管道所有人赔偿其损失。[1]

(2) 1987年《海上设施法》。

澳大利亚于1987年颁布《海上设施法》（Sea Installations Act 1987），旨在通过规范澳大利亚近海海上设施的运行，确保相关设施使用人员的安全以及设施附近的人员、船舶和飞机的安全，同时使此类海上设施的关联立法得以适当施行。

《海上设施法》对"近海"或"邻近海域"的界定与前述2000年《海上犯罪法》基本一致，但在特定海域的细则上略有差别。依据该法第5条，本法所指的各州或北方领地地区的"邻近海域"是指2006年《海上石油和温室气体封存法》（Offshore Petroleum and Greenhouse Gas Storage Act 2006）附表1下的相关海洋区域，即澳大利亚领海外部界限以外、专属经济区外部界限以内的海域，或专属经济区外部界限以外、大陆架外部界限以内的海域。该"邻近海域"的上空及底土也都与该区域拥有同等法律地位。第5条继续就珊瑚海及昆士兰地区、阿什莫尔和卡捷群岛、澳大利亚海外领地等特别区域的"邻近海域"认定作出细则说明。如，对于"澳大利亚南极领地"，其"邻近海域"的内部界限为国际法下测量该领地的领土界限的基线，而其外部界限为大陆架外部界限。同时，关于"邻近海域"的大陆架，该法明确，其范围不包括基于澳大利亚与他国间生效协定已不由澳大利亚行使主权权利的海床及底土。

依该法第6条，本法所称的"海上设施"指：安装在邻近海域，且与邻近海域的海床部分存在或即将产生实际接触的设施；安装在邻近海域，且与前款设施存在或即将产生实际接触的设施。满足上述条件的船舶或飞机也可

---

[1] "Submarine Cables and Pipelines Protection Act 1963", Australia Federal Register of Legislation, https://www.legislation.gov.au/Details/C2016C00970, January 14, 2023.

被视为本法中的海上设施，但需保持这一状态 14 天（本国船舶）或 30 天（外国船舶）以上。若某设施是通过电缆或其他设备与海床产生实际接触，该设施也应被视为本法中的海上设施。

至 2021 年《海上电力基础设施（相应修正）法》[Offshore Electricity Infrastructure (Consequential Amendments) Act 2021] 颁布，《海上设施法》已经经历了 50 次修订。当前，该法共有 5 部分 79 条，原第 2、3、4、8 部分都已废止，除第 1 部分的前导性说明外，其主要就海上设施的安装，海上设施的关联法律适用及司法管辖权划分，与海上设施有关的犯罪和处理程序，检查员的任命及其登临检查等职权，下级法规及官方声明的授权等问题进行了较详尽且严格的规定。如，为保证海上设施及其周边区域的安全，在海上设施与境外地点之间禁止直接往来通行，违反该禁令的行为将被认定为可公诉的罪行。[1]

（3）2003 年《海上运输与海上设施安全法》。

2003 年 12 月，澳大利亚颁布了《海上运输与海上设施安全法》（Maritime Transport and Offshore Facilities Security Act 2003），以保护海上运输及海上设施免受非法干预，并防止相关运输及设施被用于实施严重犯罪。为实现这一目标，该立法意在以发展船舶、其他海上运输业务及海上设施相关安全方案为核心建立规范性框架，并通过实施这一安全方案贡献于以下海事安全成效的取得：第一，履行澳大利亚在国际海事组织框架下有关人命安全、港口与船舶安保的条约义务，并落实船员相关权利、自由及福利；第二，在避免对贸易造成不适当干扰的情形下，降低澳大利亚船舶及港口、位于澳大利亚的其他船舶、澳大利亚海上设施遭受恐怖袭击的风险；第三，降低海上运输或海上设施被用于便利恐怖活动或其他非法活动的风险；第四，确保航运业参与者与对海上运输及海上设施负有安全责任的政府机构间安保信息沟通顺畅。

依据该法第 17A 条，该法中的"海上设施"是指位于某海上区域，可利用其所附设备或本身一部分从海床或其底土开采石油的设施，包括与此类作业相关的或其附带的活动中所使用的位于海上区域的各结构及船舶。浮式生产储油卸油装置（Floating Production Storage and Offloading，FPSO）与浮动式储油装置（Floating Storage Unit，FSU）都属于该法所指的"海上设施"，但离港油轮、拖船、海上设施的补给船、海上移动钻井装置及海底管道等都被

---

[1] "Sea Installations Act 1987", Australia Federal Register of Legislation, https://www.legislation.gov.au/D-etails/C2022C00172, January 15, 2023.

排除在外。海上设施所处的"海上区域"则包括了澳大利亚及其海外领地的内水、领海、专属经济区及大陆架上覆水域。

经历了2005—2021年的20余次修订后，当前《海上运输与海上设施安全法》共有16部分292条，其中：

第1部分主要就法律生效、适用范围、立法目的、术语解释作出规定，并特别对本法中的核心概念及规则进行了阐释。如，对海上运输和海上设施的非法干预的含义；对受安全管制的港口及其运营者，船舶、海上设施及其运营者的界定；未受管制的外国船舶的行为及后果认定；受管制者的一般性抗辩；等等。

第2部分主要就海事安保等级作出明确规定。随着各海事安保计划、船舶安保计划及海上安保计划中所规定的海事安保等级的生效，一系列安保措施将得以实施。同时，相关国家部门部长将有权在特殊情形下发布安保指令。

第3部分则专门就上述海事安保计划作出安排。海事安保计划应据不同海事安保等级确定相应的安保措施，各海洋产业参与方被要求制订并严格遵行相关计划。同时，有关海事安保计划的内容、形式及批准程序等也都在该部分被逐一规定。

第4部分说明了船舶安保计划与国际船舶安保证书（International Ship Security Certificates，ISSCs）间的关系，要求受管制的澳大利亚船舶应同时具备船舶安保计划与国际船舶安保证书，在遵行船舶安保计划的同时也应满足国际船舶安保证书规定的相关要求。

第5部分涉及对外国船舶的监管义务，相关国家部门部长可发布管控指令以规范外国船舶的行为，从而确保相关安保计划的执行。而后续增补的第5A、5B、5C部分则主要围绕海上安保计划展开，分别就海洋产业参与方的安保计划、澳大利亚船舶与海上设施安全、外国船舶与海上设施安全作出规定。

第6部分就海事安保区的设立作出安排。依据该部分的规定，澳大利亚可在港口、船舶之上或船舶周围、海上设施之上或其周围设立海事安保区，此类区域将适用更为严格的安保计划。

第7部分对审核、清查武器及其他被禁物品提出要求，审查对象包括：将进入特定区域、使用特定交通工具或登上特定船舶的人员；通行特定区域的车辆、货物及船舶；海事安保区内受管制的澳大利亚船舶及海上设施上的武器携带或持有情况；等等。

第8部分对本法中的6类监管官员及其权力进行规范，包括海事安保督察员、安保评估督察员、正式授权官员、警方或海关执法官员、海上安保护卫员、安检官员。

第9、10部分规定了对某些海上运输或海上安保事故的报告义务，并允许相关国家部门部长获取海洋产业参与方的安保守法信息。

第11、12、13部分则对本法相关要求的执行机制、行政上诉法庭某些判决的复核以及经济补偿、与他法的关系、效力瑕疵等其他杂项问题有所涉及或明晰。[1]

（三）海洋渔业相关立法

1. 1984年《托雷斯海峡渔业法》

为顺利执行与巴布亚新几内亚间即将生效的海洋划界条约，尤其为所涉渔业相关义务的履行准备适宜的国内法律环境，澳大利亚于1984年4月颁布了《托雷斯海峡渔业法》。该法的主要目的在于：第一，认可并保护传统居民（traditional inhabitants）的生活方式及生计，包括保护其传统捕鱼的相关权利；第二，保护并保全保护区之内及其周边的海洋环境与本土动植物；第三，采取必要措施养护生物种群，但应尽量减少此类措施对传统渔业的限制性影响；第四，合理监管所涉条约第5部分中商业捕捞相关条款的执行，以免不利于该条约第4部分中传统捕鱼相关目标的实现；第五，通过监管，以实现最优利用为目标管理商业捕捞；第六，依据所涉条约，与巴布亚新几内亚共享相关保护区内商业捕捞的许可捕捞份额；第七，在制定和实施许可政策时，充分考虑促进托雷斯海峡区域的经济发展及增加传统居民被雇用机会的需求与愿望。

2005—2016年，该法进行了20余次修订，法条正文从原有的60条扩展到112条，并随有2个附件。正文主要内容包括：（1）就澳大利亚管辖海域、巴布亚新几内亚管辖海域、保护区、传统渔业、传统居民等作出与所涉条约一致的界定并予以进一步说明或限制，如，将保护区内的昆士兰沿岸海域（Protected Zone coastal waters of Queensland）排除在本法适用范围之外；（2）就联邦政府在相关区域内的渔业管理权责作出规定，如，由联邦政府渔业部长为代表对托雷斯海峡区域的渔业活动进行管理，其有权发布捕鱼活动相关公告、管理计划；（3）就相关区域内的捕鱼许可进行规定，相关捕捞行为应在获得必要许可证的情形下实施，并对相关许可证的形式、内容、背书

---

[1] "Maritime Transport and Offshore Facilities Security Act 2003", Australia Federal Register of Legislation, https://www.legislation.gov.au/C2004A01216/latest/text, December 5, 2024.

转让等事项作出详细规定；（4）宣布由联邦政府渔业部长、昆士兰州政府渔业部长和托雷斯海峡地区管理委员会主席组建保护区联合委员会管理保护区，并就该联合委员会的组织机构、官员任命及权力行使等作出规定；（5）分别就对澳大利亚船舶及在保护区内的外国船舶的渔业捕捞活动进行监管的机制作出安排，如在相关区域内违法犯罪行为的认定及相应的行政执法与刑事处罚；等等。[1]

2. 1991 年《渔政法》

澳大利亚于 1991 年颁布《渔政法》，旨在：第一，建立澳大利亚渔业管理局，以代表澳大利亚联邦政府负责渔业监管；第二，建立渔业政策委员会，以确保渔业从业人员及利益相关人员得以参与政府渔业管理相关政策的制定。

该法共有 4 部分 128 条，其主体为：

第一，关于澳大利亚渔业管理局的第 2 部分。依该部分规定，澳大利亚渔业管理局具有独立的法人地位，代表联邦政府行使职权、承担职责。为实现高效的渔业管理目标，渔业管理局应确保渔业资源的开发利用和相关活动的开展符合生态可持续发展原则，从而使澳大利亚的渔业管理为澳大利亚社会带来最大化的净经济回报。

第二，关于渔业政策委员会的第 3 部分。依该部分规定，渔业政策委员会在履行其职能时，须致力于促进与渔业行业有利害关系的人员就影响本行业的事宜交换意见，并促成统一方法以应对影响本行业的相关事项。该法同时就该委员会的组织机构作出具体规定，包括理事会的设立、理事会职能和权务、理事会的章程和会议程序、理事会工作组等。[2]

第三，关于授权颁布相关法规的第 4 部分。依该部分规定，总督、主管部长、澳大利亚渔业管理局负责人有权制定其他层级的渔业规则，具体表现为条例、公告、决定、渔业管理计划、禁渔指示等，如 1992 年《渔业管理条例》（Fisheries Management Regulation 1992）、1995 年《渔业管理（南方蓝鳍金枪鱼渔业）条例》［Fisheries Management (Southern Bluefin Tuna Fishery) Regulations 1995］等。[3]

---

[1] "Torres Strait Fisheries Act 1984", Australia Federal Register of Legislation, https：//www. legislation. gov. au/Details/C2016C00677, January 15, 2023.

[2] 有关澳大利亚渔业管理局及经变化后的渔业政策委员会的职能，详见本书"二、海洋事务主管部门及其职能"下"（二）海洋管理相关的行政机构"部分。

[3] "Fisheries Administration Act 1991", Australia Federal Register of Legislation, https：//www. legislation. g-ov. au/Details/C2017C00373, January 15, 2023.

3. 1991年《渔业管理法》

《渔业管理法》于1991年11月10日与《渔政法》同日颁布。不同于以渔业管理机关的组建为核心目标的《渔政法》，《渔业管理法》意在作为澳大利亚的渔业基本法为海洋捕捞活动提供综合性法律依据。

该法的基本目标在于：第一，实行高效且具有成本效益的渔业管理；第二，确保渔业资源的开发利用及相关活动的开展以符合生态可持续发展原则的方式进行，尤其需要关注渔业活动对非目标物种以及海洋环境长期可持续性的影响；第三，最大化澳大利亚渔业管理对澳大利亚社会的净经济回报；第四，确保渔业管理局在渔业资源监管方面对捕捞产业和澳大利亚社会负责；第五，实现与渔业管理局成本回收有关的政府目标。除此之外，该法还要求相关主管机关考虑以下目标：第一，通过适当养护管理措施，保证澳大利亚渔区的生物资源不因过度开发而枯竭；第二，实现澳大利亚渔区内生物资源的优化利用；第三，确保通过在澳大利亚渔区及公海上的养护管理措施，履行澳大利亚在鱼类种群相关国际协定下的义务；第四，确保以澳大利亚为船旗国的船舶在捕捞活动中遵守相关国际法义务；第五，保证商业性、娱乐性及传统捕鱼的利益方都被纳入考量。依据该法第4条，澳大利亚渔区是指邻接澳大利亚及其海外领地沿岸并位于其专属经济区外部界限以内的水域，但澳大利亚各州及各领地地区内水域及其沿岸水域，由总督依该法第11条通过公告所宣布的例外水域（excepted waters）被排除在该区之外。而依据该法第5条，澳大利亚各州及各领地地区的沿岸水域是指，邻接各州或各领地地区的、从澳大利亚领海基线量起3海里以内的澳大利亚领海；不在各州或各领地地区界限内，但为基线向陆地一侧邻接各州或各领地地区的海洋或潮汐水域。

经过1993—2021年的近50次修订，该法从原有的9部分168条正文、3个附件，扩展至共11部分287条正文、4个附件。其正文内容主要包括：前置条文和概念界定；渔业和海洋环境；捕捞规则；法定捕鱼权登记；获准在公海捕鱼的船舶登记；捕鱼许可证登记；与各州和北方领地地区在渔业管理方面的合作；捕鱼业监督和执法；相关税费的征收；法定捕鱼权分配审查小组的审查和其他相关杂项；等等。该法原有的3个附件分别为：《某些太平洋岛国与美国政府间渔业协定》（Treaty on fisheries between the Governments of certain Pacific Island States and the United States of America）全文、《执行1982年12月10日〈联合国海洋法公约〉有关养护和管理跨界鱼类种群和高度洄游鱼类种群的规定的协定》[1]（Agreement for the Implementation of the Provi-

---

[1] 有关澳大利亚签署和批准此条约的情况详见本书"四、缔结和加入的国际海洋法条约"下"（一）联合国框架下的海洋法公约"部分。

sions of the United Nations Convention on the Law of the Sea of 10 December 1982 relating to the Conservation and Management of Straddling Fish Stocks and Highly Migratory Fish Stocks）全文及《促进公海渔船遵守国际养护和管理措施的协定》（Agreement to Promote Compliance with International Conservation and Management Measures by Fishing Vessels on the High Seas）全文，以锚定澳大利亚在海洋渔业管理中应履行的国际法律义务。而随着2005年正文第105Q条的加入，该法特别添加了附件1A，即有关扣留涉嫌非法捕鱼外国渔民的规定，从而进一步加强对非法、不报告和不管制捕捞活动（illegal, unreported and unregulated fishing, IUU）的监管。[1]

（四）海洋能源相关立法

1. 1994年《海上矿产法》

为规范海上矿产的勘探和开采等活动，澳大利亚于1994年颁布了《海上矿产法》（Offshore Minerals Act 1994），1981年《矿产（水下土地）法》[Minerals (Submerged Lands) Act 1981]随之被废止。依据该法第1章第4部分的说明，在开采对象上，该立法仅适用于矿物，石油的勘探和开发则由2006年《海上石油和温室气体封存法》进行规范，不属于本法适用范围。而依第4条，该法下的矿物被定义为天然存在的物质或混合物质，可以为碎石、黏土、蒸发岩、页岩、油页岩或煤等多种形态，但不包括石油和天然气。在地理范围上，该法可延伸适用于阿什莫尔和卡捷群岛、诺福克岛、圣诞岛、赫德岛和麦克唐纳群岛等海外领地，但明确将巨日升特别管理区排除在外。而在主体范围上，该法可广泛适用于所有自然人与法人，包括非澳大利亚公民、非澳大利亚及其海外领地居民、非成立于澳大利亚的公司、在澳大利亚或其海外领地无业务经营的公司。

至2019年，该法共进行了14次修订，形成了当前5章443条正文及1个附件的规范性文本。其第1章下分4部分，主要为立法背景等前导性说明，包括澳大利亚联邦与各州及各领地地区间有关矿产开发的协议，重要术语，尤其是对海洋法基础概念的界定解释，主管机关及联合主管机关的指定原则，本法的生效时间与适用范围，等等。第2章下分6部分，主要为海上矿产的开采活动提供规范，依本章规定，要在澳大利亚海域勘探和开采矿产，必须先获得相应的许可证，确保在不同需求、不同环节下的矿产开发行为受

---

[1] "Fisheries Management Act 1991", Australia Federal Register of Legislation, https://www.legislation.gov.au/Details/C2021C00546, January 15, 2023.

控。第3章下分2部分，主要就不同矿产开采活动的登记及所涉程序作出要求，包括对海上矿产开发活动的登记造册、上报公布，不同许可证的书面要求及登记程序，许可证的批准及转让，等等。第4章下分6部分，主要就海上开采行为的管理机构及管理机制作出规定，如信息管理、执行监督、对海外领地相关决定的审核、联合主管机关及其他指定机关的工作程序、监察官任命、财政运转等。第5章下分2部分，主要就本法与其他现行法律间的关系、各州及各领地地区相关立法与本法的关系、刑法典的适用、税法的适用等余留问题作出说明。

该法通过第2章规定了5种不同的许可证，以确保澳大利亚海上矿产勘探和开采活动有序、高效且符合生态可持续发展原则地进行。这5种许可证分别是：(1) 勘探许可证。该许可证涵盖采矿项目的勘探阶段，并赋予持有人申请进一步批准以进行勘探相关活动的专有权。(2) 保留许可证。对于某些在短期内不具有商业开发可行性，但客观上存在长远发展前景的待开发区域，可申请保留许可证，以确保在项目从勘探阶段过渡到商业开采阶段之前保留对该开采区域的权利。(3) 采矿许可证。该许可证涵盖项目的商业开采阶段，授权从许可证涵盖的区域回收矿物。(4) 工作许可证。该许可证授权相关作业在勘探、保留或采矿许可证区域（例如码头）之外进行。(5) 特殊（目的）许可证。该许可证授权科学调查、勘测或少量矿物的收集，但该类许可不赋予持有人任何专有权或在本区域获得其他许可证的优先权。[1]

2. 2006年《海上石油和温室气体封存法》

为在规范近海石油勘探与开发的同时，兼顾对海上温室气体的注入与储存，澳大利亚于2006年颁布了《海上石油和温室气体封存法》，为以下几类海上行为提供规范性框架：第一，石油勘探；第二，石油开采；第三，石油或温室气体相关基础设施的建造与营运；第四，石油或温室气体运输管道的建造与营运；第五，温室气体的注入与储存。

本法所称的海上区域是指以从领海基线量起的3海里为起点，向海延伸至大陆架外部界限的海域，包括澳大利亚各州、各领地地区、各海外领地及东巨日升地区的海上区域，其在上述各处的具体位置及界限由该法第8条列表作出详细说明。本法所称的石油包括：(1) 任何自然形成的碳氢化合物或各种碳氢化合物的混合物，无论其为气态、液态还是固态；(2) 硫化氢、氮、氦和二氧化碳的一种或多种混合物，无论其为气态、液态还是固态；

---

[1] "Offshore Minerals Act 1994", Australia Federal Register of Legislation, https://www.legislation.gov.au/Series/C2004A04704, January 15, 2023.

(3)管道状态下，除上述物质外，从油井直接开采的混合物，无论是否在其中添加或剔除部分物质。依据该法第1章的背景说明，各州和北方领地地区的近海石油立法应适用于本州和本地区的沿海水域，但各州和北方领地地区应按照本法规定的方式共同监管联邦海上石油立法的实施，澳大利亚联邦、各州及北方领地地区应尽量在规范和管理澳大利亚领海基线以外的海上石油勘探和开采相关原则和规则上保持一致。作为综合规制澳大利亚海上石油开采且体现海洋环保先驱行动的核心立法，《海上石油和温室气体封存法》的法条内容相当庞杂，在经历了2007—2021年的40余次修订后，更是从原来的9章791条正文及5个附件，扩展至10章1073条正文及7个附件。除第1章的前导性说明及第9章的杂项规定外，其内容主要包括：

第一，有关海上石油开采行为的授权与规范。澳大利亚相关主管机关可依据该法，分别就石油勘探许可、石油保留租约、石油生产牌照、基础设施牌照、管道牌照、特别石油勘探权、石油开采权进行赋权和管理。其中，石油勘探许可授权被许可人在许可区域内勘探石油；在可开采区域确定后，若当前无法进行商业开采但有可能在15年内实现，可以授权签署石油保留租约；石油生产牌照授权牌照持有人在牌照范围内从事石油开采活动；基础设施牌照授权牌照持有人在牌照范围内建造或营运与石油或温室气体相关的基础设施；特别石油勘探权允许权利人在授权区域内从事特定石油勘探及开采活动，但不得以钻井为目的。

第二，有关温室气体的注入与储存活动的规则安排。依据该法，相关活动需要分别申请温室气体评估许可、温室气体储存租约、温室气体注入牌照、温室气体勘察权、温室气体特别授权。其中，温室气体评估许可授权在被许可区域勘探可能的温室气体储存形式和可能的温室气体注入地点；温室气体储存租约适用于当前尚无能力注入或储存温室气体，但在15年内可能实现的申请人；温室气体注入牌照授权牌照持有人在牌照区域内开展温室气体注入及储存作业；温室气体勘察权允许权利人在授权区域内开展作业，以探查可能的温室气体储存形式或可能的温室气体注入地点，但不得以钻井为目的。

第三，石油及温室气体相关权利的转让、交易及其登记要求。依据该法，相关许可授权的管理机构必须为每个海上区域保存与该海上区域有关的石油权利和石油特别勘探授权、温室气体各项权利和温室气体勘察授权的登记记录。一项石油权利、温室气体权利的转让或交易必须得到权利管理机关的批准，相关转让及交易文书必须进行登记。任何个人未经批准不得控制或停止控制已注册权利人，否则将构成违法并引发民事责任。

第四，有关石油及温室气体活动的数据管理与信息收集。权利管理机关可以指示石油权利持有人、温室气体权利持有人留存相关记录，并通过法规制定数据管理的相关条款，同时有权获取相关信息及文件。[1]

3. 2021年《海上电力基础设施法》

2021年12月，澳大利亚颁布《海上电力基础设施法》（Offshore Electricity Infrastructure Act 2021），旨在为海上可再生能源基础设施以及海上电力输送基础设施提供有效监管框架。

依据该法第10、11条，其所称的海上可再生能源基础设施是指以下列活动为主要目的而固定或系缆的基础设施，包括：（1）勘探一种或多种可再生能源；（2）评估某一可再生能源开发的可行性；（3）开发某可再生能源；（4）储存、传输或传送可再生能源产品。该法所称的海上电力输送基础设施是指以储存或传输电力（包括非可再生能源所生产的电力）为主要目的而固定或系缆的基础设施，如海底电缆和与电缆相关的其他基础设施。但上述两种设施类型都将1994年《海上矿产法》及2006年《海上石油和温室气体封存法》中规定的固定基础设施、正在建造安装或拆除的设施、海底电缆、被其他关联法规所特别规定的设施排除在外。

自颁布以来，《海上电力基础设施法》于2022年9月和11月经《气候变化（相应修正）法》[Climate Change (Consequential Amendments) Act 2022]及《海上电力基础设施立法修正法》（Offshore Electricity Infrastructure Legislation Amendment Act 2022）修订，现共有8章311条正文。除含有上述基础概念界定的第1章外，其主要内容包括：（1）禁止未经授权在澳大利亚联邦近海地区建造海上可再生能源基础设施和海上电力输送基础设施；（2）澳大利亚总理有权宣布适合建造海上可再生能源基础设施的区域；（3）主管部长有权在澳大利亚所宣布的海上区域通过授权或许可，批准海上可再生能源基础设施和海上电力输送基础设施的建造；（4）就海上基础设施的监管机制作出安排，设立监管机构负责海上基础设施的管理和运营，同时在澳大利亚联邦海域监测、调查基础设施的合规性；（5）设立海上基础设施登记处，并指定国家海上石油安全和环境管理局为该法下的海上基础设施监管机构；（6）任命海上基础设施登记官，规定由其作为国家相关部门雇员，保管海上基础设施许可证登记册及完成其他行政任务；（7）明确2011年《工作健康与安全法》（Work Health and Safety Act 2011）在海上基础设施活动中的适用，并规

---

[1] "Offshore Petroleum and Greenhouse Gas Storage Act 2006", Australia Federal Register of Legislation, https：//www.legislation.gov.au/C2006A00014/latest/text, January 16, 2023.

范相关数据及信息的收录、上报及公开事宜。[1]

(五) 海上运输相关立法

1. 航运相关立法

(1) 1909年《海上保险法》。

澳大利亚于1909年即颁布了服务于海上运输的《海上保险法》(Marine Insurance Act 1909)，该法经1966年《制定法修订（十进制通货）法》[Statute Law Revision (Decimal Currency) Act 1966]、1973年《制定法修订法》(Statute Law Revision Act 1973)、2001年《金融服务改革（重要规定）法》[Financial Services Reform (Consequential Provisions) Act 2001]、2008年《制定法修订法》修订后，至今仍有效适用于除澳大利亚各州内保险以外的海上保险领域。

该法共有9部分95条正文及2个附件，主要内容包括：第一，海上保险的基本规则，如海上保险限额、可保利益、保险价值、相关披露及陈述义务、保险单、双重保险、保险保证、航程保险特别事项等相关规定；第二，保险单转让的相关要求，如，何种情形下以及以何种方式可以转让保险单，已经丧失保险利益的权利人转让保险单应受限制，等等；第三，保险费及其支付的相关规定；第四，灭失及委付的相关规定，如除外损失、全部损失与部分损失、失踪船舶、推定全损与实际全损、委付的通知与效果、海难救助及共同海损下的部分损失等；第五，关于保险赔偿的标准及规则，如保险人的赔偿责任、保险人在赔付中的权利等；第六，保费的返还，如，保费返还的执行、基于协议的返还、保费支付对价落空时的返还处理等。其附件1主要就部分英联邦法律及州立法在本法所涉领域的适用作出说明，附件2则就保险单的形式要求及保险单解释规则进行了规定。[2]

(2) 1991年《海上货物运输法》。

为回应海上货物运输国际立法的发展并更新本国海商事法律体系，澳大利亚于1991年颁布了《海上货物运输法》(Carriage of Goods by Sea Act 1991)，通过引入先进的、公平的和高效的海运货物责任制度，使本国相关规则与澳大利亚主要贸易伙伴国家的现有安排相一致，并妥为顾及联合国有关海运货物责任框架的新进展。

---

[1] "Offshore Electricity Infrastructure Act 2021", Australia Federal Register of Legislation, https://www.le-gislation.gov.au/Details/C2022C00346, January 16, 2023.

[2] "Marine Insurance Act 1909", Australia Federal Register of Legislation, https://www.legislation.gov.au/C1909A00011/latest/text, January 16, 2023.

为此，1991年《海上货物运输法》以1968年《修订统一提单若干法律规定的国际公约的议定书》（Protocol to Amend the International Convention for the Unification of Certain Rules of Law relating to Bills of Lading，即《维斯比规则》）及1979年部分修订《维斯比规则》的《修订（经1968年议定书修订的）统一提单若干法律规定的国际公约的议定书》[Protocol to Amend the International Convention for the Unification of Certain Rules of Law relating to Bills of Lading (as Amended by the Protocol of 1968)，即《特别提款权议定书》]为蓝本，替换原1924年《海上货物运输法》（Sea-Carriage of Goods Act 1924）中的相关条款，并在后续经审查许可进一步替换为《联合国海上货物运输公约》（United Nations Convention on the Carriage of Goods by Sea，即《汉堡规则》）相关生效内容。截至2017年，《海上货物运输法》已经历了近10次修订。鉴于该法生效后10年，相关主管部门仍未按规定发布由《汉堡规则》替换经修订的《统一提单的若干法律规则的国际公约》（International Convention for the Unification of Certain Rules of Law relating to Bills of Lading，即《海牙规则》），依该法第2条第3款，该法第3部分、附件2全部及第2A已被废止。

当前，该法共有3部分18条正文及2个附件，主要就经修订的《海牙规则》的内容及其适用作出安排。依该法第7条，经修订的《海牙规则》是指，经《维斯比规则》第1—5条及《特别提款权议定书》第2条修订后的《海牙规则》第1—10条的内容，规定在该法附件1中。其适用范围包括：经修订的《海牙规则》第10条下的海上货物运输合同；从澳大利亚某一港口前往澳大利亚另一港口的海上货物运输合同；由提单或类似权利单证外的不可转让单据记载或证明的，同意适用经修订的《海牙规则》的海上货物运输合同。但上述规则不适用于澳大利亚各州及各领地地区内港口间的运输。同时，出于扩展可适用的海上运输单证（如电子单证），在无其他国际条约适用时扩展至他国与澳大利亚间的海上运输，扩大甲板货的范围，延长承运人责任期间，规定承运人在无负责事由时为延迟交付承担责任等目的，该法还可以通过附件对经修订的《海牙规则》作出进一步修改。附件1A即此类修改的体现。[1]

（3）2012年《航海法》。

澳大利亚于2012年9月颁布《航海法》（Navigation Act 2012），以加强海上人身安全保护，促进海上航行安全，防止海洋环境污染，并确保澳大利

---

[1] "Carriage of Goods by Sea Act 1991", Australia Federal Register of Legislation, https：//www.legislation.gov.au/Details/C2017C00280, January 16, 2023.

亚海事安全局具备执行船舶检查并施行国家及国际标准的必要权力。

该法在澳大利亚境内外都准予适用，但对于外国船舶及用于休闲娱乐船舶的非澳大利亚籍船长或船东，除非违法或犯罪行为发生时该船位于澳大利亚港口、进入或离开澳大利亚港口、位于澳大利亚内水、位于澳大利亚领海且不在无害通过范围内，否则该外国船长或船东不得被认定为本法下的违法或犯罪。同时，该法不适用于：军舰及其他由澳大利亚及他国用于军事目的、由相关国家军事人员指挥、有外部国籍标志且由服从军队纪律的船舶操纵的船舶；作为海军辅助舰船且专用于政府非商业服务的政府船舶；外国用于海关或执法目的的船舶。

至 2019 年《帝汶海海洋边界条约相应修正法》颁布，该法已经历了 10 余次修改，当前共有 9 章 346 条，分别就船员管理、澳大利亚船舶及外国船舶的安全规范、污染防范、船舶吨位管理、航行安全、沉船及打捞、本法的遵守与施行、其他相关一般性事项作出规定。其中，在船员管理方面，由第 2 章围绕船员证书、澳大利亚船舶的海事劳工证书事宜、澳大利亚船舶的人员配备与船员雇佣、澳大利亚船舶及外国船舶上船员的健康问题等作出安排。在船舶安全规范方面，由第 3 章围绕澳大利亚船舶安全证书，对外国船舶应持有的在船证照的检查及违法认定，澳大利亚船舶及外国船舶不适航的违法及犯罪认定与惩处，澳大利亚船舶及外国船舶的客货作业管理（如超载、危险货物等），澳大利亚船舶或外国远洋运输船舶以及国内商船或娱乐性船舶的集合演练规范等作出要求。在船舶污染防范方面，由第 4 章围绕澳大利亚船舶的海上排污证书配备及相关违法认定，污染海洋环境的民事违法及刑事犯罪事宜，对相关防治污染公约下的外国船舶给予指示等作出规定。在航行安全方面，由第 6 章围绕强制引航要求及豁免强制引航的程序，引航员证书的颁发，引航提供方的义务，对无证上岗或顶替上岗或不遵守豁免规定的引航员的刑事、民事责任的认定，防止船舶碰撞，提供协助及报告事故的义务，赋予海事安全局有关要求设立和维护监测航行标志的权力，赋予海事安全局处理妨碍航行安全事项的权力等作出规定。[1]

（4）2012 年《海上安全（国内商业船舶）国家法》。

2012 年，在颁布《航海法》的同时，澳大利亚将《海上安全（国内商业船舶）国家法》[Marine Safety (Domestic Commercial Vessel) National Law Act 2012] 采纳为联邦立法，旨在：第一，将该法作为澳大利亚联邦与各州

---

[1] "Navigation Act 2012", Australia Federal Register of Legislation, https://www.legislation.gov.au/C2012A00128/latest/text, January 17, 2023.

及北方领地地区间合作框架的一部分,为确保国内商船运营、设计、建造安全提供统一的国家框架;第二,履行澳大利亚在国内商船安全方面的国际义务;第三,推进安全文化的形成发展,以避免或减轻海上事故的影响;第四,为制定和应用国内商船操作、设计、建造的一致性国家标准提供框架;第五,加强国内商船的高效、有序运营;第六,为相关法律规定提供有效的执行框架。

依其第 5 条,该法主要适用于以下船舶:在各州之间、各州与各领地地区之间、各领地地区之间从事商贸活动的船舶;澳大利亚境外的船舶;所有人或部分所有人为澳大利亚宪法性法人(constitutional corporation)的船舶;基于国际协定而置于澳大利亚义务之下的船舶;所有人或部分所有人为联邦或联邦机构的船舶;在各州之间、各州与各领地地区之间、各领地地区之间为从事商贸而进行航行或运输的船舶。而所谓澳大利亚境外则是指澳大利亚领海基线以外的海域,或向陆地一侧但不在一州或领地地区范围内的领海海域。

该法的 19 条正文主要为对这一联邦立法施行的说明,其实质性条款均载于附件 1 中。附件 1 共有 8 部分 165 条,主要内容包括:

第一,规定澳大利亚海事安全局为国家海上安全监管机构,并赋予其 10 项职能。具体包括:制定和维持根据第 163 条作出的海事命令;制定和维护有关海上安全的国家标准、准则和操作守则;签发本法规定的唯一标识和证书,并履行与该标识和证书有关的其他职能;根据本法或为本法目的对人员进行认证和批准的培训;根据本法或为本法目的进行调查、监测和执法活动;就与国家监管机构的活动有关的事项咨询州和地区的有关当局以及其他个人、协会和组织;收集和发布相关信息,并提供建议;就与国家监管机构的活动和本法的实施有关的事项提供建议;制订或委托制订有关海上安全的教育方案;收集、分析和传播有关海上安全的数据;等等。

第二,规定船东、船舶设计师、船舶建造师、船舶供应商、船长、船员和乘客等不同主体在国内商船相关事项中的一般安全职责。依据该法,各主体都应承担与海上安全相关的若干责任,如:船东必须在合理的范围内确保船只的正常营运和安装相关的海上安全设备;船长不但负有注意海上航行安全的义务,还负有合理注意人员安全的义务;等等。若相关主体疏于履行相应职责,将可能面临监禁或罚款。

第三,规定与船舶标识相符的相关证书和船员相关证书事宜。依据该法,国家监管机构在审查后可以向船舶颁发特别标识符、检验证书、经营证书,向船员颁发适任证书,同时有更改、暂停使用和撤销上述证书的权力。

而船舶和船员必须持有上述相关证书方能进行正常的海上活动，无特别标识符或其他证书情况下的船舶运营或航行，将构成违法或犯罪并面临相应处罚。

第四，规定由前述国家监管机构任命的海上安全检查员的资质和权力。其职权包括登船、搜查、扣押、拘留和信息收集等，但在职权行使中亦有义务出示手令或搜捕令。有关扣押、拘留、豁免等实体或程序内容也在相关章节中有所明确或作出安排。[1]

2. 船舶管理相关立法

（1）1981年《船舶登记法》。

澳大利亚于1981年3月颁布了《船舶登记法》（Shipping Registration Act 1981）以加强对澳大利亚辖下船舶的分类及监管。该法可延伸适用于澳大利亚所有领地，且对澳大利亚境外的相关作为及不作为、事项及文书同等适用。但澳大利亚国防部队所属船舶及外国海陆空部队船舶被明确排除在该法适用范围之外。

在经历了1983—2021年的20余次修改后，该法从原来的7部分95条增加至当前的9部分160条，分别就船舶登记、船舶的转让或转移及担保利益等的处置、船舶登记机关的组织机构及权责、船舶登记簿的保管及使用、被登记船舶上船员的管理及劳工福利、为施行本法的责任承担、行政程序和司法管辖、未登记船舶的处理及过渡性条款等作出规定。

依据该法，一切"澳大利亚所有的船舶"（Australian-owned ships）均应依该法进行登记。该法第8条规定，"澳大利亚所有的船舶"是指：仅由澳大利亚国有或澳大利亚国民所有的船舶；由3人及以上共同共有的船舶中，共有人多数为澳大利亚国民的船舶；由2人及以上按份共有的船舶中，共有人中一半以上份额由澳大利亚国家或国民所有的船舶。而船舶登记类型分为通用登记（General Register）与国际登记（International Register）。其中，需要进行通用登记的船舶包括："澳大利亚所有的船舶"；由澳大利亚居民所有的或由澳大利亚居民与国民共同所有的总长12米以内的小型船艇；由澳大利亚居民及国民单独或共同运营的总长12米以内的小型船艇；由总部位于澳大利亚的经营者光船租赁的船舶。而需要进行国际登记的船舶均为总长24米及以上的船舶，包括："澳大利亚所有的船舶"中的贸易船舶；完全由澳大利亚居民所有或澳大利亚居民与国民共同所有的贸易船舶；由澳大利亚居

---

[1] "Marine Safety (Domestic Commercial Vessel) National Law Act 2012", Australia Federal Register of Legislation, https：//www.legislation.gov.au/Details/C2018C00484, January 17, 2023.

民或国民单独或共同营运的贸易船舶；由总部位于澳大利亚的经营者光船租赁的贸易船舶。澳大利亚立法者希望通过国际登记的有效实施，推动澳大利亚在国际贸易中的深入参与，为促进本国航运业的长期发展提供具有国际竞争力的登记服务，同时强化澳大利亚海事技能基地地位并提升本土航运业的生存能力。[1]

(2) 2012年《沿海贸易（澳大利亚航运振兴）法》。

为就沿海贸易提供规范性框架，澳大利亚于2012年3月颁布了《沿海贸易（澳大利亚航运振兴）法》[Coastal Trading (Revitalising Australian Shipping) Act 2012]，进而推动下列立法目标的实现：第一，切实可行地推进航运业发展，以贡献于澳大利亚的整体经济；第二，促进澳大利亚航运业的长期发展；第三，作为国内运输体系组成部分，提高澳大利亚航运业的产业效能与可靠性；第四，在沿海贸易中最大化地利用澳大利亚通用登记下的船舶；第五，刺激沿海贸易中的良性竞争；第六，保证客货在澳大利亚港口间的高效流动。

为实现上述目标，《沿海贸易（澳大利亚航运振兴）法》的立法重心在于，通过规定颁发执照，授权相关船舶在澳大利亚港口间从事客货运输，以规范沿海贸易活动。具体而言：第一，确保持有通用执照的船舶在从事沿海贸易时，可不受限制地进入澳大利亚水域；第二，确保持有临时执照的船舶在从事沿海贸易时，按执照所限时间和航程行事；第三，确保持有应急执照的船舶在从事沿海贸易时，可进入执照相关应急处置所要求的水域。使用无执照的船舶从事运输将导致民事违法，从而引发罚金等责任承担。

当前，该法共有6部分115条，除第1部分的前导性说明外，其余部分围绕上述立法重心分别展开如下：第2部分主要就核心术语或概念作出界定或说明，如本法中的"沿海贸易"与"航程"的具体要件或含义；第3部分主要就本法条款的适用对象、适用范围等作出规定，包括对不同类型船舶适用以及对特定船舶或人员的豁免等；第4部分明确可授予的3种执照类型，即通用执照、临时执照及应急执照，并就各类执照的申请程序、颁发条件及吊销情形等作出规定；第5部分主要涉及本法的施行要求及违犯后果；第6部分则就行政上诉法庭的复核、相关主管官员的职能权力等杂余事项作出安排。[2]

---

[1] "Shipping Registration Act 1981", Australia Federal Register of Legislation, https://www.legislation.gov.au/Details/C2021C00553, January 17, 2023.

[2] "Coastal Trading (Revitalising Australian Shipping) Act 2012", Australia Federal Register of Legislation, https://www.legislation.gov.au/Details/C2021C00432, January 17, 2023.

3. 船员管理相关立法

(1) 1992年《船员康复和赔偿法》。

澳大利亚于1992年颁布了《船员康复和赔偿法》，专门为船员及其他特定人员的康复与工伤赔偿问题提供法律依据。该法适用于在法定船舶上对雇员的雇佣，这些船舶主要包括：在澳大利亚与澳大利亚外某地点间从事贸易或商业活动的船舶；在澳大利亚内的两个地点间从事贸易或商业活动的船舶；在澳大利亚各州间从事贸易或商业活动的船舶；在澳大利亚各领地地区间或各州与各领地地区间从事贸易或商业活动的船舶；在通用执照下从事沿海贸易的船舶；持经澳大利亚通用船舶登记在案的应急执照从事沿海贸易的船舶；《航海法》意义下的某些近海产业船舶或贸易用船舶；等等。而依该法第4条，本法下的"雇员"至少涵盖以下人员：船员；见习船员；通常作为船员受雇或从业，但实际上并未真实受雇或从业，而是在船员就业中心的要求下为获得登记资格而在指定船舶上受雇或从业的人员。

经过近30次修订，当前该法共有9部分144条，主要内容包括：第一，本法的生效与适用，关键术语及概念的界定；第二，人身伤害、伤害致死、丧失劳动能力、永久性损伤、需要家庭看护服务以及发生财产损害等各种情形下的赔偿标准与计算方式；第三，康复项目提供者的审查，雇员参与康复项目的评估，雇佣者对受伤船员康复的义务，对已自行完成康复项目或无法参与康复项目雇员的补偿，等等；第四，违反本法规定可能引发的责任，受雇船员可采取的行动，追究责任的行政及司法程序，无权向雇佣者提起赔偿请求的例外，雇佣者可能从第三方得到的赔偿，等等；第五，受雇船员的求偿条件、书面要求及信息披露，雇佣者破产时的处置，人身伤害及财产损害的求偿时效，等等；第六，船员安全、康复和赔偿局的设立、组织结构与职能；第七，行政上诉法庭对雇佣方相关决定的复议或复核，强制性保险保障，赔偿基金的设立，等等。[1]

(2) 1993年《职业健康和安全（海运业）法》。

为在更广范围内保障海洋产业中受雇劳动者的职业健康与安全，澳大利亚颁布了《职业健康和安全（海运业）法》，并于1994年1月生效。该法的基本目标在于：第一，确保海洋产业雇员在工作中的健康、安全与福利；第二，确保在相关工作场所及附近，其人员的健康和安全不因海洋产业雇员的活动而受到威胁；第三，确保可就影响海运业经营者、雇员及承包方的职业

---

[1] "Seafarers Rehabilitation and Compensation Act 1992", Australia Federal Register of Legislation, https://www.legislation.gov.au/Details/C2017C00393, January 18, 2023.

健康和安全相关事项获得专业建议；第四，改善海洋产业雇员的职业环境，以满足其健康和安全需求；第五，围绕海洋产业雇员在工作中的健康、安全及福利问题，培养海运业经营者与雇员之间的合作协商关系。

该法共 4 部分 121 条，除第 1 部分的前导性说明和第 5 部分的杂项条款外，第 2、3、4 部分主要围绕职业健康与安全、工作场所安排、外部意见与监管作出实体性规定。第 2 部分共分 2 节，明确将有关职业健康与安全的义务区分为一般义务与特别义务。一般义务涉及经营者对其雇员的义务、经营者对协议工作方的义务、经营者对第三方的义务、生产者对相关设施的义务、生产者对相关物资的义务、供应方对相关设施及物资的义务、在工作场所架设或安装相关设施的人员的义务、在工作场所维修或维护相关设施的人员的义务、在规定单位或船舶上进行装卸的人员的义务，同时规定雇员对自身的职业健康与安全也负有相应义务。而特别义务则可由依据该法颁布的相关法规另行明确。第 3 部分共分 5 节，分别就指定工作组与经营者协商、选任雇员群体的健康与安全代表、就未能纠正违法行为达成协议而颁布临时措施、相关船舶或工作单元中健康与安全委员会的设立、在雇员健康和安全受到迫近威胁时的紧急程序等作出规定。第 4 部分共分 3 节，主要就监督本法实施的视察团的成立与职责、视察团指示相关人员寻求专家建议、专职调查员的任命及调查任务与报告提交等作出安排。[1]

（六）海洋环境保护立法

1. 1981 年《环境保护（海上倾废）法》

澳大利亚于 1981 年颁布了《环境保护（海上倾废）法》[Environment Protection (Sea Dumping) Act 1981]，旨在通过规范向海中倾倒、在海上焚化以及安放人工鱼礁等相关行为以保护海洋环境。该法充分考虑了澳大利亚已缔结和加入的相关国际条约，在兼顾《南极条约》、《〈防止倾倒废物及其他物质污染海洋的公约〉1996 年议定书》（1996 Protocol to the Convention on the Prevention of Marine Pollution by Dumping of Wastes and Other Matter）、与巴布亚新几内亚间有关托雷斯海峡的条约、与印度尼西亚间海洋划界条约、与东帝汶间海洋划界条约等义务履行的情形下，不断更新、修正本法相关规定。依其第 5 条、第 7 条，该法不适用于：（1）在勘探、开发海底矿产资源及其离岸加工过程中，所直接产生或相关的受控物资的存储或处置；（2）在巨日

---

[1] "Occupational Health and Safety (Maritime Industry) Act 1993", Australia Federal Register of Legislation, https://www.legislation.gov.au/Details/C2015C00248, January 18, 2023.

升特别管理区及其上覆水域，与勘探、开发海底矿产资源及其离岸加工直接相关的船舶、飞行器及平台；(3) 武装冲突或其他紧急事态中澳大利亚国防部队的船舶或飞机；(4) 外国海陆空部队的船舶或飞机。

截至2020年，《领地立法修正法》(Territories Legislation Amendment Act 2020) 已进行了21次修订，当前共有47条正文，原附件已经全部删除。依据该法，相关人员需按要求的程序和形式向主管部长申请许可，获准后方可在海上从事排放等相关行为。在未获许可的情形下，以下均为违法行为：(1) 从船舶、飞机或平台上向澳大利亚水域倾倒受控物资，或从澳大利亚船舶、飞机或平台上向任何海域倾倒受控物资，或向澳大利亚水域弃置船舶、飞机或平台，或向任何海域弃置澳大利亚船舶、飞机或平台；(2) 在澳大利亚水域内的船舶或平台上焚烧受控物资，或在任何海域焚烧澳大利亚船舶；(3) 在明知相关物资将被倾倒入海或在海上焚烧的情形下，或在疏忽上述后果的情形下，在澳大利亚及其水域向船舶、飞机或平台装载受控物资，或在澳大利亚船舶或飞机上装载受控物资；(4) 在明知相关物资将被倾倒入海或在海上焚烧的情形下，或在疏忽上述后果的情形下，从澳大利亚向他国出口受控物资；(5) 进行人工鱼礁的安装、安放。澳大利亚联邦警察及各州警察或海关官员可作为巡查员对上述行为及相关人员进行监管。登临船舶、飞机或平台的巡查员可行使以下职权：第一，搜查、获取某一违法行为的证据；第二，搜寻、检查、摘录及复制与海上装载、倾倒、焚烧受控物资有关的文件，或与出口即将在海上倾倒、焚烧的受控物资有关的文件，或与即将作为人工鱼礁的一部分被放置的受控物资有关的文件；第三，检查各类受控物资并取样；第四，监督受控物资的装载、倾倒入海、海上焚烧及人工鱼礁的安放。除此之外，该法还就与违规船舶或违规材料有关的负责人须承担的法律后果，海洋环境恢复，联邦恢复环境所产生的费用的分配，相关许可证的申请、授予、更改、上诉审查、公布公开、暂停使用和撤销等事项，本法罪行的可公诉性，巡查员证据和专家证据的获取与采信等问题作出规定。[1]

2. 1999年《环境保护与生物多样性养护法》

1999年7月，澳大利亚颁布了《环境保护与生物多样性养护法》，该法以保护环境和生物多样性为最终目标，旨在：第一，就环境保护尤其是对国家环境具有重要意义的环境事项作出法律规定；第二，通过自然资源的可持续利用和生态保护，促进生态的可持续发展；第三，促进生物多样性的养

---

[1] "Environment Protection (Sea Dumping) Act 1981", Australia Federal Register of Legislation, https://www.legislation.gov.au/Details/C2021C00058, January 18, 2023.

护；第四，为国家遗产和世界遗产的保存和养护提供法律规范；第五，促进政府、社区、土地所有者和土著居民共同参与环境保护和管理并相互合作；第六，帮助澳大利亚能更好地承担国际环境责任；第七，对土著居民在澳大利亚生物多样性保护和生态可持续利用方面的作用作出肯定；第八，在相关知识人才的参与和合作下，学习和利用土著居民在维护生物多样性方面的知识与经验。

为了实现上述立法目标，澳大利亚于2003年添加了生态可持续发展原则贯穿全法。该法确立的生态可持续发展原则包括：第一，决策过程应有效整合长期与短期的经济、环境、社会与公平考量；第二，在存在严重或不可逆的环境损害的情形下，不应以缺乏充分科学确定性的理由推迟实施防范环境退化的措施；第三，坚持代际公平原则，当前世代应确保未来世代的利益，保护健康环境、维护生态多样性及强化生产力；第四，生物多样性与生态完整性的养护应被视为决策过程的基础性考量；第五，应不断推动评估、定价及激励机制的完善与改进。

《环境保护与生物多样性养护法》自颁布以来已进行了50余次修订，在原法基础上扩展了近500条，当前共有10章正文及1个附件。其主体框架所涉内容包括：第一，通过聚焦澳大利亚联邦在联邦区域内采取的联邦行动，关注其对具有国家环境意义事务的参与，肯定澳大利亚联邦在环境问题上的应有作用。第二，通过双边协定加强与他国政府间的合作，同时最大限度地减少不必要的重复投入。第三，为环境评估和批准程序的政府间互认提供路径。第四，采用有效和及时的联邦环境评估和批准程序，确保对可能对环境产生重大影响的活动进行恰当评估。第五，确保澳大利亚维护生物多样性能力的提升。相关措施有：（1）保护本土物种，特别注意防范濒危物种的灭绝并促进其种群恢复，同时确保对迁徙物种的养护；（2）建立澳大利亚鲸鱼保护区，以养护鲸鱼及其他海洋哺乳动物；（3）通过设立和管理自然保护区、承认和保护生态群落及促进保护区外养护措施的落实等方式来保护生态系统；（4）确认威胁各级别生态多样性的进程，并实施应对这些进程的计划。第六，纳入相关规定以加强对世界遗产的保存、养护及展示，并就"国际重要湿地"——拉姆萨尔湿地（Ramsar wetlands）的保护及合理利用作出规范。第七，确认可列入国家遗产名录与联邦遗产名录的地点，并加强对此类地点的保存、养护及展示。第八，通过多种方式促进环境保护和生物多样性养护的多方合作伙伴关系。相关方式有：（1）与各州及各领地地区达成双边协议；（2）与相关土地所有者签订养护协议；（3）认可并利用土著居民在生物多样性保护和生态可持续利用方面的知识和作用；（4）将社区纳入相关管理规划。

除上述原则的统领贯穿与法律框架的综合适用外，该法有关海洋环境及海洋生物多样性保护的内容还集中体现在：

第一，该法第2章第3部分第F分节。该分节专门围绕"海洋环境"，对在澳大利亚各州及各领地地区从事的、已经或将会影响海洋环境的多种行为作出禁止性规定，并就违反此规定的民事乃至刑事责任进行了说明。依该分节，"澳大利亚海域"是指：（1）其专属经济区向海一侧界限内的海域，但已由相关立法转归各州以及位于各州或北方领地地区界限内的水域应排除在外；（2）前述海域的上空及下覆海床；（3）其大陆架的上覆水域，但由相关立法转归各州以及位于各州或北方领地地区界限内的水域同样排除在外；（4）大陆架范围内的海床及其上空；（5）在澳大利亚联邦保护区内的其他海水及海床区域。

第二，依该法第2章第3部分第FA分节，在大堡礁海洋公园内的行为须按要求申请批准，自然人和法人不得在大堡礁海洋公园内实施对环境已经产生、将会产生或可能产生重大影响的行为，否则将面临民事或刑事处罚。

第三，该法第5章第13部分对澳大利亚鲸鱼保护区和重要的鲸类栖息地作出相关规定。依该部分的相关规定，澳大利亚鲸鱼保护区的设立是为了肯定和保证在澳大利亚联邦海域和其他规定水域内对鲸类动物提供的高水平保护和管理；政府可通过立法文书宣布澳大利亚鲸鱼保护区内的特定区域为重要的鲸类栖息地；杀死或伤害鲸类动物，获取、交易、饲养、移动或干扰鲸类动物，持有、处理非法捕杀或捕获的鲸类动物，持有、处理非法进口的鲸类动物等行为均违反本法及澳大利亚刑法，将引发刑事法律责任。

第四，依该法第5章第13部分第4节，政府必须通过立法文书制定海洋物种清单，该清单应囊括在海洋环境中生存的鱼类、鸟类、哺乳类和爬行类等各类动物。政府必须在法定时间内列明清单并向社会公布，同时向公众提供可购买的清单资料。清单公布后，若仍有个人或法人组织对清单上的动物有不利的行为，将可能面临刑事责任的承担。

第五，依该法第5B章，在经法定程序咨询磋商并经专家组评估后，相关主管部长可通过立法性文件，临时或最终宣示对商业性捕捞活动的认定。经宣示认定后，个人及组织将不得在澳大利亚联邦海域内从事商业性捕捞，否则亦将构成民事违法或刑事犯罪从而受到相应处罚。[1]

---

[1] "Environment Protection and Biodiversity Conservation Act 1999", Australia Federal Register of Legislation, https：//www.legislation.gov.au/Details/C2022C00214/Html/Volume_1#_Toc105063208, January 19, 2023.

三、国内海洋立法

3. 1975年《大堡礁海洋公园法》

大堡礁纵贯于澳大利亚昆士兰州，北起托雷斯海峡，南到南回归线以南。一如前述，作为世界最大的珊瑚礁群，其自然景观极为特殊，具有不可取代的价值和意义。1975年6月，澳大利亚颁布了《大堡礁海洋公园法》，为建立、控制、保护和发展大堡礁海洋公园提供了框架，也正因该法对大堡礁海洋公园的积极保护成效，根据自然遗产遴选依据标准（vii）（viii）（ix）（x），大堡礁于1981年被联合国教科文组织世界遗产委员会批准作为自然遗产列入《世界遗产名录》。

该法的主要目的在于实现大堡礁地区的环境、生物多样性和遗产价值的长时期保全与保护。具体而言，在与主要目的一致的前提下，该法允许以生态可持续性的方式利用大堡礁地区，包括：开放该地区供大众享受和欣赏；就该地区开展大众教育以增进公众对该地区的了解；在该地区开展具有娱乐性、经济性及文化性的活动；就该地区的自然、社会、经济和文化体系及价值展开研究。同时，该法鼓励感兴趣的个人和团体参与大堡礁地区的保护和管理，并致力于协助澳大利亚政府履行本国在保护环境和世界遗产方面的国际责任，尤其是《保护世界文化和自然遗产公约》下的责任。

为了实现上述目的，该法的规定主要涉及以下7个方面：第一，为大堡礁海洋公园的建立、管理和发展提供法律框架；第二，设立大堡礁海洋公园管理局，并就其组织机构、职能履行、人员任命等作出安排；第三，为大堡礁海洋公园各个分区计划和管理计划提供指导和规范；第四，要求以符合基于生态系统的管理和生态可持续利用原则的方式，规范大堡礁海洋公园的利用方式（如许可制度的采用）；第五，在海洋资源管理方面，促成与该区域土著居民中传统所有权人间合作伙伴关系的建立；第六，提供相关路径，从而便于与昆士兰州政府合作管理大堡礁世界遗产区；第七，对于破坏大堡礁生态环境的行为，如排放废物、非法捕鱼和疏忽航行等，明确对有关公司和个人违法行为的认定及相应的严格处罚措施。

经过多次修订，该法从原9部分共66条扩展至11部分共244条及1个附件。多部相关的法规和条例也相继出台，如1983年、1988年、1990年、1993年、2001年、2004年的《大堡礁海洋公园修正法》（Great Barrier Reef Marine Park Amendment Act 1983, 1988, 1990, 1993, 2001, 2004），2008年的《大堡礁海洋公园与其他立法修正法》（Great Barrier Reef Marine Park and Other Legislation Amendment Act 2008），2020年的《大堡礁海洋公园修正案（冠状病毒经济应对方案）法》［Great Barrier Reef Marine Park Amendment

(Coronavirus Economic Response Package) Act 2020］，其内容涵盖了排污管理、环境管理费的收取、特定区域（如圣灵群岛）的管理计划、疏浚弃土、捕捞规定、船舶停泊、基础设施建设和展望报告等诸多方面。纵然这些立法性文件有的已经失效，但自1975年起，它们都作为或者曾经作为大堡礁海洋公园管理规则体系中的重要组成部分，并贡献于《大堡礁海洋公园法》当前文本的成形。[1]

4. 履行相关国际公约义务的海洋保护立法

作为英联邦国家的一员，澳大利亚也承袭了英国在国际法与国内法关系上的"二元论"传统，原则上其缔结和加入的条约需要经相应国内立法的转化方能在澳大利亚国内法院得以适用。因此，澳大利亚有大量为履行相关国际公约义务颁布的国内立法。如，为实施1988年《制止危及海上航行安全非法行为公约》(Convention for the Suppression of Unlawful Acts against the Safety of Maritime Navigation) 和1988年《制止危及大陆架固定平台安全非法行为议定书》(Protocol for the Suppression of Unlawful Acts against the Safety of Fixed Platforms Located on the Continental Shelf) 而颁布的1992年《犯罪（船舶和固定平台）法》［Crimes (Ships and Fixed Platforms) Act 1992］，为实施1976年《海事赔偿责任限制公约》(Convention on Limitation of Liability for Maritime Claims) 而颁布的1989年《海事赔偿责任限制法》(Limitation of Liability for Maritime Claims Act 1989)，以及在与东帝汶海洋划界谈判各阶段所颁布的2003年《石油（帝汶海条约）法》［Petroleum (Timor Sea Treaty) Act 2003］、2019年《帝汶海海洋边界条约相应修正法》，等等。

同理，为推进本国加入的海洋环境保护相关国际条约在国内的执行落实，澳大利亚也颁布了以"海洋保护法"为名的系列国内立法，以保障相关条约框架下法律义务的履行，始终展现其在国际海洋环境保护中的先行者与力行者姿态。这一系列"海洋保护法"主要包括：

第一，为实施1969年《国际油污损害民事责任公约》(International Convention on Civil Liability for Oil Pollution Damage) 而颁布的1981年《海洋保护（民事责任）法》［Protection of the Sea (Civil Liability) Act 1981］。该法共有27条正文和包括上述公约及相关文件在内的3个附件，根据所实施公约的条款和精神，结合澳大利亚实际国情，规定了船舶在澳大利亚领海和专属经济区溢油污染的民事责任及损害赔偿机制。具体而言，该法规定《国际油污损

---

[1] "Great Barrier Reef Marine Park Act 1975", Australia Federal Register of Legislation, https：//www. legi-slation. gov. au/Details/C2020C00182，January 19, 2023.

害民事责任公约》的第1—6条（含），第7条的第1款、第8款和第9款，第8条的第1款和第3款，第9条，第11条的第1款，第12条的第2款[（b）项除外]，作为澳大利亚联邦法律的一部分而具有法律效力。该法同时规定，可以指定相应的规章或条款，为执行或实施《国际油污损害民事责任公约》而进行必要的便捷化，如将《国际油污损害民事责任公约》第5条第1款所指的金额换算为以澳大利亚货币表示的金额。另外，该法也就违反上述公约的行为的管辖、审理和索赔等程序性事项作出了规定。[1]

第二，为实施1969年《国际干预公海油污事故公约》（International Convention Relating to Intervention on the High Seas in Cases of Oil Pollution Casualties）而颁布的1981年《海洋保护（干预权）法》[Protection of the Sea (Powers of Intervention) Act 1981]。该法有23条正文和包括上述公约及相关文件在内的4个附件，授权澳大利亚联邦相关部门可采取措施，以保护海洋免受船舶排放的石油和其他有毒物质污染。该法允许澳大利亚海事安全局或相关主管部门部长为防止污染澳大利亚水域、沿岸海域或大堡礁区域而采取干预行动，从而使相关公约下对所规定物质污染的干预权得以实现。在该法的指示下，可采取的措施包括：将船舶或船舶的一部分移至其他地方；从船上卸下货物；打捞船舶、船舶的一部分或船舶上的任何货物；弃毁船舶或船舶上的一部分或船舶上的任何货物；接管船舶或船舶的一部分；等等。[2]

第三，为实施1973年《国际防止船舶造成污染公约》（International Convention for the Prevention of Pollution from Ships）而颁布的1983年《海洋保护（防止船舶污染）法》[Protection of the Sea (Prevention of Pollution from Ships) Act 1983]。该法通过35条正文，针对可能对海洋造成污染的物质设定了严格的排放和处置条件，并就船舶硫化物和氮化物排放进行了限制。在防止油类污染方面，该法禁止将油类或油性混合物排放入海，禁止将残油排放入海，甚至禁止在澳大利亚所主张南极地区的外国船舶运输或使用某些油类。该法同时规定了涉及澳大利亚船舶的油类货物转运的资格、计划、记录、通知等事项，也规定了污染发生后报告涉及油类或油性混合物事故的责任和相应的船上油污应急预案。在防止其他有害物质污染方面，该法禁止携带未经分类或评估的物质，更禁止将该物质排放入海。而相似地，为防止包装中有害物质造成的污染、污水污染、垃圾污染、大气污染，该法也规定了记录

---

[1] "Protection of the Sea (Civil Liability) Act 1981", Australia Federal Register of Legislation, https：//www. legislation. gov. au/Details/C2016C00625, January 20, 2023.

[2] "Protection of the Sea (Powers of Intervention) Act 1981", Australia Federal Register of Legislation, https：//www. legislation. gov. au/Details/C2019C00190, January 20, 2023.

簿、事故报告责任和应急预案"三步走"措施。为落实该法，其设置了相应的监察员，并规定违反该法造成环境污染的船舶可能被扣留并将面临检控。[1]

第四，为执行1971年《设立国际油污损害赔偿基金国际公约》（International Convention on The Establishment of an International Fund for Compensation for Oil Pollution Damage）下"国际油污赔偿基金"（The International Oil Pollution Compensation Fund）及其1976年、1992年、2003年文书的相关规定而颁布的1993年《海洋保护（油污赔偿基金）法》[Protection of the Sea (Oil Pollution Compensation Funds) Act 1993]。该法共有4部分58条正文及4个附件。其正文第2部分和第3部分分别对应公约的1992年议定书及2003年议定书，规定由"1992年基金"及"补充赔偿基金"为某些油污损害提供赔偿。其中，对于已就某些油污损害提出赔偿要求，但由于损害已经或可能超过"1992年基金"的赔偿限额而无法从"1992年基金"获得充分赔偿的人，"补充赔偿基金"可为其提供补充性赔偿。在澳大利亚港口和码头接收石油的特定人员有责任向"1992年基金"及"补充赔偿基金"缴纳款项。为保证相关款项的缴纳，该法授权澳大利亚海事安全局收集缴款者的资料并将资料提供给相应基金管理方。[2]

第五，为实施2001年《控制船舶有害防污底系统国际公约》（International Convention on the Control of Harmful Anti-fouling Systems on Ships）而颁布的2006年《海洋保护（有害防污底系统）法》[Protection of the Sea (Harmful Anti-fouling Systems) Act 2006]。依所对应公约，该法开宗明义：科学研究已经表明，船舶使用的某些防污底系统对海洋生物和海洋生态都会造成不利影响，最终会导致人体健康受到损害。而在有害防污化合物中，在防污底系统中被当作杀生物剂的有机锡化合物对环境的影响尤为突出。因此，该法的重要目标之一在于，通过一系列措施逐步杜绝将此类有机锡引入环境中。该法对有害防污底系统的应用或使用提出了具体要求，船舶或个人必须持有防污证书和防污声明，并负有进行防污申报的义务。同时，该法也为制止违法行为的发生设置专任检查员。澳大利亚海事安全局委任的人员、2012年《航海法》所指的检查员、澳大利亚联邦警察局成员或特别成员，都可以通过澳大利亚海事安全局以书面形式被任命为检查员。检查员具有一定的检察权和执法

---

[1] "Protection of the Sea (Prevention of Pollution from Ships) Act 1983", Australia Federal Register of Legislation, https://www.legislation.gov.au/Details/C2022C00356, January 20, 2023.

[2] "Protection of the Sea (Oil Pollution Compensation Funds) Act 1993", Australia Federal Register of Legislation, https://www.legislation.gov.au/Details/C2016C00871, January 20, 2023.

权,违法船舶将可能面临被扣留、赔偿、起诉等执法或司法后果。[1]

第六,为实施2001年《国际燃油污染损害民事责任公约》(International Convention on Civil Liability for Bunker Oil Pollution Damage)而颁布的2008年《海洋保护(燃油污染损害民事责任)法》[Protection of the Sea (Civil Liability for Bunker Oil Pollution Damage) Act 2008]。该法共有4部分31条正文,对所对应公约下的责任承担及与污染损害责任相关的保险证明作出了要求。依据该法,所对应公约下的责任适用于发生在澳大利亚及其专属经济区内的污染损害,也适用于为防范或最小化澳大利亚及其专属经济区内污染的防污措施。但在1969年《国际油污损害民事责任公约》下的污染损害,无论其是否得到赔偿,都不适用本法。而有关损害赔偿的保险证明适用于吨位在1000总吨以上的船舶,该部分规定同样不适用于1981年《海洋保护(民事责任)法》下的船舶。依据该法,相关船舶应进行等级注册,需要申请并持有保险证书方能在澳大利亚相关海域航行,对违反所对应公约和该法相关规定所造成的污染损害应承担赔偿等责任。[2]

除直接依据相关国际条约框架而转化的立法外,澳大利亚"海洋保护法"还包括部分与上述立法运行有关的辅助性或关联性立法,如,1981年《海洋保护(航运税)法》[Protection of the Sea (Shipping Levy) Act 1981]、1993年《海洋保护(油污赔偿基金缴纳——通用)法》[Protection of the Sea (Imposition of Contributions to Oil Pollution Compensation Funds—General) Act 1993]、1993年《海洋保护(油污赔偿基金缴纳——关税)法》[Protection of the Sea (Imposition of Contributions to Oil Pollution Compensation Funds—Customs) Act 1993]、1993年《海洋保护(油污赔偿基金缴纳——消费税)法》[Protection of the Sea (Imposition of Contributions to Oil Pollution Compensation Funds—Excise) Act 1993]等。

(七) 南极相关立法

1. 1933年《澳大利亚南极领地接纳法》

1933年6月,通过颁布《澳大利亚南极领地接纳法》(Australian Antarctic Territory Acceptance Act 1933),澳大利亚正式宣示了其在南极的领地范围及主权。英国于1936年8月发布枢密院令对澳大利亚的这一宣示表示认可。

---

[1] "Protection of the Sea (Harmful Anti-fouling Systems) Act 2006", Australia Federal Register of Legislation, https://www.legislation.gov.au/Details/C2023C00019, January 20, 2023.

[2] "Protection of the Sea (Civil Liability for Bunker Oil Pollution Damage) Act 2008", Australia Federal Register of Legislation, https://www.legislation.gov.au/Details/C2016C00123, January 20, 2023.

依据该法，澳大利亚在南极海域的领土包括位于南纬60度以南、东经160度至东经45度之间的所有岛屿及领地，仅阿德利地区（Adelie Land）除外。澳大利亚宣布，自该法生效时起，这片区域便作为"澳大利亚南极领地"被"接纳"（acceptance）为澳大利亚联邦领土地区之一，从此置于澳大利亚联邦治下。该法经最近一次的1973年修订后，至今有效。[1]

2. 1954年《澳大利亚南极领地法》

仅有两条正文的1933年《澳大利亚南极领地接纳法》并不能满足澳大利亚将所谓"南极领地"纳入治下后的管理要求。为向"澳大利亚南极领地政府"提供可资依据的法律框架，澳大利亚于1954年11月颁布了《澳大利亚南极领地法》（Australian Antarctic Territory Act 1954），在前述1933年立法基础上填充了治理细则。

该法当前共有16条正文，原第3条已被废除，但在第12条后增加了第12A、12B、12C、12D条。除第1条至第4条有关法律生效及基本术语等内容外，其第5条至第10条主要就不同层级法律在"澳大利亚南极领地"的适用作出安排。依据该法，在无相反条例规定的情形下，澳大利亚首都地区相关法律可适用于"南极领地"，在杰维斯湾领地生效的刑事法律也同样适用于"南极领地"；但除非有相关法律明文规定，联邦法律不得适用于"南极领地"。总督可就"南极领地"的和平善治制定相关条例，此类条例应在规定时限内提交议会两院审议，审议中的条例不得重拟，被驳回的条例也不得重拟，未提交审议的条例则面临失效。另外，澳大利亚首都地区各级法院对"澳大利亚南极领地"拥有司法管辖权，可按照首都地区法院的司法程序及实践对其"南极领地"的相关行为行使管辖权。[2]

该法先后经1957年《澳大利亚南极领地法》（Australian Antarctic Territory Act 1957）及1963年《澳大利亚南极领地法》（Australian Antarctic Territory Act 1963）对第12条、第13条等部分条款进行了修订。但随着2014年《1901年至1969年修正案废止法》（Amending Acts 1901 to 1969 Repeal Act 2014）的生效，该1957年及1963年法被废止，其所涉修订也不再生效。[3]

---

[1] "Australian Antarctic Territory Acceptance Act 1933", Australia Federal Register of Legislation, https://www.legislation.gov.au/Details/C2004C00416, January 20, 2023.

[2] "Australian Antarctic Territory Act 1954", Australia Federal Register of Legislation, https://www.legisla-tion.gov.au/Details/C2012C00725, January 20, 2023.

[3] "Australian Antarctic Territory Act 1957", Australia Federal Register of Legislation, https://www.legisla-tion.gov.au/Details/C1957A00035, January 20, 2023; "Australian Antarctic Territory Act 1963", Australia Federal Register of Legislation, https://www.legislation.gov.au/Details/C1963A00020, January 20, 2023.

3. 1960 年《南极条约法》

1959 年 12 月，南极会议的最终成果《南极条约》达成并开放签署。作为《南极条约》的共倡者与 12 个创始缔约国之一，澳大利亚在该条约最终生效前积极完成了国内法律环境的筹建，于 1960 年颁布《南极条约法》（Antarctic Treaty Act 1960）以明确《南极条约》在本国的生效及基本适用范围。

《南极条约法》共 4 条正文及 1 个附件。该法明确，其所适用的人员范围为：（1）《南极条约》第 7 条第 1 款所指缔约国指派的观察员；（2）《南极条约》第 3 条第 1 款（b）项下所称的进行交流的南极洲各探险队和工作站的科学人员；（3）上述人员的随行人员。上述人员均应为缔约国国民。其中，对于该法适用下的非澳大利亚国民，其在南极地区履行其职责时的作为或不作为，均不受有关"澳大利亚南极领地"现行法律的约束；对于该法适用下的澳大利亚国民，其在南极地区履行其职责时的作为或不作为，均在"澳大利亚南极领地"现行法律的约束之下，即使该作为或不作为发生在"澳大利亚南极领地"之外，也视同发生在该领地之内。1954 年《澳大利亚南极领地法》中所涉及的澳大利亚首都地区各级法院管辖权范围，依本法也延伸覆盖至前述澳大利亚国民在南极地区的作为或不作为。但同时，澳大利亚也在该法中强调，此立法无意损害或影响任何国家基于国际法对南极公海海域的权利及权利行使。[1]

4. 1980 年《南极条约（环境保护）法》

作为 1972 年《南极海豹保护公约》（Convention for the Conservation of Antarctic Seals）、1959 年《南极条约》和 1991 年《关于环境保护的南极条约议定书》（Protocol on Environmental Protection to the Antarctic Treaty）的缔约国，澳大利亚于 1980 年颁布了《南极条约（环境保护）法》[Antarctic Treaty (Environment Protection) Act 1980]，以便推进上述公约条款的国内施行，服务于南极和南极环境的养护目标。

依该法第 4 条，其适用范围包括：第一，"澳大利亚南极领地"上的任何人员及财产，外国公民及财产也不例外；第二，在澳大利亚之外的澳大利亚公民，澳大利亚探险队及其成员，澳大利亚各组织，作为澳大利亚财产的飞行器、船舶或车辆上的乘组人员，以及澳大利亚所属财产。

在经 1992 年《南极（环境保护）立法修正法》[Antarctic (Environment Protection) Legislation Amendment Act 1992]、2010 年及 2012 年《南极条约

---

[1] "Antarctic Treaty Act 1960", Australia Federal Register of Legislation, https://www.legislation.gov.au/D-etails/C2008C00398, January 20, 2023.

（环境保护）修正法》［Antarctic Treaty（Environment Protection）Amendment Act 2010，2012］等的 20 次修订后，《南极条约（环境保护）法》当前共有 7 部分 75 条正文及 3 个附件。其主要内容包括：

第一，关于南极动植物的保护。如，对需要特别保护的物种的界定，南极特别保护区的确定和设立，规范南极地区活动许可证的授予、更新、限制、变更、暂停使用和撤销，等等。

第二，关于南极的环境影响评估。其基本步骤为：首先，确定环境影响评估的对象；其次，就所筹备行动对南极环境的可能影响进行预备评估（preliminary assessment）；再次，若评估结论确定相关活动的影响可忽略不计，则行动继续，若评估结论确定相关活动可能具有轻微或暂时影响，则启动初步环境评估（initial environmental evaluation）；最后，根据初步环境评估结论，形成综合性的环境评价报告。相关主管部门需就可能轻微影响环境的活动进行授权，也可以在后续阶段对该授权作出变更、暂停或撤销的决定。

第三，关于破坏环境相关罪行的认定及处罚。除与生态环境相关的一般性破坏行为外，还涉及如，与岩石及陨石采集相关的行为、与本土物种放归相关的行为、与意外引入微生物群相关的行为、与携带食物进入南极相关的行为、未经许可破坏带入南极的非本土生物的行为等，以维护南极生态环境的封闭和安宁。同时与南极条约体系的基本立场一致，禁止在南极及"澳大利亚南极领地"实施采矿行为。

第四，关于违反本法相关规定的民事处罚。如，相关民事处罚令的签发与执行、民事处罚的证据、民事处罚令的程序要求、民事程序和刑事程序并行时的阶段安排与协调处置等。[1]

5. 1981 年《南极海洋生物资源养护法》

1980 年 8 月 1 日，《南极海洋生物资源养护公约》在堪培拉开放签署。作为该公约的签署国和保管方，澳大利亚于 1981 年 4 月颁布了《南极海洋生物资源养护法》（Antarctic Marine Living Resources Conservation Act 1981），以便该公约在澳大利亚落地实施，确保澳大利亚基于该公约第 9 条所采取的养护措施及时生效，并进一步为南极及其周边海域的海洋生物资源养护提供法律依据。

依该法第 5 条，该法同时适用于澳大利亚境内及境外，可延伸适用于澳

---

[1] "Antarctic Treaty（Environment Protection）Act 1980", Australia Federal Register of Legislation, https：//www.legislation.gov.au/Details/C2021C00351，January 21, 2023.

大利亚的所有海外领地。在澳大利亚渔区外部界限之外的水域或地点，该法的规定即使有效，也仅适用于澳大利亚国民、澳大利亚船舶及此类船舶上的船员；而在澳大利亚或澳大利亚渔区之内，该法将有效适用于一切人员和船舶，包括外国籍人与外国船舶。

当前，该法共有25条正文，以《南极海洋生物资源养护公约》约文为唯一附件，除有关本法生效适用的说明性条款外，主要就有关海洋生物组织采集与研究的禁止性规定、南极海洋生物相关活动的许可制度及规则安排、违反许可制度的情形与后果、督察员及特派督察员的选任、对非从警察选任的督察员的身份卡发放、督察员可在无逮捕令情形下执行逮捕等权限、对违法行为所涉船舶或工具的扣押或没收、对相关违法行为的指挥及起诉、南极海洋生物资源的项目规划、相关主管部长的职权及对其决定的行政复核等作出规定。

许可制度是该法的核心制度。依据该法第9条，相关主管部长可以颁发许可，以授权申请人员在《南极海洋生物资源养护公约》所涉区域或其特定范围内捕捞特定种类的海洋生物，或授权进行有关特定种类海洋生物的研究。许可的颁发需要以接收申请为前提，通过相应法定形式和程序，主管部长可在充分兼顾上述公约原则与宗旨的情形下自主决定是否授权许可。被许可人应保证遵守许可授权时所要求的条件，否则许可可能会被暂停或取消。对于违反许可制度的行为，该法下的督察员可以对涉嫌此类行为的船舶进行截停、迫近、搜查、扣押。[1]

整体而言，澳大利亚对南极固有利益的坚守及在南极秩序构建中前沿地位的维持，在其国内南极相关立法体系构建中可见一斑。除上述框架性立法外，澳大利亚还制定了大量立足于上述立法的修正法律文件或在其授权下的次级法律文件。如，1993年《南极条约（环境保护）（环境影响评价）规章》[Antarctic Treaty (Environment Protection) (Environmental Impact Assessment) Regulations 1993]、1994年《南极海洋生物资源养护规章》(Antarctic Marine Living Resources Conservation Regulations 1994)、1994年《南极条约（环境保护）（废弃物管理）规章》[Antarctic Treaty (Environment Protection) (Waste Management) Regulations 1994]、2006年《环境和遗产立法修正（南极海豹和其他措施）法》[Environment and Heritage Legislation Amendment (Antarctic Seals and Other Measures) Act 2006]、2007年《南极条约（环境保

---

[1] "Antarctic Marine Living Resources Conservation Act 1981", Australia Federal Register of Legislation, https://www.legislation.gov.au/Details/C2016C01028, January 21, 2023.

护）公告》［Antarctic Treaty（Environment Protection）Proclamation 2007］、2007 年《南极条约（环境保护-历史遗址与纪念物）公告》［Antarctic Treaty（Environment Protection-Historic Sites and Monuments）Proclamation 2007］、2011 年《海洋保护（防止船舶污染）修正（南极区域石油）法》［Protection of the Sea（Prevention of Pollution from Ships）Amendment（Oils in the Antarctic Area）Act 2011］等。

四、缔结和加入的国际海洋法条约

(一) 联合国框架下的海洋法公约

1. 1958年"日内瓦海洋法公约"体系下的条约

澳大利亚于1958年10月30日签署、1963年5月14日批准了"日内瓦海洋法公约"体系下的全部公约,即《领海及毗连区公约》(Convention on the Territorial Sea and the Contiguous Zone)、《公海公约》(Convention on the High Seas)、《捕鱼及养护公海生物资源公约》(Convention on Fishing and Conservation of the Living Resources of the High Seas)和《大陆架公约》,并于1963年5月14日作准签署《关于强制解决争端之任择议定书》(Optional Protocol of Signature concerning the Compulsory Settlement of Disputes),表示其受条约约束。

关于《领海及毗连区公约》,澳大利亚在批准时对以下保留提出反对意见:(1) 委内瑞拉在签署时对第12条所作的声明以及委内瑞拉在批准时对该条所作的保留;(2) 伊朗在签署时对第14条所作的保留;(3) 捷克斯洛伐克和匈牙利在签署时对第14条和第23条所作的并在批准时予以确认的保留;(4) 突尼斯在签署时对第16条第4款所作的保留;(5) 捷克斯洛伐克在签署时所作的并在批准时予以确认的,对第19条和第20条适用于为商业目的运营的政府船舶的保留;(6) 保加利亚在签署和批准时对第20条所作的保留;(7) 德国、白俄罗斯、罗马尼亚、乌克兰和苏联在签署时对第20条所作的并在批准时予以确认的保留;(8) 匈牙利在签署时对第21条所作的并在批准时予以确认的保留;(9) 保加利亚在签署和批准时对第23条所作的保留;(10) 白俄罗斯苏维埃社会主义共和国、罗马尼亚、乌克兰苏维埃社会主义共和国和苏维埃社会主义共和国联盟在签署时对第23条所作的并在批准时予以确认的保留;(11) 委内瑞拉在批准时对第24条第2款和第3款所作的保留。澳大利亚进一步明确,如果上述关于第23条的声明属于法律性质的声明,而不是严格意义上的保留,则澳大利亚的反对将用于记录对如此声明的异议意见。[1]

关于《公海公约》,澳大利亚于批准该公约时对以下保留提出反对意见:

---

[1] "Convention on the Territorial Sea and the Contiguous Zone-Declarations and Reservations", UNTC, https://treaties.un.org/Pages/ViewDetails.aspx?src = TREATY&mtdsg_no = XXI-1&chapter = 21&clang = _en, May 13, 2022.

（1）伊朗在签署时对第2条、第3条和第4条所作的保留；（2）伊朗在签署时对第2条第3款、第26条第1款和第2款所作的保留；（3）保加利亚在签署和批准时对第9条所作的保留；（4）德国、白俄罗斯、捷克斯洛伐克、匈牙利、波兰、罗马尼亚、乌克兰和在签署时对第9条所作的并在批准时予以确认的保留；（5）印度尼西亚、墨西哥在批准时所作的保留；（6）阿尔巴尼亚加入《公海公约》时所作的保留。[1]

2.《联合国海洋法公约》

澳大利亚于1982年12月10日签署、1994年10月5日批准《联合国海洋法公约》，该公约于1994年11月16日对澳大利亚生效。

针对菲律宾关于《公约》所提出的声明，澳大利亚于1988年8月3日致信联合国秘书长表示：第一，澳大利亚认为菲律宾共和国所作声明与《公约》第309条不符，依据该条，《公约》禁止作出保留。第二，菲律宾的声明与《公约》第310条不符，依据该条，相关"声明或说明无意排除或修改本公约规定适用于该缔约国的法律效力"方可作出。但菲方在其声明中提出，《公约》既不能影响菲律宾源于本国宪法的主权权利，也不能影响其国内立法以及菲律宾为缔约方的任何条约，由此澳大利亚认定，这意味着菲律宾并不认为其有义务使本国法律与《公约》条款相协调。菲律宾意在通过作出这一声明以达到修改《公约》条款的法律效果。第三，菲律宾的上述企图已经在其有关群岛水域地位的声明内容中得到印证。菲律宾在声明中称，《公约》中有关群岛水域的概念与菲律宾前宪法及近期由1987年菲律宾新宪法第1条所重申的内水概念相近。但《公约》明显对这两个概念进行了区分，适用于群岛水域的权利和义务与适用于内水的权利和义务并不相同，《公约》为群岛水域所规定的无害通过权和群岛海道通过权更说明了其地位的特殊。由此，澳大利亚明确，其不能接受菲律宾相关声明在《公约》生效后具有法律效力或其他任何效力，并表示不应在菲律宾声明所称的限制之下来履行《公约》相关条款。

对于澳大利亚的反对意见，菲律宾于同年10月回应称：第一，菲律宾的声明符合《公约》第310条，该声明仅是对公约相应条款的解释和说明；第二，菲律宾政府有意使其国内立法与《公约》条款相符，正在基于条约义务履行必要步骤，以颁布与群岛海道通过、群岛水域主权相关的立法；第三，

---

[1] "Convention on the High Seas-Declarations and Reservations", UNTC, https://treaties.un.org/Pages/Vie-wDetails.aspx? src = TREATY&mtdsg_no = XXI-2&chapter = 21&clang = _en, May 13, 2022.

菲律宾政府愿向澳大利亚政府及其他《公约》缔约国保证，菲律宾将遵守所提及之《公约》条款。

2002年3月22日，澳大利亚向联合国秘书长提交了其在《公约》第15部分下的争端解决声明。依据《公约》第287条第1款的规定，澳大利亚政府选择用两种方式来解决与《公约》的解释或适用有关的争端，一为《公约》附件6设立的国际海洋法法庭，二为国际法院，但澳大利亚并未具体说明二者的先后顺序。同时，澳大利亚政府进一步声明，依据《公约》第298条第1款（a）项的规定，对于与海洋划界有关的第15条、第74条和第83条的解释或适用以及涉及历史性海湾或所有权的争端，澳大利亚不接受第15部分第2节规定的任何程序（包括前述的国际海洋法法庭和国际法院）。[1]

3. 联合国海洋法条约体系下的其他公约

1990年7月，为了解决主要由工业化国家提出的有关《公约》第11部分所载海底采矿规定的某些困难，在联合国秘书长主导的一系列非正式协商之下，最终于1994年7月28日通过《关于执行1982年12月10日〈联合国海洋法公约〉第十一部分的协定》（Agreement relating to the implementation of Part XI of the United Nations Convention on the Law of the Sea of 10 December 1982）。澳大利亚于1994年7月29日签署并于1994年10月5日批准了该协定，并依据该协定第7条第2款于1994年11月16日临时适用该协定。这一临时适用已据该协定第7条第3款于1996年7月28日终止。[2]

1995年8月4日，《执行1982年12月10日〈联合国海洋法公约〉有关养护和管理跨界鱼类种群和高度洄游鱼类种群的规定的协定》在联合国跨界鱼类种群和高度洄游鱼类种群会议上通过。该协定于1995年12月4日开放签署，2001年12月11日正式生效。澳大利亚于1995年12月4日签署、1999年12月23日批准该协定，同时未作出保留。[3]

---

[1] "United Nations Convention on the Law of the Sea-Declarations and Reservations", UNTC, https://trea-ties. un. org/Pages/ViewDetailsIII. aspx? src = TREATY&mtdsg _ no = XXI-6&chapter = 21&Temp = mtdsg3&clang = _en, May 13, 2022.

[2] "Agreement relating to the implementation of Part XI of the United Nations Convention on the Law of the Sea of 10 December 1982-Declarations and Reservations", UNTC, https://treaties. un. org/Pa-ges/Vi-ewDetails. aspx? src = TREATY&mtdsg_no = XXI-6-a&chapter = 21&clang = _en, May 13, 2022.

[3] "Agreement for the Implementation of the Provisions of the United Nations Convention on the Law of the Sea of 10 December 1982 relating to the Conservation and Management of Straddling Fish Stocks and Highly Migratory Fish Stocks-Declarations and Reservations", UNTC, https://treaties. un. org/Pages/Vi-ewDetails. aspx? src = TREATY&mtdsg_no = XXI-7&chapter = 21&clang = _en, May 13, 2022.

1999年5月26日，澳大利亚签署《国际海洋法法庭特权和豁免协定》（Agreement on the Privileges and Immunities of the International Tribunal for the Law of the Sea），并于2001年5月11日批准，且未作出保留。[1]

（二）南极条约体系下的相关公约

为捍卫其宣称在南极所拥有的"巨大而长期"的利益，澳大利亚积极推进南极条约体系的搭建，并坚定本国应该并已经从这一条约体系中获益。南极条约体系主要由4项国际协定组成：1959年《南极条约》、1972年《南极海豹保护公约》、1980年《南极海洋生物资源养护公约》和1991年《关于环境保护的南极条约议定书》。[2]

1. 1959年《南极条约》

澳大利亚是《南极条约》的12个原始缔约国之一。1959年12月1日，阿根廷、澳大利亚、比利时、智利、法国、日本、新西兰、挪威、南非、英国、美国和苏联等12国在华盛顿签署了《南极条约》。该条约于1961年6月23日生效，截至2024年7月，共有57个缔约国。《南极条约》为该地区治理制定了自由进行科学调查和交换科学发现、南极洲和南大洋的非军事化以及冻结对南极的主权要求等原则性条款。12个原始缔约国是有权参加该条约第9条规定的南极条约协商会议（ATCM）的第一批国家。根据该条约第9条第2款，陆续有29个国家在南极洲的活动得到承认，获得南极条约协商国地位，其他28个非协商国应邀可出席协商会议，但不得参与决策。澳大利亚于1961年7月在堪培拉举行了第1届南极条约协商会议，又于2012年在霍巴特（Hobart）主办了第35届南极条约协商会议。

2. 1972年《南极海豹保护公约》

澳大利亚于1972年10月5日签署了《南极海豹保护公约》，该公约于1987年7月31日对其生效。该公约旨在为恢复商业捕猎海豹提供规范方法。作为缔约国，澳大利亚有义务全面保护3种南极海豹物种，并为另外3种海豹物种建立限制捕捞机制。

3. 1980年《南极海洋生物资源养护公约》

澳大利亚是《南极海洋生物资源养护公约》的原始缔约国，于1980年9月11日签署、1981年5月6日批准该公约。该公约于1982年4月7日对澳

---

[1] "CHAPTER XXI：Law of the Sea", UNTC, https：//treaties.un.org/Pages/Treaties.aspx?id = 21&subid = A&c-lang = _en, May 13, 2022.

[2] "Antarctic Treaty System", Australian Antarctic Program, https：//www.antarctica.gov.au/about-antarctica/la-w-and-treaty/, May 13, 2022.

大利亚生效，并成为唯一一个将条约下设组织总部设在澳大利亚的国际公约。《南极海洋生物资源养护公约》是第一项对海洋生物资源养护采用生态系统方法的国际协定，旨在管理整个生态系统而非仅仅着眼于单个物种的商业捕捞。南极海洋生物资源养护委员会（CCAMLR）依该公约而设立。作为南极海洋生物资源养护委员会秘书处的驻在国，南极海洋生物资源养护委员会成员国的年度会议均在澳大利亚霍巴特举行。

4. 1991年《关于环境保护的南极条约议定书》

1989年5月22日，澳大利亚确认了其反对在南极洲采矿的国家立场，并宣布不会签署1988年《南极矿物资源活动管理公约》（Convention on the Regulation of Antarctic Mineral Resource Activities）。同时，澳大利亚开始积极寻求其他南极条约缔约国的支持，以全面保护南极大陆及其周围海域的环境。在这一努力下，南极条约缔约国于1991年10月在马德里签署了《关于环境保护的南极条约议定书》。随着南极条约缔约国对南极环境的全球重要性以及保护南极环境的必要性认知的日益增加，该议定书最终于1998年正式生效。

《关于环境保护的南极条约议定书》第7条明确规定，禁止与南极矿物资源有关的一切活动，科学研究除外。在2048年之前，该议定书只能通过《南极条约》所有协商国的一致同意进行修改。此外，除非对矿物资源活动施以有效的法律规制，否则不能取消对矿物资源活动的禁令。作为该议定书的签署国，澳大利亚采取了一系列行动，特别是通过引入环境影响评估程序等，对其在南极的活动辅以更为强有力的环境保护措施。1994年，澳大利亚完成了批准该议定书的国内立法，从而使《关于环境保护的南极条约议定书》中实质性条款的履行成为所有澳大利亚公民的法律义务。

除上述南极条约体系的主要法律文本外，澳大利亚还分别于1938年、2003年与法国签署了《构成南极空中航行协定的换文》（Exchange of Notes constituting an Agreement regarding Aerial Navigation in the Antarctic）、《法属南部和南极领地、赫德岛和麦克唐纳群岛附近海域合作协定》（Agreement with the Government of the French Republic on Cooperation in the Maritime Areas adjacent to the French Southern and Antarctic Territories, Heard Island and the McDonald Islands），于1986年签署了《澳大利亚政府与南极海洋生物资源养护委员会总部协定》（Headquarters Agreement between the Government of Australia and the commission for the conservation of Antarctic Marine Living Resources）。[1]

---

[1] "Australian Treaties Database", The Australian Department of Foreign Affairs and Trade, https://www.dfat.gov.au/international-relations/treaties/australian-treaties-database, May 25, 2022.

（三）国际海事组织框架下的相关条约

澳大利亚于 1948 年 3 月 6 日签署了 1948 年《政府间海事协商组织公约》[1]（Convention on the Intergovernmental Maritime Consultative Organization），该公约于 1958 年 3 月 17 日生效，并于同日对澳大利亚生效。澳大利亚就该公约第 1 部分第 1 条第 c 款规定的本组织根据第 2 部分审议与航运企业的不公平限制性做法有关的事项作出保留。澳大利亚随后陆续接受了该公约的多项修正案，包括：1965 年《对〈国际海事组织公约〉第 28 条的修正》（Amendments to Article 28 of the Convention on the Intergovernmental Maritime Consultative Organization done at Geneva on 6 March 1948），1974 年《对〈国际海事组织公约〉第 10 条、第 16 条（d）、第 17 条、第 18 条、第 20 条、第 28 条、第 31 条和第 32 条进行的修正》[Amendments to Articles 10, 16 (d), 17, 18, 20, 28, 31 and 32 of the Convention on the Intergovernmental Maritime Consultative Organization done at Geneva on 6 March 1948]，1979 年《对〈国际海事组织公约〉第 17 条、第 18 条、第 20 条和第 51 条的修正》（Amendments to Articles 17, 18, 20 and 51 of the Convention on the Intergovernmental Maritime Consultative Organization of 6 March 1948），1991 年《对〈国际海事组织公约〉关于设立公约便利化委员会的修正案》（Amendments to the Convention on the Intergovernmental Maritime Consultative Organization of 6 March 1948 relating to the Institutionalization of the Facilitation Committee of the Convention）（尚未生效），1977 年《对〈国际海事组织公约〉序言的修正》（Amendment to the Preamble of the Convention on the Intergovernmental Maritime Consultative Organization of 6 March 1948），1993 年《对〈国际海事组织公约〉关于第 16 条、第 17 条和第 19 条（b）的修正》[Amendments to the Convention on the Intergovernmental Maritime Consultative Organization done at Geneva on of 6 March 1948 relating to Articles 16, 17 and 19 (b)]。[2]

在国际海事组织框架下，澳大利亚加入的条约主要涉及以下方面[3]。

---

[1] 根据《1975 年对〈政府间海事协商组织公约〉标题和实质性条款的修正》（Amendments to the Title and Substantive Provisions of the Convention on the Intergovernmental Maritime Consultative Organization of 6 March 1948），该公约的标题已修订为《国际海事组织公约》。

[2] "Convention on the International Maritime Organization", International Maritime Organization, https://www.imo.org/en/About/Conventions/Pages/Convention-on-the-International-Maritime-Organization.aspx, May 25, 2022.

[3] "Status of Conventions-List of the Conventions and their amendments", International Maritime Organization, https://wwwcdn.imo.org/localresources/en/About/Conventions/StatusOfConventions/Status%20-%202022.pdf, May 27, 2022.

1. 与海上航行安全有关的条约

澳大利亚分别于 1979 年、1989 年、1997 年、2001 年加入 1976 年《国际海事卫星组织公约》（Convention on the International Maritime Satellite Organization, 1976）及其 1985 年修正案、1989 年修正案、1998 年修正案；于 1980 年加入 1972 年《国际海上避碰规则公约》（Convention on the International Regulations for Preventing Collisions at Sea, 1972）；于 1981 年加入 1972 年《国际集装箱安全公约》（International Convention for Safe Containers, 1972）；于 1983 年加入 1974 年《国际海上人命安全公约》（International Convention for the Safety of Life at Sea, 1974）及其 1978 年议定书，并于 2000 年加入其 1988 年议定书；于 1985 年加入 1979 年《国际海上搜寻和救助公约》（International Convention on Maritime Search and Rescue, 1979）；于 1993 年加入 1988 年《制止危及海上航行安全非法行为公约》和《制止危及大陆架固定平台安全非法行为议定书》；于 1996 年加入 1988 年《国际搜救卫星 COSPAS-SARSAT 系统计划协定》（The International COSPAS-SARSAT Programme Agreement）；于 1998 年加入 1989 年《国际救助公约》（International Convention on Salvage, 1989）。

其中，澳大利亚在 1979 年《国际海上搜寻和救助公约》的加入书中附声明称：依澳大利亚的联邦宪政体制，其立法、行政和司法权力由联邦和各州共享或划分。澳大利亚联邦、各州和各地区当局将根据各自的宪法权力及相关施行安排，在澳大利亚全境执行《国际海上搜寻和救助公约》。1989 年《国际救助公约》的加入书则保留称，澳大利亚在该公约第 30 条第 1 款（a）、（b）和（d）项规定的情况下无义务适用此公约的规定。

2. 与防治海洋污染有关的条约

澳大利亚缔结和加入的海洋污染防治相关条约主要包括：1984 年对其生效的 1969 年《国际干预公海油污事故公约》及其 1973 年议定书；分别于 1985 年、1998 年、2006 年加入的 1972 年《防止倾倒废物及其他物质污染海洋的公约》（Convention on The Prevention Of Marine Pollution By Dumping Of Wastes And Other Matter, 1972）及其 1993 年关于工业废物的修正案和 1996 年议定书；于 1988 年加入的《关于 1973 年国际防止船舶造成污染公约的 1978 年的议定书》（International Convention for the Prevention of Pollution from Ships, 1973 as modified by the Protocol of 1978 relating thereto）；于 2007 年加入的《经 1978 年议定书修订的〈1973 年国际防止船舶造成污染公约〉的 1997 年议定书》（Protocol of 1997 to amend the International Convention for the Prevention of Pollution from Ships, 1973, as modified by the Protocol of 1978 relating thereto); 于1995年加入的1990年《国际油污防备、反应和合作公约》（International Convention on Oil Pollution Preparedness, Response and Co-operation, 1990); 于2007年加入的2000年《有毒有害物质污染事故防备、反应和合作议定书》（Protocol on Preparedness, Response And Co-operation To Pollution Incidents By Hazardous And Noxious Substances, 2000); 于2008年加入的2001年《控制船舶有害防污底系统国际公约》; 于2009年加入的2001年《国际燃油污染损害民事责任公约》。

其中，对于1969年《国际干预公海油污事故公约》，澳大利亚在其批准书中附声明重申了澳大利亚代表团在1973年出席国际海洋污染会议时所称立场：澳大利亚坚信，没有哪一个沿海国应被禁止采取任何必要的行动，以保护其管辖范围内的地区不受严重的环境损害；同时为保护其管辖范围内的区域，沿海国介入公海的权利已得到习惯国际法的承认。因此，在澳大利亚成为该公约缔约国后，它将仍然可以采取行动保护其管辖范围内的地区和资源，这既不违背习惯国际法，也不违背该公约。[1]

3. 与船舶及船员管理有关的条约

澳大利亚于1968年加入1966年《国际船舶载重线公约》（International Convention on Load Lines, 1966）及其1971年、1975年、1979年、1983年、1995年修正案和其1988年议定书；于1982年加入1969年《国际船舶吨位丈量公约》（International Convention on Tonnage Measurement of Ships, 1969）; 于1984年加入1978年《海员培训、发证和值班标准国际公约》（International Convention on Standards of Training, Certification and Watchkeeping for Seafarers, 1978); 于1986年加入1965年《便利国际海上运输公约》（Convention on Facilitation of International Maritime Traffic, 1965); 于2017年加入2004年《国际船舶压载水和沉积物控制与管理公约》（International Convention For The Control And Management Of Ships' Ballast Water And Sediments, 2004）。

4. 与损害赔偿责任有关的条约

澳大利亚于1984年加入1969年《国际油污损害民事责任公约》及其1976年议定书，又于1996年加入其1992年议定书；于1995年加入1971年《设立国际油污损害赔偿基金国际公约》及其1976年议定书，又于1996年、

---

[1] "Ratification by Australia and accessions by Bulgaria and the United Arab Emirates", Treaty Series V. 1355, UNTC, https://treaties.un.org/doc/Publication/UNTS/Volume%201355/v1355.pdf, March 20, 2023.

四、缔结和加入的国际海洋法条约

2009年加入其1992年、2003年议定书。1988年,澳大利亚就上述《国际油污损害民事责任公约》的1976年议定书向国际海事组织提交退出申请。至1998年,澳大利亚正式退出上述两公约的母约。[1]

---

[1] 其他澳大利亚缔结和加入的渔业资源及海洋环境保护相关条约详见"附录9 澳大利亚缔结和加入的国际海洋法条约"。

五、海洋争端解决

(一) 与葡萄牙、东帝汶之间的帝汶海相关争端

帝汶海东接阿拉弗拉海、西临印度洋,覆盖了约 25 万平方公里的海域。该海域普遍较浅,仅在帝汶海槽处急转直下,平均深度达 2840 米。[1] 帝汶海海域的海床被认为有丰富的油气蕴藏。

帝汶岛 (island of Timor) 位于帝汶海以北,由澳大利亚大陆与欧亚大陆板块碰撞而形成,是巽他群岛 (Sunda Islands) 最东的岛屿之一。澳大利亚北端接帝汶海以南,与东帝汶隔帝汶海相望,两国间最近距离约为 450 公里。

帝汶岛西部属印度尼西亚东努沙登加拉省 (East Nusa Tenggara),印度尼西亚群岛的其他岛屿则集中于帝汶岛以北及以东。而帝汶岛东部由东帝汶所据,其陆地领土面积约为 15000 平方公里,由帝汶岛东部、帝汶岛以北的阿陶罗岛 (island of Atauro)、距帝汶岛主岛东端不足 1 公里的雅科岛 (island of Jaco),以及位于帝汶岛西部的欧库西 - 安贝诺 (Oecussi-Ambeno) 飞地组成。

1. 葡萄牙殖民时期的帝汶海争端

葡萄牙与荷兰殖民势力于 16 世纪、17 世纪先后进入帝汶岛。几经争夺,葡萄牙与荷兰于 1859 年签订条约重新瓜分帝汶岛,划定东帝汶和西帝汶之间的陆地边界,将帝汶岛东部及欧库西 - 安贝诺划归葡萄牙,帝汶岛西部并入荷属东印度 (今印度尼西亚) 辖下。直至 1975 年,东帝汶都处于葡萄牙的实际占领之下。自 20 世纪 60 年代起,东帝汶即被承认为《联合国宪章》下的 "非自治领土" (non-self-governing territories),其人民享有民族自决权。

早在 20 世纪 50 年代,澳大利亚与葡萄牙就分别提出了其大陆架主张。1953 年 9 月,澳大利亚发布公告,宣示对邻接其海岸的大陆架海床及底土享有主权权利。1956 年 3 月,葡萄牙通过立法,宣布邻近其领土的大陆架是国家公域 (public domain) 的一部分。在该立法明确规定应适用于 "葡萄牙全境" 的情形下,根据当时有效的 1933 年《葡萄牙宪法》,这一大陆架主张也

---

[1] "Report and Recommendations of the Compulsory Conciliation Commission between Timor-Leste and Australia on the Timor Sea, Timor Sea Conciliation (Timor-Leste v. Australia)", PCA, https://pcacases.com/web/sendAttach/2327, pp. 69-70, March 23, 2023.

应延伸适用于东帝汶领土。1963年，两国先后批准1958年《大陆架公约》，并在该公约1964年生效后受其约束。20世纪70年代初，澳大利亚与葡萄牙开始就帝汶海相关大陆架划分有所接触与沟通，但正式的条约谈判从未展开。

1972年10月，澳大利亚与印度尼西亚签署了《澳大利亚联邦政府与印度尼西亚共和国政府关于在帝汶海和阿拉弗拉海地区确立某些海底边界的协定（对1971年5月18日协定之补充）》（Agreement between the Government of the Commonwealth of Australia and the Government of the Republic of Indonesia Establishing Certain Seabed Boundaries in the Area of the Timor and Arafura Seas, Supplementary to the Agreement of 18 May 1971，以下简称《1972年海底协定》）。依据该协定，澳大利亚与印度尼西亚大致沿帝汶海槽南部边缘对两国间的海底区域进行了划分。[1]《1972年海底协定》无意对邻近东帝汶的海床作出划定，但预计其将成为澳大利亚与葡萄牙间未来条约的主旨之一。对此，该协定第3条专门就连接此时"葡萄牙帝汶"东西部的印澳海底边界预留了调整空间。

2. 印度尼西亚占领时期的帝汶海争端及司法解决

1975年11月，趁着葡萄牙"康乃馨革命"（Carnation Revolution）爆发之机，东帝汶宣布从葡萄牙独立。随着葡萄牙军队的撤出，印度尼西亚迅速于当年出兵占领东帝汶。尽管印度尼西亚的军事占领与行政管理都遭到了东帝汶人民的激烈反抗，但直至1999年印度尼西亚都将东帝汶视为其行省之一。

澳大利亚于1978年即在事实上承认了印度尼西亚对东帝汶的占领地位。时任澳大利亚外长表示，尽管澳大利亚政府不赞成印度尼西亚吞并东帝汶的方式，但拒绝在事实上承认东帝汶已成为印度尼西亚的一部分并不现实。1978年12月，为推动澳大利亚与印度尼西亚间相关海床边界条约谈判的正式展开，澳大利亚更是明确表示其缔约行为应视为在法律上承认印度尼西亚对东帝汶的主权。

从1979年2月开始，这一围绕"帝汶缺口"的缔约谈判贯穿了整个20世纪80年代。1989年12月，澳大利亚与印度尼西亚签署《澳大利亚与印度尼西亚在印尼东帝汶省与北澳大利亚地区建立合作区的条约》（Treaty between Australia and the Republic of Indonesia on the Zone of Cooperation in an Area between the Indonesian Province of East Timor and Northern Australia，以下简

---

[1] 该分界线的具体坐标及走向详见本部分"（二）通过协议解决的其他海洋划界争端"中"澳大利亚与印度尼西亚之间的划界协定"下的相关内容。

称《帝汶缺口条约》)。在久拖不决的谈判波折中，两国暂时放下海洋划界的初衷，转而通过《帝汶缺口条约》建立了一个合作区（区域A），由澳大利亚与印度尼西亚通过联合管理机构共同控制相关石油作业，并平等分配其年度收益。[1]

对于澳大利亚将其排除在外，意图通过与印度尼西亚的双边安排划分帝汶海权利边界与开发收益的行为，葡萄牙表示强烈不满。1985年9月、1988年10月、1989年10月以及《帝汶缺口条约》签署后的1989年12月，葡萄牙曾多次对两国间的缔约进程及缔约成果提出抗议，但未有成效。1991年2月，葡萄牙就"澳大利亚有关东帝汶的某些行为"将澳大利亚诉至国际法院，要求法院依据两国事先提交的强制管辖声明对该案行使管辖权。

葡萄牙所称"澳大利亚有关东帝汶的某些行为"主要包括：（1）澳大利亚谈判、缔结并着手施行了1989年《帝汶缺口条约》，通过相关国内立法履行条约义务，并继续与该条约另一缔约国就帝汶缺口大陆架划界事宜展开谈判；（2）澳大利亚在有关这一区域的大陆架开发利用的谈判中进一步将管理国排除在外；（3）澳大利亚在帝汶缺口海床底土的开发利用立足于涉及多方的所有权，而这一所有权也将葡萄牙排除在外。

鉴于此，葡萄牙请求法院判决并宣告：第一，澳大利亚已经侵犯并正在侵犯东帝汶人民的民族自决权，东帝汶的领土完整和统一及对其财富和资源的永久主权，并因未能尊重上述权利而违反其国际法义务。第二，澳大利亚已经侵犯并正在侵犯葡萄牙作为东帝汶管理国的权力，妨碍其履行对东帝汶人民及国际社会的应尽职责，侵犯葡萄牙承担相应责任的权利，并因未能尊重葡萄牙权责而违反其国际法义务。第三，澳大利亚的行为与联合国安理会第384号及第389号决议相抵触，违反了《联合国宪章》下接受并执行安理会决议的义务，无视联合国相关机构有关东帝汶决议的拘束力，违背了联合国会员国善意合作的义务。第四，在东帝汶人民于联合国所设条件下行使其民族自决权之前，澳大利亚必须停止有关东帝汶人民、葡萄牙及国际社会的上述行为，包括：对于帝汶缺口区域的大陆架划界、开发利用或管辖权行使，澳大利亚须避免与管理国以外的他国谈判、签署或批准任何相关协定；有关帝汶缺口区域大陆架的开发利用或管辖权行使，若该行为立足于涉及多方的所有权，而该所有权未将作为东帝汶管理国的葡萄牙纳入其中，澳大利

---

[1] 有关《帝汶缺口条约》的其他规定，参见 "Chapter 4-The Timor Gap (Zone of Co-operation) Treaty", Parliament of Australia, https：//www.aph.gov.au/Parliamentary_Business/Committees/Senate/Foreign_Affairs_Defence_and_Trade/Completed_inquiries/1999-02/east_timor/report/c04, March 20, 2023.

五、海洋争端解决

亚须避免涉及该行为。[1]

对于葡萄牙提出的上述主张，澳大利亚在程序上对案件管辖权及可受理性提出反对意见，并在实体上请求国际法院驳回葡萄牙全部诉讼请求。相关反对意见主要包括：第一，澳大利亚与葡萄牙之间事实上并无争端；第二，葡萄牙的请求将令法院对一个非本案当事方的国家（印度尼西亚）的权利和义务作出裁决；第三，葡萄牙不具备向国际法院提起本案的诉讼资格，其在本案中既没有充分的本国利益，也无权代表东帝汶人民，且其所提事项也并无法律性质，而应通过政治方法解决。其中，第一及第二项反对意见成为国际法院在审理该案时的争议焦点。[2]

（1）关于第一项反对意见的判决结论。

第一项反对意见聚焦于"是否存在争端"。澳大利亚提出：其一，葡萄牙人为地将问题限定为澳大利亚行为的合法性，但本案的真实相对方应是印度尼西亚而非澳大利亚。澳大利亚替代印度尼西亚被诉，而印度尼西亚并未向国际法院提交过强制管辖声明。其二，葡萄牙并未质疑过澳大利亚缔结1989年《帝汶缺口条约》的能力，也无意争论该条约的效力，因而澳大利亚与葡萄牙之间并无实际的争端存在。但葡萄牙始终坚持其所提交至国际法院的争端是真实且唯一的。

针对这一反对意见，国际法院再次回顾了从常设国际法院以来相关司法实践中对"争端"含义的澄清与确认，申明"争端是有关法律或事实的分歧，是当事方间法律观点或利益的冲突"。在这一界定结论之上，所谓"真实的争端"到底存在于葡萄牙与印度尼西亚之间还是葡萄牙与澳大利亚之间，已无关紧要。无论正确与否，葡萄牙都明确阐述了针对澳大利亚的事实及法律的诉请，而这一诉请已被澳大利亚否认。一项法律争端即经由这一否认而生成。因此，国际法院认为，当事方间确实存在法律及事实的分歧，即澳大利亚谈判、缔结并着手施行1989年《帝汶缺口条约》的行为，是否违反了澳大利亚在国际法下应对葡萄牙承担的义务。[3]

（2）关于第二项反对意见的判决结论。

第二项反对意见需要判明"法院是否被要求裁定印度尼西亚的权利与义务"。澳大利亚提出：其一，葡萄牙对国际法院提出的诉讼请求，将不可避免地要求法院在未获得第三国印度尼西亚同意的情形下，对该第三国行为的

---

[1] Judgment of 30 June 1995, East Timor (Portugal v. Australia), pp. 8-9.
[2] Judgment of 30 June 1995, East Timor (Portugal v. Australia), pp. 12-13.
[3] Judgment of 30 June 1995, East Timor (Portugal v. Australia), pp. 13-14.

合法性作出裁决。澳大利亚同时援引了国际法院在"1943年从罗马运走的货币黄金案"中的裁决结论作为支撑。其二,即使葡萄牙在撤离东帝汶后仍然保留其管理国地位,但据一般国际法,其仍有可能在此后将权力移交给另一国家,而它也确实将权力移交给了印度尼西亚。

葡萄牙则反驳称:其一,葡萄牙的诉讼请求仅与澳大利亚的客观行为相关,该行为完全可与印度尼西亚的行为区分开来,澳大利亚的行为本身构成了对相关国际义务的违反,对作为非自治领土的东帝汶及作为管理国的葡萄牙造成了威胁。其二,"1943年从罗马运走的货币黄金案"相关结论不适用于本案,因为澳大利亚侵犯的权利为"对所有人"的权利,葡萄牙可以单独要求澳大利亚尊重这些权利,而不论另一国是否采取了类似的非法行为。其三,东帝汶作为非自治领土及葡萄牙作为该领土管理国的权力,已在联合国大会及安理会决议中得以确认,法院无须重新裁定这些"既定事实"。[1]

对于双方的相峙立场,国际法院首先重申了"当事国同意原则"是《国际法院规约》下的基本原则,并进一步阐释其立场为:

第一,葡萄牙的请求源于其一项主张,即只有作为管理国的葡萄牙才有权代表东帝汶缔结条约,但澳大利亚已通过与印度尼西亚缔结1989年《帝汶缺口条约》的行为表明,澳大利亚将印度尼西亚视为有权方。

第二,要评估澳大利亚的行为,必须先解决一个问题,即为何印度尼西亚缔结1989年《帝汶缺口条约》为非法但葡萄牙却为合法。由此,国际法院作出判决的核心问题就在于,考虑到印度尼西亚已经进入东帝汶并在此地持续存在,印度尼西亚能否获得相应权力以代表东帝汶缔结有关其大陆架资源的条约。而在未获得印度尼西亚同意的情形下,国际法院无法就该问题作出裁定。

第三,国际法院认可民族自决权具有"对所有人"的性质,其已经得到《联合国宪章》和国际法院司法实践的承认,民族自决原则是现代国际法的一项基本原则。但国际法院仍坚持认为,一项规范所具有的"对所有人"的性质,与一项同意行使管辖权的规则是两码事。无论所援引的义务有何性质,在法院的判决将涉及评判案件非当事国行为的合法性时,法院都无法对案件当事国行为的合法性作出裁定。

第四,当事国双方都同意,东帝汶领土仍然为非自治领土,其人民享有民族自决权。这一领土性质也得到了联合国有权机关联合国大会及安理会的确认。但对作为管理国的葡萄牙可从东帝汶的非自治领土地位获取何种法律

---

[1] Judgment of 30 June 1995, East Timor (Portugal v. Australia), pp. 14-17.

地位尚存在分歧。国际法院认为，不能仅仅因为联合国大会及安理会在一些决议中将葡萄牙称为东帝汶的管理国，就断定这些决议旨在规定第三国有义务只与葡萄牙讨论东帝汶的大陆架问题。事实上，已有数个国家与印度尼西亚缔结了可能影响东帝汶的条约，而未对这一非自治领土作出任何保留。因此，在不损害联合国相关决议拘束力的前提下，法院无法将这些决议视为"既定因素"，也不能将其作为确定当事国之间争端的充分依据。

由此，国际法院认定，葡萄牙的诉讼请求意味着法院需裁判印度尼西亚进入及驻留东帝汶是非法的，且因此并无就东帝汶大陆架资源谈判缔约的权力。印度尼西亚的权利与义务因而构成了未经该国同意的本案判决的关键主题（the very subject-matter），并令该判决直接与《国际法院规约》下早已被接受的国际法原则"当事国同意原则"相悖。[1]

（3）有关"东帝汶案"（葡萄牙诉澳大利亚）的最终判决结果。

国际法院对该案的审理止步于对前两项反对意见的判定。在阐明对澳大利亚第二项反对意见的支持立场后，法院判定，为裁判葡萄牙的相关诉讼请求，作为一项先决条件，法院将不可避免地在未经印度尼西亚同意的情形下对该国行为的合法性作出裁定。由此，国际法院不能基于《国际法院规约》第36条第2款对本案行使管辖权，法院不必再审议澳大利亚的其他反对意见，也无须对有关葡萄牙诉求的实体问题进行裁判。"东帝汶案"于1995年6月由国际法院作出无管辖权判决而告终。[2] 澳大利亚与印度尼西亚也于1997年再次尝试缔约划定两国间的专属经济区及大陆架界限。[3]

3. 东帝汶公投独立后的帝汶海争端解决

1999年8月，东帝汶在联合国监督下从印度尼西亚公投独立。经过艰难的过渡期后，东帝汶于2002年5月正式宣布成为独立国家。澳大利亚积极介入东帝汶独立后的相关过渡行动，并在2002年该国正式独立前即与相关方就帝汶海相关条约的实施展开接触。

（1）2002年前过渡期的相关协议安排。

2000年2月，澳大利亚与联合国东帝汶过渡行政当局（United Nations Transitional Administration in East Timor，UNTAET）就继续执行《帝汶缺口条约》相关条款签署换文。随着印度尼西亚于1999年10月宣布放弃对东帝汶的领土主张，该条约已经无法在澳大利亚与印度尼西亚之间继续适用。

---

[1] Judgment of 30 June 1995, East Timor (Portugal v. Australia), pp.16-19.
[2] Judgment of 30 June 1995, East Timor (Portugal v. Australia), pp.19-20.
[3] 参见本部分"（二）通过协议解决的其他海洋划界争端"中"澳大利亚与印度尼西亚之间的划界协定"下"1997年《珀斯条约》"相关内容。

2001年7月，澳大利亚与联合国东帝汶过渡行政当局签署《有关帝汶海安排的谅解备忘录》（Memorandum of Understanding of Timor Sea Arrangement，以下简称《帝汶海安排》）。通过该谅解备忘录所设立的"联合石油开发区"（Joint Petroleum Development Area，JPDA）正与《帝汶缺口条约》中的区域A边界相对应。不过，不同于在《帝汶缺口条约》下由澳大利亚与印度尼西亚两国平均分享区域A的石油收益，《帝汶海安排》为"联合石油开发区"规定了更有利于东帝汶的9∶1的收益划分比例。[1]

（2）2002年《帝汶海条约》。

2002年5月，在东帝汶正式重获独立当日，东帝汶与澳大利亚两国政府成功缔结《帝汶海条约》（Timor Sea Treaty），旨在将《帝汶海安排》中的相关框架及规定进一步细化。

《帝汶海条约》共有正文25条，主要内容包括：条约所涉的术语界定；本条约与其他重要条约间的关系；依条约设立的"联合石油开发区"（《帝汶海安排》下的"联合石油开发区"）；石油收益分享；财政安排及税收制度；监管机构设置及职责；相关石油开采规章的制定；油气管道的铺设与管理；联合石油开发协议；联合开发区域的海洋环境保护；劳工雇佣及劳工安全与健康管理；相关税收法律的适用；相关刑事程序的适用；条约所涉区域中海关、移民、卫生事项的监管；相关水文及地质测量的要求；石油作业船舶的安全航行营运标准及船员管理；联合开发区域的监督执行权归属；联合开发区域的安保及空中飞越事宜；有关争端解决、条约有效期、条约生效及修订等程序性事项。[2]

除正文外，《帝汶海条约》还通过7个附件分别就"联合石油开发区"的位置及范围，条约相关的争端解决程序，本条约第6条所指定管理机关（Designated Authority）及联合委员会（Joint Commission）的权利与职能，巨日升地区的联合开发，特定油田的财政计划，在"联合石油开发区"防止逃税并避免双重征税等作出安排。其中，依据附件A，"联合石油开发区"由连接15个坐标点的测地线包围划定。[3] 这15个坐标点的位置如表14所示：

---

[1] "Report and Recommendations of the Compulsory Conciliation Commission between Timor-Leste and Australia on the Timor Sea，Timor Sea Conciliation（Timor-Leste v. Australia）"，PCA，https：//pcacases.com/web/sendAttach/2327，10，March 23，2023.

[2] "Timor Sea Treaty"，UN，https：//www.un.org/Depts/los/LEGISLATIONANDTREATIES/PDF-FILES/TREAT-IES/AUS-TLS2002TST.PDF，March 21，2023.

[3] "Timor Sea Treaty"，Annex A under article 3 of this Treaty Designation and description of the JPDA，UN，https：//www.un.org/Depts/los/LEGISLATIONANDTREATIES/PDFFILES/TREATIES/AUS-TLS2002TST.PDF，March 21，2023.

五、海洋争端解决

表14　澳大利亚与东帝汶间"联合石油开发区"的边界坐标点[1]

坐标点	纬度（南）	经度（东）
a	9°22′53″	127°48′42″
b	10°06′40″	126°00′25″
c	10°28′00″	126°00′00″
d	11°20′08″	126°31′54″
e	11°19′46″	126°47′04″
f	11°17′36″	126°57′07″
g	11°17′30″	126°58′13″
h	11°14′24″	127°31′33″
i	10°55′26″	127°47′04″
j	10°53′42″	127°48′45″
k	10°43′43″	127°59′16″
l	10°29′17″	128°12′24″
m	9°29′57″	127°58′47″
n	9°28′00″	127°56′00″
o	沿西北测地线返回 a 点	

《帝汶海条约》基本全盘接受了《帝汶海安排》中有关联合开发的协商成果，包括两国在"联合石油开发区" 9∶1 的石油收益分配比例。两国更在条约签订当日另行换文[2]，同意在《帝汶海条约》生效前继续临时适用《帝汶海安排》。上述条约及换文均声明，该条约及换文所载内容不得妨害或影响两国间后续的海洋边界划定。上述换文还进一步明确，在同意《帝汶海安排》继续生效的情形下，东帝汶将不再承认澳大利亚与印度尼西亚间《帝汶缺口条约》的效力，也不承认将东帝汶"并入"印度尼西亚的合法性。[3]

---

[1] "Timor Sea Treaty", UN, https：//www.un.org/Depts/los/LEGISLATIONANDTREATIES/PDF-FILES/TREATIES/AUS-TLS2002TST.PDF, March 21, 2023.

[2] 即2002年5月20日《澳大利亚政府与东帝汶民主共和国政府间有关在澳大利亚与东帝汶间的帝汶海某区域勘探开发石油的安排达成协定的换文》（Exchange of Notes constituting an Agreement between the Government of Australia and the Government of the Democratic Republic of East Timor concerning Arrangements for Exploration and Exploitation of Petroleum in an Area of the Timor Sea between Australia and East Timor, Dili, 20 May 2002）。

[3] See "Exchange of Notes constituting an Agreement between the Government of Australia and the Government of the Democratic Republic of East Timor concerning Arrangements for Exploration and Exploitation of Petroleum in an Area of the Timor Sea between Australia and East Timor, Dili, 20 May 2002", article 7, article 8, UN, https：//www.un.org/Depts/los/LEGISLATIONANDTREATIES/PDFFILES/TREATIES/AUS-TLS2002EX.PDF, March 21, 2023.

(3) 2003 年《澳大利亚政府与东帝汶民主共和国政府间关于联合开发巨日升与吟游诗人油田的协定》。

依据《帝汶海条约》附件 E，"由于巨日升与吟游诗人油田有 20.1% 都位于联合石油开发区内"，东帝汶与澳大利亚同意联合开发巨日升地区。两国同样于《帝汶海条约》签订当日附随了一份谅解备忘录[1]，以巩固两国开发帝汶海石油资源的合作意愿，并尽快促成对巨日升油田联合开发协定的善意签订。2003 年 3 月，在确认巨日升地区的石油生产收益中的 20.1% 归属"联合石油开发区"、79.9% 归属澳大利亚的基础上，《澳大利亚政府与东帝汶民主共和国政府间关于联合开发巨日升与吟游诗人油田的协定》（Agreement between the Government of Australia and the Government of the Democratic Republic of Timor-Leste relating to the Unitization of the Sunrise and Troubadour fields，以下简称《联合开发协定》）得以正式订立。

该协定共含 27 条正文及 5 个附件，分别就条约术语界定、单元储油层开采条件、可适用法律、与相关合资石油企业的协议、单元石油开采的分摊、单元开采区（Unit Area）的管理、单元开采区内的财产税收、相关开发计划、开采区内设施废弃、非为巨日升开采作业而使用开采区内财产、劳工雇佣与培训、环境保护、信息流动、关税及安保、争端解决等作出规划和安排。同时，两国在协定中再次申明，"澳大利亚与东帝汶已分别提出海洋主张且尚未划定海洋边界，对巨日升所在的帝汶海区域同样如此"，两国进一步强调该协定不能被解释为损害任何一方的海洋主张或边界立场。[2]

该协定附件 1 就本协定中的核心区域即单元开采区的位置进行了划定。依据附件 1，该开采区由连接以下坐标点（表 15）的连续恒向线（rhumb line）包围而成：

---

[1] 参见《东帝汶民主共和国政府与澳大利亚政府间有关巨日升油田国际联合开发协定的谅解备忘录》，载联合国网站，https：//www.un.org/Depts/los/LEGISLATIONANDTREATIES/PDFFILES/TREA-TIES/AUS-TLS2002SUN.PDF，最后访问日期：2024 年 9 月 15 日。

[2] "Agreement between the Government of Australia and the Government of the Democratic Republic of Timor-Leste relating to the Unitization of the Sunrise and Troubadour fields, Dili, 6 March 2003", UN, https：//www.un.org/Depts/los/LEGISLATIONANDTREATIES/PDFFILES/TREATIES/AUS-TLS2003UNI.PDF, March 21, 2023.

五、海洋争端解决

表15 《联合开发协定》下单元开采区的边界坐标点[1]

坐标点	纬度（南）	经度（东）
1	9°50′00″	127°55′00″
2	9°50′00″	128°20′00″
3	9°40′00″	128°20′00″
4	9°40′00″	128°25′00″
5	9°30′00″	128°25′00″
6	9°30′00″	128°20′00″
7	9°25′00″	128°20′00″
8	9°25′00″	128°00′00″
9	9°30′00″	127°53′20″
10	9°30′00″	127°52′30″
11	9°35′00″	127°52′30″
12	9°35′00″	127°50′00″
13	9°37′30″	127°50′00″
14	9°37′30″	127°45′00″
15	9°45′00″	127°45′00″
16	9°45′00″	127°50′00″
17	9°47′30″	127°50′00″
18	9°47′30″	127°55′00″

（4）2006年《澳大利亚与东帝汶民主共和国间关于帝汶海某些海上安排条约》。

乘着《联合开发协定》的东风，澳大利亚与东帝汶于2003年11月紧锣密鼓地开启了海洋划界的又一轮谈判。2006年1月，两国几经调整后签署了《澳大利亚与东帝汶民主共和国间关于帝汶海某些海上安排条约》（Treaty between Australia and the Democratic Republic of Timor-Leste on certain maritime arrangements in the Timor Sea，以下简称《海上安排条约》）[2]。

---

[1] "Agreement between the Government of Australia and the Government of the Democratic Republic of Timor-Leste relating to the Unitization of the Sunrise and Troubadour fields, Dili, 6 March 2003", Annex I, UN, https：//www.un.org/Depts/los/LEGISLATIONANDTREATIES/PDFFILES/TREATIES/AUS-TLS2003UNI.PDF, March 21, 2023.

[2] 《海上安排条约》在后续强制调解程序中由双方同意终止。详见后文"帝汶海调解案"（东帝汶诉澳大利亚）。

2006年《海上安排条约》共有13条正文及2个附件，主要内容包括：第一，将《帝汶海条约》的有效期延长至《海上安排条约》生效后的50年；第二，规定由东帝汶对"联合石油开发区"的上覆水域行使管辖权；第三，规定巨日升地区油气产出所获的直接收益由两国平均分享，而不再适用《帝汶海条约》及《联合开发协定》中的分配比例。[1] 总体而言，这一2006年条约沿袭了2002年《帝汶海条约》与2003年《联合开发协定》的基本框架与协商成果，仅就最具争议的巨日升油田的收益分配问题另行安排，谈判初衷的海洋划界问题仍然处于搁置状态。

依据《海上安排条约》第2条，任何一方都不得将本条约解释为损害或影响两国各自海洋主张的立场或权利，不得被解释为对己方在帝汶海任何区域的权利或主张的重申，也不得被解释为对另一方在帝汶海任何区域的权利或主张的承认或肯定。该条约第4条进一步规定：在本条约存续期间，澳大利亚与东帝汶均不得以任何方式向对方伸张、寻求实现主权权利、管辖权及海洋边界的相关主张；在本条约存续期间，双方也无义务与对方就永久海洋边界的划定进行谈判。而依据该条约第12条，这一海洋划界的"冻结期"将跟随条约的有效期，或为该条约生效后的50年，或为"联合石油开发区"开采停止后的5年。[2] 事实上，根据相关研究，就争议油田的开采生命周期而言，该条约第12条可以有效地保证在帝汶海油气资源耗尽前两国不必再胶着于永久海洋边界的划定。[3]

《海上安排条约》受到了澳大利亚官方的高度赞扬，其认为此次缔约成果既有益于澳大利亚也"慷慨"施惠于东帝汶。但对东帝汶而言，这一条约的缔结既令人鼓舞也令人失望。东帝汶未能大幅扩展其得以行使管辖权并获得高比例份额的"联合石油开发区"，未能保证澳大利亚就以往在争议油田的开采对东帝汶进行补偿，也未能就相关油气开采的下游活动与澳大利亚达成一致。这意味着，东帝汶无法确保本应有权获得的全部收益，也几乎注定

---

[1] "Treaty between Australia and the Democratic Republic of Timor-Leste on certain maritime arrangements in the Timor Sea, 12 January 2006", Centre for International Law, https：//cil. nus. edu. sg/wp-content/uploa-ds/2019/02/2006-Treaty-Between-Australia-And-The-Democratic-Republic-Of-Timor-1. pdf, March 22, 2023.

[2] "Treaty between Australia and the Democratic Republic of Timor-Leste on certain maritime arrangements in the Timor Sea, 12 January 2006", article 2, article 4, article 12, Centre for International Law, https：//cil. nus. edu. sg/wp-content/uploads/2019/02/2006-Treaty-Between-Australia-And-The-Democratic-Republi-c-Of-Timor-1. pdf, March 22, 2023.

[3] Smith, Madeleine, "Australian claims to the Timor sea's petroleum resources: Clever, cunning, or criminal?", *Monash University Law Review*, Vol. 3, 2012, p. 65.

将失去来自巨日升油田的利润丰厚的油气加工机会。[1]

(5) 2006年后的法律解决尝试。

2002年3月，澳大利亚依据《公约》第298条第1款对海洋法下的争端解决作出任择性声明，排除国际法院与国际海洋法法庭对其海洋边界争端的强制管辖。2002年5月，《帝汶海条约》第23条规定，与该条约解释和适用相关的争端应通过协商和谈判解决；若通过协商和谈判未能解决的，应将争端提交至依该条约附件B成立的仲裁庭解决。2006年1月，《海上安排条约》第11条亦规定，任何与本条约解释和适用有关的争端均应通过协商和谈判解决。该条约第4条更进一步限定：澳大利亚与东帝汶双方均不得就帝汶海划界问题，在任何争端解决机构直接或间接地启动针对另一方的相关程序；任何法院、法庭或其他争端解决机构均不得在聆讯等程序中，直接或间接地审议、评论或判定涉及帝汶海划界问题的事宜；任何一方均不得在国际组织中提出或谋求帝汶海海洋边界划界事项的解决。[2] 在上述条约框架之下，于双边谈判中难获优势的东帝汶只能尝试通过国际仲裁或迂回诉诸国际法院，寻求在海洋边界划定及争议区油气资源配比的后续拉锯中取得相对理想的结果。

东帝汶于2013年2月正式加入《公约》。同年4月，东帝汶依据《帝汶海条约》关于第23条的附件B（b）款对澳大利亚提起国际仲裁，要求仲裁庭就《海上安排条约》订立时的情势、《海上安排条约》的效力及其延长《帝汶海条约》有效期的合法性作出裁定。2014年9月1日以来，澳大利亚和东帝汶多次请求仲裁庭中止庭审程序，以便双方可以尝试通过谈判友好解决争端。但经过近一年的谈判，双方的协商进程并无明确突破。[3] 2015年9月，东帝汶再次依据《帝汶海条约》下的争端解决条款提起仲裁，并要求仲裁庭裁定：《帝汶海条约》中有关澳大利亚对其铺设的管道具有管辖权的条款，是否可理解为赋予澳大利亚专属管辖权，从而排除了东帝汶对铺设于

---

[1] Smith, Madeleine, "Australian claims to the Timor sea's petroleum resources: Clever, cunning, or criminal?", *Monash University Law Review*, Vol. 3, 2012, p. 69.

[2] "Timor Sea Treaty", article 23, UN, https://www.un.org/Depts/los/LEGISLATIONANDTREATIES/PDFFILES/TREATIES/AUS-TLS2002TST.PDF, March 22, 2023; "Treaty between Australia and the Democratic Republic of Timor-Leste on certain maritime arrangements in the Timor Sea, 12 January 2006", article 4, article 11, Centre for International Law, https://cil.nus.edu.sg/wp-content/uploads/2019/02/2006-Treaty-Be-tween-Aust-ralia-And-The-Democratic-Republic-Of-Timor-1.pdf, March 22, 2023.

[3] "Termination Order, Arbitration under the Timor Sea Treaty (Timor-Leste v. Australia), 20 March 2017", PCA, https://pcacases.com/web/sendAttach/2110, March 22, 2023.

"联合石油开发区"的海底管道行使管辖的权利。[1]2017年1月,随着2016年强制调解程序的推进,双方均表示相关仲裁程序的进行已无意义,并共同致函仲裁庭同意中止上述2013年及2015年仲裁。[2]

在依双边协定提起仲裁的同时,东帝汶也不放弃借助某些关联事项迂回寻求国际法院层面的支持。2013年12月,东帝汶就"某些文件被收缴和扣押"一事在国际法院对澳大利亚提起诉讼。东帝汶在诉讼申请中称,澳大利亚官员收缴并扣押了"属于东帝汶或东帝汶根据国际法有权保护的文件、数据和其他财产",被收缴的物品中包括东帝汶与其法律顾问之间的往来文件、数据和信函,其内容涉及根据2002年5月20日《帝汶海条约》正在进行的待决仲裁。

在东帝汶的请求下,国际法院于2014年3月3日发布临时措施指示,要求:第一,澳大利亚应确保在本案结案前任何人员不得以任何方式或在任何时候利用所收缴材料的内容使东帝汶处于不利地位;第二,在法院作出进一步裁定之前,澳大利亚应封存所收缴的文件和电子数据及其任何副本;第三,对于《帝汶海条约》下的待决仲裁案,未来关于海洋划界的任何双边谈判,或两国间任何其他相关诉讼(包括国际法院正在审理的本案),澳大利亚不应以任何方式干涉东帝汶与其法律顾问之间的通信。[3]

2014年9月,东帝汶和澳大利亚联名致信国际法院,请求推迟原定的聆讯程序,以便双方能够自行寻求方法友好解决争端。经过双方协商,国际法院部分修改了原临时措施指示,澳大利亚在该指示下于2015年5月确认向东帝汶归还了其2013年12月所收缴的文件和数据。2015年5月,东帝汶致信国际法院,表示澳大利亚已经归还东帝汶的合法财产,东帝汶已经成功实现了它向国际法院提出诉求的目的,请求终止诉讼程序。2015年6月,在澳大利亚未予反对的情形下,国际法院决定终止"收缴和扣押某些文件和数据的问题案"。[4]

---

[1] "Arbitration under the Timor Sea Treaty (Timor-Leste v. Australia)", PCA, https://pca-cpa.org/en/cases/141/, March 22, 2023.

[2] "Termination Order, Arbitration under the Timor Sea Treaty (Timor-Leste v. Australia), 20 March 2017", PCA, https://pcacases.com/web/sendAttach/2110, March 22, 2023.

[3] "Order of 3 March 2014, Questions relating to the Seizure and Detention of Certain Documents and Data (Timor-Leste v. Australia)", ICJ, https://www.icj-cij.org/public/files/case-related/156/156-20140303-ORD-01-00-EN.pdf, pp. 17-18, March 22, 2023.

[4] "Order of 11 June 2015, Questions relating to the Seizure and Detention of Certain Documents and Data (Timor-Leste v. Australia)", ICJ, https://www.icj-cij.org/public/files/case-related/156/156-20150611-ORD-01-00-EN.pdf, March 22, 2023.

(6) 2016年"帝汶海调解案"(东帝汶诉澳大利亚)。

在经过双边谈判、国际仲裁、国际法院的多番尝试之后,东帝汶最终决定将帝汶海海洋划界争端的解决交托于《公约》下的强制调解程序。2016年4月,东帝汶依据《公约》第298条第1款(a)项及附件5第2节启动与澳大利亚间的强制调解程序,要求"解释和适用《公约》第74条和第83条以划定东帝汶与澳大利亚间的专属经济区及大陆架界限,并为两国确立永久海洋边界"。这也是《公约》生效后对强制调解程序的首次援引适用。

依据《公约》附件5,调解委员会由5名调解员组成,以"听取争端各方的陈述,审查其权利主张和反对意见,并向争端各方提出建议,以便达成和睦解决"。该调解委员会有权"确定其本身的程序",当事方对"调解委员会是否有管辖权如有争议,应由调解委员会加以解决"。调解委员会在调解程序中可"提请争端各方注意便于和睦解决争端的任何措施"。[1] 经双方指派调解员协商确定调解委员会主席,"帝汶海调解案"调解委员会于2016年6月正式成立。

2016年7月—2018年2月,调解委员会依程序定期与当事方会面并就特定问题多次组织非正式的单方沟通,依职权作出判定,并为促进两国间共识提出阶段性建议:

第一,关于调解委员会的管辖权。澳大利亚于程序一开始即提出了对调解委员会管辖资格与管辖权限的质疑,主要理由在于:诉诸强制调解的程序已经被《海上安排条约》所排除,且该条约也为双方准备了适宜的争端解决方式。在作为初步程序审议澳大利亚的反对意见及东帝汶的回应后,调解委员会分别围绕《公约》第281条与第298条、《公约》第311条与《海上安排条约》间的关系、调解程序与"可受理性"、提交调解的事项范围、《公约》附件5第7条与12个月期限的适用等对管辖权及关联问题进行分析判定。[2]

在基于《公约》第281条的分析中,调解委员会认为:首先,两国总理于2003年的来往信函不能构成一项在《公约》第281条下的有效协议,澳大利亚也并未主张这些信件往来有意"排除后续的任何程序"。其次,《海上安排条约》中没有提供任何旨在解决海洋边界问题的程序,相反,这一条约排除了解决有关海洋边界争端的所有可能途径,并在其第4条第7款中否定

---

[1] 参见《公约》附件4第4条、第5条、第6条、第13条。
[2] "Annex 9 to Report-Decision on Competence, Timor Sea Conciliation (Timor-Leste v. Australia)", PCA, https://pcacases.com/web/sendAttach/10062, March 23, 2023.

了缔约国在本条约存续期间就永久海洋边界的划定进行谈判的义务。即使上述的2003年信函可以构成一项有约束力的协议以促成双方谈判,这一谈判义务也被2006年的《海上安排条约》所否定。因此,《海上安排条约》未就"自行选择的和平方法"达成协议;同时调解委员会也不认为,一项不诉诸任何争端解决办法的协议,可以合理地被视为当事方自行选择的争端解决方式。调解委员会由此确认,《海上安排条约》不是《公约》第281条下的协议,不能据《海上安排条约》排除《公约》第298条及附件5下强制调解程序的适用。[1]

基于《公约》第298条,调解委员会的重心在于:当事方间的争端是否"发生于本公约生效之后";"争端各方的谈判"是否"未能在合理期间内达成协议"。对于前者,调解委员会认为,从通常意义来看,"公约生效"应是指《公约》作为整体的生效,《公约》多个条款中的"公约生效"一词的使用也都表明其意指《公约》在所有相关方间发生效力。因此,第298条中的"公约生效"应指《公约》作为整体生效于1994年,而非指在澳大利亚与东帝汶之间于2013年生效,因此当事方的争端确属"发生于本公约生效之后"。而对于后者,调解委员会认为,《海上安排条约》第4条并未排除《公约》第298条第1款(a)项所设想的双边谈判。尽管《海上安排条约》第4条第7款暂停了双方就永久海洋边界进行谈判的义务,但并未禁止此类谈判本身。更何况,《海上安排条约》并未排除就该条约本身及其下的临时性安排进行谈判。调解委员会由此确定,"争端各方的谈判"存在"合理期间",且确实"未能在合理期间内达成协议"。[2]

最终,针对澳大利亚提出的管辖权异议,调解委员会认定:对于东帝汶2016年4月11日"依《公约》附件5第2节提起调解的通知"中所涉事项,调解委员会有进行强制调解的管辖权;本案不存在将调解委员会从相关程序中排除的可受理性问题或礼让问题;附件5第7条中的12个月期限将从该管辖权裁定作出之日起算。[3]

第二,关于海洋边界的划定。2017年3月,调解委员会出具了一份供当事双方参考的非正式文件(Non-Paper)。该非正式文件附有一份划界草图,

---

[1] "Annex 9 to Report-Decision on Competence, Timor Sea Conciliation (Timor-Leste v. Australia)", PCA, https://pcacases.com/web/sendAttach/10062, pp. 10-16, March 23, 2023.

[2] "Annex 9 to Report-Decision on Competence, Timor Sea Conciliation (Timor-Leste v. Australia)", PCA, https://pcacases.com/web/sendAttach/10062, pp. 17-22, March 23, 2023.

[3] "Annex 9 to Report-Decision on Competence, Timor Sea Conciliation (Timor-Leste v. Australia)", PCA, https://pcacases.com/web/sendAttach/10062, p. 31, March 23, 2023.

调解委员会建议双方考虑采取该草图所标注的单一海洋边界方法。该草图所建议的边界东段将延伸至"联合石油开发区"以外，但仍有部分穿过巨日升地区，并将与《1972年海底协定》所划界限的交会处留待未来谈判。为促成双方在最具争议的巨日升地区的划界和解，调解委员会进一步建议：委员会并不认为任何一方的公开法律立场是完全正确的；东帝汶的海洋权利不能被局限于"联合石油开发区"的边界或澳大利亚与印度尼西亚间《1972年海底协定》的边界范围；委员会认为存在需要考虑的相关情况，中间线需要依据相关情况进行调整以获得更为公平的结果；不排除对中间线东段的调整会令相关海底边界穿过巨日升地区；委员会不认为分割巨日升地区的海底边界会显失公平或与《公约》不符。[1]

第三，关于资源管理与收益分配。在调解委员会的建议下，当事双方同意将巨日升问题与海底边界的划定分开讨论。为推进协商进程，调解委员会出具了《关于巨日升特别制度无争议事项的非正式文件》，认为双方可以较易达成一致的事项包括：特别制度的目标应是共同发展、开采和管理巨日升油田，包括管理东帝汶和澳大利亚共同参与巨日升油田开发所带来的整体利益；特别制度将仅适用于巨日升地区以及《联合开发协定》下的相应区域；特别制度将对联合管辖权区及专属管辖权区作出清晰划分；关于开发路线的选择，将由东帝汶与巨日升合资企业（The Greater Sunrise Joint Venture）协商后决定，但应作为特别制度整体协议的一部分；在特别制度区对油气作业进行日常监督的指定机关为东帝汶国家石油与矿产管理局；新的产品分成合同（Production Sharing Contracts）应由东帝汶国家石油与矿产管理局和巨日升合资企业签订，以替代或认证现有同类合同，并以与现在文件相当的条件保留涉及巨日升地区的租约；应成立一个或多个管理机构或上诉机构负责高级别战略决策，并确保相关战略决策的可靠性；收益分享应将对上游及下游活动的考量纳入其中，将直接、间接税收及其他经济收益都纳入其中。[2]

第四，关于2017年8月30日的一揽子协定。立足已进行的多轮讨论，调解委员会试图整合所有争端解决要素以形成当事各方都可以接受的一揽子方案，同时以符合《公约》及海洋划界国际法规则的方式公平划定两国海洋

---

[1] "Report and Recommendations of the Compulsory Conciliation Commission between Timor-Leste and Australia on the Timor Sea, Timor Sea Conciliation (Timor-Leste v. Australia)", PCA, https：//pcacases.com/web/sendAttach/2327, pp. 69-70, March 23, 2023.

[2] "Report and Recommendations of the Compulsory Conciliation Commission between Timor-Leste and Australia on the Timor Sea, Timor Sea Conciliation (Timor-Leste v. Australia)", PCA, https：//pcacases.com/web/sendAttach/2327, pp. 70, 72-73, March 23, 2023.

边界。由调解委员会建议形成的2017年8月30日一揽子协定也成为后来两国正式海洋划界条约的基础。按照该一揽子协定：除可能影响印度尼西亚在上覆水域相关权利的西南方向，两国的南部海洋边界将采取单一海洋界限，部分沿中间线、部分沿中间线以北的商定路线展开；西部边界将仅为大陆架边界，并延伸至"联合石油开发区"以西，从而将巴法罗油田（Buffalo oil field）划归东帝汶，将卡拉丽娜油田（Corallina oil fields）及拉米那瑞尔油田（Laminaria oil fields）划归澳大利亚；东部与西部海底边界将分别与《1972年海底协定》的A16点及A17点相会，但作为临时性边界，应根据相关条约宗旨在某些情形下进行调整。[1]

第五，关于巨日升地区的开发利用。根据上述一揽子协定，若当事双方无法在2017年12月15日前按照相关标准就开发概念达成一致，调解委员会应与双方积极接触，以期双方在2018年2月1日前就开发概念达成协议。为获得在技术和财政方面的专家援助，调解委员会在当事方的共同许可下任命了1名油气发展规划专家，作为补充行动计划的一部分。同时，在两国政府及相关合资企业的参与下，调解委员会尝试拟定了涵盖3种情形的协议草案框架，分别为：东帝汶液化天然气（Timor LNG）概念下的草案框架；达尔文液化天然气（Darwin LNG）概念下的草案框架；以上概念均未被选择下的草案框架。至调解程序结束时，澳大利亚与东帝汶仍未能就巨日升地区的开发概念达成一致。[2]

2018年5月，调解委员会依职权发布了《东帝汶与澳大利亚间有关帝汶海的强制调解委员会报告与建议》，并依规则交存联合国秘书长。调解委员会确认，该报告完成于当事方和解进程完结之后，争端国间已就帝汶海的海洋边界达成了一项全面协议。在这一情形下，调解委员会已经不再承担向缔约国提供争端解决建议的任务。在当事方已经自行解决争端的前提下，调解委员会报告的目的更在于为当事方达成协议的过程提供背景记录与上下文支撑。调解委员会认为，尽管当事国最终达成的条约本身就是对两国海洋边界争端的法律解决，但两国政府及其人民都将受益于调解委员会对该协议促成途径及方式的中立性阐述。作为《公约》下强制调解程序的首次实践，调解

---

[1] "Report and Recommendations of the Compulsory Conciliation Commission between Timor-Leste and Australia on the Timor Sea, Timor Sea Conciliation (Timor-Leste v. Australia)," PCA, https：//pcacases.com/web/sendAttach/2327, pp. 76-78, March 23, 2023.

[2] "Report and Recommendations of the Compulsory Conciliation Commission between Timor-Leste and Australia on the Timor Sea, Timor Sea Conciliation (Timor-Leste v. Australia)," PCA, https：//pcacases.com/web/sendAttach/2327, pp. 81-83, March 23, 2023.

委员会对当事双方在调解程序中的参与给予了高度肯定，并专门就本次调解进程中有助于成果获得的关键要素进行了反思与总结。[1]

（7）澳大利亚与东帝汶之间的划界协定。

在经历了冗长跌宕的国际政治及法律程序之后，澳大利亚与东帝汶间有关帝汶海区域的划界及海洋资源利用纷争终见曙光。作为2016年启动的《公约》下强制调解程序的重要成果，在联合国秘书长和调解委员会的见证下，两国政府于2018年3月6日签订了《澳大利亚与东帝汶民主共和国确立在帝汶海海洋边界的条约》（Treaty between Australia and the Democratic Republic of Timor-Leste Establishing Their Maritime Boundaries in the Timor Sea）。该划界条约于次年8月30日生效，旨在：第一，立足《公约》第74条第1款、第83条第1款，为澳大利亚与东帝汶划定专属经济区及大陆架分界线；第二，在依据《公约》第298条及附件5所组建的调解委员会协助下，协商永久解决两国的海洋争端；第三，为巨日升油田建立特别制度，从而为两国间海床底土的石油开采活动提供长期稳定的基础，以惠及缔约双方；第四，以经济及环境层面的可持续方式开发和管理帝汶海的生物及非生物资源，促进澳大利亚与东帝汶的投资及长期发展。[2]

依据该条约第2条，澳大利亚与东帝汶在帝汶海的大陆架分界线为连接13个坐标点的测地线。但其中部分线段（TA-1至TA-2，TA-11至TA-13）具有临时性，需随澳大利亚与印度尼西亚的《1972年海底协定》及东帝汶与印度尼西亚未来可能达成的大陆架划界协定而有所调整。这13个坐标点的位置如表16所示：

表16　澳大利亚与东帝汶在帝汶海的大陆架分界线坐标点[3]

坐标点	纬度（南）	经度（东）
TA-1	10°27′54.91″	126°00′04.40″
TA-2	11°24′00.61″	126°18′22.48″

---

[1] "Report and Recommendations of the Compulsory Conciliation Commission between Timor-Leste and Australia on the Timor Sea, Timor Sea Conciliation (Timor-Leste v. Australia)", PCA, https://pcacases.com/web/sendAttach/2327, pp. 2, 84, 90, March 23, 2023.

[2] "Treaty between Australia and the Democratic Republic of Timor-Leste Establishing Their Maritime Boundaries in the Timor Sea", Australasian Legal Information Institute, http://www.austlii.edu.au/au/other/dfat/t-reaties/ATS/2019/16.html, March 25, 2023.

[3] "Australian Treaties Database", The Australian Department of Foreign Affairs and Trade, https://www.dfat.gov.au/sites/default/files/treaty-maritime-arrangements-australia-timor-leste.pdf, May 25, 2024.

续表

坐标点	纬度（南）	经度（东）
TA-3	11°21′00.00″	126°28′00.00″
TA-4	11°20′00.00″	126°31′00.00″
TA-5	11°20′02.90″	126°31′58.40″
TA-6	11°04′37.65″	127°39′32.81″
TA-7	10°55′20.88″	127°47′08.37″
TA-8	10°53′36.88″	127°48′49.37″
TA-9	10°43′37.88″	127°59′20.36″
TA-10	10°29′11.87″	128°12′28.36″
TA-11	09°42′21.49″	128°28′35.97″
TA-12	09°37′57.54″	128°30′07.24″
TA-13	09°27′54.88″	127°56′04.35″

依据该条约第4条，澳大利亚与东帝汶在帝汶海的专属经济区分界线为连接6个坐标点的测地线。这6个坐标点的位置如表17所示：

表17　澳大利亚与东帝汶在帝汶海的专属经济区分界线坐标点[1]

坐标点	纬度（南）	经度（东）
TA-5	11°20′02.90″	126°31′58.40″
TA-6	11°04′37.65″	127°39′32.81″
TA-7	10°55′20.88″	127°47′08.37″
TA-8	10°53′36.88″	127°48′49.37″
TA-9	10°43′37.88″	127°59′20.36″
TA-10	10°29′11.87″	128°12′28.36″

除划定两国间的专属经济区及大陆架界限外，建立巨日升特别管理体制也是该条约的核心内容之一。依据该条约第7条，两国将设立巨日升特别管理区，由双方依据《公约》第77条共同行使沿海国权利。这一特别管理区的治理工作与管辖权行使将由巨日升特别管理体制作出安排，而对本条约未规定的内容，双方的权利义务以《公约》为准。若未来巨日升特别管理体制不再运行，双方将按《公约》第77条以本条约所划定的大陆架界限为基础

---

[1] "Australian Treaties Database", The Australian Department of Foreign Affairs and Trade, https://www.dfat.gov.au/sites/default/files/treaty-maritime-arrangements-australia-timor-leste.pdf, May 25, 2024.

各自行使作为沿海国的权利。同时，除本条约第 3 条已明确的情形（界限调整的可能情形）外，东帝汶与印度尼西亚间未来大陆架划界协定的生效将不会对巨日升特别管理体制产生影响。该条约通过附件 B 共 23 条对巨日升特别管理体制作出了具体规定，通过附件 C 对巨日升特别管理区的位置及边界进行了划定。

依据附件 C，巨日升特别管理区为连接 18 个地理坐标点的恒向线所包围的大陆架地区。这 18 个坐标点的位置如表 18 所示：

表 18　巨日升特别管理区边界线坐标点[1]

坐标点	纬度（南）	经度（东）
GS-1	09°49′ 54.88″	127°55′ 04.35″
GS-2	09°49′ 54.88″	128°20′ 04.34″
GS-3	09°39′ 54.88″	128°20′ 04.34″
GS-4	09°39′ 54.88″	128°25′ 04.34″
GS-5	09°29′ 54.88″	128°25′ 04.34″
GS-6	09°29′ 54.88″	128°20′ 04.34″
GS-7	09°24′ 54.88″	128°20′ 04.34″
GS-8	09°24′ 54.88″	128°00′ 04.34″
GS-9	09°29′ 54.88″	127°53′ 24.35″
GS-10	09°29′ 54.88″	127°52′ 34.35″
GS-11	09°34′ 54.88″	127°52′ 34.35″
GS-12	09°34′ 54.88″	127°50′ 04.35″
GS-13	09°37′ 24.88″	127°50′ 04.35″
GS-14	09°37′ 24.89″	127°45′ 04.35″
GS-15	09°44′ 54.88″	127°45′ 04.35″
GS-16	09°44′ 54.88″	127°50′ 04.35″
GS-17	09°47′ 24.88″	127°50′ 04.35″
GS-18	09°47′ 24.88″	127°55′ 04.35″

除上述内容外，该条约还就其他关联事项作出了规定，如：对于跨越界限的石油资源，缔约双方应就如何有效开采和公平分享该矿床达成协议；在本条约生效后 5 年内，任何关于本条约解释或适用的争端，如在任何一方通

---

[1]　"Australian Treaties Database", The Australian Department of Foreign Affairs and Trade, https://www.dfat.gov.au/sites/default/files/treaty-maritime-arrangements-australia-timor-leste.pdf, May 25, 2024.

知另一方存在争端后的6个月内未能通过谈判解决的，可由缔约双方共同提交调解委员会，或由任一缔约方提交仲裁解决；等等。

（二）通过协议解决的其他海洋划界争端

1. 澳大利亚与法国之间的划界协定

为准确划定两国可行使主权的海洋区域，并促进作为友好邻邦的国家间关系，澳大利亚和法国于1982年1月4日签订了《澳大利亚政府与法兰西共和国政府间海洋划界协定》（Agreement on Maritime Delimitation between the Government of Australia and the Government of the French Republic）。该协定以两国间1980年的谈判进程为参照，立足于相关国际法规则及第三次联合国海洋法会议的工作成果，于1983年1月10日正式生效。

依据该协定第1条，在澳大利亚以东的太平洋海域，于澳大利亚珊瑚海上诸岛、诺福克岛及其他澳大利亚岛屿向海一侧，与法国新喀里多尼亚岛（New Caledonia）、切斯特菲尔德群岛（Chesterfield Islands）及其他法属岛屿向海一侧，有关澳大利亚渔区与法国经济区（French Economic Zone）间的分界线以及两国间大陆架的分界线，由两国协商确定的22个地理坐标点间的连线构成。这22个坐标点的位置如表19所示：

表19 澳大利亚与法国在珊瑚海诸岛间的海上界限坐标点[1]

坐标点	纬度（南）	经度（东）
R1	15°44′07″	158°45′39″
R2	16°25′28″	158°22′49″
R3	16°34′51″	158°16′26″
R4	17°30′28″	157°38′31″
R5	17°54′40″	157°21′59″
R6	18°32′25″	156°56′44″
R7	18°55′54″	156°37′29″
R8	19°17′12″	156°15′20″
R9	20°08′28″	156°49′34″
R10	20°32′28″	157°03′09″
R11	20°42′52″	157°04′34″

---

[1] "Australian Treaty Series 1983 No. 3", Australasian Legal Information Institute, http：//www.austlii.edu.au/au/other/dfat/treaties/1983/3.html, March 26, 2023.

续表

坐标点	纬度（南）	经度（东）
R12	20°53′33″	157°06′25″
R13	21°12′57″	157°10′17″
R14	21°47′21″	157°14′36″
R15	22°10′31″	157°13′04″
R16	22°31′38″	157°18′43″
R17	23°14′54″	157°48′04″
R18	25°08′48″	158°36′39″
R19	26°26′30″	163°43′30″
R20	26°12′04″	165°51′37″
R21	25°50′42″	168°44′18″
R22	25°55′51″	169°25′54″

依据该协定第2条，在南印度洋的南极周边海域，于澳大利亚的赫德岛和麦克唐纳群岛向海一侧，与法国的凯尔盖朗群岛（Kerguelen Islands）向海一侧，有关澳大利亚渔区与法国经济区间的分界线以及两国间大陆架的分界线，由两国协商确定的8个地理坐标点间的连线构成。这8个坐标点的位置如表20所示：

表20　澳大利亚与法国在赫德岛和麦克唐纳群岛及凯尔盖朗群岛间（南印度洋）的海上界限坐标点[1]

坐标点	纬度（南）	经度（东）
S1	53°14′07″	67°03′20″
S2	52°42′28″	68°05′31″
S3	51°58′18″	69°44′02″
S4	51°24′32″	71°12′29″
S5	51°03′09″	72°28′28″
S6	50°54′23″	72°49′21″
S7	49°49′34″	75°36′08″
S8	49°24′07″	76°42′17″

在划定以上海上界限的基础上，澳大利亚和法国进一步明确：第一，前述第1条及第2条所划定的两条分界线的端点，均不必然代表两国大陆架外

---

[1] "Australian Treaty Series 1983 No. 3", Australasian Legal Information Institute, http://www.austlii.edu.au/au/other/dfat/treaties/1983/3.html, March 26, 2023.

缘的位置；第二，若有必要延伸第 1 条及第 2 条所划定的分界线，以进一步明确邻接澳大利亚与法国领土的大陆架边界，该延伸界限将由两国政府依据国际法协议定之；第三，两国将在依上述界限所划定的海域内，依国际法行使各自主权权利及管辖权；第四，两国就本协定的解释或适用所产生的任何分歧，应依国际法以和平方式解决。[1]

2. 澳大利亚与新西兰之间的划界协定

作为在地理上亲密相依、在历史及政治经济上同源相伴的友好邻邦，澳大利亚和新西兰政府于 2004 年 7 月 25 日签订了《澳大利亚和新西兰政府间确立某些专属经济区边界和大陆架边界的条约》（Treaty between the Government of Australia and the Government of New Zealand Establishing Certain Exclusive Economic Zone Boundaries and Continental Shelf Boundaries），以鼓励并促进对相关区域海洋资源的可持续性开发利用，并进一步加强对两国邻近水域海洋环境的保护。该协定已于 2006 年 1 月 25 日正式生效。[2]

立足《公约》第 74 条与第 83 条，两国通过该条约第 2 条划定了澳大利亚豪勋爵岛、诺福克岛和新西兰之间的专属经济区和大陆架界限，并通过该条约第 3 条划定了澳大利亚麦夸里岛和新西兰奥克兰群岛（Auckland Islands）、坎贝尔群岛（Campbell Islands）之间的专属经济区和大陆架界限。

其中，依据该条约第 2 条，在澳大利亚豪勋爵岛与新西兰北岛之间，以及澳大利亚诺福克岛和新西兰三王群岛（Three Kings Islands）之间，两国的专属经济区和大陆架界限为 29 个地理坐标点间的连线。这 29 个坐标点的位置如表 21 所示：

表 21　澳大利亚豪勋爵岛与新西兰北岛、澳大利亚诺福克岛与新西兰三王群岛间专属经济区和大陆架分界线坐标点[3]

坐标点	纬度（南）	经度（东）
ANZ1	25°41′58.77″	173°59′27.48″
ANZ2	27°05′37.98″	171°54′30.61″

[1] "Australian Treaty Series 1983 No. 3", Australasian Legal Information Institute, http://www.austlii.edu.au/au/other/dfat/treaties/1983/3.html, March 26, 2023.

[2] "Treaty between the Government of Australia and the Government of New Zealand Establishing Certain Exclusive Economic Zone Boundaries and Continental Shelf Boundaries", Australasian Legal Information Institute, http://www.austlii.edu.au/au/other/dfat/treaties/2006/4.html, March 26, 2023.

[3] "Treaty between the Government of Australia and the Government of New Zealand Establishing Certain Exclusive Economic Zone Boundaries and Continental Shelf Boundaries", Australasian Legal Information Institute, http://www.austlii.edu.au/au/other/dfat/treaties/2006/4.html, March 26, 2023.

续表

坐标点	纬度（南）	经度（东）
ANZ3	27°29′53.98″	171°58′42.98″
ANZ4	27°52′50.38″	171°58′51.31″
ANZ5	28°13′20.83″	171°56′10.22″
ANZ6	28°52′49.54″	171°56′16.16″
ANZ7	30°25′42.70″	171°56′30.44″
ANZ8	30°43′29.25″	171°28′45.57″
ANZ9	30°53′11.23″	171°13′28.85″
ANZ10	31°16′01.68″	170°37′06.34″
ANZ11	31°19′31.67″	170°31′15.10″
ANZ12	31°40′26.30″	169°56′12.27″
ANZ13	31°47′23.99″	169°44′25.06″
ANZ14	32°04′50.57″	169°14′37.00″
ANZ15	32°06′52.74″	169°11′06.79″
ANZ16	32°25′18.55″	168°39′03.72″
ANZ17	32°22′18.95″	166°58′54.37″
ANZ18	32°09′22.23″	166°17′34.30″
ANZ19	31°53′49.17″	165°46′20.73″
ANZ20	31°30′	165°13′27.08″
ANZ21	32°30′	163°06′58.81″
ANZ22	33°52′40.25″	162°21′59.44″
ANZ23	36°36′25.68″	163°15′37.64″
ANZ24	37°26′21.31″	161°04′38.06″
ANZ25	37°30′11.12″	161°00′14.00″
ANZ26	37°43′11.18″	160°49′46.53″
ANZ27	37°52′48.02″	160°41′59.88″
ANZ28	38°03′21.95″	160°33′24.99″
ANZ29	38°19′36.19″	160°23′49.32″

依据该条约第3条，在澳大利亚麦夸里岛和新西兰奥克兰群岛、坎贝尔群岛之间，两国的专属经济区和大陆架界限为25个地理坐标点间的连线。这25个坐标点的位置如表22所示：

表22　澳大利亚麦夸里岛和新西兰奥克兰群岛、坎贝尔群岛间专属经济区和大陆架分界线坐标点[1]

坐标点	纬度（南）	经度（东）
ANZ30	51°04′48.96″	158°01′25.98″
ANZ31	51°01′38.44″	158°59′53.57″
ANZ32	51°10′36.30″	160°37′30.11″
ANZ33	51°26′17.80″	160°57′46.87″
ANZ34	52°11′26.54″	161°57′11.15″
ANZ35	52°15′53.24″	162°03′07.43″
ANZ36	52°27′43.12″	162°18′59.49″
ANZ37	52°40′46.86″	162°36′30.28″
ANZ38	52°46′50.62″	162°44′42.77″
ANZ39	52°47′42.61″	162°45′53.41″
ANZ40	53°42′58.16″	164°03′13.39″
ANZ41	53°50′59.84″	164°14′42.04″
ANZ42	54°13′58.99″	164°26′41.46″
ANZ43	54°40′13.65″	164°40′40.22″
ANZ44	54°41′43.03″	164°41′28.44″
ANZ45	54°56′14.18″	164°39′00.39″
ANZ46	55°00′11.94″	164°38′17.35″
ANZ47	55°10′06.11″	164°36′21.26″
ANZ48	55°14′12.61″	164°35′21.12″
ANZ49	55°42′50.10″	164°26′46.41″
ANZ50	55°52′23.70″	164°23′57.71″
ANZ51	56°38′56.15″	163°56′44.86″
ANZ52	56°52′19.72″	163°44′04.71″
ANZ53	57°09′53.30″	163°23′17.53″
ANZ54	57°48′21.07″	163°24′47.01″

在明确相关管辖海域分界线的基础上，为有效利用海上资源，该条约进一步规定：如果任何单一石油积聚（无论是气态、液态或固态）或海床下的任何其他矿藏，延伸跨越了前述第2条或第3条所述的分界线，而位于界限一侧的部分石油积聚或矿藏可全部或部分从该分界线的另一侧采收，则双方将促成进一步协议，以寻求最有效开发利用这一石油积聚或矿藏的方式，并

---

[1] "Treaty between the Government of Australia and the Government of New Zealand Establishing Certain Exclusive Economic Zone Boundaries and Continental Shelf Boundaries", Australasian Legal Information Institute, http://www.austlii.edu.au/au/other/dfat/treaties/2006/4.html, March 26, 2023.

保证该开发收益的公平分享。[1]

3. 澳大利亚与印度尼西亚之间的划界协定

(1) 1971年《澳大利亚联邦政府与印度尼西亚共和国政府关于确立某些海底边界的协定》。

澳大利亚政府和印度尼西亚政府于1971年5月18日签订了《澳大利亚联邦政府与印度尼西亚共和国政府关于确立某些海底边界的协定》(Agreement between the Government of the Commonwealth of Australia and the Government of the Republic of Indonesia Establishing Certain Seabed Boundaries),该协定于1973年11月8日生效。[2]

该协定共有9条,主要内容包括:第一,两国共同确定划分海床边界的地理坐标,分别就东经133度23分以东的阿拉弗拉海(邻接及附属于澳大利亚的海床区域与邻接及附属于印度尼西亚的海床区域)、东经140度49分30秒以西(邻接及附属于巴布亚领土的海床区域与邻接及附属于印度尼西亚的海床区域)、新几内亚(伊里安)北方海岸之外(邻接及附属于新几内亚托管地之海床区域与邻接及附属于印度尼西亚的海床区域),作出了划界的安排;第二,规定了跨界限的海底矿藏的开采方式及双方应协商确定利益分配;第三,两国之间因本协定的解释或适用而产生的任何争端,应通过协商或谈判和平解决。

该协定划定了澳大利亚和印度尼西亚在东经133度23分以东的阿拉弗拉海的海床分界线,其为12个坐标点间的连线。这12个坐标点的位置如表23所示:

表23 澳大利亚和印度尼西亚在阿拉弗拉海的海床分界线坐标点[3]

坐标点	纬度(南)	经度(东)
A1	9°52′	140°29′
A2	10°24′	139°46′

---

[1] "Treaty between the Government of Australia and the Government of New Zealand Establishing Certain Exclusive Economic Zone Boundaries and Continental Shelf Boundaries", Australasian Legal Information Institute, http://www.austlii.edu.au/au/other/dfat/treaties/2006/4.html, March 27, 2023.

[2] "Agreement between the Government of the Commonwealth of Australia and the Government of the Republic of Indonesia Establishing Certain Seabed Boundaries", Australasian Legal Information Institute, http://www.austlii.edu.au/au/other/dfat/treaties/ATS/1973/31.html, March 27, 2023.

[3] "Agreement between the Government of the Commonwealth of Australia and the Government of the Republic of Indonesia Establishing Certain Seabed Boundaries", Australasian Legal Information Institute, http://www.austlii.edu.au/au/other/dfat/treaties/ATS/1973/31.html, March 27, 2023.

续表

坐标点	纬度（南）	经度（东）
A3	10°50′	139°12′
A4	10°24′	138°38′
A5	10°22′	138°35′
A6	10°09′	138°13′
A7	9°57′	137°45′
A8	9°08′	135°29′
A9	9°17′	135°13′
A10	9°22′	135°03′
A11	9°25′	134°50′
A12	8°53′	133°23′

该协定划定了澳大利亚和印度尼西亚在新几内亚岛南部沿海相关区域海床的分界线，其为阿拉弗拉海的海床分界线与2个坐标点间的连线。这2个坐标点的位置如表24所示：

表24　澳大利亚和印度尼西亚在新几内亚岛南部的海床分界线坐标点[1]

坐标点	纬度（南）	经度（东）
B1	9°24′30″	140°49′30″
A1	9°52′	140°29′

该协定划定了澳大利亚和印度尼西亚在新几内亚岛北部沿海相关区域海床的分界线，其为连接2个地理坐标点间的直线段。这2个坐标点的位置如表25所示：

表25　澳大利亚和印度尼西亚在新几内亚岛北部的海床分界线坐标点[2]

坐标点	纬度（南）	经度（东）
C1	新几内亚托管地与西伊里安间的陆地边界线同新几内亚岛北部海岸线的交点	
C2	2°08′30″	141°01′30″

---

[1]　"Agreement between the Government of the Commonwealth of Australia and the Government of the Republic of Indonesia Establishing Certain Seabed Boundaries", Australasian Legal Information Institute, http：//www.austlii.edu.au/au/other/dfat/treaties/ATS/1973/31.html, March 27, 2023.

[2]　"Agreement between the Government of the Commonwealth of Australia and the Government of the Republic of Indonesia Establishing Certain Seabed Boundaries", Australasian Legal Information Institute, http：//www.austlii.edu.au/au/other/dfat/treaties/ATS/1973/31.html, March 27, 2023.

五、海洋争端解决

（2）1972年《澳大利亚联邦政府与印度尼西亚共和国政府关于在帝汶海和阿拉弗拉海地区确立某些海底边界的协定（对1971年5月18日协定之补充）》。

澳大利亚政府和印度尼西亚政府于1972年10月9日签订了《澳大利亚联邦政府与印度尼西亚共和国政府关于在帝汶海和阿拉弗拉海地区确立某些海底边界的协定（对1971年5月18日协定之补充）》，该协定于次年11月8日生效。[1]

该协定的主要实体内容包括：第一，两国共同确定了划分海底边界的地理坐标，并以其连线作为两国在塔宁巴尔群岛（Tanimbar Islands）以南地区、罗地岛（Roti Island）和帝汶群岛（Timor Islands）以南地区的海底边界；第二，规定了跨界限的海底矿藏的开采方式，并要求双方应协商确定利益分配；第三，规定了澳大利亚在其已经不具有主权权利的海床区域所颁发的且仍然有效的石油勘探许可证或石油生产许可证的后续效力问题；第四，两国之间因本协定的解释或适用而产生的任何争端，应通过协商或谈判和平解决。

该协定划定了澳大利亚和印度尼西亚在塔宁巴尔群岛以南地区的海底边界，其为5个坐标点间的连线。这5个坐标点的位置如表26所示：

表26　澳大利亚和印度尼西亚在塔宁巴尔群岛以南地区的海底边界坐标点[2]

坐标点	纬度（南）	经度（东）
A12	8°53′	133°23′
A13	8°54′	133°14′
A14	9°25′	130°10′
A15	9°25′	128°00′
A16	9°28′	127°56′

该协定划定了澳大利亚和印度尼西亚在罗地岛和帝汶群岛以南地区的海底边界，其为9个坐标点间的连线。这9个坐标点的位置如表27所示：

---

[1]　"Agreement between the Government of the Commonwealth of Australia and the Government of the Republic of Indonesia Establishing Certain Seabed Boundaries in the Area of the Timor and Arafura Seas, Supplementary to the Agreement of 18 May 1971", Australasian Legal Information Institute, http：//www.aus-tlii.edu.au/au/other/dfat/treaties/ATS/1973/32.html, March 27, 2023.

[2]　"Agreement between the Government of the Commonwealth of Australia and the Government of the Republic of Indonesia Establishing Certain Seabed Boundaries in the Area of the Timor and Arafura Seas, Supplementary to the Agreement of 18 May 1971", Australasian Legal Information Institute, http：//www.aus-tlii.edu.au/au/other/dfat/treaties/ATS/1973/32.html, March 27, 2023.

表27　澳大利亚和印度尼西亚在罗地岛和帝汶群岛以南地区的海底边界坐标点[1]

坐标点	纬度（南）	经度（东）
A17	10°28′	126°00′
A18	10°37′	125°41′
A19	11°01′	125°19′
A20	11°07′	124°34′
A21	11°25′	124°10′
A22	11°26′	124°00′
A23	11°28′	123°40′
A24	11°23′	123°26′
A25	11°35′	123°14′

（3）1973年《澳大利亚和印度尼西亚关于巴布亚新几内亚和印度尼西亚之间某些边界的协定》。

澳大利亚政府和印度尼西亚政府于1973年2月12日签订了《澳大利亚和印度尼西亚关于巴布亚新几内亚和印度尼西亚之间某些边界的协定》（Agreement between Australia and Indonesia concerning Certain Boundaries between Papua New Guinea and Indonesia，以下简称《1973年协定》），该协定于次年11月26日生效。[2]

该协定的主要实体内容包括：第一，两国共同确定了划分海底边界的地理坐标，并以其连线作为两国在新几内亚岛南部海岸的海底边界；第二，规定了跨界限的海底矿藏的开采方式，并要求双方应协商确定利益分配；第三，巴布亚新几内亚船只为进入或离开在巴布亚新几内亚境内流经的本斯巴赫河（Bensbach River），应有权通过邻近的印度尼西亚水域；第四，澳大利亚和印度尼西亚两国政府之间因解释或适用本协定而产生的任何争端，应按照《联合国宪章》第33条所规定的程序和平解决。

该协定划定了澳大利亚和印度尼西亚在新几内亚岛南部海岸的海底边界，其为3个坐标点间的连线。这3个坐标点的位置如表28所示：

---

[1] "Agreement between the Government of the Commonwealth of Australia and the Government of the Republic of Indonesia Establishing Certain Seabed Boundaries in the Area of the Timor and Arafura Seas, Supplementary to the Agreement of 18 May 1971", Australasian Legal Information Institute, http：//www.aus-tlii.edu.au/au/other/dfat/treaties/ATS/1973/32.html, March 27, 2023.

[2] "Agreement between Australia and Indonesia concerning Certain Boundaries between Papua New Guinea and Indonesia", Australasian Legal Information Institute, http：//www.austlii.edu.au/au/other/dfat/treaties/ATS/1974/26.htm, March 28, 2023.

表28 澳大利亚和印度尼西亚在新几内亚岛南部海岸的海底边界坐标点[1]

坐标点	纬度（南）	经度（东）
B1	9°24′30″	140°49′30″
B2	9°23′	140°52′
B3	9°08′08″	141°01′10″

（4）1973年《澳大利亚政府（代表其本国并代表巴布亚新几内亚政府）与印度尼西亚政府关于巴布亚新几内亚和印度尼西亚之间边界行政区边界安排的协定》。

1974年，澳大利亚对巴布亚新几内亚的托管即将结束。鉴于《1973年协定》涉及对新几内亚岛上的陆地边界与该岛南北沿岸的领海边界的划定，在巴布亚新几内亚即将独立之际，澳大利亚政府、印度尼西亚政府和巴布亚新几内亚政府于1973年11月13日签订了《澳大利亚政府（代表其本国并代表巴布亚新几内亚政府）与印度尼西亚政府关于巴布亚新几内亚和印度尼西亚之间边界行政区边界安排的协定》［Agreement between the Government of Australia (acting on its own behalf and on behalf of the Government of Papua New Guinea) and the Government of Indonesia concerning Administrative Border Arrangements as to the Border between Papua New Guinea and Indonesia］，将《1973年协定》中涉巴布亚新几内亚一侧边界的相关安排交由巴布亚新几内亚政府执行，并明确该国独立后澳大利亚对《1973年协定》中的相关划界安排不再承担责任。该协定于1974年11月26日正式生效。

该协定共有14条，主要就边境联络制度及联络官员的设置与职责、尊重边境居民出于传统习俗的跨境活动、对跨境土地及河流的权利、边境争端的解决、其他穿越边境的行为、边境安全与边境贸易、界河上航行设施的保护、边境污染防治等作出安排。[2]

（5）《澳大利亚政府与印度尼西亚政府关于印尼传统渔民在澳大利亚专属渔区与大陆架作业的谅解备忘录》。

《澳大利亚政府与印度尼西亚政府关于印尼传统渔民在澳大利亚专属渔

---

[1] "Agreement between Australia and Indonesia concerning Certain Boundaries between Papua New Guinea and Indonesia", Australasian Legal Information Institute, http：//www.austlii.edu.au/au/other/dfat/treaties/ATS/1974/26.htm, March 28, 2023.

[2] "Agreement between the Government of Australia (acting on its own behalf and on behalf of the Government of Papua New Guinea) and the Government of Indonesia concerning Administrative Border Arrangements as to the Border between Papua New Guinea and Indonesia", Australasian Legal Information Institute, http：//www.austlii.edu.au/au/other/dfat/treaties/ATS/1974/27.html, March 27, 2023.

区与大陆架作业的谅解备忘录》（Memorandum of Understanding between the Government of Australia and the Government of the Republic of Indonesia Regarding the Operations of Indonesian Traditional Fishermen in Areas of the Australian Exclusive Fishing Zone and Continental Shelf）签署于1974年11月7日。该备忘录共有8条规定，分别就印尼传统渔民可以作业的特定区域、限制条件、可捕捞的海产物种以及管辖权等问题作出了相应规定。

根据该备忘录第2条，澳大利亚政府允许印尼传统渔民在阿什莫尔礁（Ashmore Reef）（12°15′S, 123°03′E），卡地亚岛（Cartier Islet）（12°32′S, 123°33′E），斯科特礁（14°03′S, 121°47′E），塞林伽巴丹礁（Soringapatam Reef）（11°37′S, 122°03′E），布劳斯岛（Browse Islet）（14°06′S, 123°32′E）附近作业，但受制于以下条件：第一，印尼在该区域的作业仅限于其传统渔民；第二，印尼传统渔民仅能出于获得淡水补给的目的在阿什莫尔礁的东部岛（12°15′S, 123°07′E）与中部岛（12°15′S, 123°03′E）登陆；第三，印尼传统捕鱼船可在上述允许捕鱼的区域避难，但船上人员除为获得淡水补给外不得上岸。

在管辖协调方面，印尼政府承认，除第2条规定的区域外，在澳大利亚专属渔区捕鱼或在澳大利亚开采资源的印尼传统渔民，应受澳大利亚管辖。同时，印尼政府将尽最大努力将备忘录的内容告知可能在澳大利亚周围作业的印尼传统渔民。双方政府应为交换有关印尼渔船在帝汶海西部作业的信息提供便利。[1]

（6）《澳大利亚与印度尼西亚在印尼东帝汶省与北澳大利亚地区建立合作区的条约》。

在印度尼西亚军事占领东帝汶期间，为尽快明晰海洋权利的行使边界，澳大利亚以印度尼西亚为东帝汶事实上的合法政府，推进关于帝汶海的划界谈判。在视东帝汶为印尼领土组成的情形下，澳大利亚与印度尼西亚前述所签署的《1972年海底协定》所划定的两国海床分界线便出现了一个所谓的"帝汶缺口"。围绕"帝汶缺口"问题，澳大利亚与印度尼西亚于1989年12月签署了《澳大利亚与印度尼西亚在印尼东帝汶省与北澳大利亚地区建立合作区的条约》（前文所称《帝汶缺口条约》）。

该条约将"帝汶缺口"相应地域分为区域A、区域B、区域C三部分。

---

[1] "Memorandum of Understanding between the Government of Australia and the Government of the Republic of Indonesia Regarding the Operations of Indonesian Traditional Fishermen in Areas of the Australian Exclusive Fishing Zone and Continental Shelf", UNEP Law and Environment Assistance Platform, https://leap.unep.org/sites/default/files/treaty/TRE-151704.pdf, March 27, 2023.

其中，区域 B 位于该地域的南部，由澳大利亚管理；区域 C 位于该地域的北部，由印度尼西亚管理；而最大的区域 A 位于中部，两国在该区域内的权利义务由依该条约建立的部长理事会（Minister Council）与联合管理局（Joint Authority）确定，后者对前者负责。[1] 随着东帝汶在 2002 年独立，该条约被《帝汶海条约》所取代。[2]

(7)《澳大利亚政府与印度尼西亚共和国政府确立专属经济区边界与某些海底边界的条约》。

《澳大利亚政府与印度尼西亚共和国政府确立专属经济区边界与某些海底边界的条约》（Treaty between the Government of Australia and the Government of the Republic of Indonesia Establishing an Exclusive Economic Zone Boundary and Certain Seabed Boundaries，简称《珀斯条约》）签署于 1997 年 3 月 14 日，从未生效。该条约大致依中间线划定了两国的海洋边界，但与《1972 年海底协定》中的界限走向并不完全相符。澳大利亚在后续的强制调解程序中曾表示，尽管该条约未能生效，但该条约相关规定仍在实践中得到了澳大利亚及印度尼西亚政府的遵行。[3]

4. 澳大利亚与巴布亚新几内亚之间的划界协定

澳大利亚与巴布亚新几内亚于 1978 年 12 月 18 日签订了《澳大利亚与巴布亚新几内亚独立国关于两国间区域（包括所称托雷斯海峡）的主权和海洋边界及相关事宜的条约》（Treaty between Australia and the Independent State of Papua New Guinea concerning Sovereignty and Maritime Boundaries in the area between the two Countries, including the area known as Torres Strait, and Related Matters），该条约于 1985 年 2 月 15 日生效。[4] 以托雷斯海峡为核心区域，两国旨在通过该条约保障托雷斯海峡上的澳大利亚岛民及巴布亚新几内亚人民的传统生活方式与基本民生，并在养护海洋环境的同时确保两国船舶及飞

---

[1] "Chapter 4-The Timor Gap (Zone of Co-operation) Treaty", Parliament of Australia, https：//www.aph. gov. au/Parliamentary_Business/Committees/Senate/Foreign_Affairs_Defence_and_Trade/Completed_inquiries/1999-02/east_timor/report/c04, April 1, 2023.

[2] 有关《帝汶缺口条约》和《帝汶海条约》的进一步内容，参见本部分"（一）与葡萄牙、东帝汶之间的帝汶海相关争端"中的相关小节。

[3] "Report and Recommendations of the Compulsory Conciliation Commission between Timor-Leste and Australia on the Timor Sea, Timor Sea Conciliation (Timor-Leste v. Australia)", PCA, https：//pcacases. com/web/sendAttach/2327, p. 9, March 23, 2023.

[4] "Treaty between Australia and the Independent State of Papua New Guinea concerning Sovereignty and Maritime Boundaries in the area between the two Countries, including the area known as Torres Strait, and Related Matters", Australasian Legal Information Institute, http：//www. austlii. edu. au/au/other/dfat/treaties/ATS/1985/4. html, April 1, 2023.

机在托雷斯海峡的航行及飞越自由。

该条约共有6大部分32条及9个附件，其主要内容包括：（1）条约中的重要术语界定；（2）有关岛屿、领海及其他管辖海域的主权及管辖权；（3）与行使主权及管辖权相关的其他事宜，如油气开采牌照的颁发、对特定海床底土区域的开发、航行及飞越自由、航行互助、船舶及飞行器残骸的处置等；（4）保护区设立及管理事宜，如传统捕鱼权等传统活动自由的权利、传统习惯性权利、海洋环境保护、本土动植物保护、海关移民卫生的监管、托雷斯海峡联合咨询委员会的设立及职责等；（5）保护区商业捕捞相关事宜，如保障传统捕鱼活动的优先地位、对保护区资源的养护管理及最优利用、保护区内渔获的分享、捕捞执照的颁发、对第三国在保护区商业捕捞的检查与监管等；（6）争端解决及磋商相关条款。

为明确权利行使范围并落实相关执行条款，该条约通过附件1至附件9分别就澳大利亚与巴布亚新几内亚在托雷斯海峡地区的领海界限、海床管辖区域界限、渔区界限、保护区界限以及澳大利亚在该地区诸岛的领海外部界限作出了划定。其中，依据条约附件1，在澳大利亚的奥布西、博伊古和莫伊米诸岛（Islands of Aubusi, Boigu and Moimi）与巴布亚新几内亚之间，两国的领海分界线为8个地理坐标点间的连线。这8个坐标点的位置如表29所示：

表29 奥布西岛、博伊古岛和莫伊米岛与巴布亚新几内亚之间的领海边界坐标点[1]

坐标点	纬度（南）	经度（东）
1	9°15′43″	142°03′30″
2	9°12′50″	142°06′25″
3	9°11′51″	142°08′33″
4	9°11′58″	142°10′18″
5	9°11′22″	142°12′54″
6	9°11′34″	142°14′08″
7	9°13′53″	142°16′26″
8	9°16′04″	142°20′41″

同依附件1，在澳大利亚的道安、考马格和赛拜各岛（Islands of Dauan,

---

[1] "Treaty between Australia and the Independent State of Papua New Guinea concerning Sovereignty and Maritime Boundaries in the area between the two Countries, including the area known as Torres Strait, and Related Matters", Australasian Legal Information Institute, http：//www.austlii.edu.au/au/other/dfat/treaties/ATS/1985/4.html, April 1, 2023.

Kaumag and Saibai）与巴布亚新几内亚之间，两国的领海分界线为7个地理坐标点间的连线。这7个坐标点的位置如表30所示：

表30 道安岛、考马格岛和赛拜岛与巴布亚新几内亚之间的领海边界坐标点[1]

坐标点	纬度（南）	经度（东）
9	9°22′04″	142°29′41″
10	9°21′48″	142°31′29″
11	9°22′33″	142°33′28″
12	9°21′25″	142°35′29″
13	9°20′21″	142°41′43″
14	9°20′16″	142°43′53″
15	9°19′26″	142°48′18″

依该条约附件3，奥布西岛、博伊古岛和莫伊米岛的领海外部界限由两部分组成：其一为从附件1（表29）中的坐标点1开始依次连接至坐标点8的测地线；其二为一系列以40个地理坐标点为圆心、以3海里为半径的圆弧相交所连接成的弧线段。这40个坐标点的位置如表31所示：

表31 奥布西岛、博伊古岛和莫伊米岛的领海外部界限坐标点[2]

坐标点	纬度（南）	经度（东）
1	9°15′53″	142°17′39″
2	9°16′26″	142°17′36″
3	9°16′28″	142°17′36″
4	9°16′31″	142°17′30″
5	9°17′06″	142°17′30″
6	9°17′15″	142°17′30″
7	9°17′26″	142°17′15″
8	9°17′50″	142°16′46″

---

[1] "Treaty between Australia and the Independent State of Papua New Guinea concerning Sovereignty and Maritime Boundaries in the area between the two Countries, including the area known as Torres Strait, and Related Matters", Australasian Legal Information Institute, http：//www.austlii.edu.au/au/other/dfat/treaties/ATS/1985/4.html, April 1, 2023.

[2] "Treaty between Australia and the Independent State of Papua New Guinea concerning Sovereignty and Maritime Boundaries in the area between the two Countries, including the area known as Torres Strait, and Related Matters", Australasian Legal Information Institute, http：//www.austlii.edu.au/au/other/dfat/treaties/ATS/1985/4.html, April 1, 2023.

续表

坐标点	纬度（南）	经度（东）
9	9°17′55″	142°16′39″
10	9°17′56″	142°16′30″
11	9°17′53″	142°16′11″
12	9°17′52″	142°16′07″
13	9°17′44″	142°14′52″
14	9°17′45″	142°14′49″
15	9°17′44″	142°14′38″
16	9°17′44″	142°14′30″
17	9°17′38″	142°14′06″
18	9°17′38″	142°13′59″
19	9°17′36″	142°13′47″
20	9°17′34″	142°13′31″
21	9°17′33″	142°13′20″
22	9°17′32″	142°12′56″
23	9°17′32″	142°12′46″
24	9°17′33″	142°12′26″
25	9°17′38″	142°11′56″
26	9°17′39″	142°11′51″
27	9°17′38″	142°11′34″
28	9°17′37″	142°11′30″
29	9°17′33″	142°10′20″
30	9°17′30″	142°10′13″
31	9°17′15″	142°09′08″
32	9°17′13″	142°09′00″
33	9°17′02″	142°08′35″
34	9°16′56″	142°08′23″
35	9°16′52″	142°08′15″
36	9°16′47″	142°08′01″
37	9°16′46″	142°07′58″
38	9°16′21″	142°06′2″
39	9°16′19″	142°06′51″
40	9°15′08″	142°06′28″

同依附件3，道安岛、考马格岛和赛拜岛的领海外部界限亦由两部分组成：其一为从附件1（表30）中的坐标点9开始依次连接至坐标点15的测地线；其二为一系列以58个地理坐标点为圆心、以3海里为半径的圆弧相交所连接成的弧线段。这58个坐标点的位置如表32所示：

表32　道安岛、考马格岛和赛拜岛的领海外部界限坐标点[1]

坐标点	纬度（南）	经度（东）
1	9°22′24″	142°47′49″
2	9°22′28″	142°47′53″
3	9°22′39″	142°47′57″
4	9°22′48″	142°48′00″
5	9°22′58″	142°48′01″
6	9°23′02″	142°48′01″
7	9°23′06″	142°47′59″
8	9°23′12″	142°47′55″
9	9°23′28″	142°47′46″
10	9°23′44″	142°47′41″
11	9°25′46″	142°46′36″
12	9°25′48″	142°46′36″
13	9°25′53″	142°46′29″
14	9°26′05″	142°46′12″
15	9°26′10″	142°46′03″
16	9°26′15″	142°45′47″
17	9°26′15″	142°45′34″
18	9°26′12″	142°45′25″
19	9°26′09″	142°45′12″
20	9°26′06″	142°45′07″
21	9°25′57″	142°44′39″
22	9°25′48″	142°43′07″
23	9°25′54″	142°42′42″

---

[1]　"Treaty between Australia and the Independent State of Papua New Guinea concerning Sovereignty and Maritime Boundaries in the area between the two Countries, including the area known as Torres Strait, and Related Matters", Australasian Legal Information Institute, http：//www. austlii. edu. au/au/other/dfat/treaties/ATS/1985/4. html, April 1, 2023.

续表

坐标点	纬度（南）	经度（东）
24	9°25′53″	142°42′13″
25	9°25′52″	142°41′59″
26	9°25′51″	142°41′51″
27	9°25′48″	142°41′15″
28	9°25′47″	142°41′04″
29	9°25′46″	142°40′55″
30	9°25′43″	142°40′20″
31	9°25′44″	142°40′04″
32	9°25′50″	142°39′30″
33	9°25′51″	142°39′22″
34	9°25′50″	142°39′13″
35	9°25′48″	142°39′03″
36	9°25′35″	142°38′05″
37	9°25′31″	142°37′46″
38	9°25′28″	142°37′36″
39	9°25′23″	142°37′22″
40	9°25′22″	142°37′19″
41	9°25′04″	142°36′35″
42	9°24′50″	142°36′03″
43	9°25′25″	142°33′03″
44	9°25′27″	142°32′58″
45	9°25′54″	142°32′17″
46	9°26′11″	142°33′00″
47	9°26′15″	142°31′55″
48	9°26′17″	142°31′52″
49	9°26′17″	142°31′48″
50	9°26′15″	142°31′46″
51	9°26′06″	142°31′47″
52	9°25′38″	142°31′35″
53	9°25′28″	142°31′34″
54	9°25′24″	142°31′33″
55	9°25′05″	142°31′27″

续表

坐标点	纬度（南）	经度（东）
56	9°24′39″	142°31′18″
57	9°24′37″	142°31′17″
58	9°24′32″	142°31′24″

同依附件3，锚礁（Anchor Cay）和东礁（East Cay）的领海外部界限为一系列以44个地理坐标点为圆心、以3海里为半径的圆弧相交连接，将相关岛礁包围其中的弧线段。这44个坐标点的位置如表33所示：

表33　锚礁和东礁的领海外部界限坐标点[1]

坐标点	纬度（南）	经度（东）
1	9°21′27″	144°07′30″
2	9°21′25″	144°07′28″
3	9°21′25″	144°07′38″
4	9°21′26″	144°07′44″
5	9°21′29″	144°07″50″
6	9°21′31″	144°07′55″
7	9°21′44″	144°08′24″
8	9°21′45″	144°08′27″
9	9°21′49″	144°08′33″
10	9°21′54″	144°08′37″
11	9°23′09″	144°12′43″
12	9°23′02″	144°12′55″
13	9°23′02″	144°13′23″
14	9°23′04″	144°13′29″
15	9°23′06″	144°13′33″
16	9°23′09″	144°13′40″
17	9°23′13″	144°13′44″
18	9°23′30″	144°13′59″

---

[1] "Treaty between Australia and the Independent State of Papua New Guinea concerning Sovereignty and Maritime Boundaries in the area between the two Countries, including the area known as Torres Strait, and Related Matters", Australasian Legal Information Institute, http：//www.austlii. edu. au/au/other/dfat/treaties/ATS/1985/4. html, April 1, 2023.

续表

坐标点	纬度（南）	经度（东）
19	9°23′40″	144°14′11″
20	9°23′44″	144°14′18″
21	9°23′50″	144°14′25″
22	9°23′59″	144°14′30″
23	9°24′05″	144°14′31″
24	9°24′19″	144°14′33″
25	9°24′29″	144°14′37″
26	9°24′40″	144°14′40″
27	9°24′44″	144°14′40″
28	9°24′49″	144°14′35″
29	9°24′53″	144°14′33″
30	9°24′57″	144°14′27″
31	9°24′57″	144°14′20″
32	9°24′56″	144°14′14″
33	9°24′44″	144°13′19″
34	9°24′40″	144°13′02″
35	9°24′36″	144°12′58″
36	9°24′31″	144°12′56″
37	9°23′47″	144°12′34″
38	9°22′06″	144°08′38″
39	9°22′07″	144°08′31″
40	9°21′59″	144°07′57″
41	9°21′47″	144°07′32″
42	9°21′44″	144°07′29″
43	9°21′40″	144°07′26″
44	9°21′35″	144°07′24″

同依附件3，黑岩礁（Black Rocks Cay）和布兰布尔礁（Bramble Cay）的领海外部界限为一系列以16个地理坐标点为圆心、以3海里为半径的圆弧相交连接，将相关岛礁包围其中的弧线段。这16个坐标点的位置如表34所示：

表34　黑岩礁和布兰布尔礁的领海外部界限坐标点[1]

坐标点	纬度（南）	经度（东）
1	9°10′28″	143°49′59″
2	9°08′40″	143°52′19″
3	9°08′33″	143°52′22″
4	9°08′26″	143°52′32″
5	9°08′24″	143°52′41″
6	9°08′23″	143°52′48″
7	9°08′24″	143°52′54″
8	9°08′27″	143°53′06″
9	9°08′32″	143°53′12″
10	9°08′43″	143°53′19″
11	9°08′48″	143°53′19″
12	9°08′52″	143°53′17″
13	9°09′00″	143°53′13″
14	9°09′04″	143°53′07″
15	9°09′08″	143°53′00″
16	9°09′07″	143°52′49″

同依附件3，拯救岛（Deliverance Island）和科尔岛（Kerr Islet）的领海外部界限为一系列以40个地理坐标点为圆心、以3海里为半径的圆弧相交连接，将相关岛礁包围其中的弧线段。这40个坐标点的位置如表35所示：

表35　拯救岛和科尔岛的领海外部界限坐标点[2]

坐标点	纬度（南）	经度（东）
1	9°32′39″	141°32′15″
2	9°32′35″	141°32′11″

---

[1] "Treaty between Australia and the Independent State of Papua New Guinea concerning Sovereignty and Maritime Boundaries in the area between the two Countries, including the area known as Torres Strait, and Related Matters", Australasian Legal Information Institute, http://www.austlii.edu.au/au/other/dfat/treaties/ATS/1985/4.html, April 1, 2023.

[2] "Treaty between Australia and the Independent State of Papua New Guinea concerning Sovereignty and Maritime Boundaries in the area between the two Countries, including the area known as Torres Strait, and Related Matters", Australasian Legal Information Institute, http://www.austlii.edu.au/au/other/dfat/treaties/ATS/1985/4.html, April 1, 2023.

续表

坐标点	纬度（南）	经度（东）
3	9°32′07″	141°31′50″
4	9°32′02″	141°31′54″
5	9°31′56″	141°31′58″
6	9°31′51″	141°32′02″
7	9°31′29″	141°32′17″
8	9°31′27″	141°32′19″
9	9°31′24″	141°32′21″
10	9°30′40″	141°33′32″
11	9°30′08″	141°34′01″
12	9°30′01″	141°34′05″
13	9°29′57″	141°34′08″
14	9°29′51″	141°34′14″
15	9°29′51″	141°34′19″
16	9°29′58″	141°36′13″
17	9°30′04″	141°36′16″
18	9°30′12″	141°36′16″
19	9°30′28″	141°36′18″
20	9°30′47″	141°36′18″
21	9°31′00″	141°36′15″
22	9°31′11″	141°36′10″
23	9°31′29″	141°36′02″
24	9°31′38″	141°35′55″
25	9°31′47″	141°35′46″
26	9°31′50″	141°35′42″
27	9°32′02″	141°35′21″
28	9°36′21″	141°34′33″
29	9°36′24″	141°34′34″
30	9°36′35″	141°34′33″
31	9°36′49″	141°34′26″
32	9°36′56″	141°34′21″
33	9°37′05″	141°34′02″
34	9°37′14″	141°33′47″

续表

坐标点	纬度（南）	经度（东）
35	9°37′15″	141°33′28″
36	9°37′13″	141°33′25″
37	9°37′09″	141°33′22″
38	9°37′03″	141°33′21″
39	9°36′58″	141°33′22″
40	9°36′52″	141°33′27″

同依附件3，皮尔斯礁（Pearce Cay）的领海外部界限位于该条约第4条第1款中所称的两国海床及底土分界线以北，起于东经143度14分51秒、南纬9度33分00秒处，经一系列以9个地理坐标点为圆心、以3海里为半径的圆弧相交连接的线段后，最终通过东经143度19分46秒、南纬9度33分00秒处返回起点。其中所涉9个坐标点的位置如表36所示：

表36 皮尔斯礁的领海外部界限坐标点[1]

坐标点	纬度（南）	经度（东）
1	9°30′56″	143°17′03″
2	9°30′53″	143°17′03″
3	9°30′50″	143°17′08″
4	9°30′46″	143°17′19″
5	9°30′43″	143°17′26″
6	9°30′42″	143°17′34″
7	9°30′41″	143°17′43″
8	9°30′48″	143°17′42″
9	9°30′50″	143°17′40″

同依附件3，坦纳根岛（Turnagain Island）的领海外部界限为一系列以74个地理坐标点为圆心、以3海里为半径的圆弧相交连接，将相关岛礁包围其中的弧线段。这74个坐标点的位置如表37所示：

---

[1] "Treaty between Australia and the Independent State of Papua New Guinea concerning Sovereignty and Maritime Boundaries in the area between the two Countries, including the area known as Torres Strait, and Related Matters", Australasian Legal Information Institute, http：//www.austlii.edu.au/au/other/dfat/treaties/ATS/1985/4.html, April 1, 2023.

表37 坦纳根岛的领海外部界限坐标点[1]

坐标点	纬度（南）	经度（东）
1	9°32′54″	142°10′47″
2	9°32′54″	142°10′44″
3	9°32′54″	142°10′40″
4	9°32′52″	142°10′36″
5	9°32′49″	142°10′35″
6	9°32′44″	142°10′36″
7	9°32′23″	142°10′54″
8	9°32′11″	142°11′39″
9	9°32′10″	142°11′45″
10	9°32′15″	142°11′54″
11	9°32′37″	142°14′59″
12	9°32′36″	142°15′08″
13	9°32′37″	142°15′14″
14	9°32′40″	142°15′24″
15	9°32′44″	142°15′40″
16	9°32′44″	142°15′47″
17	9°32′45″	142°15′53″
18	9°32′48″	142°16′04″
19	9°32′51″	142°16′16″
20	9°32′53″	142°16′28″
21	9°32′54″	142°16′34″
22	9°32′56″	142°16′39″
23	9°32′58″	142°16′49″
24	9°33′02″	142°17′01″
25	9°33′03″	142°17′12″
26	9°33′05″	142°17′18″
27	9°33′11″	142°17′30″
28	9°33′14″	142°17′40″

---

[1] "Treaty between Australia and the Independent State of Papua New Guinea concerning Sovereignty and Maritime Boundaries in the area between the two Countries, including the area known as Torres Strait, and Related Matters", Australasian Legal Information Institute, http://www.austlii. edu. au/au/other/dfat/treaties/ATS/1985/4. html, April 1, 2023.

五、海洋争端解决

续表

坐标点	纬度（南）	经度（东）
29	9°33′16″	142°17′50″
30	9°33′18″	142°18′00″
31	9°33′21″	142°18′09″
32	9°33′23″	142°18′16″
33	9°33′28″	142°18′27″
34	9°33′33″	142°18′42″
35	9°33′35″	142°18′51″
36	9°33′38″	142°19′03″
37	9°33′41″	142°19′12″
38	9°33′42″	142°19′19″
39	9°33′44″	142°19′25″
40	9°33′47″	142°19′38″
41	9°33′49″	142°19′40″
42	9°34′15″	142°20′11″
43	9°34′19″	142°20′16″
44	9°34′23″	142°20′17″
45	9°34′29″	142°20′14″
46	9°34′34″	142°20′10″
47	9°34′42″	142°20′03″
48	9°34′46″	142°19′58″
49	9°34′49″	142°19′52″
50	9°34′52″	142°19′32″
51	9°34′52″	142°19′24″
52	9°34′52″	142°19′15″
53	9°34′50″	142°19′05″
54	9°34′48″	142°18′54″
55	9°34′46″	142°18′39″
56	9°34′43″	142°18′28″
57	9°34′40″	142°18′11″
58	9°34′38″	142°18′05″
59	9°34′35″	142°17′56″
60	9°34′30″	142°17′39″

145

续表

坐标点	纬度（南）	经度（东）
61	9°34′23″	142°17′09″
62	9°34′21″	142°16′55″
63	9°34′19″	142°16′39″
64	9°34′16″	142°16′29″
65	9°34′07″	142°15′58″
66	9°34′05″	142°15′49″
67	9°34′01″	142°15′41″
68	9°33′50″	142°15′17″
69	9°33′48″	142°15′10″
70	9°33′44″	142°15′00″
71	9°33′35″	142°14′48″
72	9°33′24″	142°14′31″
73	9°33′09″	142°13′59″
74	9°33′08″	142°13′53″

同依附件3，图鲁礁（Turu Cay）的领海外部界限为一系列以20个地理坐标点为圆心、以3海里为半径的圆弧相交连接，将相关岛礁包围其中的弧线段。这20个坐标点的位置如表38所示：

表38　图鲁礁的领海外部界限坐标点[1]

坐标点	纬度（南）	经度（东）
1	9°49′53″	141°24′42″
2	9°49′39″	141°24′44″
3	9°49′31″	141°24′52″
4	9°49′25″	141°25′02″
5	9°49′23″	141°25′13″
6	9°49′20″	141°25′25″
7	9°49′19″	141°25′36″
8	9°49′18″	141°25′43″

---

[1] "Treaty between Australia and the Independent State of Papua New Guinea concerning Sovereignty and Maritime Boundaries in the area between the two Countries, including the area known as Torres Strait, and Related Matters", Australasian Legal Information Institute, http：//www.austlii. edu. au/au/other/dfat/treaties/ATS/1985/4. html, April 1, 2023.

续表

坐标点	纬度（南）	经度（东）
9	9°49′18″	141°25′53″
10	9°49′17″	141°26′07″
11	9°49′23″	141°26′09″
12	9°49′26″	141°26′06″
13	9°49′32″	141°25′58″
14	9°49′38″	141°25′49″
15	9°49′44″	141°25′38″
16	9°49′47″	141°25′31″
17	9°49′53″	141°25′19″
18	9°49′56″	141°25′09″
19	9°49′57″	141°24′54″
20	9°49′56″	141°24′45″

依附件5，澳大利亚和巴布亚新几内亚在托雷斯海峡地区的海底管辖权分界线为21个地理坐标点间的连线。这21个坐标点的位置如表39所示：

表39 澳大利亚和巴布亚新几内亚在托雷斯海峡地区的海底管辖权分界线坐标点[1]

坐标点	纬度（南）	经度（东）
a	10°50′00″	139°12′00″
b	11°09′00″	139°23′00″
c	10°59′00″	140°00′00″
d	9°46′00″	142°00′00″
e	9°45′24″	142°03′30″
f	9°42′00″	142°23′00″
g	9°40′30″	142°51′00″
h	9°40′00″	143°00′00″
i	9°33′00″	143°05′00″
j	9°33′00″	143°20′00″

---

[1] "Treaty between Australia and the Independent State of Papua New Guinea concerning Sovereignty and Maritime Boundaries in the area between the two Countries, including the area known as Torres Strait, and Related Matters", Australasian Legal Information Institute, http：//www.austlii. edu.au/au/other/dfat/treaties/ATS/1985/4.html, April 1, 2023.

续表

坐标点	纬度（南）	经度（东）
k	9°24′00″	143°30′00″
l	9°22′00″	143°48′00″
m	9°30′00″	144°15′00″
n	9°51′00″	144°44′00″
o	12°20′00″	146°30′00″
p	12°38′30″	147°08′30″
q	13°10′30″	148°05′00″
r	14°38′00″	152°07′00″
s	14°45′00″	154°15′00″
t	14°05′00″	156°37′00″
u	14°04′00″	157°00′00″

依附件8，澳大利亚和巴布亚新几内亚在托雷斯海峡地区的渔业管辖权分界线为35个地理坐标点间的连线。这35个坐标点的位置如表40所示：

表40　澳大利亚和巴布亚新几内亚在托雷斯海峡地区的渔业管辖权分界线坐标点[1]

坐标点	纬度（南）	经度（东）
a	10°50′00″	139°12′00″
b	11°09′00″	139°23′00″
c	10°59′00″	140°00′00″
d	9°46′00″	142°00′00″
e	9°45′24″	142°03′30″
f	9°15′43″	142°03′30″
g	9°12′50″	142°06′25″
h	9°11′51″	142°08′33″
i	9°11′58″	142°10′18″
j	9°11′22″	142°12′54″
k	9°11′34″	142°14′08″

---

[1] "Treaty between Australia and the Independent State of Papua New Guinea concerning Sovereignty and Maritime Boundaries in the area between the two Countries, including the area known as Torres Strait, and Related Matters", Australasian Legal Information Institute, http：//www.austlii.edu.au/au/other/dfat/treaties/ATS/1985/4.html, April 1, 2023.

续表

坐标点	纬度（南）	经度（东）
l	9°13′53″	142°16′26″
m	9°16′04″	142°20′41″
n	9°22′04″	142°29′41″
o	9°21′48″	142°31′29″
p	9°22′33″	142°33′28″
q	9°21′25″	142°35′29″
r	9°20′21″	142°41′43″
s	9°20′16″	142°43′53″
t	9°19′26″	142°48′18″
u	9°23′40″	142°51′00″
v	9°40′30″	142°51′00″
w	9°40′00″	143°00′00″
x	9°33′00″	143°05′00″
y	9°33′00″	143°20′00″
z	9°24′00″	143°30′00″
za	9°22′00″	143°48′00″
zb	9°30′00″	144°15′00″
zc	9°51′00″	144°44′00″
zd	12°20′00″	146°30′00″
ze	12°38′30″	147°08′30″
zf	13°10′30″	148°05′00″
zg	14°38′00″	152°07′00″
zh	14°45′00″	154°15′00″
zi	14°05′00″	156°37′00″

在托雷斯海峡地区划定专门的保护区是该条约较具特色的内容。根据该条约第 10 条，澳大利亚和巴布亚新几内亚意在通过确定这一保护区东、南、西、北的四面边界，确认和保障该区域内土著居民的传统生活方式与基本民生，包括其传统捕鱼权与自由行动的权利，同时更好地保护海洋环境，保护本土动物及植物。依附件 9，这一保护区的边界为沿特定方向经 17 个地理坐标点间的连线。这 17 个坐标点的位置及连线相关走向如表 41 所示：

表41　托雷斯海峡保护区的边界坐标点[1]

坐标点	纬度（南）	经度（东）
a	10°28′00″	144°10′00″
b	10°28′00″	141°20′00″
c	9°33′00″	141°20′00″
d	9°13′00″	141°57′00″
e	沿141°57′00″E向北与新几内亚岛南部在低潮时的海岸线的交点	
f	向东沿新几内亚岛的南部海岸线穿过各河口与142°36′00″E的交点	
g	9°21′00″	142°36′00″
h	9°09′00″	143°47′20″
i	越黑岩礁西北至黑岩礁领海外部界限与布兰布尔礁领海外部界限的交点	
j	9°10′50″	143°55′40″
k	9°18′40″	144°06′10″
l	越锚礁北部至锚礁领海外部界限与东礁领海外部界限的交点	
m	9°26′50″	144°16′50″
n	9°35′15″	144°28′00″
o	9°54′00″	144°28′00″
p	10°15′00″	144°12′00″
q	沿测地线向西南方向延伸至起点（坐标点a）	

5. 澳大利亚与所罗门群岛之间的划界协定

澳大利亚与所罗门群岛于1988年9月13日签订了《澳大利亚政府与所罗门群岛政府间确立某些海洋和海底边界的协定》（Agreement between the Government of Australia and the Government of Solomon Islands Establishing Certain Sea and Seabed Boundaries），以明晰两国行使主权权利海域的准确界限。该协定以《公约》及相关国际法规则为基础，于次年4月14日生效。

依据该协定第1条，在珊瑚海上的澳大利亚群礁（Australian reefs）向海

---

[1] "Treaty between Australia and the Independent State of Papua New Guinea concerning Sovereignty and Maritime Boundaries in the area between the two Countries, including the area known as Torres Strait, and Related Matters", Australasian Legal Information Institute, http：//www.austlii.edu.au/au/other/dfat/treaties/ATS/1985/4.html, April 1, 2023.

一侧与所罗门群岛群礁之间，澳大利亚渔区与所罗门群岛专属经济区之间的分界线以及两国大陆架之间的分界线，为连接3个坐标点的测地线。这3个坐标点的位置如表42所示：

表42 澳大利亚渔区与所罗门群岛专属经济区间分界线以及两国大陆架间分界线坐标点[1]

坐标点	纬度（南）	经度（东）
U	14°04′00″	157°00′00″
V	14°41′00″	157°43′00″
R1	15°44′07″	158°45′39″

该协定进一步明确：第一，两国共同确定了划分大陆架边界的地理坐标，并以其连线作为两国大陆架的边界；第二，规定了跨界限的海底矿藏的开采方式，并要求双方应协商确定利益分配；第三，两国政府之间因本协定的解释或适用而产生的任何争端，应通过协商或谈判和平解决。

如果有任何液烃（liquid hydrocarbons）及天然气积聚或在海床下有任何其他矿藏延伸跨越了前述第1条所定分界线，而位于界限一侧的部分油气积聚或矿藏可全部或部分从该分界线的另一侧采收，则双方政府将促成进一步协议，以寻求最有效开发利用这一油气积聚或矿藏的方式，并保证该开发收益的公平分享。[2]

（三）通过法律方法解决的海洋渔业相关争端

作为四面环海、独踞一个大陆的国家，自视为印太地区重要海洋力量及南大洋海洋秩序维护者的澳大利亚，一直以来都在海洋航行、海洋环境及海洋资源利用等方面表现出规则捍卫者的积极姿态。除上述的海洋划界争端外，澳大利亚也数次就南太平洋海域上的生物资源捕捞纠纷向国际法院、国际海洋法法庭及国际仲裁庭寻求解决之道。

1. 南方蓝鳍金枪鱼案

南方蓝鳍金枪鱼是被列入《公约》附件1下的高度洄游的深海鱼类之

---

[1] "Agreement between the Government of Australia and the Government of Solomon Islands Establishing Certain Sea and Seabed Boundaries", Australasian Legal Information Institute, http：//www. austlii. edu. au/au/other/dfat/treaties/ATS/1989/12. html, April 10, 2023.

[2] "Agreement between the Government of Australia and the Government of Solomon Islands Establishing Certain Sea and Seabed Boundaries", Australasian Legal Information Institute, http：//www. austlii. edu. au/au/other/dfat/treaties/ATS/1989/12. html, April 10, 2023.

一。这一鱼类广泛分布于南半球的公海之中，但也时常穿梭于某些国家如澳大利亚、新西兰和南非的领海及专属经济区。南方蓝鳍金枪鱼的主要销售市场在日本，由金枪鱼做成的刺身是享誉全球的美食。面对南方蓝鳍金枪鱼被过度捕捞的严峻情势，自20世纪80年代起，澳大利亚、新西兰与日本即开始就相关限制及管理措施展开谈判和协商。对于该鱼类的总许可渔获量（total allowable catch）的设定、该鱼类的当前状态与种群恢复前景以及通过何种方式可以减少科学上的不确定性，澳大利亚、新西兰与日本之间一直存在较大分歧。

1993年，澳大利亚、新西兰与日本签订了《南方蓝鳍金枪鱼养护公约》（Convention for the Conservation of Southern Bluefin Tuna，以下简称《1993年公约》），并依据该公约成立了南方蓝鳍金枪鱼养护委员会（以下简称"养护委员会"）。日本从1994年起不断要求提高总许可渔获量及本国捕捞配额，但屡遭澳大利亚与新西兰驳回。在1998年的养护委员会会议上，日本提出将启动一项单方的、为期3年的"实验捕捞项目"（Experimental Fishing Program），旨在前往停止捕捞区收集相关数据，以减少有关种群恢复的科学上的不确定性。尽管澳大利亚与新西兰对这一项目表示强烈反对，但日本仍于1998年夏天实施了一项试点计划。

1998年8月31日，澳大利亚与新西兰同时向日本发出照会，声明其与日本间就养护和管理南方蓝鳍金枪鱼问题存在争端。同时，澳大利亚与新西兰依据《1993年公约》第16条第1款正式要求与日本进行紧急磋商与谈判，但各方未能在这一条约框架下顺利达成协议。1999年7月15日，澳大利亚与新西兰依据《公约》下附件7相关规定对日本提起仲裁。这也是在《公约》附件7下成立的第一个仲裁庭。[1]

（1）南方蓝鳍金枪鱼（临时措施）案。

在等待仲裁庭成立期间，澳大利亚与新西兰依据《公约》第290条第5款于1999年7月30日请求国际海洋法法庭指示临时措施，以阻止日本的单方"实验捕捞项目"及相关行动。日本则在提出管辖权异议的同时，请求对澳大利亚及新西兰反向指示临时措施，要求两国在6个月内以善意重启紧急谈判以促成合意。

为在本案中指示临时措施，国际海洋法法庭须满足两项要件：其一，

---

[1] "Southern Bluefin Tuna (New Zealand-Japan, Australia-Japan), 4 August 2000", United Nations-Office of Legal Affairs, https://legal.un.org/riaa/cases/vol_XXIII/1-57.pdf, pp. 8-14, April 10, 2023.

"初步证明"即将组建的仲裁庭对该案具有管辖权；其二，判定在仲裁庭组建期间"情况紧急"，指示临时措施"有此必要"。

对于前者，法庭审理后认为：第一，澳大利亚与新西兰所援引的《公约》相关条款可以作为即将组成的仲裁庭的依据；第二，适用于争端各方间的《1993年公约》并不排斥《公约》第15部分第2节程序在当事方间的适用；第三，在争端解决的各种可能都已穷尽的情形下，缔约国并无义务通过《公约》第15部分第1节的程序以解决争端；第四，援引《公约》第15部分第2节下程序的要件已经得到满足。因此，法庭认为，可"初步证明"即将组建的仲裁庭对本案具有管辖权。[1]

对于后者，法庭审理后认为：第一，双方已经确认，对南方蓝鳍金枪鱼的商业捕捞会在1999年及以后继续进行；第二，当事方应在这一情形下谨慎行事，以确保采取有效措施防止对南方蓝鳍金枪鱼种群的严重伤害；第三，尽管无法对当事方提交的科学证据作出决定性评估，但法庭仍然认为应采取紧急措施以保全当事方的权利，并避免南方蓝鳍金枪鱼种群的进一步衰减；第四，除非符合已商定的标准，在"实验捕捞项目"框架下的捕捞量不应超过最近确定的各方等级。基于上述理由，法庭认为，在当前情形下指示临时措施是适当的。[2]

1999年8月27日，法庭发布关于临时措施的命令，要求：第一，对于已提交至仲裁庭的争端，澳大利亚、日本和新西兰应各自确保不采取可能激化或扩大争端的行动；第二，对于仲裁庭就实体问题作出的可能裁定，澳大利亚、日本和新西兰应各自确保不采取可能妨碍执行上述裁定的行动；第三，除另有协议外，澳大利亚、日本和新西兰应确保，它们的年度捕鱼量不超过缔约国最后商定的年度国家分配额，且在计算1999年和2000年的年度渔获量时，在不影响仲裁庭的任何决定的情况下，应将1999年期间的渔获量作为"实验捕捞项目"的一部分考虑在内；第四，澳大利亚、日本和新西兰均应避免进行涉及捕获南方蓝鳍金枪鱼的"实验捕捞项目"，除非得到其他当事方的同意或实验捕获量计入其年度国家分配额；第五，澳大利亚、日本和新西兰应毫不拖延地恢复谈判，以期就南方蓝鳍金枪鱼的养护和管理措施

---

[1] "Order of 27 August 1999, Southern Bluefin Tuna Cases (New Zealand v. Japan; Australia v. Japan), Provisional Measures", ITLOS, https：//www.itlos.org/fileadmin/itlos/documents/cases/case_no_3_4/published/ C34-O-27_aug_99.pdf, pp. 293-295, April 11, 2023.

[2] "Order of 27 August 1999, Southern Bluefin Tuna Cases (New Zealand v. Japan; Australia v. Japan), Provisional Measures", ITLOS, https：//www.itlos.org/fileadmin/itlos/documents/cases/case_no_3_4/published/ C34-O-27_aug_99.pdf, pp. 295-297, April 11, 2023.

达成协议。[1]

（2）南方蓝鳍金枪鱼仲裁案。

2000年1月，仲裁庭组建完毕，当事方开始就程序性问题进行磋商。日本再次对仲裁庭的管辖权及可受理性问题提出初步反对意见。仲裁庭自认，作为依据《公约》附件7组建的第一个仲裁庭，本案当事方的说理论证及仲裁庭的法律实践，不仅对本次争端解决至关重要，更对《公约》下和平争端解决程序的演进极具意义，同时对理解和发展与这一造法性条约有关的执行性条约或关联性条约多有助益。管辖权问题被视为仲裁庭程序推进的首要问题。围绕争议各方的观点及理据，仲裁庭对管辖权问题作出以下回应：

第一，关于本案是否存在争端、仲裁程序是否应予中止。仲裁庭认为，如果当事方能够就"实验捕捞项目"达成一致，捕捞限制将超过当前事实上的总许可渔获量，但仍限制在1500吨以内，则当事方争端中的最大争议点确实将因此得以解决。但澳大利亚和新西兰绝不可能接受日本的这一提议或限额标准。而即便日本的提议能够获得另外两国的接纳，也不足以使整个争端得以解决。日本已经提议在"实验捕捞项目"中将捕捞量限制在1500吨以内，但其并未承诺在养护委员会未就有关总捕捞量及分配各国捕捞量作出决定的情形下，在未来会放弃或限制在公海上捕捞南方蓝鳍金枪鱼的权利。因此，本案并非虚幻无意义，仲裁程序也不应中止。[2]

第二，关于本案争端的产生依据与适用法律。仲裁庭认为，本案的核心问题之一在于，申请方提交至仲裁庭的争端到底是关于《1993年公约》的适用，还是关于《公约》的适用，或是关于两者的适用。在仲裁庭看来，无论是在国际法层面还是国内法层面，都既存在着适用特别法支配在先条约或立法中一般性条款的情形，也存在着某一特定争端同时涉及多个条约的情形。无论是实体性内容还是其中的争端解决条款，多条约并行的情形都不鲜见。在国家实践中，缔结一项执行性条约并不必然免除框架性公约下该执行性条约当事方的义务。因此，于仲裁庭而言，一项有关《1993年公约》解释和实施的争端并不能完全与《公约》的解释和适用区分开来，因为《1993年公约》的缔结目的就在于落实《公约》所确立的宽泛原则。由上，日本管

---

[1] "Order of 27 August 1999, Southern Bluefin Tuna Cases (New Zealand v. Japan; Australia v. Japan), Provisional Measures", ITLOS, https：//www.itlos.org/fileadmin/itlos/documents/cases/case_no_3_4/published/C34-O-27_aug_99.pdf, pp. 297-301, April 12, 2023.

[2] "Southern Bluefin Tuna (New Zealand-Japan, Australia-Japan), 4 August 2000", United Nations-Office of Legal Affairs, https：//legal.un.org/riaa/cases/vol_XXIII/1-57.pdf, pp. 37-38, April 12, 2023.

理南方蓝鳍金枪鱼尤其是进行单方"实验捕捞项目"的行为,既涉及《1993年公约》核心内容,也应立足《公约》进行判定。[1]

第三,关于本案是否可适用《公约》第15部分第2节的强制争端解决程序。作为依据《公约》附件7所成立的仲裁庭,对这一问题的回应构成了判定仲裁庭管辖权的关键。为此,仲裁庭主要从以下3个方面阐明了对《公约》第15部分第2节中强制争端解决程序适用的立场。

首先,基于对《公约》第15部分第1节的考量。仲裁庭注意到,依据《公约》第286条,《公约》第15部分第2节下强制争端解决程序的适用受到其上下相关条款的限制。《公约》第286条需与其第281条、第279条及第280条一并考量。而《公约》第281条明确规定,"有关本公约的解释或适用的争端各方的缔约各国,如已协议用自行选择的和平方法来谋求解决争端",则只有在两种情形下可适用《公约》第15部分的相关规定。这两种情形分别是:其一,"诉诸这种方法而仍未得到解决";其二,"争端各方间的协议并不排除任何其他程序"。

对于上述情形一,仲裁庭表示,《1993年公约》第16条可以视为当事方间"用自行选择的和平方法来谋求解决争端"的合意,符合《公约》第280条及第281条的措辞与意图。《1993年公约》第16条为缔约方提供了一系列争端解决方式,但显而易见的是,当事方并未穷尽该条所列的所有争端解决方式,所采用的争端解决方式也未取得成效。各方未通过谈判获得任何成果,也并未通过《1993年公约》下的调解和仲裁达成协议。由此,本案与《公约》第281条所要求的"诉诸这种方法而仍未得到解决"的情形相符。

对于上述情形二,仲裁庭承认,《1993年公约》第16条并未以明文直截了当地排除对包括《公约》第XV部分第2节在内的其他程序的适用。但仲裁庭认为,就通常意义而言,该第16条已经清晰表明,不能"经争端任何一方请求"(《公约》第286条)就将争端提交至国际法院、国际海洋法法庭或国际仲裁庭。争端各方在每一案件中的同意都是必需的。《1993年公约》明确规定,当事各方有义务通过第16条所列方式继续寻求争端的解决。在仲裁庭看来,这不但意味着任何争端都应基于合意方能提交司法解决或仲裁,也意味着第16条有意将其排除在《公约》第XV部分第2节的强制程序之外,以免未经所有当事方同意的程序适用于某一争端。由此,仲裁庭认

---

[1] "Southern Bluefin Tuna (New Zealand-Japan, Australia-Japan), 4 August 2000", United Nations-Office of Legal Affairs, https://legal.un.org/riaa/cases/vol_XXIII/1-57.pdf, pp. 38-41, April 12, 2023.

定，《1993年公约》第16条符合《公约》第281条下"排除任何其他程序"的情形。[1]

其次，基于对《公约》第XV部分第3节的考量。仲裁庭认为，《公约》第XV部分第3节为第2节强制程序的适用设置了重要的限制与例外条款。其中，《公约》第297条对于沿海国适用强制程序的限制尤为重要，其第1款至第3款分别从主权争端、海洋科学研究争端、渔业争端等对第2节的适用作出限制或排除。在逐一考察了《公约》第XV部分第3节下第297条至第299条后，仲裁庭认定，《公约》显然未能真正建立起一个全面的强制管辖制度。

最后，基于对其他国际条约实践的考量。据仲裁庭观察，有相当数量的在《公约》生效后缔结的涉海国际协定，都不同程度地明确将单方提交司法或仲裁程序的争端解决方式排除在外。有诸多协定都明文要求，无论采取何种争端解决方式都需要经过当事各方的同意。一些条约不但明确规定当事一方提交强制争端解决程序需经所有当事方同意，还如《1993年公约》第16条一样，要求当事方通过其自行选择的和平方法继续寻求争端解决。仲裁庭认为，无论在《公约》缔结之前还是之后，这类条约实践都意在证实：在符合《公约》第281条的情形下，《公约》的缔约方可以通过彼此间的协定排除《公约》第XV部分第2节对其争端的适用。[2]

由上，仲裁庭认可当事方间存在国际争端，仲裁程序也并非不具意义，本案在立足于《1993年公约》的同时也不应将《公约》的适用排除；但正是《公约》自身对其第XV部分第2节强制程序的限制，使《公约》附件7下的仲裁庭在本案中的立足存在缺陷。仲裁庭最终遗憾裁定其对本案没有管辖权。依据《公约》第290条第5款，国际海洋法法庭于1999年8月27日所指示的临时措施从仲裁裁决作出之日起停止生效。尽管对于仲裁庭管辖权的成立，国际海洋法法庭与仲裁庭作出了相反裁决，但仲裁庭仍然强调，争端被先后提交至两个争端解决机构并非对程序的滥用，两个机构下的程序运行都具有建设意义。[3]

---

[1] "Southern Bluefin Tuna (New Zealand-Japan, Australia-Japan), 4 August 2000", United Nations-Office of Legal Affairs, https://legal.un.org/riaa/cases/vol_XXIII/1-57.pdf, pp. 42-44, April 12, 2023.

[2] "Southern Bluefin Tuna (New Zealand-Japan, Australia-Japan), 4 August 2000", United Nations-Office of Legal Affairs, https://legal.un.org/riaa/cases/vol_XXIII/1-57.pdf, pp. 44-46, April 12, 2023.

[3] "Southern Bluefin Tuna (New Zealand-Japan, Australia-Japan), 4 August 2000", United Nations-Office of Legal Affairs, https://legal.un.org/riaa/cases/vol_XXIII/1-57.pdf, pp. 46-47, April 12, 2023.

2. "伏尔加号案"

(1) 争端背景。

"伏尔加号"是一艘悬挂俄罗斯国旗的远洋渔船。2002年2月,澳大利亚军方人员以"伏尔加号"在澳大利亚专属经济区非法捕鱼为由,在澳大利亚赫德岛和麦克唐纳群岛的专属经济区界限外海域登上该船,并将其带回位于西澳大利亚的弗里曼特尔港。澳大利亚将该船及其渔获、渔网、设备全部扣押,同时将其渔获全部售卖。"伏尔加号"的船长、大副及引航员均被澳大利亚指控犯有刑事罪行。2002年12月2日,俄罗斯依据《公约》第292条将澳大利亚诉至国际海洋法法庭,要求澳大利亚释放"伏尔加号"及其船员。至国际海洋法法庭开始审理之时,"伏尔加号"被扣押的3名船员已经在满足一定保释条件后离开澳大利亚回到其本国。但为释放"伏尔加号",澳大利亚要求俄罗斯提供300万澳元以上的担保,并称这一金额经过了其基于多因素的计算考量。[1]

(2) 双方的主张。

俄罗斯向国际海洋法法庭主张,澳大利亚未能遵照《公约》第73条第2款的规定,在提出合理担保的情形下迅速释放其船舶及3名船员。俄罗斯提出,依据《公约》第73条第2款,澳大利亚就释放船舶及3名船员所设定的条件要么不被允许,要么并不合理。

澳大利亚坚称,其就释放"伏尔加号"所设定的保证金是合理的。确定这一金额的依据在于:对船舶、燃料及捕捞设备等的估值;相关罪行的严重性及可能的刑罚;有关非法捕捞的国际关注程度;在相关国内法律程序完结前,确保澳大利亚法律及相应国际义务得以遵行的需要。澳大利亚同时主张,其就释放3名船员所设定的保证金也是合理的。[2]

(3) 争议焦点及判决结果。

毫无疑问,该案的核心问题就在于《公约》第73条第2款是否得以遵行。对此,国际海洋法法庭一则就可用于评估保证书或其他财政担保合理性的相关因素作出判定,二则尝试就第73条中关键术语的含义予以明确。

关于澳大利亚确定保证金的关联因素。立足于在先司法判决中的相关结

---

[1] "Judgment of 23 December 2002, The 'Volga' Case (Russian Federation v. Australia), Prompt Release", ITLOS, https://www.itlos.org/fileadmin/itlos/documents/cases/case_no_11/11_judgment_231202_en.pdf, pp. 14-17, April 13, 2023.

[2] "Judgment of 23 December 2002, The 'Volga' Case (Russian Federation v. Australia), Prompt Release", ITLOS, https://www.itlos.org/fileadmin/itlos/documents/cases/case_no_11/11_judgment_231202_en.pdf, p. 31, April 13, 2023.

论，国际海洋法法庭首先关注了因素之一的"所涉罪行的严重性"。法庭注意到，所称罪行与"专属经济区渔业资源的养护相关"。澳大利亚向法庭呈交的相关材料中，特别说明了南大洋相关南极鱼类种群的衰减，国际社会对非法、不报告和不管制捕鱼的关注，并表示了对包括《南极海洋生物资源养护公约》缔约方在内的各国应对努力的赞赏。但国际海洋法法庭强调，本案程序旨在于扣押国法庭司法程序完结前，依据《公约》第 292 条评估澳大利亚所确定保证金的合理性。作为评估考量因素的惩罚，应是依据扣押国法律可能施加于所指罪行的惩罚。正是参照这些惩罚，法庭才可能评估所指称罪行的严重性。同时，法庭注意到，俄罗斯也并未否认被指控的罪行在澳大利亚法律下被视为严重罪行。

对于船舶及其货物的价值，国际海洋法法庭注意到，当事双方对相关价值数额并无异议。因此，法庭认定，基于各部分的价值总和，在双方并无争议的情形下，澳大利亚就释放船舶所确定的 1920000 澳元保证金依《公约》第 292 条是合理的。而在 3 名船员已经获释离开澳大利亚的情形下，有关释放船员保证金的审理已无意义。[1]

关于《公约》第 73 条第 2 款中"保证书或其他担保"的解释。澳大利亚就释放"伏尔加号"还附加有两项非财政条件，即要求在澳大利亚国内法律程序完结前：安装全面运行的船舶监控系统（Vessel Monitoring System, VMS）；遵行南极海洋生物资源养护委员会的相关养护措施。对于澳大利亚就释放船舶所提出的上述额外条件，国际海洋法法庭认为，对于《公约》下沿海国是否可为行使主权权利而施加相关条件，不宜在本案程序中进行审理；而关于《公约》第 73 条第 2 款下的"保证书或其他担保"是否可以包含这类条件，才是在本案程序中应予判定的问题。

国际海洋法法庭认为，对于"保证书或其他担保"之措辞，应按其上下文并参照条约之目的及宗旨进行解释。其相关的上下文包括《公约》中有关在提供保证书或担保时迅速释放船舶及船员的各款规定，这些条款包括：第 292 条、第 220 条第 7 款以及第 226 条第 1 款（b）项。这些条款中使用的措辞为"保证书或其他财政担保"或"保证书或其他适当财政担保"。从这一上下文来看，第 73 条第 2 款中的"保证书或其他担保"应被解释为一份具有财政性质的保证书或一项具有财政性质的担保。国际海洋法法庭同时发

---

〔1〕 "Judgment of 23 December 2002, The 'Volga' Case (Russian Federation v. Australia), Prompt Release", ITLOS, https://www.itlos.org/fileadmin/itlos/documents/cases/case_no_11/11_judgment_231202_en.pdf, pp. 31-34, April 13, 2023.

现，基于这一上下文，凡《公约》有意设定在财政担保以外的其他条件的，都已在相关条款中明示。如，《公约》在其第226条第1款（c）项中规定："在不妨害有关船只适航性的可适用的国际规则和标准的情形下，无论何时如船只的释放可能对海洋环境引起不合理的损害威胁，可拒绝释放或以驶往最近的适当修船厂为条件予以释放。"这意味着，因违反《公约》第73条第2款而适用第292条时，非财政条件不能被认为是保证书或其他财政担保的一部分。结合《公约》第292条，第73条第2款的宗旨与目的在于为船旗国提供机制，允许其通过提出可以依财政条款合理评估的具有财政性质的担保，使其被扣押的船舶及船员获得迅速释放。若将额外的非财政条件包含在这类担保之中，将背离其宗旨与目的。

同理，对于澳大利亚为保证安装船舶监控系统及遵行南极海洋生物资源养护委员会相关养护措施所提出的"良好行为保证金"（good behaviour bond），国际海洋法法庭认为，仍需依据《公约》第73条第2款及第292条中保证书或担保的含义来判定。在法庭看来，《公约》第73条整体上是为被控违反沿海国法律法规的行为所设计的执法手段。而结合《公约》第292条，防止未来违反沿海国法律法规的"良好行为保证金"并不能被认为是《公约》第73条第2款意义下的保证书或担保。[1]

由此，国际海洋法法庭最终判决，澳大利亚所主张的保证金不为《公约》第292条意义下合理的保证金。俄罗斯关于澳大利亚的行为不符合《公约》第73条第2款的主张得以成立。澳大利亚须在俄罗斯提供法庭所认定的保证书或其他财政担保后迅速释放"伏尔加号"。[2]

3. 南极捕鲸案

（1）争端背景。

20世纪上半叶，随着配备加工设施的捕鲸船的出现及其他技术的创新，国际捕鲸业迅速发展。人们可以前往远离陆上基地的水域，如南极水域，进行大规模的捕鲸活动。1931年，出于对捕鲸业可持续性的担忧，美国、英国和丹麦等26个国家缔结了《管制捕鲸公约》（Convention for the Regulation of Whaling）。该公约禁止捕杀部分种类的鲸鱼，要求缔约国的捕鲸船必须申领

---

[1] "Judgment of 23 December 2002, The 'Volga' Case (Russian Federation v. Australia), Prompt Release", ITLOS, https：//www.itlos.org/fileadmin/itlos/documents/cases/case_no_11/11_judgment_231202_en.pdf, pp. 34-37, April 13, 2023.

[2] "Judgment of 23 December 2002, The 'Volga' Case (Russian Federation v. Australia), Prompt Release", ITLOS, https：//www.itlos.org/fileadmin/itlos/documents/cases/case_no_11/11_judgment_231202_en.pdf, p. 37, April 14, 2023.

捕鲸作业许可证，但没能解决渔获总量上升的问题。捕获量的增加与鲸油价格的下降迅速促成了1937年《国际管制捕鲸协议》（International Agreement for the Regulation of Whaling）的通过。该协定进一步禁止捕捞部分种类的鲸鱼，为不同种类的鲸鱼规定捕鲸季，关闭某些海域禁止捕鲸，对捕鲸业采取更多管制措施，但同时规定缔约国政府可向国民颁发特别许可证，授权其为科学研究目的而捕获、击杀和加工处理鲸鱼。

1946年，在美国政府的推动下，15个主要捕鲸国召开了一次国际捕鲸会议，并于1946年12月2日在华盛顿签署了《国际捕鲸公约》（International Convention for the Regulation of Whaling）。该公约分别于1948年及1951年对澳大利亚和日本生效。新西兰于1949年交存批准书后，曾于1968年退出，后于1976年再次加入该公约。

不同于上述1931年及1937年所订条约，1946年《国际捕鲸公约》并未就保护鲸鱼种群和管理捕鲸业作出实质性规定，而是在其"附件"中予以明确。依据该公约第1条，"附件"作为《国际捕鲸公约》的有机组成部分，可以被修正，且其修正应由国际捕鲸委员会（以下简称"委员会"）通过。如缔约国未对修正提出异议，则该修正将对缔约国具有法律约束力。委员会的这一职能正是《国际捕鲸公约》不断发展完善的重要途径。

依据该公约第5条第2款，"附件"的修正需要满足若干前提，包括：第一，"应该是为了执行本公约目的和任务，并为了谋求鲸类资源的保护、发展和最适当的利用上所必需者"；第二，"应该以科学的判断为基础"。在1982年的委员会会议上，缔约各方通过援引该第5条对"附件"作出修正，将商业捕鲸的限额削减为零，从而在事实上全面禁止了商业捕鲸行为。

对于1982年的商业捕鲸禁令，日本最初以"不具备科学依据"而表示反对，称这一决定主要是对其他缔约国国内社会政治关切的回应。尽管日本后来撤回了这一反对意见并一度停止远洋商业捕鲸，但同时也宣布将执行"科学捕鲸方案"以证明1982年禁令本身就缺乏"可靠科学"基础。1987—2014年，以《国际捕鲸公约》第8条为授权依据，日本连续执行了两阶段的"南极特别许可下的日本鲸鱼研究方案"（Japanese Whale Research Programme under Special Permit in the Antarctic，JARPA）。在两轮方案执行中，鲸鱼尸体最终都被出售食用。

大部分《国际捕鲸公约》的缔约国都对日本的上述研究方案提出疑问，尤其对其采取致死方式对鲸鱼取样的行为多有批评。澳大利亚是对日本的南大洋捕鲸行为抨击最为猛烈的国家之一。2010年5月，澳大利亚以"日本凭借南极特别许可证，以第二阶段日本鲸鱼研究方案（JARPA II）的名义，持续开展大规模捕鲸行动"为由将日本诉至国际法院，指称日本违反了其在《国际捕鲸公约》下应承担的义务，同时还违背了养护海洋哺乳动物及海洋环境的相关国际义务。2012年11月，新西兰根据《国际法院规约》第63条第2款向国际法院提交《参加诉讼声明》，要求"作为非当事方参加澳大利亚对日本提出的诉讼"，因为法院对《国际捕鲸公约》的相关决定对于同为该公约缔约国的新西兰有直接利益关联。2013年2月，国际法院发布命令裁定允许新西兰参加该诉讼程序。[1]

（2）双方的主张。

澳大利亚向国际法院主张，由于第二阶段日本鲸鱼研究方案不是《国际捕鲸公约》第8条所指的以科学研究为目的的方案，日本已经违反并仍在持续违反"附件"规定的3项实质性义务及1项程序性要求，包括：第一，有关遵守禁令的义务，即为商业目的而捕杀各类鲸鱼的总捕获量限额为零；第二，有关不在南大洋保护区对长须鲸进行商业捕捞的义务；第三，暂停使用渔业加工船或与渔业加工船相连的鲸鱼船捕获、击杀和加工处理鲸鱼的义务；第四，"附件"第30条规定的颁发特别许可证的相关程序要求。

日本驳斥了上述澳大利亚的全部主张。关于实质性义务，第二阶段日本鲸鱼研究方案是以科学研究为目的，应属《国际捕鲸公约》第8条第1款所规定的豁免范围，澳大利亚援引的各项条款对该研究方案均不适用。关于程序性要求，日本相关行为未违反"附件"第30条的任何规定。[2]

（3）争议焦点及判决结果。

一如争议双方主张所昭示，对《国际捕鲸公约》第8条中关键术语的解释以及该条款对日本鲸鱼研究方案的适用，是本案是非判定的着力关键。而其他争议如日本对"附件"义务的遵行等在很大程度上都需以该第8条的认定结论为前提。

《国际捕鲸公约》第8条第1款规定："尽管有本公约的规定，缔约政府对本国国民为科学研究的目的而对鲸进行捕获、击杀和加工处理，可按该政府认为适当的限制数量，得发给特别许可证。按本条款的规定对鲸的捕获、

---

[1] See "Overview of The Case, Whaling in the Antarctic (Australia v. Japan: New Zealand intervening)", ICJ, https://www.icj-cij.org/en/case/148, April 14, 2023; Dawid Bunikowski et al., "Philosophies of Polar Law (1st ed.)", https://doi.org/10.4324/9780429461149, April 14, 2023.

[2] "Judgment of 31 March 2014, Whaling in the Antarctic (Australia v. Japan: New Zealand intervening)", ICJ, https://www.icj-cij.org/public/files/case-related/148/148-20140331-JUD-01-00-EN.pdf, p. 27, April 14, 2023.

击杀和加工处理，均不受本公约的约束。各缔约政府应将所有发出的上述的特别许可证迅速通知委员会。各缔约政府可在任何时期取消其发出的上述特别许可证。"围绕这一关键条款，国际法院作出了以下分析与回应：

第一，关于《国际捕鲸公约》第8条的作用。国际法院并不认同日本最初关于第8条已经"完全超出《国际捕鲸公约》范围"、应与该公约其他条款区分开来独立解读的观点。国际法院指出，作为《国际捕鲸公约》的有机组成部分，该第8条应依据该公约的目的和宗旨予以解读，同时还需要顾及包括"附件"在内的该公约的其他规定。但国际法院同时也确认，既然第8条第1款已经明确，"按本条款的规定对鲸的捕获、击杀和加工处理，均不受本公约的约束"，则对于依据满足第8条各项条件的特别许可证而开展的捕鲸作业，应不受"附件"下关于商业目的捕鲸、在南大洋保护区商业捕鲸以及渔业加工船等禁令或限制的约束。[1]

第二，关于第8条与《国际捕鲸公约》的目的和宗旨之间的关系。国际法院认为，联系《国际捕鲸公约》序言及其他关联条款，对于第8条的限制解释或扩充解释都是站不住脚的。法院指出，以科学研究为目的的方案应有助于科学知识的增长，也可以力求实现除保护或可持续利用鲸鱼种群之外的其他目的。委员会发布的科学委员会（Scientific Committee）对特别许可证的审查准则也体现出这一点。科学委员会于1950年由委员会设立，负责在缔约国根据《国际捕鲸公约》第8条第1款向国民发放以科学研究为目的的特别许可证之前，审查这些许可证并发表评论意见。20世纪80年代中期以来，科学委员会依据委员会发布或核准的"准则"来审查特别许可证。有关第二阶段日本鲸鱼研究方案的适用准则分别收录于案件材料"附件Y"（Annex Y）和"附件P"（Annex P）中。其中，"附件Y"不仅涉及"对加强鲸群合理管理至关重要的信息"的方案，与对于暂停商业捕鲸禁令"进行综合评估"有关的方案，同时还涉及为满足"其他重要研究需要"而开展的方案；"附件P"除旨在"改善鲸鱼种群的保护和管理"的方案之外，还设计了旨在"改善其他海洋生物资源或鲸鱼种群赖以生存的生态系统的保护和管理"的方案，以及旨在"检验与海洋生物资源管理没有直接关系的科学假设"的方案。[2]

---

[1] "Judgment of 31 March 2014, Whaling in the Antarctic (Australia v. Japan: New Zealand intervening)", ICJ, https://www.icj-cij.org/public/files/case-related/148/148-20140331-JUD-01-00-EN.pdf, pp. 27-29, April 14, 2023.

[2] "Judgment of 31 March 2014, Whaling in the Antarctic (Australia v. Japan: New Zealand intervening)", ICJ, https://www.icj-cij.org/public/files/case-related/148/148-20140331-JUD-01-00-EN.pdf, pp. 29-30, April 14, 2023.

第三，关于国家颁发特别许可证的权力。国际法院认为，《国际捕鲸公约》第8条赋予该公约缔约国自由裁量权，允许缔约国驳回对特别许可证的申请，或具体说明给予特别许可证的各项条件。但国际法院同时强调，凭借申请到的特别许可证捕获、击杀和加工处理鲸鱼的行为是否以科学研究为目的，这一问题不能简单地依据该国的看法而定。

第四，关于适用于第8条第1款下授权捕获、击杀和加工处理鲸鱼的特别许可证发放的审查标准。国际法院认为，首先，应评估这些活动所属的方案是否涉及科学研究；其次，在采用致命性方法的问题上，应考虑方案的设计和执行工作对实现其既定目标而言是否合理。国际法院同时明确，在适用上述审查标准时，法院无意解决科学政策或捕鲸政策问题。国际社会的成员对于鲸及捕鲸的适当政策持有不同观点，但这些分歧不应交由国际法院消除。本案中，法院的任务仅限于确定颁发给第二阶段日本鲸鱼研究方案的特别许可证是否在《国际捕鲸公约》第8条第1款规定的范围之内。[1]

第五，关于第8条下"以科学研究为目的"的含义。国际法院认为，"科学研究"和"以……为目的"在第8条这一用语中为叠加一体的两个要素。因此，除非相关活动是以科学研究"为目的"的，否则即便捕鲸方案涉及科学研究工作，根据此类方案对鲸鱼进行捕获、击杀和加工处理依然不符合第8条的规定。

对于要素一的"科学研究"，国际法院指出，《国际捕鲸公约》并未对"科学研究"一词作出界定。而据澳大利亚所提供的专家意见，《国际捕鲸公约》下的"科学研究"应具备4项基本特征：确定的和可实现的目标（问题或假设）；旨在增长对于种群保护和管理具有重要意义的知识；"适当的方法"，包括在其他任何手段均无法实现研究目标时，方可采用致命性方法；避免对种群产生不良影响。这一专家意见并未得到法院的认同。国际法院认为，第8条所指的"科学研究"不必符合澳大利亚提出的4项标准。这些标准更多反映出澳大利亚专家对于严谨的科学研究的认知，而不能作为对《公约》所用术语的解释。同时，国际法院也并不认为有必要针对"科学研究"制定新的标准或提出普遍定义。[2]

---

[1] "Judgment of 31 March 2014, Whaling in the Antarctic (Australia v. Japan; New Zealand intervening)", ICJ, https://www.icj-cij.org/public/files/case-related/148/148-20140331-JUD-01-00-EN.pdf, pp. 30-32, April 14, 2023.

[2] "Judgment of 31 March 2014, Whaling in the Antarctic (Australia v. Japan; New Zealand intervening)", ICJ, https://www.icj-cij.org/public/files/case-related/148/148-20140331-JUD-01-00-EN.pdf, pp. 32-36, April 15, 2023.

对于要素二"以……为目的"的含义，国际法院首先明确，一项研究方案所述的研究目标是该方案设计的基础，但一方面，法院无须通过评判这些目标的科学价值或重要性来评估根据此项方案捕杀鲸鱼的目的，另一方面，法院也无须判定相关方案的设计和执行工作是否为实现其既定目标的最佳可行方式。为确定方案采用致命性方法是否以科学研究为目的，国际法院将分析方案设计和执行工作中的某些内容对实现其既定目标而言是否合理。这些内容包括：关于采用致命性方法的决定；方案采用致命性取样的范围；确定样本数量的方法；目标样本数量和实际获取量的对比；与方案有关的时间框架；方案的科学产出；方案与相关研究项目的协作水平。

针对澳大利亚提出的认定一个研究方案是否"以科学研究为目的"的两大特征，国际法院认为：其一，关于鲸鱼肉能否售出。本案当事国和参加诉讼国都认同，第8条第2款允许加工处理和出售由于根据第8条第1款发放的特别许可证捕杀鲸鱼而产生的鲸鱼肉。若一项研究方案出售鲸鱼肉和利用售卖所得资助研究工作，仅凭这一点并不足以认定特别许可证不符合第8条的规定。尤其需要考虑，缔约国为资助获得特别许可证的研究工作，采用致命性取样的范围不得超出实现方案既定目标所需的合理范围。其二，关于追求科学研究以外的目标是否会与第8条相悖。国际法院认为，国家在推行某项政策时往往会争取同时实现多项目标。客观地检验一项方案是否用于科学研究并不取决于个别政府官员的意图，而是取决于该项方案的设计和执行与实现所述研究目标的关系是否合理。因此，国际法院认为，无论某些政府官员是否怀有科学研究之外的动机，都不能排除某项方案符合第8条意义下的"以科学研究为目的"。与此同时，若该方案采用致命性取样的范围超出了实现这一方案既定研究目标所需的合理范围，上述动机也不能为对此类方案发放特别许可证的行为作出合理解释。一项方案的研究目标本身即必须足以证明方案的设计和执行确当无误。[1]

基于上述对《国际捕鲸公约》第8条及其关键术语的解析结论，国际法院在考察日本采用致命性方法的政策决定、第二阶段日本鲸鱼研究方案采用致命性取样的范围、第二阶段日本鲸鱼研究方案的设计和执行工作的其他关联方面后，最终认定：尽管第二阶段日本鲸鱼研究方案开展的活动可以被笼统地定性为科学研究，但相关证据没能证明该方案的设计和执行工作对实现

---

[1] "Judgment of 31 March 2014, Whaling in the Antarctic (Australia v. Japan; New Zealand intervening)", ICJ, https://www.icj-cij.org/public/files/case-related/148/148-20140331-JUD-01-00-EN.pdf, pp. 36-38, April 15, 2023.

其既定目标而言是合理的。因此,日本颁发给第二阶段日本鲸鱼研究方案的捕获、击杀和加工处理鲸鱼的特别许可证不符合《国际捕鲸公约》第8条第1款规定的"为科学研究的目的"。在这一结论之下,国际法院在判决中进一步裁定,日本应撤销与第二阶段日本鲸鱼研究方案有关的,关于捕获、击杀和加工处理鲸鱼的任何现有授权、许可或特许,而且今后不得再根据该项方案,颁发《国际捕鲸公约》第8条第1款规定的许可证。[1]

---

[1] "Judgment of 31 March 2014, Whaling in the Antarctic (Australia v. Japan: New Zealand intervening)", ICJ, https://www.icj-cij.org/public/files/case-related/148/148-20140331-JUD-01-00-EN.pdf, pp. 71, 76-78, April 15, 2023.

六、国际海洋合作

（一）海洋防务合作

在经历了从依附英国到追随美国再到尝试区域独立的战略转变之后，澳大利亚在其《2013年国防白皮书》（2013 Defence White Paper）中首次正式提出"印太战略"。[1] 自此，"印太"概念开始频繁在澳大利亚的外交和防务政策中出现。随着《2016年国防白皮书》（2016 Defence White Paper）、《2020年国防战略更新》（2020 Defence Strategic Update）、《2020年部队结构规划》（2020 Force Structure Plan）的不断修订充实，澳大利亚于2023年4月发布《国防战略评论》（Defence Strategic Review 2023）将印太地区明确为其"关键性战略地理框架"（key strategic geographical framework），并将该地区力量对比的深刻变化和主要势力间的竞争作为主导防务策略的唯一核心背景。在印太地区加深与伙伴国间的外交与防务合作已进入澳大利亚政府国防工作的优先列表，而作为四面环海国，海洋防务合作无疑是澳大利亚实现相关目标及规划的最优先项。

在有关海洋防务合作的现状及预期中，美国一直并仍然将是澳大利亚海洋安全与防务合作中的最重要伙伴，通过包括核潜艇、部队轮换在内的军备及军工合作，该地位还将进一步提升；深化与太平洋地区包括东南亚伙伴国的接触与合作，是澳大利亚海洋防务合作的第二重心；拓展与日本和印度等主要大国的关系和务实合作，是稳固其印太地区防务架构的另一关键方向。[2]

1. 与美国的合作

澳美军事同盟起步于1951年《澳新美安全条约》（Security Treaty between Australia, New Zealand and the United States of America, ANZUS）。《澳新美安全条约》是澳外交和防务政策的基石，也将与美国间的紧密合作确立为澳大利亚保证自身安全的最重要的外部力量。澳美军事同盟使得澳大利亚积

---

[1] "2013 Defence White Paper", Parliament of Austrailia, https：//www. aph. gov. au/About_Parliament/Parlia-mentary_Departments/Parliamentary_Library/pubs/rp/rp1516/DefendAust/2013，June 7, 2023.

[2] "National Defence: Defence Strategic Review 2023", Australian Defence, https：//www. defence. gov. au/a-bout/reviews-inquiries/defence-strategic-review, pp. 7, 8, 18, June 7, 2023.

极支持美国参与亚太事务。如，冷战后每次澳大利亚对华政策的调整几乎都与美国对华政策紧密相关。而在数次因台海危机导致中美关系紧张之时，都不乏澳大利亚的积极介入。在中美因南海撞机事件关系紧张之时，澳大利亚3艘舰艇驶过台湾海峡，被认为是澳海军为"配合美国在东亚加强军事前沿部署"而实施的一次典型行动。[1]

除了在越南战争、印尼—马来西亚对抗（Konfrontasi conflict）、"9·11"后反恐战争等军事行动中援引或试图援引这一条约框架，澳美两国的日常海洋防务合作实践主要体现在：第一，澳美年度部长级磋商（Australia-U. S. Ministerial Consultations, AUSMIN）；第二，相关情报及技术共享；第三，部队轮换及其他军事交流项目；第四，国际性军事演习或实战演练。[2]

其中，在澳美两国外长与防长间定期举行的部长级磋商，是两国交换对全球及地区政治事务意见、加强对外安全和防务合作的首要双边对话平台。自1985年首轮对话开始，该部长级磋商已经持续了近40年，并成功开展了33次。在2023年7月的第33届澳美外长、防长的部长级磋商中，双方重申将致力于强化跨陆、海、空领域的兵力合作，继续合作升级在澳大利亚北部的皇家空军基地，在澳大利亚轮换美国海军海上巡逻和侦察飞机，以加强空中合作、增强地区海域意识，并吸引更多"伙伴"方的加入；将大力发展后勤、维持和养护联合工业，筹备在昆士兰州建立一个长期后勤支援区，以加强两国部队互操性和快速应对区域危机的能力；将密切合作以确定可以扩大双边合作的领域和活动范围，在关岛和印太其他地区加强与一体化反导防空系统相关的军事演习的业务合作。[3]

在军备建设方面，澳美双边防务合作在近10年不断扩大深化。2019年，澳大利亚海军的"布里斯班号"防空驱逐舰在美国完成了"宙斯盾"战斗系统的首次海外部署测试，包括首次使用美国军舰远程提供的遥测技术并练习对目标实施打击。[4] 2021年9月，"美英澳三方安全伙伴关系"成立，旨在

---

[1] 苏浩：《从哑铃到橄榄：亚太合作安全模式研究》，世界知识出版社2003年版，第112页。

[2] "The National Museum of Australia", The National Museum of Australia, https：//www. nma. gov. au/defin-ing-moments/resources/anzus-treaty, August 8, 2023.

[3] "AUSMIN fact sheet: dates and locations", The Australian Department of Foreign Affairs and Trade, https：// www. dfat. gov. au/geo/united-states-of-america/ausmin/ausmin-fact-sheet-dates-and-locations, August 8, 2023; "Joint Statement on Australia-U. S. Ministerial Consultations（AUSMIN）2023", U. S. Department of State, https：//www. state. gov/joint-statement-on-australia-u-s-ministerial-consultations-ausmin-2023/, August 8, 2023.

[4] "— RAAF takes to the skies in Guam training serials, ‖ July 2020", Australia Government DOD, https：//news. defence. gov. au/international/raaf-takes-skies-guam-training-serials, August 8, 2023.

三国间已有的双边关系基础上,加强澳大利亚政府对安全防务的支持力度,深化信息和技术共享,推动安全防务相关科技、产业基础及供应链的深度融合。这一伙伴关系的建立开启了为期 18 个月的三边磋商,所涉的两项主要倡议为:第一,承诺支持澳大利亚政府为澳大利亚皇家海军购买核动力潜艇;第二,以网络能力、人工智能、量子技术和额外的水下能力建设为重心,加强澳大利亚与美英间的军事联合能力和互操作性。[1] 2023 年 3 月,"美英澳三方安全伙伴关系"伙伴国领导人发布联合声明,表示将向澳大利亚交付由三国共同开发的 SSN-AUKUS 潜艇,并在 10 年内帮助其在国内造船厂建造该型号潜艇。为尽早实现相关常规及核动力潜艇的交付目标,美英承诺从 2023 年起安排澳大利亚军事和文职人员进入美国海军及英国皇家海军相关部门,并在美国和英国的潜艇工业基地加速培训澳大利亚技术人员。其远期目标是,预计于 2030 年后由美国向澳大利亚出售 3—5 艘"弗吉尼亚级"潜艇,于 2040 年前由英国向澳大利亚海军交付第一艘 SSN-AUKUS 潜艇,并于 2040 年后实现该类潜艇在澳大利亚的自主建造。[2]

在部队交流、军情及技术共享方面,从 2020 年 7 月 21 日开始,超过 150 名澳大利亚皇家空军人员前往美国关岛的空军基地参加"地区存在"部署。这些人员主要为空中打击部队与监视侦察部队的成员。[3] 美国计划从 2023 年开始增加攻击核潜艇对澳大利亚港口的访问,澳大利亚船员将加入美国船员的培训和发展计划。同时,美英两国都计划从 2027 年开始向澳大利亚轮换核潜艇,以加速澳大利亚海军人员、劳动力、基础设施和监管系统的发展更新,从而建立澳大利亚自主核潜艇能力。[4] 另外,双方同意在 2024 年前在澳大利亚国防情报组织内建立澳大利亚联合情报中心。该中心将进一步加强澳大利亚国防情报局和美国国防情报局之间的长期情报合作,重点分析印太地区共同关心的战略问题。[5]

---

[1] "AUKUS: The Trilateral Security Partnership Between Australia, U. K. and U. S.", U. S. Department of Defense, https://www.defense.gov/Spotlights/AUKUS/, August 8, 2023.

[2] "Joint Leaders Statement on AUKUS", The White House, https://www.whitehouse.gov/briefing-room/stat-ements-releases/2023/03/13/joint-leaders-statement-on-aukus-2/, August 8, 2023.

[3] "— RAAF takes to the skies in Guam training serials,‖ July 2020", Australia Government DOD, https://news.defence.gov.au/international/raaf-takes-skies-guam-training-serials, August 8, 2023.

[4] "AUKUS: The Trilateral Security Partnership Between Australia, U. K. and U. S.", U. S. Department of Defense, https://www.defense.gov/Spotlights/AUKUS/, August 8, 2023.

[5] "Joint Statement on Australia-U. S. Ministerial Consultations (AUSMIN) 2023", U. S. Department of State, https://www.state.gov/joint-statement-on-australia-u-s-ministerial-consultations-ausmin-2023/, August 8, 2023.

在国际化联合军演方面,"护身军刀"演习(Talisman Sabre)和"环太平洋"演习(Rim of the Pacific)是澳大利亚最为重视也最具代表性的两项海上军演行动。

"护身军刀"系列演习是由澳大利亚与美国主导并欢迎其他伙伴国加入的多国联合及多军种联合演习。该演习自 2005 年开始,每两年举办一次,主要地点为澳大利亚昆士兰州以及珊瑚海邻近的海上和空域,旨在展示澳美两国军事同盟的紧密和强大,测试和提高双方部队及伙伴国之间的联合行动能力,并增强地区内伙伴国家对澳美两国的军事信任。[1] 2023 年 7 月,由美国和澳大利亚主导、13 个国家参与、演习兵力超过 3 万人,被称为史上规模最大的"护身军刀 2023"联演在澳大利亚昆士兰州等地举行。此次演习从 7 月 22 日开始,有美国、澳大利亚、法国、英国、德国、加拿大、新西兰、斐济、巴布亚新几内亚、汤加、印度尼西亚、日本、韩国 13 个国家参演,而印度、泰国、新加坡及菲律宾则派员以观察员身份参加演习。为参加此次演习,美国派出了美国两栖准备群(ARG),包括两栖攻击舰"美国号"(LHA-6),登陆平台船坞"新奥尔良号"(LPD-18)和"绿湾号"(LPD-20),以及舰载的第 31 海军陆战队远征部队(MEU)。[2] 日本自卫队则首次在澳大利亚发射 12 式岸舰导弹,该款机动式陆基反舰导弹是日本政府 2022 年推出新版国家安保战略、允许自卫队拥有所谓"反击能力"后,日本自卫队实施远程精确打击的主要武器之一。而继 2019 年以观察员身份参演以后,韩国于 2023 年首次派出作战部队参与"护身军刀"演习,参演装备包括韩军现役吨位最大的水面舰艇——"马罗岛号"两栖攻击舰。[3] 一方面,澳大利亚海军部长表示,此类演习意在"准备共同行动,捍卫我们的安全利益,捍卫我们作为西方国家和非西方国家共同分享的核心价值观"。[4] 另一方面,针对所谓的"中国舰船监视军演"问题,澳大利亚国防部长明确回应,"中

---

[1] "Exercise Talisman Sabre", Australian Defence, https://www.defence.gov.au/exercises/talisman-sabre, August 9, 2023; "Official opening of Exercise Talisman Sabre", Australian Defence Ministers, https://www.mi-nister.defence.gov.au/media-releases/2023-07-21/official-opening-exercise-talisman-sabre, August 9, 2023.

[2] "Chinese Spy Ship Off Coast of Australia as Talisman Sabre Exercise Begins", USNI News, https://news.usni.org/2023/07/21/chinese-spy-ship-off-coast-of-australia-as-talisman-sabre-exercise-begins, August 8, 2023.

[3] 《美澳最大军演将启动,日韩赴澳大利亚测试武器》,载新浪网,https://finance.sina.com.cn/jjxw/2023-07-21/doc-imzcmfyx7689683.shtml,最后访问日期:2023 年 8 月 9 日。

[4] "Chinese Spy Ship Off Coast of Australia as Talisman Sabre Exercise Begins", USNI News, https://news.usni.org/2023/07/21/chinese-spy-ship-off-coast-of-australia-as-talisman-sabre-exercise-begins, August 8, 2023.

国舰船是符合国际法规则的,本次军演并不是在模拟对中国的战争"[1]。

"环太平洋"系列联合军事演习始于1971年,1974年后调整为每两年举办一次,号称"全球最大规模的多国联合海上演习"。与"护身军刀"演习不同,该军演由美国海军太平洋舰队领导,澳大利亚是这一系列演习的主要参加国之一。2022年6—8月,"环太平洋-2022"联合军演在夏威夷群岛、南加州及周边海域举行,旨在加强盟友间的海上合作,提升联合作战能力,巩固并维持美军印太前沿存在。此次军演由第3舰队与盟友共同开展,参演国主要包括英国、澳大利亚、加拿大和新西兰等。作为该系列的第28届演习,"环太平洋-2022"演习为期37天,共有26国约2.5万人参加,参演兵力主要包括38艘水面舰艇、4艘潜艇、约170架飞机、30多套无人系统和9支陆上部队。按照惯例,"环太平洋"系列演习课目分为多个层次,普通参演国舰艇能参与的仅限于前期的联合巡逻、海上搜救、海上拦截与登舰检查等非传统安全领域课目,只有美国的核心盟友才能参与联合作战和实弹射击环节。"环太平洋-2022"的演练内容聚焦于与战略对手的全域对抗,主要从联合反舰、两栖作战、无人系统演练、联合后勤补给4个方面,演练了面向高端海战的联合作战场景。约1600名澳大利亚国防军人员参与了此次国际海上演习,参演军舰包括"堪培拉级"两栖攻击舰、"供应号"综合补给舰、"瓦拉蒙加号"护卫舰、"海神"(P-8A Poseidon)飞机、1艘具备布雷及下潜扫雷能力的潜艇,以及1支由澳大利亚皇家团第2营带领的联合登陆部队。[2]

2. 与日本的合作

澳大利亚与日本间的双边关系早已由原来以经济性质为主逐步转向政治和安全合作层面。当前,日本是除美国之外最重要的"印太战略"构建方,而澳大利亚则是"印太战略"重要的支持者。对澳大利亚而言,澳日关系是除澳美同盟关系外最受其重视的对外大国关系之一。

2007年3月,澳大利亚与日本签署了《安全合作联合宣言》(Joint Declaration on Security Cooperation)。这是二战后日本与除美国之外的国家所签订的第一个防务协定,也是澳美签订同盟条约之后的又一个着眼于国家安全

---

[1] "Television interview, Sky News Weekend Edition", Australian Defence Ministers, https://www.minister.d-efence.gov.au/transcripts/2023-07-22/television-interview-sky-news-weekend-edition, August 8, 2023.

[2] 王金志:《多国航母云集"环太平洋2022"联合演习》,载新华网,http://www.news.cn/mil/2022-06/30/c_1211662453.htm,最后访问日期:2023年6月20日;刘从众等:《美盟"环太平洋-2022"联合军事演习情况分析》,载网易网,https://www.163.com/dy/article/HK2ES G5U0515E3KM.html,最后访问日期:2023年6月20日。

的防务协定。该宣言提出，澳日应在美日澳三边以及东盟地区论坛、东亚峰会等多边框架下强化安全合作，强调两国应强化技术、情报交流，建立外交、国防和其他有关部门间的务实对话机制，并在具体合作中明确海洋安全等为两国重点合作领域。[1] 2022年10月，澳日签署新的《安全合作联合宣言》，作为前述2007年宣言的升级版。更新后的联合宣言在重申2007年关于加强防务和安全合作承诺的基础上，将在未来10年推动两国防务和安全交流的扩大和深化，包括在防务能力方面更为密切的合作以及防务部队之间更为复杂的协同训练，为澳大利亚和日本在未来的合作提供了指引。2022年新的《安全合作联合宣言》强调，澳日之间极为重要的"特殊战略伙伴关系"是全面构建"自由开放的印太区域"的坚实支柱。两国均认为，签署新版《安全合作联合宣言》是两国战略同盟关系更为紧密的重要里程碑。[2]

在高层对话互访方面，以《安全合作联合宣言》的签署为契机，澳日两国于2007年开始定期举行由两国外长及防长参与的"2+2"安全保障磋商。2008年，两国之间的关系提升为"全方位的战略、安全、经济伙伴关系"；2009年，两国发布双边安全合作行动计划的主要内容。2022年12月，澳日第10次外长与防长"2+2"磋商在东京举行。磋商重申了2022年10月《安全合作联合宣言》中表达的雄心与愿景，既表示将重点关注双边合作的扩大和深化，也强调了美日澳三边合作的重要性，同时提出将致力于在"四方安全对话"等框架下与包括印度和美国在内的伙伴合作，以实现印太地区及其他地区的和平、稳定和繁荣。直接与海洋防务相关的磋商内容还包括：加强战略能力合作，包括远程制导武器、综合防空和导弹防御系统以及海下作战相关领域；深化合作，支持太平洋基础设施、互联互通和海上安全需求，支持加强太平洋岛国的海上安全能力；推动作战单位交流和进行更复杂的演练，加快审议日本海上自卫队和澳大利亚皇家海军之间的潜艇搜索和救援训练项目。[3]

---

[1] "安全保障協力に関する日豪共同宣言（仮訳）"，Ministry of Foreign Affairs of Japan, http://www.mo-fa.go.jp/mofaj/area/australia/visit/0703_ks.html, July 8, 2023.

[2] 《澳日签署新安全合作联合声明》，载网易网，https://www.163.com/dy/article/HKHV6M9G0553R3LX.html，最后访问日期：2023年7月12日；"Australia and Japan strengthen security cooperation", Australian Defence Ministers, https://www.minister.defence.gov.au/media-releases/2022-10-22/australia-and-japan-strengt-hen-security-cooperation, July 12, 2023.

[3] "International cooperation and defence", Australian Embassy Tokyo, https://japan.embassy.gov.au/tkyo/de-fence.html, July 12, 2023; "Tenth Japan-Australia 2+2 Foreign and Defence Ministerial Consultations", Australian Minister for Foreign Affairs, https://www.foreignminister.gov.au/minister/penny-wong/media-release/te-nth-japan-australia-22-foreign-and-defence-ministerial-consultations?_gl=1*1wy502c*_ga*MTY1MDM2ODE4OS4xNjkxNTg2OTQ0*_ga_8Z18QMQG8V*MTY5MTcxOTQyMy4yLjEuMTY5MTc0NTM5MC42MC4wLjA, July 12, 2023.

在军备及技术共享方面，2013 年，两国签署了《物品劳务相互提供协议》（Japan-Australia Acquisition and Cross-servicing Agreement，ACSA），据此日本自卫队与澳大利亚军队在行动中可共享食物、水、燃料以及其他供应；2014 年，两国签订了《防卫装备与技术转移协定》（Agreement concerning the Transfer of Defence Equipment and Technology），为日本和澳大利亚两国政府参与联合研究、联合生产国防装备、合作开发国防技术以及相关装备和技术在两国间的转让建立了法律框架。2023 年 6 月，在新加坡举行的香格里拉对话上，澳日签署了《研究、开发、测试与评估安排》（Research, Development, Test and Evaluation Arrangement），以简化两国之间进行联合技术研究和开发的程序，加快技术转移，减少审批时间，从而更有效地开发和生产防务装备。[1]

日本在澳大利亚主办或共举的各多边海上联合军演中有较多参与。除前述"护身军刀"及"环太平洋"系列演习外，两国在由美印主导的"马拉巴尔"（Malabar）海上军演中也有积极表现。"马拉巴尔"军演最初为美国与印度自 1992 年起共同举行的双边海上军事演习。2007 年，日本加入"马拉巴尔"军事演习，并在 2015 年正式成为该联合演习的固定成员。继 2007 年首次参演后，澳大利亚于 2020 年 11 月再度加入这一联合演习，此次演习也成为美、日、澳、印四方机制首次联合实施的军事演习。澳大利亚"巴拉瑞特号"护卫舰（HMAS Ballarat）以及日本"大波号"护卫舰（JS Ōnami）参加了此次演习。自此，"马拉巴尔"系列演习成为提升美、日、澳、印四国海军协同作战能力的重要演练场。[2]

澳大利亚与日本也不乏更为直接亲密的双边海上联合军事演习。2013 年 6 月，日本海军与澳大利亚海军在日本东京附近海域开展了为期 3 天的军演，此次联合演习演练了空中防御以及反潜作战等项目，澳大利亚"悉尼号"护

---

[1] "Key documents", The Australian Department of Foreign Affairs and Trade, https：//www.dfat.gov.au/geo/japan/key-documents, July 13, 2023; "Signing of the Agreement between the Government of Japan and the Government of Australia concerning the Transfer of Defence Equipment and Technology", Ministry of Foreign Affairs of Japan, https：//www.mofa.go.jp/press/release/press4e_000349.html#：~：text=This%20Agreement%20establishes%20the%20legal%20framework%20for%20the，countries%20in%20the%20areas%20of%20security%20and%20defence., July 13, 2023; "Joint Statement-Implementing our shared ambition", Australian Government, https：//www.minister.defence.gov.au/statements/2023-06-04/joint-statement-implementing-our-shared-ambition, July 13, 2023.

[2] "India Hosts Japan, Australia, U.S. in Naval Exercise MALABAR 2020［EB/OL］", US Navy, https：//www.navy.mil/Press-Office/News-Stories/Article/2402780/india-hosts-japan-australia-us-in-naval-exercise-malab-ar-2020/, July 15, 2023.

卫舰（HMAS Sydney）以及日本"村雨号"驱逐舰（Murasame）参与演习。[1] 2016年4月，澳大利亚海军和日本海军在澳大利亚新南威尔士附近海域举行联合军演，澳大利亚海军"巴拉瑞特号"（Ballarat）、"阿德莱德号"（Adelaide）和"成功号"（Success），以及日本驱逐舰"海雾号"（JS Umigiri）、"朝雪号"（JS Asayuki）和"白龙号"（JS Hakuryu）潜艇参与了反潜作战等任务，并与澳大利亚空军AP-3C"猎户座"（AP-3C Orion）和Hawk 127战机展开联合演练。[2]

3. 与印度的合作

随着双边关系的整体提升和各自海洋战略的调整，澳大利亚和印度间的海洋合作逐步加强。同为印度洋实力出众且有海洋雄心和抱负的国家，两国都确信加强彼此间海洋防务合作将会对本国安全、亚太地区稳定、印度洋乃至印太地区的地缘政治产生重要影响。

印度和澳大利亚于2008年签署了《安全与合作联合公报》（Joint Declaration on Security and Cooperation），希望通过"安全合作框架"将两国的战略观点相融合。该公报的主要内容之一是要在战略层面巩固两国海上合作的优势地位。澳大利亚是印度雄心勃勃希望成为区域"网络安全提供者"（Net Security Provider）愿景的支持者之一，其旨在通过与印度建立更深入的海上合作关系作为对华的平衡力量。[3]

两国于2011年后逐步建立起了国防部长固定对话机制、海军参谋长年度会晤机制及双边海洋安全对话机制。2011年，澳大利亚国防部长访问印度，同印度国防部长讨论了进一步推动两国防务合作特别是海洋安全合作的问题。2012年4月，印度海军参谋长访问澳大利亚。2013年6月，印度国防部长首次访问澳大利亚，双方同意定期进行防长对话，并决定于2015年举行双边海军演习。2015年10月，印度海军参谋长访问澳大利亚，并参加了澳大利亚举办的海权大会。2015年，印度与澳大利亚举行了首次双边海洋安全对话。2016年8月，印度海军参谋长与澳大利亚海军参谋长举行了包括水文地

---

[1] "HMAS Sydney and JDS Murasame Exercise off Tokyo Bay, Japan [EB/OL]", Royal Australian Navy, https://news.navy.gov.au/en/Jun2013/Fleet/51/HMAS-Sydney-and-JDS-Murasame-exercise-off-Tokyo-Bay-Japan.htm#.X9WDItgzbD4, July 15, 2023.

[2] "Australia-Japan Bilateral Exercise Concludes [EB/OL]", Royal Australian Navy, https://news.navy.gov.au/en/Apr2016/Fleet/2878/Australia-Japan-bilateral-exercise-concludes.htm#.X9WPidgzbD4, July 15, 2023.

[3] "Challenges and Prospects for India-Australia Maritime Cooperation", Kanchi Mathur, https://www.youn-g-diplomats.com/india-australia-maritime-cooperation-challenges-and-prospects/, July 16, 2023.

理、人员培训、双边演习在内的多项海洋合作会谈。2017年7月，印度海岸警卫队总司令访问了澳大利亚，与澳大利亚海上边境指挥部负责人探讨了加强合作和进行人员培训事宜。2017年10月，一支由海军副参谋长带队的印度海军代表团参加了在悉尼举行的海权大会和太平洋国际海事博览会。2017年12月，两国举行了由国防秘书和外交秘书参加的首次"2+2"会谈。

较长时间以来，澳大利亚都通过目标多样的海上演习，来加强与印度的安全合作。2015年9月，两国在孟加拉湾举行了第一次双边海军演习。演习共持续了一周，内容包括反潜、水面和防空演练、驾驶操作技术等。两国海军相关负责人都表示，两国海军在促进印度洋和平与繁荣方面享有共同利益，"这次演习发出了一个明确信号，就是双方都希望加强防务合作。这是两国海军关系取得的自然进展"[1]。在接下来的4年内，双方又于2017年、2019年进行了联合军事演习。澳大利亚驻印度高级专员表示，此类演习"是两国强有力而又不断增长的战略伙伴关系的一部分。两国应携手合作促进印太地区的和平与繁荣"[2]。2020年9月，澳印海军在东印度洋地区进行了一次"通行演习"（PASSEX）。此次演习旨在加强互操性，增强互相了解和吸收彼此最佳实践方法，再次展现出澳印作为全面战略伙伴的实力，特别是在海上领域的防务合作能力日益增强[3]。

除进行双边海军演习外，两国都还积极参加由对方主导的多国海军演习。除已知的"护身军刀""环太平洋""马拉巴尔"系列多国联合演习外，自2003年以来，澳大利亚已多次参加了由印度主导的"米兰"（Milan）海军演习。2016年12月，印度参加了由澳大利亚主导的"卡卡杜"（Kakadu）多国海军演习。2018年8月，印度再次参加了这一演习[4]。

4. 与南太平洋周边国家的合作

澳大利亚一直自视为南太平洋地区安全与经济发展的主要支柱国。为了在该地区持续推进和更新相关国防倡议，澳大利亚外交贸易部下的国际政策司特别设立加强介入印太事务的专门机构，以便通过与本地区伙伴国对话确

---

[1] The Economic Times, "India-Australia Naval Exercise 'AUSINDEX 15' to Begin Tomorrow", https://economictimes.indiatimes.com/news/defence/india-australia-naval-exercise-ausindex-15-to-begin-tomorrow/articleshow/48916014.cms, September 10, 2018.

[2] David Brewster, "The India-Australia Security and Defence Relationship: Developments, Constraints and Prospects", *Security Challenges*, Vol. 10, 2014, p. 76.

[3] 《印度澳大利亚海上联合军演：因疫情双方人员不许身体接触》，载环球网，https://world.huanqiu.com/article/400DsNPH4Zu，最后访问日期：2023年7月22日。

[4] 时宏远：《印度—澳大利亚海洋合作：动力与制约》，载《南亚研究季刊》2020年第1期，第101—102页。

六、国际海洋合作

定优先合作事项，升级防务合作计划，为太平洋区域合作国家提供量身定做的海陆训练活动，并为各太平洋岛国军队及其他安保部队的优先需求提供支持，从而实现安全、稳定和繁荣的地区目标。

一如前述，印太地区的防务伙伴关系对澳大利亚及其核心军事利益至关重要。而被称为"朋友、伙伴和盟友"的新西兰[1]，则是澳大利亚在地区内进一步推行多边主义，通过援助、救灾等方式打通防务合作路径的最重要伙伴。基于历史的同源和地缘的亲近，澳新两国在多个历史阶段的不同战场都曾并肩作战。2023年4月，澳大利亚和新西兰在军事伙伴层面升级了两国历史性的"跨塔斯曼关系"（Trans-Tasman，即"澳新关系"），达成了一项全新的"澳新军团计划"（Plan Anzac）。这一计划将允许澳大利亚和新西兰两国军队共享情报、技术和培训资源，以提高两国军队的作战能力。此外，两国还将加强在反恐、海上安全、人道主义援助等领域的合作，共同应对地区安全挑战。该计划的推出，标志着澳大利亚和新西兰两国在军事领域的合作关系迈上了一个新的台阶。两国都认为，此次升级的"澳新军团计划"将有助于两国共同应对地区安全挑战，维护地区的和平与稳定。为此，澳新两国的陆军总司令计划一同前往斐济和瓦努阿图，向这两个较小的太平洋邻国"提供其军事经验"，同时进一步解释两国的合作计划，并邀请一些较小的太平洋岛国与之合作。[2]

当前，澳大利亚在南太平洋区域的防务及海洋安全合作主要在太平洋岛国论坛（Pacific Islands Forum）的《关于地区安全的博埃宣言》（Boe Declaration on Regional Security，以下简称《博埃宣言》）区域框架下，与部分太平洋岛国间的双边军事或安全合作协定及澳大利亚本国推出的"防务合作计划"（Defence Cooperation Program）、"太平洋海上安全计划"（Pacific Maritime Security Program，以下简称"海安计划"）下展开。其中：

澳大利亚与巴布亚新几内亚的防务合作，被称为迄今为止澳大利亚与周边国家的最大防务合作规划。在"海安计划"之下，澳大利亚于2023年之前向巴布亚新几内亚移交了4艘"守护者级"巡逻艇。澳巴两国的安全和战略合作，已经延伸到警察、海关和移民相关工作中，并肩应对影响巴布亚新

---

[1] H. E. Harinder Sidhu, "Australia and New Zealand-Friends, Partners, Allies", https：//newzealand. emb-assy. gov. au/wltn/HOM_Speech_DSSC. html, July 23, 2023.

[2] 熊超然：《澳大利亚和新西兰达成"澳新军团计划"，扩大军事合作并共享情报和技术》，载观察者网，https：//www. guancha. cn/internation/2023_04_20_689131. shtml，最后访问日期：2023年6月22日；"Plan builds on partnership", Australian Defence, https：//www. defence. gov. au/news-events/news/2023-04-20/plan-builds-partn-ership, July 10, 2023.

175

几内亚、澳大利亚和周边太平洋区域的海上犯罪和安全问题。为履行《博埃宣言》的承诺，澳巴两国计划在2022—2026年通过"肩并肩"顾问、有针对性的指导及新兴领导人培训等方式推动两国警务伙伴关系建设。[1]

澳大利亚国防军和斐济军队已经依据《博埃宣言》共同部署应对区域危机。据"海安计划"，澳大利亚于2020年3月向斐济移交了1艘"守护者级"巡逻艇，并随之为斐济的斯坦利布朗码头（Stanley Brown Wharf）翻修升级提供支持。同时，与斐济合作建设海事基本服务中心（Maritime Essential Services Centre），以提高斐济的海上安全能力，加强澳斐两国在海上安全、人道主义援助和灾难救助、维和训练等领域的合作。[2]

澳大利亚于2021年11月首次启动了与所罗门群岛间的《2017年双边安全条约》。当前，澳大利亚已经通过"海安计划"向所罗门群岛交付了2艘"守护者级"巡逻艇，并通过升级奥拉基地码头（Aola Base Wharf）、建设所罗门群岛东西边境巡逻前哨，继续支持所罗门群岛内的安全稳定及其在地区秩序中的合作参与。[3]

澳大利亚分别于1989年和2022年向库克群岛赠送了2艘巡逻艇——太平洋巡逻艇"和平鸽（Dove of Peace）Ⅰ号"和"守护者级"巡逻艇"和平鸽Ⅱ号"，以协助库克群岛海警部门在本国专属经济区内执行巡航监视，提高搜索和救援能力。在"防务合作计划"下，澳大利亚还向该国提供了相应的技术和专业技能培训、行动规划支持、巡逻及持续维护的资金支持。[4]

2021年，澳大利亚向瓦努阿图赠送了1艘新的"守护者级"巡逻艇。2022年12月，澳大利亚与瓦努阿图签署双边安全协议，建立起更为密切的安全协作关系。同时，作为两国长期海上安全合作的一部分，澳大利亚将新开发的马拉基地码头（Mala Base Wharf）移交给瓦努阿图，以满足巡逻艇的系泊基础设施要求，并随赠了1艘警用船。[5]

---

[1] "Australia-Papua New Guinea engagement", The Australian Department of Foreign Affairs and Trade, https://www.dfat.gov.au/geo/papua-new-guinea/australia-papua-new-guinea-engagement, August 8, 2023.

[2] "Australia-Fiji engagement", The Australian Department of Foreign Affairs and Trade, https://www.df-at.gov.au/geo/fiji/australia-fiji-engagement, August 8, 2023.

[3] "Pacific Engagement in Solomon Islands", The Australian Department of Foreign Affairs and Trade, https://www.dfat.gov.au/geo/solomon-islands/pacific-engagement-in-solomon-islands, August 8, 2023.

[4] "Cook Islands country brief", The Australian Department of Foreign Affairs and Trade, https://www.df-at.gov.au/geo/cook-islands/cook-islands-country-brief, August 8, 2023.

[5] "Australia's engagement in Vanuatu", The Australian Department of Foreign Affairs and Trade, https://www.dfat.gov.au/geo/vanuatu/engagement-in-vanuatu, August 8, 2023.

5. 与东南亚国家的合作

一直以来，澳大利亚都在其战略规划中，将覆盖东北印度洋、能够通过东南亚进入太平洋的邻近区域视为国家防御的首要军事利益区。确立本国"印太战略"后，东南亚国家既是澳大利亚保卫本国安全时不可忽略的北方友邦，也是维护本地区和平、安宁与繁荣的最重要区域伙伴。因此，澳大利亚在东南亚有了较为广泛、深入的长期防务伙伴关系基础，且通过东盟等区域组织机构不断加强与该区域国家的军事联系。

在相关高层对话和防务协定签署方面，澳大利亚既积极搭建与东南亚各国间的双边条约框架，也通过支持东盟防长扩大会（ADMM-Plus）寻求公开对话和促进防务合作。东盟防长扩大会聚焦海上安全、反恐、人道主义援助与灾害管理、维和行动、军事医学、人道主义排雷行动、网络安全共七大领域的务实合作，并成立相关专家工作组。澳大利亚参加了全部7个专家工作组，并与文莱共同主持了2021—2024年军事医学工作组的工作。在单个国家层面，澳大利亚在所有东盟国家都有武官或军事顾问。2006年，澳大利亚与印度尼西亚签订了第一份安全合作条约《龙目条约》（Lombok Treaty），加强了双方在国防建设、联合执法、反恐、海洋安全和应急管理等多方面的合作承诺。两国分别于2017年、2018年发表《海上合作联合声明》（Joint Declaration on Maritime Cooperation）和《海上合作行动计划》（Maritime Cooperation Plan of Action），海洋安全合作顶层设计渐趋完善。2020年2月，两国外长签署的《全面战略伙伴关系行动计划》（Plan of Action for Philippines-Australia Comprehensive Strategic Partnership）第89—110项细则，详细阐明了2020—2024年海洋安全合作的重点事项。[1] 在菲律宾方面，2007年《菲律宾与澳大利亚互访军队地位协定》（Status of Visiting Forces Agreement between the Philippines and Australia）于2012年正式生效，澳大利亚据此不断帮助菲律宾提高海防能力，以协助保障其海上边界免受威胁。[2] 2023年，澳大利亚宣布了针对菲律宾的一揽子海事合作倡议，包括为菲律宾海岸警卫队提供技术援助和能力建设支持，如为包括棉兰老岛（Mindanao Island）和平进程

---

[1] 王玥：《印太语境下澳大利亚与印度尼西亚的海洋安全合作》，载《印度洋经济体研究》2022年第4期，第71—88页、第158页。

[2] "Exploring Philippines and Australias Maritime Security Cooperation", Royal Australian Navy, https://www.navy.gov.au/sites/default/files/documents/Exploring_Philippines_and_Australias_Maritime_Security_Cooperati-on, August 8, 2023.

在内的多项倡议增加官方发展援助。[1]

在部队交流和军事演习方面，为加强同东盟国家海军的合作和交流，充分发挥海军的外交职能，澳大利亚积极派出海军舰艇访问有关国家和地区的海军基地。同时，澳大利亚十分重视海军军事人员的培训和交流，积极向东盟国家"出借军事基地"，提供军事人员培训项目，为东盟国家的约1000名军官提供了赴澳学习的机会。此外，澳大利亚还积极促成了多种形式的地区联合军事演习，如多国海军联合演习、多国海空联合演习、多国多兵种协同演习、澳新海军联合演习等。据澳大利亚国防部统计，每年澳大利亚与东南亚伙伴国家共同参与的演习约50场。其中，较具特色的机制及行动主要为"五国联防"（Five Power Defence Arrangements）和"印太奋进"（Indo-Pacific Endeavour）。[2]

"五国联防"是由澳大利亚、马来西亚、新西兰、新加坡和英国于1971年建立的地区安全机制，最初的创建动机在于防范彼时的印尼政府危及马来西亚和新加坡的安全，同时为马来西亚和新加坡之间的防务事务提供沟通渠道，并建立两国之间的战略信任。随着地区局势的演变，这一安全机制早已超越了其初始目标，成为机制内国家增强军事互信、提高军事能力、保障在印太地区集体安全的长效平台。"五国联防"机制定期举行的演习活动包括："五国之盾"（Bersama Shield）年度联合演习、"苏曼勇士"（Suman Warrior）年度地面演习、"五国团结"（Bersama Lima）联合演习、"五国联合"（Bersama PADU）演习以及"苏曼保护者"（Suman Protector）联合演习。2023年的"五国之盾"联合演习在马来西亚举行，澳大利亚派遣"海神"飞机和"空中之王"（KA350 King Air）战术机动性飞机、"澳新军团号"护卫舰（HMAS Anzac）以及约250名军人参加此次演习。[3]

"印太奋进"军事巡访演练行动由澳大利亚于2017年启动。澳大利亚希望

---

[1] "Australia Announces Maritime Cooperation Package for PH Increased Oda", Presidential Communications Office, http：//pco. gov. ph/news_releases/australia_announces-maritime-cooperation-package-for-ph-increased-o-da/，August 8，2023.

[2] "Southeast Asia", The Australian Department of Foreign Affairs and Trade, https：//www. dfat. gov. au/geo/southeast-asia#：~：text = Australia% 20has% 20broad% 2C% 20deep% 20and% 20longstanding% 20defence% 20partnerships，Australia% 20has% 20Defence% 20Attach% C3% A9s% 2FAdvisers% 20in% 20all% 20ASEAN% 20countries. ，August 8，2023.

[3] Tim Huxley, "Developing the Five Power Defence Arrangements", https：//www. iiss. org/online-analysis/online-analysis/2017/06/fpda/，July 10，2023；"Five Power Defence Arrangement exercise concludes", Australian Defence, https：//www. defence. gov. au/news-events/releases/2023-05-14/five-power-defence-arrangement-exe-rcise-concludes，July 10，2023.

通过这一本区域的年度"旗舰"(flagship)活动,确保其在本地区的"强大存在",并加强与伙伴国间的友好交流。2017年9月,首次"印太奋进"行动派遣1200多名澳大利亚军人,搭载"堪培拉级"两栖攻击舰"阿德莱德号"等6艘舰艇,在9—11月巡访文莱、柬埔寨、密克罗尼西亚联邦、印度、印度尼西亚、日本、马来西亚、菲律宾、韩国、新加坡、泰国和东帝汶共12国,并参加一系列重要军事演习。2022年及2023年,"印太奋进"行动范围扩展为东南亚的14个国家[1],澳大利亚投身其中与印度等多个国家进行联合训练,并在菲律宾等国参与了联合军演,同时通过研讨会、体育赛事和文化活动等,围绕人道主义救灾救援、性别平等、和平与安全等议题进行了交流。[2]

6. 与中国的合作

中澳军事交往始于1978年。1982年,中澳开始互派武官。1994年,澳大利亚在其国防白皮书中提出,"支持中国以各种方式参与区域安全对话,维护该地区的稳定"[3]。自此,澳大利亚正式将其与中国的互动与合作纳入本国外交计划。在这一认知之下,中澳两国的军事交往在20世纪90年代逐渐密切,两国组织的海上活动也日益频繁。1997年,中澳建立防务战略磋商机制。在双方的共同努力下,中澳防务战略磋商机制健康发展,为增进相互理解、扩大共识发挥了积极作用,推动了一系列军事交流互访和海上联训联演。2019年11月,中央军委联合参谋部参谋长李作成访问澳大利亚并主持了中澳两军第22次防务战略磋商。

在军事交流互访方面,1996年9月,澳大利亚国防军司令对中国进行了正式友好访问。1997年,澳皇家空军参谋长、国防军副司令相继访华。此后至2020年前,中澳基本实现了两国防长及军队领导人的年度高级别互访。1997年8月底,澳海军3艘军舰访问青岛。1998年5月,中国海军3艘军舰访问悉尼。

---

[1] 这14个国家是孟加拉国、文莱、柬埔寨、印度、印度尼西亚、老挝、马来西亚、马尔代夫、菲律宾、新加坡、斯里兰卡、东帝汶、泰国和越南。"Indo-Pacific Endeavour 2023 to strengthen regional partnerships", Australian Defence, https://www.defence.gov.au/news-events/releases/2023-07-05/indo-pacific-endea-vour-2023-strengthen-regional-partnerships, July 12, 2023.

[2] "Indo-Pacific Endeavour", Australian Defence, https://www.defence.gov.au/operations/indo-pacific-endeav-our, July 12, 2023;"Task Group deployment to strengthen regional military cooperation", Australian Defence Ministers, https://www.minister.defence.gov.au/media-releases/2017-09-04/task-group-deployment-strengthe-n-regional-military-cooperation, July 12, 2023.

[3] "The Defence of Australia (1994 Defence White Paper)", Parliament of Australia, https://www.aph.gov.au/About_Parliament/Parliamentary_Departments/Parliamentary_Library/pubs/rp/rp1516/DefendAust/1994#:~:text=The%20Keating%20Government%20tabled%20the%201994%20Defence%20White, engagement%20with%20regional%20neighbours%20and%20the%20United%20States., July 18, 2023.

1998—2000年，澳舰艇编队连续3年访问上海。2001年10月，中国海军舰艇编队访问悉尼港。2005年4月，澳海军"堪培拉号"护卫舰访问湛江和上海。2010年9月，澳海军"瓦拉蒙加号"护卫舰访问青岛、湛江。同月，中国海军舰艇编队访澳。2012年3月，中国人民解放军总参谋长助理戚建国中将访澳。5月，澳海军"巴拉瑞特号"护卫舰访问上海港。同月，由"益阳号"、"常州号"2艘新型导弹护卫舰、"千岛湖号"综合补给舰组成的中国海军第12批护航编队访问悉尼。2016年11月，海军"郑和号"训练舰访澳。2018年9月，澳海军"墨尔本号"护卫舰访问湛江。2019年4月，澳海军"墨尔本号"护卫舰访问青岛，并参加了中国人民海军成立70周年海上阅兵活动。同年6月，中国海军第31批护航编队访问澳大利亚悉尼。[1]

在联合军事学习方面，2004年10月，中国和澳大利亚海军在青岛附近黄海海域首次举行联合演习，中国北海舰队"哈尔滨号"导弹驱逐舰和澳大利亚海军"安扎克号"导弹护卫舰参加军演。这是中澳两军首次进行非传统安全领域的合作。2007年10月，海军北海舰队副参谋长率中国海军舰艇编队访澳，并与澳大利亚、新西兰海军举行海上联合搜救演习。2011年11月，中澳两军在成都举行首次人道主义救援减灾联合演练。在2012年后的5年间，中澳海上联合训练行动尤为频繁。2013年8月，中、澳、新、美在新西兰克赖斯特彻奇（Christchurch）举行"凤凰精神—2013"四边人道主义救援减灾联合室内推演；同年9月，中澳军事文化友谊周在澳举行；同年10月，中国海军舰艇应邀赴澳参加"国际海上阅兵式"活动，并与澳海军共同参加了海上安全联合演练。2015年10月，澳2艘军舰访问湛江，并与我国海军舰船举行海上联演。除上述单项活动外，中澳间的系列联训联演还包括：

第一，"熊猫袋鼠"中澳双边联训。该联训是一项中澳年度军事交流项目，被认为是中澳两国军队保持良性互动、加深相互了解、增进彼此信任的重要平台。第二，"合作精神"系列联合演练。该联合演练是中澳参与的非战争军事行动领域的军事合作项目之一，旨在提升演练国军队应对非传统安全问题的行动能力。2012年10月，中国、澳大利亚、新西兰三国军队在澳大利亚共同举行"合作精神—2012"三边人道主义救援减灾联合演练。2015年起，美国加入该联合演练，将其扩展为四边人道主义救援减灾联合室内推

---

[1]《中澳磋商防务战略澳方首次由国防军司令参加》，载新浪网，http://news.sina.com.cn/c/2008-07-21/012314191159s.shtml，最后访问日期：2023年7月21日；《中国同澳大利亚的关系》，载中华人民共和国外交部网站，https://www.mfa.gov.cn/web/gjhdq_676201/gj_676203/dyz_681240/1206_681242/sbgx_681246/，最后访问日期：2023年7月21日。

演。"合作精神—2015"至"合作精神—2017"分别在澳大利亚、新西兰、中国南京举行。[1]

必须明确的是，美澳同盟被澳大利亚视为外交与防务政策的基石，尽管澳大利亚一直尝试寻求在中美之间保持"平衡"，但在中美关系发生深刻变化的背景下，澳大利亚在中美之间的选择倾向越来越明显，澳大利亚对中国发展强大的焦虑和不安全感也在不断被"唤醒"。澳大利亚政府近年来在南海问题及台湾、香港等问题上与美国同步的捆绑表态，给中澳关系蒙上了阴霾，也使得中澳防务合作推进在2020年后遭遇波折。尽管澳大利亚在其2023年《国防战略评论》中承认"一个稳定的澳中关系符合两国和本地区的利益"，却也谨慎地表示澳大利亚将仅在"可以合作"的方面与中国合作，且并未将中国纳入其防务伙伴和防务合作的后续构想。[2]

（二）海洋油气资源合作

澳大利亚富天然气而贫石油。依据美国能源信息署（Energy Information Administration）发布的相关报告，截至2021年年底，澳大利亚已探明石油储量仅为2.4亿桶。大部分储量位于西澳大利亚州卡那封（Carnarvon）盆地和布劳斯（Browse）盆地、维多利亚州吉普斯兰（Gippsland）盆地以及北方领地地区波拿巴（Bonaparte）盆地的近海海域。[3]而在天然气方面，研究表明，该国天然气已探明可采储量达3.7万亿立方米，居全球第10位，天然气储采比67.6年。澳大利亚大陆内部常规油气资源储量规模小，探明程度高，储量增长潜力有限，有利储量增长点主要位于该国西北大陆架（North West Shelf）。由此，一方面，深水海域天然气勘探及液化天然气开发成为澳大利亚国际油气合作最具前景的两个领域；另一方面，海域天然气勘探成本高，风险相对较大，同时受海洋环境保护的政策趋向与舆论压力的影响，澳大利

---

[1]《中澳首次举行联合军演获得巨大军事财富》，载新浪网，http://mil.news.sina.com.cn/2004-10-19/1047236079.html，最后访问日期：2023年7月21日；《"合作精神—2012"中澳新人道主义救援减灾实兵联合演练闭幕》，载中国军网，http://photo.chinamil.com.cn/pla/2012-10/31/content_5677537.htm，最后访问日期：2023年7月21日；《中国同澳大利亚的关系》，载中华人民共和国外交部网站，https://www.mfa.gov.cn/web/gjhdq_676201/gj_676203/dyz_681240/1206_681242/sbgx_681246/，最后访问日期：2023年7月21日。

[2] "National Defence: Defence Strategic Review 2023", Australian Defence, https://www.defence.gov.au/about/reviews-inquiries/defence-strategic-review, June 7, 2023.

[3] "Country Analysis Executive Summary: Australia", U.S. Energy Information Administration (EIA), https://www.eia.gov/international/content/analysis/countries_long/Australia/australia.pdf, July 13, 2023.

亚海洋油气合作开发的规模难免受限。[1]

在天然气开发项目的商业合作领域，西北大陆架项目是澳大利亚最大的液化天然气生产项目，年产能为1690万吨；其次是戈尔贡（Gorgon，又译为"高更"）项目，年产能为1560万吨；而惠斯通（Wheatstone）项目、"依系"（Ichthys）项目及"序曲"（Prelude）项目则是近年来较具代表性的新开发合作项目。[2]

西北大陆架项目位于澳大利亚西北海岸的卡那封盆地，是澳大利亚第一个液化天然气项目，从1989年开始将海上天然气、石油和凝析油开采输送至澳大利亚及国际市场。该项目由5家公司共同参与经营，其主要经营方为澳大利亚最大的独立石油天然气公司伍德赛德能源公司（Woodside Energy），其占有该项目33.33%的份额。余下份额由4家外国公司或合资公司平均分配，分别是：英国石油澳大利亚发展有限公司（BP Australia Developments Pty Ltd）、雪佛龙澳大利亚有限公司（Chevron Australia Pty Ltd）、日本澳大利亚液化天然气有限公司（Japan Australia LNG Pty Ltd）、壳牌澳大利亚有限公司（Shell Australia Pty Ltd）。当前，中国海洋石油集团有限公司也进入了西北大陆架合资业务，但并未参与该项目的基础设施建设。[3]

戈尔贡项目是世界最大液化天然气项目之一，也是澳大利亚历史上最大的单一资源项目。该项目位于西澳大利亚州巴罗岛（Barrow Island），其戈尔贡油田于1980年由西澳大利亚石油有限公司（West Australian Petroleum Pty Ltd）发现，2009年开始建设模块化液化天然气工厂，2016年正式向外输送液化天然气。目前，该项目的国内工厂每天向西澳大利亚州供应300兆焦耳能量的天然气，是澳大利亚经济的重要支柱，也是全球清洁燃料供应方。戈尔贡项目以雪佛龙澳大利亚有限公司为主要经营商，包括埃克森美孚公司（Exxon Mobil）、壳牌澳大利亚有限公司、日本大阪燃气有限公司（Osaka Gas Limited Company）、日本东京燃气有限公司（Tokyo Gas Limited Company）等

---

[1] 杜贵超、仓辉、胡双全等：《澳大利亚油气资源潜力及油气合作前景》，载《海峡科技与产业》2016年第2期，第72—73页。

[2] "LNG Majors Seek To Avoid Strikes At Australian Projects", Irina Slav, https://oilprice.com/Latest-En-ergy-News/World-News/LNG-Majors-Seek-To-Avoid-Strikes-At-Australian-Projects.html, July 13, 2023; "Australian LNG Export Projects", Incorrys, https://incorrys.com/liquefied-natural-gas-lng-forecast/australian-lng-p-rojects/, July 13, 2023.

[3] "NORTH WEST SHELF", Woodside Energy, https://www.woodside.com/what-we-do/australian-operations/north-west-shelf, July 13, 2023; "Participants", NWSG, http://www.nwsg.com.au/project-and-operations/parti-cipants/, July 13, 2023.

六、国际海洋合作

在内的多国多家公司共同参与其中。[1]

惠斯通项目被称为澳大利亚第一个天然气枢纽。2004年8月，位于澳大利亚西北海岸约225公里处的惠斯通气田被发现。2009年，惠斯通项目进入前端工程的设计和建设阶段。该项目液化天然气1号线和2号线分别于2017年10月和2018年6月成功投产，并于2019年3月开始国内天然气的商业生产。当前，惠斯通项目由1个海上油气平台、1个陆上处理厂、1个国内天然气工厂及相关基础设施组成，负责开发和处理来自惠斯通气田、埃古（Iago）气田、朱力马（Julimar）气田和布鲁内罗（Brunello）气田的天然气。惠斯通海上油气平台则是迄今为止在澳大利亚安装的最大海上天然气处理平台，其上部重量约为37000吨，也是雪佛龙澳大利亚有限公司在全球交付的最大的浮式装置。惠斯通项目由雪佛龙澳大利亚有限公司主导经营，由科威特外国石油勘探公司（Kuwait Foreign Petroleum Exploration Company）、伍德赛德能源公司、日本九州电力公司（Kyushu Electric Power Company）以及由日本JERA公司部分控股的PE惠斯通有限公司（PE Wheatstone Limited Company）合作管理开发。[2]

"依系"液化天然气项目于2018年正式投产，是世界上最大、最复杂的液化天然气项目之一。为开发距西澳大利亚州北部海岸约220公里的海上油气田，该项目建造了南半球最长的输气管道，横跨882公里的海洋和8公里的陆地。该大型液化天然气项目以日本国际石油开发帝石控股公司（INPEX）和法国道达尔能源公司（Total Energies）为主要经营方，日本东京燃气有限公司、日本大阪燃气有限公司、日本关西电力有限公司（Kansai Electric Power Limited Company）、东邦燃气有限公司（Toho Gas Limited Company）等也参与其中。"依系"液化天然气项目于2018年10月开始商业化生产，并开始凝析油和液化天然气运输。[3]

位于布劳斯盆地的"序曲"项目中有世界上最大的浮式液化天然气设施。该项目以2007年发现的序曲气田和协奏曲（Concerto）气田为主要开采

---

[1] "the gorgon project", Chevron Australia, https://australia.chevron.com/our-businesses/gorgon-project, July 13, 2023.

[2] "Australia's first natural gas hub", Chevron, https://www.chevron.com/projects/wheatstone, July 13, 2023; "WHEATSTONE", Woodside Energy, https://www.woodside.com/what-we-do/operations/wheatstone-project, July 13, 2023.

[3] "Ichthys LNG Project", NS Energy, https://www.nsenergybusiness.com/projects/ichthys-lng-project/, July 13, 2023; "Ichtys: a bold LNG project off the coast of Australia", Total Energies, https://totalenergies.com/energy-expertise/projects/oil-gas/lng/ichthys-a-bold-lng-project-off-the-coast-of-australia, July 13, 2023.

对象，于 2012 年 10 月开工建设，2018 年 12 月正式投入生产。该项目由壳牌澳大利亚有限公司主导运营，日本国际石油开发帝石控股公司、韩国天然气公司（Korea Gas Corporation）等公司与之共同拥有和开发。"序曲"项目每年生产 530 万吨液化气和凝析油，包括 360 万吨液化天然气、130 万吨凝析油和 40 万吨液化石油气。[1]

（三）海洋渔业合作

澳大利亚拥有全世界第三大专属经济区，是世界上最重要的渔业国家之一，其海洋渔业也相当发达，海洋渔业产值和海洋渔业的就业贡献，在澳大利亚海洋经济发展中占有重要位置。自 20 世纪 80 年代将海产品出口转向亚洲市场以来，澳大利亚的渔业出口额不断实现飞跃式增长。与此同时，海水养殖产值呈现逐步上升趋势。2021—2022 年，澳大利亚渔业和水产养殖总产值增长了 9%；2023—2024 年，澳大利亚渔业和水产养殖总产值预计仍将增长 0.5%，达到 35.6 亿美元。[2] 澳大利亚海洋生物资源的合作开发具有较大潜力。与此同时，为了确保渔业活动对受保护物种和海洋环境的影响降至最低，保护澳大利亚海洋生态的多样性，澳大利亚尤其重视海洋渔业捕捞监管，并有着良好口碑和成效。无论是海洋生物资源的商业捕捞，还是海洋渔业的监测监控，澳大利亚都主要在区域性国际组织和多边条约框架下推进和实现相关国际合作。[3]

通过区域性渔业管理组织和多边条约，澳大利亚与缔约他方合作提供相关科学建议、制定捕捞限额和捕捞控制程序、评估相应规则遵守和义务履行情况、协调在相关海域的数据监测与行为监管，共同推进国际渔业生产、鱼类种群养护及关联环境影响等的可持续管理。在区域性渔业管理组织中积极

---

[1] 周乐萍：《澳大利亚海洋经济发展特性及启示》，载《海洋开发与管理》2021 年第 9 期，第 5 页；"Australian fisheries and aquaculture outlook 2024", The Australian Department of Agriculture, Fisheries and Forestry, https：//www.agriculture.gov.au/abares/research-topics/fisheries/fisheries-economics/fisheries-forecasts, July 14, 2024.

[2] 周乐萍：《澳大利亚海洋经济发展特性及启示》，载《海洋开发与管理》2021 年第 9 期，第 5 页；"Australian fisheries and aquaculture outlook 2023", The Australian Department of Agriculture, Fisheries and Forestry, https：//www.agriculture.gov.au/abares/research-topics/fisheries/fisheries-economics/fisheries-forecasts#：~：text=Following%20a%20strong%20post-pandemic%20recovery%20in%202021%E2%80%9322%2C%20the，vol-ume%20and%20prices%20for%20prawns%2C%20oysters%20and%20tuna.，July 14, 2023.

[3] "Managing Australian fisheries", The Australian Department of Agriculture, Fisheries and Forestry, https：//www.agriculture.gov.au/agriculture-land/fisheries/domestic/managing-australian-fisheries, July 14, 2023.

参与相关活动，确保了对澳大利亚渔民目标种群（targeted stocks）的可持续管理。对于可共享的高度洄游物种渔获，澳大利亚合作的主要区域性组织是中西太平洋渔业委员会、南方蓝鳍金枪鱼养护委员会以及印度洋金枪鱼委员会；对于非高度洄游物种渔获，澳大利亚所依托的组织或条约框架主要为南太平洋区域渔业管理组织、《南印度洋渔业协定》以及南极海洋生物资源养护委员会。除此之外，其他可作为合作框架的国际性或区域性渔业机构或条约安排还包括：太平洋岛国论坛渔业局、《关于南太平洋区域渔业监督和执法合作的纽埃条约》（Niue Treaty on Cooperation in Fisheries Surveillance and Law Enforcement in the South Pacific Region）及其后的《纽埃条约附属协定》（Niue Treaty Subsidiary Agreement）、《促进负责任捕捞活动（包括打击本区域非法、不报告和不管制捕捞）的区域行动计划》（Regional Plan of Action to Promote Responsible Fishing Practices including Combating Illegal, Unreported and Unregulated Fishing in the Region，以下简称《区域行动计划》）等。[1]

在上述框架下，澳大利亚与周边太平洋岛国展开紧密合作，支持太平洋渔业生产的可持续发展，从而帮助合作国家维持经济发展、粮食安全和民生健康。每年，澳大利亚分别向太平洋岛国论坛渔业局和太平洋共同体（Pacific Community）提供500万美元及300万美元的援助。通过支持区域性渔业管理组织，澳大利亚帮助太平洋岛国对生存性捕捞和商业性捕捞进行有效治理，并从有益于生态保护的可持续性管理机制中获益。如，通过太平洋岛国论坛的合作关系，协助确保所有太平洋岛国从金枪鱼的可持续利用中受益；通过在太平洋共同体下的合作，为高价值近海鱼类资源的养护、沿海渔业的良性发展以及沿海国粮食安全提供科学监测和评估；通过澳大利亚国际农业研究中心（Australian Centre for International Agricultural Research）为各太平洋岛国的社区渔业管理和水产养殖援助提供支持，其第3阶段（2020—2024年）的支持经费为800万美元，将为基里巴斯、所罗门群岛和瓦努阿图扩展和更新当地渔业管理方案。同时，澳大利亚在与太平洋岛国合作共同打击本地区非法、不报告和不管制捕捞活动方面有着悠久的历史。通过太平洋岛国论坛渔业局、国际渔业管理组织系统以及澳大利亚"海安计划"的协调合作，共同应对非法、不报告和不管制捕捞活动的挑战，确保域内外船只实施本区域内国家及地区为管理渔业资源而采取的措施，保证太平洋鱼类资源管

---

[1] "International Engagement", Australian Fisheries Management Authority, https://www.afma.gov.au/fisheri-es-management/international-fisheries-management/international-engagement, July 14, 2023.

理有序，维护海上安全。[1]

　　澳大利亚与东南亚的渔业管理合作则主要在《区域行动计划》框架下运行。《区域行动计划》是澳大利亚和印度尼西亚联合倡议的成果，于 2007 年 5 月由 11 个国家的渔业部长商定，旨在加强和深化东南亚海域有关渔业管理和海洋治理的合作。《区域行动计划》强调了非法、不报告和不管制捕捞活动在世界各国海事管辖区中的复杂性，明确区域行动的协调是打击非法、不报告和不管制捕捞活动的较优解。以促进负责任捕捞活动相关国际条约及其他法律文件为基础，《区域行动计划》的目标是提升该地区渔业管理的总体水平，既协助实现各国捕鱼能力的现代化，又督促框架下合作各方采用负责任的捕鱼措施。在该计划下组织的协调委员会（Coordination Committee）每年均举行会议，讨论决定战略合作方向和优先事项，更新《区域行动计划》的年度工作计划，以加强法律、行政和政策框架为重点，不断调整措施以加强区域及国际合作，尤其在监测、控制和督查渔业合规作业等方面取得了较好的工作成果。当前，已形成的主要成果性文件包括：（1）东南亚渔业发展援助框架，该成果报告帮助指导供资机构为渔业机构提供财政援助，以便相关投入有效用于野生捕捞渔业管理及渔业科学各方面的能力建设和培训；（2）东南亚示范渔业立法框架，该成果报告逐一分析各合作国家在改善区域渔业立法和打击非法捕鱼中的优势、劣势和机会。[2]

（四）海洋研究合作

　　澳大利亚为其独特的海洋地理和丰富的海洋资源而自豪，也为不断衰退的海洋生态和来源广泛的环境威胁而担忧。为应对国家蓝色经济发展路上的各种挑战，澳大利亚需要创新海洋技术，改进海洋产业的规划和管理框架，整合海洋观测系统，促进海洋知识的获取和交流，因此需要澳大利亚海洋科学界的积极参与与广泛合作带来的支持与活力。依据对《澳大利亚国家海洋

---

[1] "Pacific regional-fisheries assistance", The Australian Department of Foreign Affairs and Trade, https：//www. dfat. gov. au/geo/pacific/development-assistance/fisheries-assistance#：~：text = Australia% 20supports% 20incr-eased% 20benefits% 20to% 20Pacific% 20island% 20countries, support% 20is% 20largely% 20implemented% 20throu-gh% 20regional% 20fisheries% 20organisations. , July 15, 2023; "Regional cooperation in the Pacific", Australian Fisheries Management Authority, https：//www. afma. gov. au/fisheries-management/international-fisheries-management/regional-cooperation-pacific, July 15, 2023.

[2] "Regional fisheries issues affecting Australia", The Australian Department of Agriculture, Fisheries and Forestry, https：//www. agriculture. gov. au/agriculture-land/fisheries/international/cooperation/issues, July 15, 2023.

科学计划（2015—2025）》（Australia's National Marine Science Plan 2015 – 2025）执行进展的审查报告，澳大利亚海洋科学在制订国家海洋研究基础设施计划、加强海洋生物多样性评估和建立国家海洋公园网络等多个领域取得了重大进展，然而海洋科学研究也存在如研究资金有限等持续挑战，需要加强国际、国内多部门之间的协调与合作。[1] 澳海科所、国家海洋科学委员会（National Marine Science Committee）、澳大利亚海洋科学协会（Australian Marine Sciences Association）是澳大利亚海洋科学研究及研究合作项目开展的主要力量。其中，澳大利亚海洋科学研究所为联邦政府官方研究机构，其热带海洋研究处于世界领先地位；国家海洋科学委员会是由澳大利亚联邦和州政府海洋科学机构、学术界和工业界的代表组成的机构，重在促进利益相关者之间的合作，并就海洋科学问题向政府和其他组织提供战略指导和建议；澳大利亚海洋科学协会则是澳大利亚历史最悠久的海洋科学专业组织之一，当前已发展成澳大利亚各学科海洋科学家的主要专业协会。[2]

澳海科所成立50多年来，与60多个澳大利亚组织以及散布在25个国家的75个国际机构进行过合作，分别在国家海洋政策制定、国际合作框架、研究与发展协作项目以及相关谅解备忘录签署等方面发挥主导作用。澳海科所于2005年与澳大利亚国立大学共同设立"阿拉弗拉帝汶研究机构"（Arafura Timor Research Facility），以支持邻接澳大利亚以北阿拉弗拉海和帝汶海的印度尼西亚、巴布亚新几内亚及东帝汶等多国的海洋科学研究，同时作为北澳大利亚海洋研究联盟（North Australia Marine Research Alliance）的合作核心。[3] 该研究机构与美国国家海洋和大气管理局（National Oceanic and Atmospheric Administration）也建立了战略联盟，主要围绕全球珊瑚礁普查在国际层面上共同开展项目。当前，双方参与合作的"珊瑚礁观察"（Coral Reef Watch）项目于2005年启动，是海洋生物普查的珊瑚礁部分。该普查项目是

---

[1] Benjamin Arthur al et., "Ocean Outreach in Australia: How a National Research Facility is Engaging with Community to Improve Scientific Literacy", https://www.frontiersin.org/articles/10.3389/fenvs.2021.610115/full, July 15, 2023; "New NMSC reports guide future of Australian marine science", National Marine Science Committee, https://www.marinescience.net.au/new-nmsc-wg-reports-march-2023/, July 15, 2023.

[2] "About AIMS", The Australian Institute of Marine Science, https://www.aims.gov.au/about-aims, July 15, 2023; "National Marine Science Committee: who we are and what we do", National Marine Science Committee, https://www.marinescience.net.au/aboutnmsc/, July 15, 2023; "History", Australian Marine Sciences Association, https://www.amsa.asn.au/history, July 15, 2023.

[3] "ATRF", The Australian Institute of Marine Science, https://www.aims.gov.au/partnerships/research-partnerships/atrf, July 15, 2023.

由80多个国家的研究人员参与的一项为期10年的全球性倡议，旨在评估和解释海洋中过去、现在和未来海洋生物的多样性、分布和丰富程度。澳海科所与美国国家海洋和大气管理局通过共同部署海洋仪器将海面温度变化与珊瑚礁上的精细变化相联系，并合作改进大堡礁上的水动力模型，从而更好地研究气候变化与珊瑚健康之间的关联。[1]

除"阿拉弗拉帝汶研究机构"外，澳大利亚与连通其北部关键海域的东南亚及南亚各国一直都有较密切的海洋科研往来。2018年11月，澳大利亚詹姆斯库克大学（James Cook University）校长与菲律宾政府科技部签署了谅解备忘录。该备忘录基于澳菲两国高校在与热带地区相关的特色学科与教学联盟方面的共建需求确立了双方的合作伙伴关系，以海洋科学、生物多样性、热带生态和环境、全球变暖、旅游、热带医学和特殊人群的公共卫生保健等为重点方向，共同促进相关专题的研究共享，增加学生和科学家的交流，并加强有关改善热带地区生活的技术信息交流。[2] 同年11月，澳大利亚总理在会见印度总统时交换了对强化澳印合作的意见，双方同意设立的澳印战略研究基金，旨在帮助研究人员解决两国共同面临的问题，尤其合作应对在能源储存、海洋科学和植物基因组学等领域的新挑战。[3]

澳大利亚与中国间也有较好的海洋科研合作基础。2014年7月，海南省带队国内相关海洋与渔业科学团队访问澳大利亚。在澳海科所，中国科研人员与海科所所长一行进行了交流，并参观了澳大利亚国家海洋模拟馆。在交流中，澳海科所介绍了其在大堡礁海洋公园珊瑚礁生态与保护研究方面的成果，包括全面系统的珊瑚礁生态监测、水质监测、保护区生态评价与规划、人类活动对珊瑚礁生态的影响、珊瑚礁与全球气候变化等多个方面。海南省海洋与渔业科学院科研人员则介绍了中国方面在水产养殖研究、珊瑚礁生态监测、环境保护与保护区规划、海岸工程研究与防护、国际交流合作等领域的研究情况，并提出了今后希望开展合作的具体方向。双方在珊瑚礁生态监测、人类活动对珊瑚礁生态的影响、生态保护与评估等领域达成合作意向，

---

[1] "NOAA", The Australian Institute of Marine Science, https：//www.aims.gov.au/partnerships/research-partn-erships/noaa, July 15, 2023; "CReefs", The Australian Institute of Marine Science, https：//www.aims.gov.au/docs/about/partnerships/creefs.html, July 15, 2023.

[2] "James Cook University teams up with Philippines' Department of Science and Technology", SBS Filipino, https：//www.sbs.com.au/language/english/james-cook-university-teams-up-with-philippines-department-of-s-cience-and-technology, July 15, 2023.

[3] "Australian Government Unveils Road Map to Boost Economic Ties with India 1", SBS Filipino, https：//www.sbs.com.au/language/english/australian-government-unveils-road-map-to-boost-economic-ties-with-india_1, July 15, 2023.

并签署了合作备忘录。该合作备忘录的签署，开启了海南海洋科学研究团队与澳大利亚进行科技合作的新篇章，对于争取双方国家政府的后续支持、深化科技与人才的合作具有重要意义。[1] 2017年5月，青岛海洋科学与技术试点国家实验室（以下简称"海洋国家实验室"）和澳大利亚联邦科学与工业研发组织共建的国际南半球海洋研究中心在澳大利亚霍巴特正式启用，海洋国家实验室主任吴立新和澳大利亚联邦科学与工业研发组织首席执行官共同为中心剪彩揭牌。澳大利亚工业创新与研究部部长及中国驻悉尼总领事馆科技参赞均发文或出席表示祝贺，澳大利亚新南威尔士大学（University of New South Wales）、塔斯马尼亚大学（University of Tasmania）也派代表出席活动。国际南半球海洋研究中心的启用标志着海洋国家实验室全球分布式协同创新网络建设取得实质性进展，与澳大利亚的海洋科研合作进入新阶段，相关国际化战略又迈出了坚实一步。[2]

（五）区域性国际合作

1. 东盟伙伴关系与东盟地区论坛

澳大利亚于1974年成为东盟第一个对话伙伴国。通过东盟主导的东亚峰会、东盟地区论坛、东盟防长扩大会等相关安排，澳大利亚与东盟国家在东南亚及太平洋地区的贸易和经济议题合作十分密切。2021年10月，东盟与澳大利亚建立全面战略伙伴关系（Comprehensive Strategic Partnership）。澳大利亚多次表示，东盟是维持东南亚和平、稳定、繁荣和安全的中心架构，相关国家都应为该地区的战略平衡作出贡献。作为澳大利亚北部邻接海域的"关键通道"，东南亚地区及东盟国家在战略、经济及外交等方面都对澳大利亚的未来具有深远意义。而在与东盟的合作领域中，海上安全、蓝色经济及可持续发展都是双方合作的优先选项。[3]

东盟地区论坛是冷战结束后亚太国家多边安全对话需求下的外交成果。1993年7月，东盟6个成员国、7个对话伙伴国、3个观察员国和2个来宾国外长参加了"非正式晚宴"，各国外长同意召开东盟地区论坛，就地区政治安全问题举行非正式磋商。1994年7月25日，东盟地区论坛首届外长会

---

[1]《我省科技合作代表团访澳成果丰硕》，载海南省科学技术厅网站，https://dost.hainan.gov.cn/zt/kjhz/201609/t20160902_705197.html，最后访问日期：2024年7月15日。

[2]《共享发展成果，推动海洋文明——海洋国家实验室国际南半球海洋研究中心正式启用》，载《科技日报》2017年5月26日，第6版。

[3] "ASEAN and Australia", The Australian Department of Foreign Affairs and Trade, https://www.dfat.gov.au/geo/southeast-asia/asean-and-australia, July 16, 2023.

在泰国曼谷召开。目前，东盟地区论坛已成为亚太地区主要的官方多边安全对话与合作平台，迄今为止已举行了 31 届外长会。除每年轮流在东盟主席国举行的外长会外，东盟地区论坛还举行过 1 次高官会、1 次安全政策会议、1 次建立信任措施与预防性外交间辅助会议、5 次会间会和 2 次国防官员对话会。其中，海上安全是这 5 次会间会的主议题之一。[1]

澳大利亚是东盟地区论坛的 27 个成员国之一，也是其创始成员国。自东盟地区论坛成立以来，澳大利亚一直在反恐和跨国犯罪、信息和通信技术安全、救灾、海上安全、防扩散与裁军五大领域积极参与该论坛的相应活动。澳大利亚近期已结束了与越南和欧盟联席担任 2018—2021 年东盟地区论坛海上安全工作组主席的任期。在这一任期内，澳大利亚的主要工作成果包括：（1）于 2018 年与马来西亚和东帝汶共同主持海上安全会间会；（2）于 2020 年与越南和欧盟共同主持关于争端解决和海洋法的东盟地区论坛研讨会；（3）于 2018—2022 年连续 4 年与越南和欧盟共同主持关于加强区域海上执法合作的东盟地区论坛研讨会；（4）于 2022 年与越南和欧盟共同主持国际海事安全会议线上会；（5）于 2019 年与越南共同主持关于执行《公约》及其他法律文件以解决新兴海洋问题的两个讲习班；（6）于 2021 年与印度尼西亚和印度共同主持关于海洋法与渔业的线上讲习班。[2]

2. 太平洋岛国间区域性组织

澳大利亚是太平洋地区多个主要政治及技术组织的创始成员和积极参与者。澳大利亚在这些组织框架下推动制订了区域性规划及工作方案，以应对蓝色太平洋面临的包括气候变化、海洋健康等在内的挑战。这些组织还包括太平洋岛国论坛、太平洋共同体、太平洋区域环境规划署秘书处（Secretariat of the Pacific Regional Environment Programme）。

太平洋岛国论坛源自于 1971 年成立的"南太平洋论坛"（South Pacific Forum），于 2000 年 10 月正式更名为"太平洋岛国论坛"。包括澳大利亚在内的 18 个成员国旨在通过该组织加强成员国间在贸易、经济发展、航空、海运、电信、能源、旅游、教育等领域及其他共同关心问题上的合作和协调。近年来，该论坛尤其加强了在政治、安全等领域的对外政策协调与区域合作。太平洋岛国论坛的财政预算由澳大利亚和新西兰各支付 1/3，其余部分由其他岛

---

[1]《东盟地区论坛》，载中华人民共和国外交部网站，https://www.mfa.gov.cn/web/gjhdq_676201/gjhdqzz_681964/lhg_682614/jbqk_682616/，最后访问日期：2024 年 7 月 16 日。

[2] "ASEAN Regional Forum（ARF）", The Australian Department of Foreign Affairs and Trade, https://www.dfat.gov.au/international-relations/regional-architecture/asean-regional-forum-arf, July 16, 2023.

国成员分摊。目前，还有包括中国在内的14个非成员国家、地区及组织向该论坛秘书处提供捐助。自2014年起，澳大利亚与论坛秘书处建立了伙伴关系。通过长期向论坛秘书处提供主要资金支持，澳大利亚协助秘书处就政治治理、经济合作、安全和贸易等地区政策问题开展工作，并根据秘书处的授权，共同努力应对本地区面临的挑战。2020年，澳大利亚为论坛秘书处贡献了约36%的预算。2022—2024年，澳大利亚向该论坛提供的款项共为1872万美元。[1]

太平洋共同体于1947年依美国、英国、法国、澳大利亚、新西兰和荷兰6国签署的《堪培拉协议》（Canberra Agreement）成立，于1998年由原"南太平洋委员会"（South Pacific Commission）更名为"太平洋共同体"。该组织共有27个成员国。1983年，根据澳大利亚的提议，将原仅由美、英、法、澳等13个成员国享有的选举权扩展至全部27个成员国。当前，太平洋共同体是太平洋地区最大的科学技术性区域组织，旨在通过提供技术、科研、政策及培训相关服务来增强和补充成员国相关能力，促进南太平洋各国（地区）的经济发展、社会福利和进步，同时与其他国际组织合作，向南太平洋岛国提供经济技术援助。太平洋共同体每两年召开一届会议，制定相关政策并决定总干事人选。总干事及副总干事下设的具体项目部门有地质科学司，经济发展司，社会发展司，渔业、水产养殖和海洋生态系统司，陆地资源司，公共卫生司，发展数据司，等等。澳大利亚、美国、法国和新西兰承担了太平洋共同体会费的90%，并在会费外向该组织提供项目援助。2014年，澳大利亚与太平洋共同体建立了伙伴关系，支持共同愿景，密切合作以取得更好的发展成果，并可持续地改善所有太平洋岛国人民的生活。2020年11月，双方更新了伙伴关系协议，以更好地支持在公共卫生、渔业科学、粮食安全、教育标准、发展统计和性别平等等领域的项目合作与能力建设。2021—2023年，澳大利亚向太平洋共同体交纳会费及捐赠款项共约4250万美元。[2]

---

[1]《太平洋岛国论坛》，载中华人民共和国外交部网站，https：//www. mfa. gov. cn/web/gjhdqz_676201/gjhdqzz_681964/lhg_683142/jbqk_683144/，最后访问日期：2023年7月16日；"Pacific islands regional organisations", The Australian Department of Foreign Affairs and Trade, https：//www. dfat. gov. au/international-relations/regional-architecture/pacific-islands/pacific-islands-regional-organisation, July 16, 2023.

[2]《太平洋共同体》，载中华人民共和国外交部网站，https：//www. mfa. gov. cn/w-eb/gjhdq_676201/gjhdqzz_681964/lhg_683166/jbqk_683168/，最后访问日期：2023年7月16日；"Pacific Regional-effective regional institutions", The Australian Department of Foreign Affairs and Trade, https：//www. df-at. gov. au/geo/pacific/development-assistance/effective-governance-pacific-regional, July 16, 2023.

太平洋区域环境规划署构想最初源于20世纪70年代南太平洋委员会与联合国环境规划署间关于本区域环境管理综合方案的磋商。1980年，在联合国亚洲及太平洋经济社会委员会（Economic and Social Commission for Asia and the Pacific）的资助下，在南太平洋论坛和南太平洋委员会的联合倡议下，南太平洋区域环境规划署（South Pacific Regional Environment Programme）正式成立。1991年，在审议了南太平洋区域环境规划署的行动计划、财政状况和法律影响后，太平洋区域环境规划署获得了独立于其他南太平洋地区组织的自主地位。当前，太平洋区域环境规划署是负责保护和管理太平洋环境和自然资源的区域性组织，总部设在萨摩亚（Samoa）的阿皮亚（Apia），共26个成员方，包括对该区域有"直接利益"的5个大国（澳大利亚、法国、新西兰、英国、美国）和21个太平洋岛国及地区。

太平洋区域环境规划署的任务是促进太平洋地区的合作并提供援助，以保护和改善本区域环境，并确保今世后代的可持续发展，同时保存太平洋自然遗产，让生存和发展与海洋文化和谐共存。该机构运行的区域性目标在于：（1）使太平洋人民受益于加强对气候变化的抵御能力；（2）使太平洋人民受益于健康和有复原力的岛屿及海洋生态系统；（3）使太平洋人民受益于废物管理和污染控制的日渐改善；（4）使太平洋人民及环境受益于对环境治理的承诺和最佳实践。[1]

澳大利亚坚定支持太平洋海洋保护计划及其他区域的环境保护规划，其每年向太平洋区域环境规划署提供430万美元的核心资金以及额外的具体项目援助。澳大利亚是《澳大利亚、新西兰及太平洋岛国塑料公约》（Australian, New Zealand and Pacific Islands Plastics Pact）的主要缔约方，该区域性公约以行业为主导，以加速塑料包装的循环经济为规范核心，以减少太平洋岛国所在海域的塑料废物和污染。为打击塑料污染，澳大利亚与太平洋岛国在2021年联合国环境大会（United Nations Environment Assembly）上成功推动了新兴全球条约的谈判。2022—2024年，澳大利亚向太平洋区域环境规划署秘书处提供了共计72.9万美元的资金，用于支援相应国家能力建设和支持太平洋岛国筹备并参与条约谈判。同时，澳大利亚在该组织的"太平洋垃圾项目"（Pacific Ocean Litter Project，2019-2025）中投入了1600万美元，旨在减少海洋环境中一次性塑料的来源，通过改变塑料消费者和生产者的行为，逐步淘汰一次性塑料在本区

---

[1] "About Us", Secretariat of the Pacific Regional Environment Programme, https：//www.sprep.org/about-us, July 16, 2023；"Our Backstory", Secretariat of the Pacific Regional Environment Programme, https：//www.sprep.org/our-history, July 16, 2023.

域国家中的使用。[1]

3. 印度洋国家区域性组织

澳大利亚自视为印度洋的重要国家，以西澳大利亚州为面向印度洋的门户。作为拥有最长印度洋海岸线和最大印度洋搜救区的太平洋国家，澳大利亚致力于在该地区的机遇和挑战中发挥更具领导性的作用：通过深化区域合作，为打击恐怖主义、跨国犯罪、非法捕鱼等提供区域性办法；通过引导规则制定，促进贸易及应对气候变化挑战；通过提升建设和平的区域化能力，为印度洋区域的稳定作出贡献。为此，澳大利亚成了多个印度洋区域组织或论坛的创始成员或主要支持者。其中，印度洋海军研讨会（Indian Ocean Naval Symposium，IONS）旨在通过提供一个开放论坛来讨论区域海上安全问题，从而加强印度洋沿岸国家海军之间的海上合作。印度洋金枪鱼委员会意在督促成员国养护和管理措施的改善和落实，以确保印度洋及邻近海域金枪鱼和类金枪鱼物种的可持续和最佳利用。印度洋港口国管制备忘录组织（Indian Ocean Memorandum of Understanding on Port State Control）旨在核验进入本区域的外国船只在安全、环境等问题上对所适用国际海事公约的遵守情况。而环印度洋联盟是唯一一个通过年度外交部长会议将印度洋沿岸大多数国家联系起来的区域论坛，是澳大利亚参与的若干印度洋区域组织中最具政治和外交意义的合作框架。[2]

环印度洋联盟成立于1997年。[3]作为政府间国际组织，环印度洋联盟现有23个成员国、11个对话伙伴国及2个观察员，其秘书处设于毛里求斯的埃比尼（Ebene）。环印度洋联盟的核心任务是促进成员国间的贸易和投资，旨在通过开展一致同意的区域性合作，增进成员间特别是印度洋沿岸成员间

---

[1] "Pacific islands regional organisations", The Australian Department of Foreign Affairs and Trade, https://www.dfat.gov.au/international-relations/regional-architecture/pacific-islands/pacific-islands-regional-organisation, July 16, 2023; "Australia and the Pacific: partnering to support sustainable oceans and livelihoods", The Australian Department of Foreign Affairs and Trade, https://www.dfat.gov.au/geo/pacific/engagement/suppo-rting-sustainable-oceans-and-livelihoods, July 16, 2023.

[2] "Australia and the Indian Ocean region", The Australian Department of Foreign Affairs and Trade, https://www.dfat.gov.au/international-relations/regional-architecture/indian-ocean/Pages/indian-ocean-region, July 16, 2023; "Indian Ocean regional forums", The Australian Department of Foreign Affairs and Trade, https://www.dfat.gov.au/international-relations/regional-architecture/indian-ocean/Pages/indian-ocean-regional-forums, July 16, 2023.

[3] 环印度洋地区14国于1997年3月成立环印度洋地区合作联盟（The Indian Ocean Rim Association for Regional Cooperation，IOR-ARC）。该组织于2013年11月由其第13届部长理事会会议决定更名为环印度洋联盟（The Indian Ocean Rim Association，IORA）。

的互信与合作,为更广范围和更具深度的合作构建顺畅良好的运行机制。[1]

澳大利亚是环印度洋联盟的创始成员国之一,其积极致力于该联盟框架下的各项合作事宜,于2013—2014年担任该组织主席国。2011年班加罗尔峰会上,副主席国澳大利亚与主席国印度共同推动联盟六大优先议题的确立,海事议题便占据其中3项。澳大利亚还在2013年和2014年利用主席国身份推动女性赋权与蓝色经济两个跨领域议题成为特别关切点。在合作中,有关蓝色经济的讨论最初只包括渔业和水产养殖业、可再生海洋能源、海港和航运、离岸碳氢化合物和海床矿产4个方面,而后又扩展到深海采矿与海洋旅行、海洋生物技术调查与发展等。2018年4月,孟加拉国总理谢赫·哈西娜(Sheikh Hasina)访问澳大利亚期间提出,希望能够获得澳大利亚的技术援助来发展水产养殖并推动海洋研究教师的交换学习。[2]

4."四方安全对话"机制

"四方安全对话"是美、日、印、澳四国近年来成立的小范围多边机制。2021年9月,该机制的首次峰会在美国华盛顿举行。澳大利亚将与印度、日本和美国间的这一四方伙伴关系视为澳大利亚外交政策的"关键支柱",希望通过由该四国组成的外交网络,支持印太地区的开放、稳定、繁荣、包容。"四方安全对话"参加国同意每年举行一次领导人会晤。2023年的四方领导人峰会由澳大利亚举办。

"四方安全对话"将一系列所谓"本地区面临的最紧迫挑战"列入议程,包括卫生安全、气候变化、基础设施、关键和新兴技术、网络安全、人道主义援助和救灾、太空、打击虚假信息和反恐等,海上安全合作是其中重要内容之一。澳大利亚意在以该合作机制补充本国现有的双边、区域和多边框架,尤其是与东盟国家和太平洋伙伴的合作。通过该四方机制,澳大利亚与其他三国:一则,试图以东盟长期对话伙伴身份进一步表达对东盟中心地位、东盟主导架构和东盟印太观的支持;二则,有意与"蓝色太平洋大陆2050发展战略"相对接,从而深入参与太平洋岛国论坛诸多太平洋地区事务;三则,支持环印度洋联盟作为应对印度洋地区挑战的主要论坛,大力配合其在印度洋地区的工作并肯定其贡献。[3]

---

[1] "About IORA", Indian Ocean Rim Association, https://www.iora.int/en/about/about-iora, October, 25, 2022.

[2] 卓振伟:《澳大利亚与环印度洋联盟的制度变迁》,载《太平洋学报》2018年第12期,第12—23页。

[3] "Quad", The Australian Department of Foreign Affairs and Trade, https://www.dfat.gov.au/international-relations/regional-architecture/quad, July 15, 2023.

（六）全球性国际组织框架下的合作

1. 国际海事组织

国际海事组织成立于1959年1月，总部设在伦敦，原名"政府间海事协商组织"（Inter-Governmental Maritime Consultative Organization），1982年5月改称"国际海事组织"。国际海事组织是负责全球海上航行安全、防止船舶污染的联合国专门机构，其宗旨在于促进各国间的航运技术合作，鼓励各国在促进海上安全、提高船舶航行效率、防止和控制船舶对海洋污染方面采取统一的标准，并处理随之产生的相关法律问题。[1]

澳大利亚是国际海事组织的创始成员国之一，自1985年以来一直是国际海事组织理事会的当选国。澳大利亚在负责国际航运安全、安保的联合国专门机构中发挥着关键作用。澳大利亚坚定地致力于制定公平和有效的航运标准，与每个成员国合作，确保国际海事组织的公平和有效运转。2017年，澳大利亚成为第一个从理事会C类成员上升为B类成员的国家，这正是澳大利亚作为世界大宗商品出口国在该类别成员中地位的应有反映。[2]澳大利亚在国际海事组织中的工作目标主要包括：（1）实施强有力的国际标准，确保航运更安全；（2）提高海员福利；（3）保护海洋环境；（4）协调本地区的搜救工作，确保其有效开展；（5）提高印度洋和太平洋地区的海上技术能力和搜救能力。[3]

为提高国际海事组织的公开度和透明度，便利信息获取，澳大利亚于2018年启动了一项改革建议，推动国际海事组织向更为现代化、民主和充满活力的标准制定机关迈进。2023年，为实现国际海事组织2050年航运脱碳目标，澳大利亚政府与亚太经济合作组织（Asia-Pacific Economic Cooperation，以下简称"亚太经合组织"）国家共同发起了一项"APEC绿色海事合作项目"。该项目的重点是，通过关注亚太经合组织成员港口与运输机构间的合作，推动低排放与零排放海运业务。此项目在美国底特律举行的亚太经合组织运输部长会议上启动，它将支持参与其中的亚太国家在确

---

[1] International Maritime Organization, http：//www.imo.org/en/About/page/Default.aspx, July 16, 2023.

[2] "Australia and the International Maritime Organization", Australian High Commission (UK), http：//uk.emb-assy.gov.au/lhlh/AustraliaIMO.html, July 16, 2023.

[3] "Australia and the International Maritime Organization", Australian High Commission (UK), https：//uk.hi-ghcommission.gov.au/lhlh/AustraliaIMO.html#：~：text=Australia%20is%20a%20foundation%20member%20of%20the%20IMO, commitment%20to%20develop%20fair%20and%20effective%20shipping%20standards., July 16, 2023.

保其港口维持竞争力的同时,将气候变化问题纳入其航运政策与投资统筹考虑。[1]

2. 国际水道测量组织

国际水道测量组织(International Hydrographic Organization)为1921年成立的政府间国际组织,旨在促进航海资料的统一,推广可靠有效的海洋测绘方法,促进海道测量数据在航海中的应用。国际水道测量组织每5年召开1次大会,由成员国政府的代表参加。当前,该组织共有100个成员国,各国均由本国负责提供水文和海图服务的国家机构为代表。

无论是由于气候变化造成的极端事件,还是日常的潮汐和洋流运动,都将带来海洋环境的不断变化。对于大多数船只来说,海图上所显示的30厘米的额外深度意味着至少可以多运载2000吨货物。掌握最新的海洋环境信息所带来的经济利益可能是相当可观的。国际水道测量组织的工作正是为了帮助各国监测这种变化,以最大限度地利用水文调查数据,引导各成员国适时调整其相关活动,并提升各成员国国内的水文测量能力。[2]

澳大利亚于1921年即已加入该组织。当前,澳大利亚水文局是国际水道测量组织的重要成员,在为国际利益攸关团体作出贡献的同时,也大力倡导澳大利亚在海洋地理空间的利益。通过在国际组织框架下的合作,澳大利亚努力保持其在制定相关国际规范和标准方面的影响力,以持续获取国家行政及军事安全所需的国际数据。澳大利亚水道测量局在邻近海域的工作成果主要有:第一,通过签署水文测量、专家培训和航海制图相关的双边协定,与巴布亚新几内亚建立伙伴关系;第二,在所罗门群岛承担主要制图机构职能,并与该国共同制作和传播所罗门群岛的官方海图及相关出版物;第三,积极加入西南太平洋水道测量委员会(South West Pacific Hydrographic Commission),与其他成员合作发展水道测量的主权能力,从而服务于整个西南太平洋地区的航行安全、海洋环境保护、海洋利用强化以及海上贸易扩大。[3]

3. 其他联合国专门机构

除国际海事组织外,澳大利亚在多个联合国专门机构中都保持着长期投

---

[1] 《澳大利亚承诺:制定"海事减排国家行动计划"创建绿色航运走廊》,载中国船东网,http://csoa.cn/doc/25241.jsp,最后访问日期:2023年7月17日。

[2] "About the IHO", IHO, https://iho.int/en/about-the-iho, July 16, 2023; "Importance of Hydrography", IHO, https://iho.int/en/importance-of-hydrography, July 16, 2023.

[3] "International Obligations", Australian Government, https://www.hydro.gov.au/aboutus/roles.htm, July 16, 2023.

入和参与，并在这些专业性政府间国际组织的涉海议题或项目中发挥了积极作用。

第一，联合国粮食及农业组织（Food and Agriculture Organization of the United Nations，以下简称"粮农组织"）。粮农组织是联合国系统内最早的常设专门机构之一，其宗旨是：提高各国人民的营养水平和生活水准；提高所有粮农产品的生产和分配效率；改善农村人口的生活状况，促进世界经济的发展，并最终消除饥饿和贫困。[1] 澳大利亚是粮农组织创始成员国之一。作为世界主要粮食生产国和农产品贸易国，澳大利亚在粮农组织中的工作重心主要在于：促进农业、渔业和林业统计数据的收集和信息交流；参与粮农组织对农业和食品标准的编纂；促进国际贸易；推动渔业和林业资源的可持续管理；监测粮食剩余处理及粮食援助交易；等等。[2]

第二，世界贸易组织（World Trade Organization，以下简称"世贸组织"）。世贸组织的核心是通过一系列多边条约和诸边协议，为国际货物、服务和知识产权贸易制定法律规则。自1995年世贸组织成立以来，澳大利亚一直是该组织的成员。澳大利亚政府坚决支持世贸组织及其规则框架，其有助于促进和保护开放的全球贸易体系，而澳大利亚的经济发展依赖于一个强大且开放的全球贸易环境。澳大利亚在受益于世贸组织的贸易规则和争端解决程序的同时，也积极关注和推动世贸组织的改革，以确保世贸架构的有效运作能够继续满足成员国在现代全球贸易环境中的需求。[3]

2022年，澳大利亚及其太平洋伙伴国在世贸组织第12届部长级会议上就渔业补贴达成了一项新协议，以应对因补贴加剧的过度捕捞导致全球鱼类资源减少的严峻问题。该协议在世贸组织现有补贴规则的基础上，进一步禁止和约束对渔业可持续性发展有害的补贴。为确保该协议在太平洋地区发挥最佳作用和提供最大环境效益，澳大利亚与斐济等太平洋岛国紧密合作，推出针对太平洋远洋船队的补贴条款，以限制主要捕鱼国在公海上的过度捕捞，并尝试在数年内通过条款升级应对与之相关的产能过剩问题。澳大利亚高度评价了这一协议及其新规，称其为世贸组织近10年来谈判达成的最具

---

[1]《联合国粮食及农业组织》，载中华人民共和国外交部网站，https：//www.mfa.gov.cn/web/wjb_673085/zzjg_673183/gjjjs_674249/gjzzyhygk_674253/lhglsjnyzz_674409/gk_674411/，最后访问日期：2024年12月23日。

[2] "UN specialised agencies and regional com-missions", The Australian Department of Foreign Affairs and Trade, https: //www.dfat.gov.au/international-relations/international-organisations/un/Pages/un-specialised-ag-encies-and-regional-commissions, July 17, 2023.

[3] "World Trade Organization", The Australian Department of Foreign Affairs and Trade, https://www.dfat.gov.au/trade/organisations/wto/Pages/the-world-trade-organization, July 17, 2023.

实质性的条约，也是世贸组织第一个以环境问题为重点关注的条约；该协议的成功达成将为太平洋岛国经济体及多边贸易体系提振信心，也将有助于实现联合国可持续发展目标之一的"海洋可持续性"。[1]

---

[1] "Australia and Pacific Partners secure new global fisheries subsidies deal-at the WTO", Senator the Hon Tim Ayres, https：//www.trademinister.gov.au/minister/don-farrell/media-release/australia-and-pacific-partners-secure-new-global-fisheries-subsidies-deal-wto, July 17, 2023.

七、对中国海洋法主张的态度

（一）对"南海仲裁案"的态度

澳美关系始终是左右澳大利亚南海立场的逻辑核心。为履行澳美同盟义务，澳大利亚早在 20 世纪 70 年代就开始关注中国南海地区。为在冷战时期监控苏联军事行动的途经区域，澳大利亚曾派飞机飞越南海水域监视苏联船只和潜艇的行进。1994 年，澳大利亚发布《1994 年国防白皮书》（1994 Defence White Paper）明确其南海政策，在表达对南海声索国领土主权争端的担忧、呼吁有关各方"谨慎应对"的同时，基本确立了在较长时期内的相对中立立场。[1] 在 2007—2013 年的陆克文（Kevin Rudd）及吉拉德（Julia Gillard）两届政府执政时期，澳大利亚官方有关南海问题的表态都相对克制，措辞和行动基本体现了其在南海地区争端中重申的中立姿态。2009 年，美国在东盟会议上首提"重返亚太"。这一战略自 2010 年开始牵动澳大利亚的"神经"。澳大利亚的南海政策从"并无介入南海的意图和实际行动"逐渐向南海争端"利益攸关方"的自我定位转变，从"仅敦促南海争端有关各方遵守国际法，维持南海地区现状以及制定南海地区统一行为准则"向高调介入南海争端的地区秩序看守者转向。随着 2013—2016 年"南海仲裁案"的推进，澳大利亚迅速完成了从"观望中立"到"谨慎介入"再到"积极介入"的角色转换，并倚仗 2016 年的该仲裁裁决与美国步调一致地高频指摘中国南海相关海洋主张。

1. 以仲裁裁决的承认与执行为和平解决南海争端的标杆

一直以来，澳大利亚都以呼吁南海争端各方保持克制、避免事态恶化、遵守国际法为其基本表态。但在 2013 年菲律宾单方提请仲裁程序之前，澳大利亚对依国际法和平解决南海争端方式的表述都是宽泛而开放的，并多次明

---

[1] "The Defence of Australia（1987 Defence White Paper）", Parliament of Australia, https：//www.aph.gov.au/About_Parliament/Parliamentary_Departments/Parliamentary_Library/pubs/rp/rp1516/DefendAust/1987, July 18, 2023; "The Defence of Australia（1994 Defence White Paper）", Parliament of Australia, https：//www.aph.gov.au/About_Parliament/Parliamentary_Departments/Parliamentary_Library/pubs/rp/rp1516/DefendAust/1994#：~：text=The%20Keating%20Government%20tabled%20the%201994%20Defence%20White，engagement%20with%20regional%20neighbours%20and%20the%20United%20States.，July 18, 2023.

确响应中国与东盟国家间已有共识的谈判协商方式。如，2012年7月，澳大利亚国防部长在接受澳大利亚国家广播电台及"天空新闻"（Sky News）等媒体采访时表示，"希望所有的领海主权争端能够遵循国际法，依据国际海洋法来解决"，而解决方式建议"可以由牵涉各方和平的协商来解决"，或"可以通过像东亚峰会和东盟国防部长会议这样一些国际性或区域性的机制或会议来商讨解决之法"。[1]但随着2016年"南海仲裁案"裁决的作出，澳大利亚有关符合国际法的南海争端解决之道就迅速具象为由第三方介入的法律解决方案，或者就是国际仲裁裁决执行本身，其他和平解决争端选项则多作为附加项或是仲裁裁决的执行实践而被顺带讨论。

2013年起，澳大利亚开始密切关注"南海仲裁案"进展，并表态支持菲律宾提起国际仲裁。至2016年年初，澳大利亚的常态化表述格式为，澳方在南海问题上不选边站但支持有关国际仲裁。2016年2月，澳大利亚外交部长毕晓普（Julie Bishop）力挺菲律宾将南海纷争诉诸国际仲裁庭，要求其他国家尊重菲律宾的南海领土主权，尤其要求中国和平地，使菲律宾"不受威胁"地解决与中国的领土纠纷，批评中国捍卫南海主权的行为无益于地区的和平与稳定。2016年7月12日"南海仲裁案"裁决出台当天，澳大利亚外交部发布题为《澳大利亚支持和平解决南海争端》的官方新闻，确认：第一，该仲裁庭依《公约》合法成立，其仲裁裁决虽与主权无关，但与《公约》下的海洋权利相关；第二，仲裁裁决对争端双方都是最终且具有拘束力的，中菲双方应遵守仲裁裁决。同时高度评价该仲裁裁决，指出其重要贡献包括：第一，该裁决是所涉地区和平解决争端方式的一次重要试验；第二，该裁决澄清了诸多海洋权利，有利于南海地区各声索国重启对话，有利于地区团结；第三，该仲裁程序及裁决的作出意味着，所有声索国都可以从"基于规则"的国际秩序中获益匪浅。最后澳大利亚试图作出强硬表态，敦促各声索国不要采取旨在改变争议地区现状的强制行为和单方面行动，以保障澳大利亚及他国继续行使航行和飞越自由的国际法权利，保证地区和平与稳定。[2]在随后的澳大利亚—东盟部长级会议开幕致辞中，澳大利亚外长再次

---

[1] 参见庄国土、卢秋莉：《近年来澳大利亚官方对南海争端的基本立场》，载《南洋问题研究》2013年第3期，第98页。

[2] Julie Bishop, "Australia supports peaceful dispute resolution in the South China Sea", https：//www.foreignminister.gov.au/minister/julie-bishop/media-release/australia-supports-peaceful-dispute-resolution-south-china-sea#：~：text = Australia% 20urges% 20all% 20South% 20China% 20Sea% 20claimants% 20to, to% 20change% 20the% 20status% 20quo% 20in% 20disputed% 20areas., July 12, 2023.

表示鼓励中菲两国遵守这一具有最终约束力的裁决,并恢复接触、解决分歧;同时称,有关南海问题的裁决明确了有关南海海域海洋权利的国际法,如何处理这一仲裁结果将是对东盟介入和平解决争端的重要考验。[1]

2017年6月,澳美外长和防长的年度部长级磋商发表联合声明,认为2016年据《公约》作出的仲裁裁决为进一步和平解决南海争端提供了有益基础,同时强调维护合法的航行和飞越自由以及坚持"基于规则"的秩序的重要性。[2] 同年10月,澳大利亚外长在外交政策讲话中再称澳大利亚在南海领土争端中不选边站,但仲裁庭就南海问题作出的裁决是终局的、具有约束力的;澳大利亚认为仲裁庭的裁决是对国际法的权威阐释,也是对《公约》的适用。[3] 2021年7月,时任澳大利亚外长佩恩(Marise Payne)发表关于"南海仲裁案"裁决的声明,声明回顾了2016年仲裁庭作出裁决时是"明确的""一致的",明确呼吁争端各方遵守终局的、有约束力的仲裁裁决是澳大利亚的一贯立场。声明称,澳大利亚的这一立场源于对国际法和《公约》规则的支持,正是《公约》规定了所有海洋活动进行的法律框架。声明强调,国际法允许"无论大小"的所有国家都可以和平解决争端,因而遵守国际法对相关区域的持续和平、繁荣和稳定至关重要。[4] 2021年8月23日,澳大利亚与菲律宾两国部长会议发布联合声明,再次提出希望中国尊重"南海仲裁案"的裁决结果。[5]

以高调支持由仲裁解决南海争端、高声疾呼应尊重"南海仲裁案"裁决为契机,澳大利亚大力塑造其恪守国际法则、坚守以法律方法解决国际争端的文明国家形象。在警告中国无视"南海仲裁案"裁决可能"付出巨大声誉成本"的同时,澳大利亚既多次鼓励南海争端其他声索国积极诉诸国际法庭,更将其与东帝汶间的调解案作为对照示范,力证自己在遵循《公约》强

---

[1] Julie Bishop, "ASEAN-Australia Ministerial Meeting-Opening remarks", https://www.foreignminister.gov.au/minister/julie-bishop/speech/asean-australia-ministerial-meeting-opening-remarks, July 25, 2023.

[2] Julie Bishop, "Joint statement AUSMIN 2017", https://www.foreignminister.gov.au/minister/julie-bishop/media-release/joint-statement-ausmin-2017, June 5, 2023.

[3] Julie Bishop, "Foreign Policy in an Uncertain World", https://www.foreignminister.gov.au/minister/julie-bishop/speech/foreign-policy-uncertain-world, October 16, 2023.

[4] Marise Payne, "Marking the 5th Anniversary of the South China Sea Arbitral Award", https://www.foreignminister.gov.au/minister/marise-payne/media-release/marking-5th-anniversary-south-china-sea-arbitral-award, July 12, 2023.

[5] Marise Payne, "The Philippines-Australia Ministerial Meeting", https://www.foreignminister.gov.au/minister/marise-payne/media-release/philippines-australia-ministerial-meeting-joint-ministerial-statement, March 21, 2023.

制性争端解决方法上"以身作则"。

2016年8月，澳大利亚外长在有关澳大利亚与东帝汶调解案的专栏文章中表示，澳大利亚正据其法律义务参加不具拘束力的调解程序，同时澳大利亚也正在参与由东帝汶发起的两项仲裁程序，澳大利亚"将遵守仲裁人的裁决，正如我们呼吁菲律宾和中国在南中国海的做法一样"。[1] 2017年10月，澳大利亚外长在接连两场演讲中提出，澳大利亚支持《公约》争端解决机制、国际刑事法院等诸多法律框架，最坚定地维护国际法庭权威。为证明这一点，澳大利亚再次将中菲在《公约》下的仲裁与澳东（帝汶）在《公约》下的调解作比：对于前者，澳大利亚强调无论仲裁裁决有利于哪方，都应作为最终裁决得到双方尊重；而后者，正是同一时期澳大利亚解决与周边国家海洋划界争端的成功范例。[2] 2018年5月，澳大利亚外长在接受电视采访时又表示，如果南海争端中的各声索国无法解决分歧，那么"它们可以自由地诉诸仲裁或调解，就像澳大利亚根据《公约》对东帝汶所做的那样"。[3] 同年7月，在接受"天空新闻"采访时，澳大利亚外长再次提出，澳大利亚与东帝汶的海洋主权主张存在的冲突已经依据《公约》通过谈判得以解决并签署了条约；对于经过数个世代都未能解决的海洋争端，各国应该"像澳大利亚那样，通过谈判解决彼此之间的分歧"。[4]

2. 视仲裁裁决为追随美国"保障"航行自由的法理底气

保证本国在南海区域的航行和飞越自由不受干扰或侵害，是澳大利亚在南海问题上的最基本诉求。即使在反复申明对南海争端不持立场的谨慎中立时期，澳大利亚政府也从不回避对南海航行自由问题的高度关注，而2016年的"南海仲裁案"裁决则进一步被澳大利亚视为在保障航行和飞越自由的前提下，其采取更为强硬甚至激进行动的背书。

2012年11月，澳大利亚总理吉拉德在东亚峰会上的发言强调，尽管澳大利亚政府"不站在声称拥有大部分战略海域归属权的中国这一方，也不站

---

[1] Julie Bishop, "Conciliation between Australia and Timor-Leste", https：//www.foreignminister. gov.au/minister/julie-bishop/news/conciliation-between-australia-and-timor-leste, August 30, 2023.

[2] Julie Bishop, "UWA In The Zone conference", https：//www.foreignminister.gov.au/minister/julie-bishop/speech/uwa-zone-conference, October 2, 2022; Julie Bishop, "Sir John Downer O-ration", https：//www.foreignminister.gov.au/minister/julie-bishop/speech/sir-john-downer-oration, October 6, 2022.

[3] Julie Bishop, "Doorstop-Canberra", https：//www.foreignminister.gov.au/minister/julie-bishop/transcript-eoe/doorstop-canberra-1, May 30, 2023.

[4] Julie Bishop, "Interview with Graham Richardson-Sky News", https：//www.foreignminister.gov.au/minister/julie-bishop/transcript-eoe/interview-graham-richardson-sky-news, July 11, 2023.

在声称拥有部分海域归属权的其他各方",但南海作为海上航线是"一条通向世界各地的航海要道",也是一条对澳大利亚而言"十分重要的海上贸易通道",这一海上要道的安全对澳大利亚非常重要。2013年2月,澳大利亚外交贸易部秘书在澳大利亚"亚洲连线"(Asialink)的演说中称,在亚洲力量再次崛起时,印度洋和太平洋航线对澳大利亚战略和国防计划中的海上环境将更为重要。他进一步表示,澳大利亚当前面临的海上问题就在于南海区域争端对深海开发自由和航海自由的潜在挑战。[1] 2016年2月,澳大利亚外长在访华前夕除挑衅式支持菲律宾将南海争端提交国际仲裁外,亦圈出与中方会晤时的重点包括"重申澳希继续维护南海地区海空、军民航行自由"[2]。

"南海仲裁案"裁决一经作出,澳大利亚立即将该裁决与所谓《公约》下航行和飞越自由主张紧密捆绑。2016年后,澳美部长级磋商的年度联合声明均反复提及以下内容:第一,强烈反对任何南海声索国采取可能改变现状、加剧紧张局势的强制性单边行动;第二,强调维护航行、飞越和其他合法利用海洋的自由以及所有国家按照国际法行事的重要性;第三,强调中菲"南海仲裁案"的裁决具有约束力,对地区的和平和秩序极为重要;第四,要求南海地区的所有行为准则都与国际法尤其是《公约》相符合。[3] 2018年3月,在首届澳大利亚—东盟特别峰会之前,澳大利亚和印度尼西亚举行了外长和防长"2+2"会谈并发表联合声明称,双方部长认识到,"南海仲裁案"裁决及其对争端的解决直接影响本地区;在此背景下,双方一致强调"维护南海和平、安全与稳定以及航行和飞越自由的重要性"。[4] 2023年5月,在与菲律宾外交部共同举办的新闻发布会上,澳大利亚外长表示,

---

[1] 参见庄国土、卢秋莉:《近年来澳大利亚官方对南海争端的基本立场》,载《南洋问题研究》2013年第3期,第97—98页。

[2] 《外交部回应"澳大利亚希望中方停止南海岛礁建设"》,载环球网,https://world.huanqiu.c-om/article/9CaKrnJTRX,最后访问日期:2023年7月21日。

[3] See Julie Bishop, "Joint Statement Australia-U. S. Ministerial Consultations (AUSMIN) 2018", Minister for Foreign Affairs, https://www.foreignminister.gov.au/minister/julie-bishop/media-release/joint-statement-australia-us-ministerial-consultations-ausmin-2018, July 24, 2023; "Joint Statement Australia-US Ministerial Consultations (AUSMIN) 2019", U. S. Department of Defense, https://www.defense.gov/News/Releases/Release/Article/1925222/joint-statement-australia-us-ministerial-consultations-ausmin-2019/, August 4, 2023.

[4] Julie Bishop, "Joint Statement on the Fifth Indonesia-Australia Foreign and Defence Ministers 2 + 2 Meeting", Minister for Foreign Affairs, https://www.foreignminister.gov.au/minister/julie-bishop/media-release/joint-statement-fifth-indonesia-australia-foreign-and-defence-ministers-22-meeting, March 16, 2023.

澳大利亚将继续致力于在"西菲律宾海"或"南中国海"地区的长期存在，澳大利亚"对与所有伙伴合作行使航行和飞越自由权持开放态度"，并强调"菲律宾是我们长期以来重要的安全伙伴"。[1]

由此，在锚定支持南海仲裁程序及其裁决就是在遵守《公约》、维护国际法的策略方向之后，澳大利亚迅速成为追随美国在南海"自由航行"行动的"正义伙伴"。2015年10月，美国首次派遣军舰巡航南海。美国导弹驱逐舰"拉森号"（USS Lassen DDG-82）闯入中国渚碧礁和美济礁12海里的水域，以此表明美国不承认中国依南海相关岛礁及其人工建设所主张的领海主权。澳大利亚国防部长于美舰行动次日即发表声明，肯定美国开展的"自由航行"行动符合国际法，"澳大利亚坚决支持"世界各国在南海所享有的航行和飞越自由。该声明特别强调，由于澳大利亚"在维护南中国海的和平与稳定、尊重国际法、不受阻碍的贸易以及航行和飞越自由方面有正当利益"，其将"继续在海上安全问题上与美国和其他区域伙伴密切合作"。[2] 同年11月，澳大利亚总理在对美国事访问中称，澳美"在亚太地区问题上观点一致"，并公开表态维护南海航行自由是澳坚持不懈的目标。[3] 2016年2月，澳大利亚防长再次发声，要求政府派军舰进入南海有争议地区的12海里水域。自此，澳大利亚政府口径一致地坚称其有"不可动摇"的义务维护南海航行和飞越自由。2020年7月，时任澳大利亚总理莫里森（Scott Morrison）在回答记者提问时表示，将继续与美国保持一致立场，继续"非常坚决地"主张南海航行自由；澳大利亚会"以自身行动、主张及声明予以支持"这一行动，就像澳大利亚海军舰船曾与美方一起在南海开展"航行自由"巡逻一样。[4] 2021年11月，针对现身澳大利亚附近的中国侦察船，莫里森故作真诚地称希望中国也支持澳大利

---

[1] Penny Wong, "Press conference with the Hon Enrique Manalo, Philippine Secretary for Foreign Affairs", https：//www.foreignminister.gov.au/minister/penny-wong/transcript/press-conference-hon-enrique-manalo-philippine-secretary-foreign-affairs, August 16, 2023.

[2] "Minister for Defence-Statement-Freedom of Navigation in the South China Sea", Australian Defence Ministers, https：//www.minister.defence.gov.au/statements/2015-10-27/minister-defence- statement-freedom-navigation-south-china-sea #：~：text = Australia% 20strongly% 20supports% 20these% 20rights. % 20Australia% 20is% 20not, navigation% 20and% 20overflight% 20in% 20the% 20South% 20China% 20Sea, July 25, 2023.

[3] "Remarks by President Obama and Prime Minister Malcolm Turnbull of the Commonwealth of Australia after Bilateral Meeting", Obama White House Archives, https：//obamawhitehouse.archives.gov/the-press-of-fice/2015/11/17/remarks-president-obama-and-prime-minister-malcolm-turnbull-commonwealth, July 25, 2023.

[4] 《不说航行自由了？澳媒炒作"中国侦察船监视"：这是威胁澳大利亚》，载百度网站，https：//baijiahao.baidu.com/s? id = 1705319033573219418&wfr = spider&for = pc, 最后访问日期：2024年12月10日。

亚军舰在南海争议海域享有同等权利，中国军舰当然可以在"国际海域"自由航行，就像澳大利亚军舰在南海也可以自由航行一样。[1] 2023 年 3 月，在对"美英澳三方安全伙伴关系"最新协议内容的回应中，澳大利亚国防部长马尔思（Richard Marles）表示，采购美国制造的核潜艇并不意味着将参与可能发生的台海冲突，澳大利亚只是希望通过这一协议保护印太地区用于贸易的关键海上通道。马尔思强调："维护基于规则的秩序，即航行自由和飞越自由，这完全符合澳大利亚的利益，我们需要确保我们有能力保护这种利益。"[2] 同年 8 月，美日澳三国在菲律宾附近的南海海域举行联合军演，被媒体解读为发出"强烈信息"以重申他们维护南海航行自由的"承诺"，这也是澳大利亚参与的又一次以南海"自由巡航"为目标的武力施压。[3]

3. 依仲裁裁决全面否定中国南海的"九段线"及历史性权利主张

澳大利亚的"印太战略"选择推动着其在外交平衡及防务依赖中愈加倾身于美国。为巩固美国在澳大利亚对外关系中独一无二的显要地位以及澳美同盟关系持续深化的亲密前景，仅仅笼统地肯定"南海仲裁案"裁决、塑造国际规则维护者形象，已经不足以展现澳大利亚在南海问题上追随美国的坚定和一致。在宣扬航行自由的基本权利之外，澳大利亚政府还进一步地向世界表达了否定中国南海具体主张的官方立场。这一表态是对 2014 年美国《海洋中的界限》第 143 号报告的应和，也得到了美国 2022 年《海洋中的界限》第 150 号报告的支持。[4]

2020 年 7 月 23 日，澳大利亚就南海问题致函联合国，对中国不接受"南海仲裁案"裁决约束的主张提出异议。澳大利亚认为，中国方面有关仲裁裁决不能约束中国的理由缺乏国际法支持。相反，根据《公约》第 296 条

---

[1] "Australia has the right to send warships in South China Sea, says Prime Minister Scott Morrison", Global Defense Corp, https：//www.globaldefensecorp.com/2021/11/29/australia-has-the-right-to-send-warships-in-south-china-sea-says-prime-minister-scott-morrison/, July 26, 2023.

[2] 达乔、陈子帅：《澳防长称没为核潜艇承诺参战台海，还说"很努力"稳定对华关系》，载环球网，https：//b-aijiahao.baidu.com/s? id = 1760838539994512175&wfr = spider&for = pc，最后访问日期：2023 年 7 月 26 日。

[3] "3 PH allies to hold joint sea drills", The Manila Times, https：//www.manilatimes.net/2023/08/21/news/3-ph-allies-to-hold-joint-sea-drills/1906324, July 26, 2023.

[4] See "China's Maritime Claims in the South China Sea", Limits in the Seas No. 143, Bureau of Oceans and International Environmental and Scientific Affairs, https：//www.state.gov/wp-content/uploads/2019/10/LIS-143.pdf, May 19, 2023; "People's Republic of China: Maritime Claims in the South China Sea", Limits in the Seas No. 150, Bureau of Oceans and International Environmental and Scientific Affairs, https：//www.s-tate.gov/wp-content/uploads/2022/01/LIS150-SCS.pdf, May 19, 2023.

及附件7第11条，仲裁庭的裁决是终局的，对争端双方均有约束力。立足该仲裁裁决，澳大利亚所谓中国"与《公约》不符"海洋法主张的针对性意见如下。

第一，澳大利亚拒绝接受中国在南海经"长期历史实践"确立的"历史性权利"或"海洋权益"相关主张。澳大利亚充分肯定2016年"南海仲裁案"裁决结论，完全认同"历史性权利"相关主张与《公约》不符且因此无效。第二，基于认定中国直线基线划定不符合《公约》，进而否定"九段线"及相关海域主张。澳大利亚声称，没有法律依据支持中国可以通过连接南海中诸岛或海洋地形的最外缘各点来划定直线基线，包括划定包围"四沙"或大陆国家"远洋"群岛的直线基线。由此，澳大利亚也不接受任何基于此类直线基线的内水、领海、专属经济区及大陆架主张。澳大利亚政府援引了《公约》第7条第1款有关直线基线以及《公约》第47条第1款有关群岛直线基线的划定条件，并否认中国符合相关法条下的特定情形，认为应回归《公约》第5条的规定。第三，基于仲裁裁决对中国所主张的南海岛礁地位的全盘否定，澳大利亚进一步否认中国对"水下地物"或"低潮高地"的领土主权或主权权利。澳大利亚宣称，岛礁只能在自然状态下产生《公约》规定的海洋权利，陆地建设活动或其他形式的人工改造不能改变《公约》对海洋地物的分类。因此，澳大利亚政府既不接受人工改造地物可以根据《公约》第121条第1款获得岛屿地位，又依《公约》第60条第8款规定认定此类"人工岛屿"不具有岛屿地位。在澳大利亚看来，中国所主张的南海岛礁没有自己的领海，不需要在领海、专属经济区和大陆架划界时被纳入考量，相关主权要求也没有"得到国际社会的广泛承认"。第四，澳大利亚政府对中国在2019年12月、2020年3月、2020年4月、2020年6月致联合国照会中提出的其他方面主张持保留立场。[1]

上述正式函件发出后不久，2020年澳美部长级磋商于7月28日发表联合声明，再次强调2016年"南海仲裁案"裁决的终局性和对争端双方的约束力，同时称根据2016年的仲裁裁决，两国"确认"中国的海洋主张在国际法下无效：中国不能基于"九段线"、历史性权利或整个南海岛屿群在南中国海主张海洋主权。在否定了中国南海主张或权利的合法性后，该联合声明貌似公道地表示所有南海岛礁的主权声索国都"有权在不受骚扰和胁迫的

---

[1] "Australian Mission to the United Nations, diplomatic note No. 20/026, July 23, 2020", UN, https://www.un.org/Depts/los/clcs_new/submissions_files/mys_12_12_2019/2020_07_23_AUS_NV_UN_001_OLA-2020-00373.pdf, July 28, 2023.

情况下，合法开采海上资源，包括长期存在的南海油气项目和渔业资源"[1]。与致联合国照会几乎完全一致的措辞也出现在2021年7月澳大利亚外长发表的关于"南海仲裁案"裁决的声明中。该声明开篇即表示，中国在南海"长期历史实践"过程中确立的"历史性权利"或"海洋权益"主张与《公约》不符，因而是无效的，这也正是"南海仲裁案"裁决的结论。[2] 2021年11月，因菲律宾补给船非法进入我国南沙群岛仁爱礁，中国海警船依法依规全程值守并监视，却被澳大利亚曲解为"中国海警封锁并用水炮对付菲律宾船只"，声明"对在南海以危险方式使用或胁迫使用海岸警卫队船只等破坏稳定的行动表示关切"。这一声明再次以"南海仲裁案"裁决为理据，全盘否定中国有关"九段线"及历史性权利，错误认定仁爱礁"位于菲律宾专属经济区和大陆架范围内"，因而中国对仁爱礁附近海域的任何权利都没有法律依据。[3]

4. 恃仲裁裁决反对岛礁建设

无论是定位为"谨慎观望"还是"积极介入"，无论是自视为"中立观察者"还是"利益攸关方"，澳大利亚都无法改变其本质上作为南海问题域外国家的地缘事实。由是，密切关注南海争端的直接利益方及其他地理相近方的国家举措，尤其是对军事或准军事行动保持高度警惕，就成为澳大利亚保障己方利益免受波及或侵扰的权重选项。

2013年1月，在菲律宾提交仲裁申请的第二日，澳大利亚防长就在新闻访谈中表达了对相关国家在南海地区军费增长现象的关注，称："无论是日本还是中国的军费开支，都不能解决南中国海或是东中国海的紧张局势。南中国海和东中国海的紧张局势只有通过外交途径，在所有国家都遵循准则和国际海洋法以及海洋法公约的情况下才能得到解决。"[4] 2015年10月，澳美外长和防长联合发声，表示"对中国最近在南中国海的填海造陆和建设活

---

[1] "Joint Statement Australia-U. S. Ministerial Consultations (AUSMIN) 2020", The Australian Department of Foreign Affairs and Trade, https：//www.dfat.gov.au/geo/united-states-of-america/ausmin/joint-statement-ausmin-2020, July 28, 2023.

[2] Marise Payne, "Marking the 5th Anniversary of the South China Sea Arbitral Award", https：//www.foreignminister.gov.au/minister/marise-payne/media-release/marking-5th-anniversary-south-china-sea-arbitral-award, July 12, 2023.

[3] "Recent incidents in the South China Sea", The Australian Department of Foreign Affairs and Trade, https：//www.dfat.gov.au/news/media-release/recent-incidents-south-china-sea, November 22, 2022.

[4] 参见庄国土、卢秋莉：《近年来澳大利亚官方对南海争端的基本立场》，载《南洋问题研究》2013年第3期，第98页。

动表示强烈关注",呼吁停止一切填海造陆、海上建设和军事化活动,"敦促声索国保持克制,采取措施缓和紧张局势,避免采取可能使紧张局势升级的挑衅行动"。[1]

随着"南海仲裁案"的推进,澳大利亚也在对中国南海意图进行重新评估。在澳大利亚的观察之下,南海岛礁建设工作有序开展、中国对"南海仲裁案"的态度,都让澳大利亚开始对中国岛礁军事部署的性质及最终目的产生忧虑,并在其自身"战略利益"安排中转化为高敏感内容。2016年2月,澳大利亚发布《2016年国防白皮书》,首次明确表达了对中国南海行动的"特别关切"。尽管澳大利亚在该白皮书中仍然保留了"澳大利亚在南海争端中不采取任何立场"的表述,却特别表达了对"中国以前所未有的速度与规模开展陆地建设活动"的担忧。澳大利亚在白皮书中反对在南海构建存在军事目的的人工设施,反映的正是其对中国崛起的审慎立场、警惕姿态,即在澳大利亚的战略视野中,南海问题的影响已经不限于岛礁主权归属争端所蕴含的冲突风险。澳大利亚所谓新崛起的强国"对经济、军事力量的胁迫性使用"将可能危害澳大利亚赖以立足的航行自由甚或是"基于规则的国际秩序"。[2]

2017年6月,澳大利亚外长在接受采访时言辞激烈地称:"中国单方面填海造陆,在岛屿上修建军事设施,这是对基于国际规则的秩序的直接无视。"[3] 同年8月,美日澳在菲律宾举行三国外长会谈并发表联合声明,表示"强烈反对"中国在南海和东海的"单方面行动",要求南海声索国"避免从事填海活动、建设前哨基地以及将争议海洋地物予以军事化"。[4] 同年11月,澳大利亚政府发布《2017年外交政策白皮书》(2017 Foreign Policy White Paper),基本延续《2016年国防白皮书》的立场表述对中国在南海地区正常的维权固权行为展开批评,称"已敦促所有声索国不要采取可能加剧

---

[1] "Joint statement AUSMIN 2015", The Australian Department of Foreign Affairs and Trade, https://www.dfat.gov.au/geo/united-states-of-america/ausmin/Pages/joint-statement-ausmin-2015, October 13, 2022.

[2] "2016 Defence White Paper", Australian Defence, https://www.defence.gov.au/sites/default/files/2021-08/2016-Defence-White-Paper.pdf, August 9, 2023.

[3] Julie Bishop, "Interview with Kieran Gilbert-First Edition, Sky News", https://www.foreignminister.gov.au/minister/julie-bishop/transcript-eoe/interview-kieran-gilbert-first-edition-sky-news-0, June 5, 2023.

[4] "Australia-Japan-United States Trilateral Strategic Dialogue Ministerial Joint Statement", U.S. Department of State, https://2017-2021.state.gov/australia-japan-united-states-trilateral-strategic-dialogue-ministerial-joint-statement/, October 20, 2024.

紧张局势的行动,并呼吁停止填海造陆和建设活动",并表示"尤其关注中国空前的步伐和规模的活动"。[1]

随着《中华人民共和国海上交通安全法》的修订以及 2018 年《全国人民代表大会常务委员会关于中国海警局行使海上维权执法职权的决定》、2021 年《中华人民共和国海警法》的颁布实施,中国海警机构改革推进带来的法律属性及行动力度的变化引来包括澳大利亚在内的西方国家的持续关注和挑剔目光。2018 年 8 月,美日澳三国外长在参加东盟地区论坛之际举行三国安全对话,发表联合声明表达"对在南海争议地区配置先进武器的担忧,反对单边采取填海、基地建设、军事化等行动"。[2] 2019 年 8 月,美日澳外长在第 9 次三边战略对话部长级会议上发表声明,指称中国的海洋维权行动为"负面事态",称对"在争议地物上部署先进武器系统表示严重关切",给中国在南海岛礁上的正当国土防卫设施建设行为贴上"建设前哨基地、在争议岛礁上进行军事化行动以及对待划界海域的海洋环境造成永久性物理改变"等标签。[3] 2021 年 8 月,澳大利亚外交贸易部负责人在第 5 次澳菲部长级会议上为"南海仲裁案"裁决出台五周年摇旗呐喊,特别提及对"南海争议岛礁持续军事化、以危险方式使用和强制使用海警船和海上民兵以及干扰他国资源开发活动的行为表示严重关切"。会议声明数次明确提及国家海警行动及其相关法律框架必须符合国际法,试图将中国海警力量的使用影射为对航行和飞越自由的威胁。[4] 在 2021 年 9 月及 2022 年 1 月的澳美年度部长级磋商中,两国外长及防长都在联合声明中采用了更为直白的表述:先是定性中国在南海的海洋主张是"扩张性的""毫无法律依据的";再明示或暗示地质疑中国国内法的正当性,"呼吁"中国以符合《公约》的方式"实施包括《海上交通安全法》在内的相关国内立法",甚至"点名"包括中国的"《海警法》和《海上交通安全法》在内的国内立法的实施必须符合《联合

---

[1] "2017 Foreign Policy White Paper", The Australian Department of Foreign Affairs and Trade, https://www.dfat.gov.au/sites/default/files/minisite/static/4ca0813c-585e-4fe1-86eb-de665e65001a/fpwhitepaper/index.ht-ml, August 9, 2023.

[2] "Trilateral Strategic Dialogue Joint Ministerial Statement", Ministry of Foreign Affairs of Japan, https://www.mofa.go.jp/files/000387762.pdf, August 9, 2023.

[3] Marise Payne, "Trilateral Strategic Dialogue Joint Ministerial Statement", https://www.foreignminister.gov.au/minister/marise-payne/media-release/trilateral-strategic-dialogue-joint-ministerial-statement, August 2, 2023.

[4] "The Philippines-Australia Ministerial Meeting-Joint Ministerial Statement", The Australian Department of Foreign Affairs and Trade, https://www.dfat.gov.au/geo/philippines/philippines-australia-ministerial-meeting-joint-ministerial-statement, August 23, 2023.

国海洋公约》";最后仍剑指中国海警,称"以危险方式使用海岸警卫队和海上民兵"是在"破坏其他国家海上资源开采活动的努力",是在"有争议的岛礁上军事化",是"破坏稳定的行动"。[1]

(二) 对《南海各方行为宣言》及"南海行为准则"的态度

一如前述,在菲律宾单方面提起南海仲裁程序之前,澳大利亚曾在较长时间内对南海问题的解决方案持观望态度。其中,鼓励中国与东盟国家间通过谈判达成具有一致性的南海行为约束规范,就是澳大利亚较为欢迎的符合其预期的方案之一。

2011年6月,澳大利亚国防部长在新加坡香格里拉安全对话会议上的演讲中表示,澳大利亚鼓励所有国家都耐心冷静地通过多边安全协商机制和遵循国际法律准则等方式来解决领海争端,并特别指明东盟有关行为准则的提出在这方面就是一个很好的起点。同年7月,澳防长史密斯(Stephen Smith)在华盛顿布鲁金斯学会(The Brooking Institute)的主题发言中再次表示,澳大利亚支持所有国家耐心并沉着地通过多边安全协商机制,遵循国际法律准则解决领海争端,而不是诉诸武力威胁。由此,澳大利亚支持通过"一套指导方针来落实南中国海行为准则",并对相关国家间致力推动该准则实现的决定表示欢迎。2012年11月,澳大利亚总理在东亚峰会上表达了对"南海行为准则"的关注,称澳大利亚"相信行为准则可以既遵循国际法又有助于确保解决南中国海争端的任何问题",并表示这是"澳大利亚一直以来的立场,也是值得澳大利亚长期坚持推进的立场"。[2]

2013年2月,澳大利亚政府外交贸易部秘书表示,尽管有习惯国际法及《公约》的存在,但是有关主权、资源管辖权及其所有权的相关规则仍然处在形成阶段。同年3月,澳大利亚国防部长在电视访谈中重申澳大利亚对"南海行为准则"的支持。他表示,作为东盟对话伙伴、东亚峰会及东盟防长扩大会的一员,澳大利亚支持东盟通过"行为准则来解决南中国海的领海和领土争端"。同年5月,澳大利亚发布《2013年国防白皮书》首次明确提

---

[1] "The Australia-U. S. Ministerial Consultations Joint Statement: An Unbreakable Alliance for Peace and Prosperity", The Australian Department of Foreign Affairs and Trade, https://www.dfat.gov.au/news/news/australia-us-ministerial-consultations-joint-statement-unbreakable-alliance-peace-and-prosperity, September 17, 2022; "AUKMIN 2022 Joint Statement", The Australian Department of Foreign Affairs and Trade, https://www.dfat.gov.au/news/news/aukmin-2022-joint-statement, January 21, 2023.

[2] 参见庄国土、卢秋莉:《近年来澳大利亚官方对南海争端的基本立场》,载《南洋问题研究》2013年第3期,第99页。

及中国与菲律宾、马来西亚、越南等国的南海领土争端，同时将利用"基于国际法的南海行为准则"来共同管控南海争端作为重要建议方向。[1] 这一表态在当年7月的澳大利亚与韩国的部长级会议中得到了延续，两国表示就海上安全和航行自由、贸易安全及畅通、遵循国际法以和平解决南海争端等达成一致意见，为此两国共同支持继续推进"南海行为准则"。2015年10月，澳美年度部长级磋商发出更为清晰的信号，呼吁东盟和中国确保切实落实《南海各方行为宣言》下的承诺，并尽快就实质性的"南海行为准则"达成一致。[2]

对于《南海各方行为宣言》及"南海行为准则"，澳大利亚似乎保持了高度的政策连贯性。无论是南海仲裁程序开始前抑或"南海仲裁案"裁决作出后，澳大利亚政府似乎都表达了对《南海各方行为宣言》的认可和对"南海行为准则"的期待。但值得注意的是，在看似罕见的与中国"合拍"的表态中，夹杂着并不隐晦的政治导向：第一，在有关南海行为规则体系的表述中多以"东盟"为叙事主体，力推东盟在"南海行为准则"谈判构建中的主导地位；第二，强行将南海仲裁拉入《南海各方行为宣言》及"南海行为准则"的实施或谈判中，热切期盼落实《南海各方行为宣言》是为配合"南海仲裁案"裁决的执行，呼吁尽早达成的"南海行为准则"则应以仲裁裁决为动力和契机；第三，推动有法律拘束力的"准则"的形成，而需要得以约束的目标内容已预设为"不损害第三方的利益或所有国家根据国际法享有的权利""巩固现有包容性地区架构""停止将争议复杂化或升级，包括将争议地物军事化"等，以便与澳美"以规则为基础的地区和国际秩序"的共识相对接，并试图为介入中国东海问题创造条件。

2017年3月，澳大利亚外长毕晓普称，东盟应尽快与中国签订"南海行为准则"，同时表示：既然（菲律宾南海）仲裁已经将建议和结果表述得非常清楚，那么这应该成为"南海行为准则"的基础。[3] 同年4月，澳日第7次外长与防长"2+2"磋商发表联合声明，"重申东盟国家和中国有必要全面有效落实《南海各方行为宣言》"，同时"在国际法基础上"，"并考虑到2016

---

[1] "2013 Defence White Paper", Parliament of Australia, https://www.aph.gov.au/About_Parliament/Parliame-ntary_Departments/Parliamentary_Library/pubs/rp/rp1516/DefendAust/2013, August 10, 2023.

[2] "Joint statement AUSMIN 2015", The Australian Department of Foreign Affairs and Trade, https://www.dfat.gov.au/geo/united-states-of-america/ausmin/Pages/joint-statement-ausmin-2015, October 13, 2022.

[3] 《澳外长妄称南海仲裁案可成为〈南海行为准则〉基础》，载中国南海研究院网站，https://www.nanhai.org.cn/info--detail/22/4414.html，最后访问日期：2022年4月4日。

年 7 月 12 日《联合国海洋法公约》下仲裁庭的裁决","鼓励"各方"尽早达成有效的'南海行为准则'"。[1] 同年 8 月,在中国和东盟外长签署谅解备忘录、顺利通过"南海行为准则"框架文件、进展良好之际,美日澳却发表联合声明谴责中国,妄图通过南海问题来离间中国与东盟的关系。[2]

2018 年 3 月,在澳大利亚与印度尼西亚的部长级磋商中,双方强调"东盟国家和中国承诺全面有效落实《南海各方行为宣言》",认可东盟国家和中国为早日达成"符合国际法、有效"的"南海行为准则"所做的努力。[3] 2018 年 8 月,美日澳在菲律宾举行三国外长会谈并发表联合声明,"强烈反对"中国在南海和东海的所谓"单方面行动",在要求南海声索国"避免从事填海活动、建设前哨基地、将争议海洋地物予以军事化","敦促"中国和菲律宾"遵守'南海仲裁案'裁决"的同时,呼吁东盟成员国尽快与中国签订"具有法律约束力"的"南海行为准则"。同时,澳大利亚驻菲律宾大使提出,要达成"南海行为准则"并不容易。虽然相应行为准则应能强化东盟已有的体系结构及东盟的向心力,强化各方停止使争议升级的承诺,但该大使同意美国的立场,即第三方的关切也应包括在"南海行为准则"内,该"准则的结论不应伤害非签署国的利益及权利"。[4]

2019 年 8 月,新一轮的美日澳三国外长会谈继续肯定"南海行为准则"的谈判努力,但再次强调相关"准则"应"符合现行国际法""不损害第三方的利益或所有国家根据国际法享有的权利""巩固现有包容性地区架构""停止将争议复杂化或升级的行动"。[5] 2020 年 7 月,澳美年度部长级磋商发表联合声明,"欢迎东盟领导人近日发表的'南海行为准则'应与《联合国海洋法公约》相一致的声明",强调"任何准则都不应损害各国根据国际法享有的权利或利益,也不应破坏现有的地区架构""应加强各方不采取使

---

[1] "Joint statement-Seventh Japan-Australia 2 + 2 Foreign and Defence Ministerial Consultations", Australian Defence, https://www.minister.defence.gov.au/statements/2017-04-21/joint-statement-seventh-japan-australia-22-foreign-and-defence-ministerial-consultations, April 20, 2023.

[2]《南海行为准则稳定局势 美日澳立马联手煽风点火》,载观察者网,https://www.guancha.cn/military-affairs/2017_08_08_421812.shtml,最后访问日期:2024 年 9 月 10 日。

[3] "Joint Statement on the Fifth Indonesia-Australia Foreign and Defence Ministers 2 + 2 Meeting", The Australian Department of Foreign Affairs and Trade, https://www.dfat.gov.au/news/news/Pages/joint-statement-on-the-fifth-indonesia-australia-foreign-and-defence-ministers-2-2-meeting, March 16, 2023.

[4]《澳大利亚在中国与东盟间横插一刀!称南海行为准则不能伤害第三方》,载网易网,https://www.163.com/dy/article/DPIMV30B0512DAHC.html,最后访问日期:2023 年 4 月 4 日。

[5] Marise Payne, "Trilateral Strategic Dialogue Joint Ministerial Statement", https://www.foreignminister.gov.au/minister/marise-payne/media-release/trilateral-strategic-dialogue-joint-ministerial-statement, August 12, 2023.

争端复杂化或扩大化的行动的承诺，特别是不将争议岛礁军事化"。2022 年 1 月，澳美年度部长级磋商在联合声明中再次强调，"任何行为准则都必须完全符合国际法""不得损害各国根据国际法享有的权利或利益""不得破坏现有的包容性地区架构"。[1]

综上，正如澳大利亚联邦议会在"东盟与南海"专题报告所述及的，澳大利亚认同中国和东盟签署《南海各方行为宣言》表明了各方有在南海地区开展相关活动时遵守国际法相关规则的意愿，各方已据此承诺了保持自我克制，不将南海地区军事化。但澳大利亚同时认定，中国不仅没有遵守《南海各方行为宣言》，还加快了在南海的"扩张"以及在南海的"军事设施建设"。由此，澳大利亚认为：第一，关于南海问题的争端，尚不存在一项各方都能接受的行为准则，而若不对中国的主权主张加以限制，恐怕南海问题永远都得不到解决；第二，中国所希望达成的"南海行为准则"不可能符合2016 年"南海仲裁案"裁决的结论，据此在中国与东盟间形成的"南海行为准则"预期将损害澳大利亚的利益，这一准则将不可能得到澳大利亚的支持；第三，为避免因不接受"南海行为准则"而导致的与中国及东盟国家间的关系恶化，澳大利亚将在美国的压力下积极介入中国与东盟国家间的"南海行为准则"谈判，通过与东南亚沿海国家的多途径协商合作，对未来的谈判行为施加影响，并持续"鼓励"东盟国家签署的"南海行为准则"不会"违反国际法"。[2]

（三）在"一带一路"框架下与中国合作的态度

2015 年 3 月，国家发展和改革委员会、外交部及商务部联合印发了《推动共建丝绸之路经济带和 21 世纪海上丝绸之路的愿景与行动》，明确："21 世纪海上丝绸之路重点方向是从中国沿海港口过南海到印度洋，延伸至欧洲；从中国沿海港口过南海到南太平洋。"[3] 作为"21 世纪海上丝绸之路"的南线，从南海至南太平洋的太平洋方向是"一带一路"倡议不可或缺的重要一环，区域内海洋资源丰富和基础设施严重落后的矛盾现实也使南线建设

---

[1] "AUKMIN 2022 Joint Statement", The Australian Department of Foreign Affairs and Trade, https://www.dfat.gov.au/news/news/aukmin-2022-joint-statement, January 21, 2023.

[2] See "ASEAN and the South China Sea", Parliament of Australia, https://www.aph.gov.au/About_Parliament/Parliamentary_Departments/Parliamentary_Library/pubs/rp/rp2122/ASEANSouthChinaSea, March 21, 2022; "Australia's South China Sea challenges", Lowy Institute, https://www.lowyinstitute.org/sites/default/files/COO-K SCS Challenges FINAL PDF.pdf, April 4, 2022.

[3] 《推动共建丝绸之路经济带和 21 世纪海上丝绸之路的愿景与行动》，载人民网，http://ydyl.people.com.cn/n1/2017/0425/c411837-29235511.html，最后访问日期：2023 年 8 月 21 日。

极具可行空间。毫无疑问，澳大利亚是南太平洋国土面积最大、人口数量最多、经济实力最强的国家，也是对同在"21世纪海上丝绸之路"南线上的东南亚地区有较强影响力的国家。对于"一带一路"建设在域内的推进与延伸，澳大利亚的立场和态度极具意义。

依据2017年3月澳大利亚洛伊国际政策研究所（Lowy Institute for International Policy）发布的《理解中国"一带一路"》（Understanding China's Belt and Road Initiative）研究报告，澳大利亚对"一带一路"根本属性的认知存在两种代表性观点：一是将其定位为单纯的国际经济合作机制；二是将其识别为具有经济属性但实质上为战略性质的政策工具。前者多为澳地方政府和商界的期待，认可"一带一路"倡议带来的发展机遇，希望在改善基础设施条件的同时，通过加强双边经贸合作提振实体经济。后者则体现出澳大利亚政界及部分学界对中国政治和经济影响力以及中国塑造和引领国际规范的"软实力"在澳本土乃至整个南太平洋地区持续强化的忧虑，并随着"中国威胁论"和"中国渗透论"在澳大利亚国内持续蔓延。[1]在这一认知对立之下，澳大利亚官方对"一带一路"倡议的态度经历了从观望、犹豫到拒绝、否定的阶段性转变。其节点正是美国对华战略大转向下的2017年。随着2018年6月澳大利亚反外国干涉相关法案及2020年12月新《对外关系法》的出台，中澳经贸合作更是接连遭遇重挫，澳官方趋于负面的"一带一路"认知不断得到强化。

1. 经济利益与安全焦虑间的试探与摇摆

2013年4月，习近平主席在海南省博鳌会见澳大利亚总理吉拉德，宣布中澳构建相互信任、互利共赢的战略伙伴关系，并同意启动两国总理年度定期会晤机制及中澳外交与战略对话机制。[2] 2014年11月，习近平主席在堪培拉同澳大利亚总理阿博特（Tony Abbott）举行会谈，将中澳关系提升为全面战略伙伴关系，同时建立起中澳高级别对话会议平台。[3]习近平主席也在这次访问中明确表示："大洋洲地区是古代海上丝绸之路的自然延伸，中方

---

[1] Peter Cai, "Understanding China's Belt and Road Initiative", Lowy Institute, https://www.lowyinstitute.org/sites/default/files/documents/Understanding%20China%E2%80%99s%20Belt%20and%20Road%20Initiative_WEB_1.pdf, 2017, pp.1-2.

[2]《习近平7日在海南省博鳌会见澳大利亚总理吉拉德》，载中华人民共和国中央人民政府网站，https://www.gov.cn/ldhd/2013-04/07/content_2371991.htm，最后访问日期：2023年8月20日。

[3]《习近平同澳大利亚总理阿博特举行会谈》，载央广网，https://news.cnr.cn/native/gd/20160707/t20160707_522615977.shtml，最后访问日期：2024年9月10日。

七、对中国海洋法主张的态度

对澳大利亚参与21世纪海上丝绸之路建设持开放态度。"[1] 2015—2016年，在与时任澳大利亚总理特恩布尔（Malcolm Turnbull）的3次会面中，中国国家主席习近平均表示，希望双方做好"一带一路"倡议同澳大利亚"北部大开发"计划的对接。如，2015年11月，习近平主席同澳大利亚总理特恩布尔在土耳其会面时提出，中澳同处亚太地区，两国拥有重要的共同利益和广阔的合作空间；中国愿同澳方在互信互利的基础上，深化各领域的友好交流和务实合作，双方要发挥互补优势，推进"一带一路"倡议同澳方"北部大开发"计划的对接。2016年4月，习近平主席在澳大利亚总理受邀访问中国时再次提出，希望双方做好中方"一带一路"倡议同澳方"北部大开发"计划、中国创新驱动发展战略同澳方"国家创新与科学议程"的对接，探讨开展更多务实合作项目。[2]

面对中国共赢互益的"君子之朋"的诚挚之邀，澳大利亚官方一方面态度谨慎，尤其避免在公开场合作出倾向性表态；另一方面却从未否定加入"一带一路"倡议的可能性，并不乏试探或迂回地与中方就开展"一带一路"合作进行接洽。以贸易部门为代表的澳大利亚政府官员大都对"一带一路"倡议持正面看法，希望通过这一框架下的合作为澳大利亚企业提供更多发展机遇。由此，中澳间的"一带一路"合作在2014—2017年因较为密集的实践推进似乎进入了令人振奋的良性发展轨道。

2014年11月，习近平主席访澳期间，双方签署了《中华人民共和国政府和澳大利亚政府关于实质性结束中澳自贸协定谈判的意向声明》。2015年6月，中澳双方签署了《中华人民共和国政府和澳大利亚政府自由贸易协定》。同年12月，中澳自贸协定正式生效。也是在2015年3月，澳大利亚加入亚投行筹建，成为亚投行创始成员国。2016年4月，澳大利亚总理特恩布尔访华期间，与中国领导人围绕"一带一路"倡议交换意见，习近平主席在会面时再次提出，希望双方做好中方"一带一路"倡议同澳方"北部大开发"计划、中国创新驱动发展战略同澳方"国家创新与科学议程"的对接。随之而来的是，中国在澳大利亚堪培拉、维多利亚州、西澳大利亚州等多项

---

[1]《习近平在澳联邦议会演讲：携手追寻中澳发展梦想 并肩实现地区繁荣稳定》，载新华网，http://www.xinhuanet.com/world/2014-11/17/c_1113285659_2.htm，最后访问日期：2023年8月21日。

[2] 刘乐、王宗英：《习近平会见澳大利亚总理特恩布尔》，载央广网，http://china.cnr.cn/gdgg/20151116/t20151116_520518202.shtml，最后访问日期：2023年8月21日；李忠发：《习近平会见澳大利亚总理特恩布尔》，载中华人民共和国人民政协网，https://www.rmzxb.com.cn/c/2016-04-15/769171.shtml，最后访问日期：2023年8月21日。

215

大型交通基础设施项目的开展或完成，包括堪培拉城市轻轨一期项目、维多利亚州政府高运量地铁车项目等。2017年3月，中国国务院总理李克强成功访澳，两国领导人一致同意努力打造"两国自贸繁荣新时代"，深入推进"一带一路"倡议与澳"北部大开发"计划以及两国创新发展战略的对接，两国有关企业签署了关于澳北部基础设施合作协议。在中澳两国总理的见证下，中国建筑工程总公司与澳大利亚BBIG公司（Balla Balla Infrastructure Group）签署了一项金额达50亿澳元的西澳大利亚州基础设施一揽子建设项目合作备忘录。该项目是包括港口、铁路基础设施和PIOP铁矿石资源矿山为一体的大型综合建设开发项目，是推进与澳大利亚"北部大开发"计划对接的重要项目之一。[1] 同年4月，中澳举行了首次高级别安全对话。同年5月，澳贸易、旅游与投资部长乔博（Steven Ciobo）代表澳政府来华出席"一带一路"国际合作高峰论坛。在随后9月的第3次中澳战略经济对话期间，两国政府部门签署了《关于开展第三方市场合作的谅解备忘录》，鼓励和支持两国企业在"一带一路"沿线国家和地区推进能源资源、基础设施、农业和食品、服务业、先进制造业等领域的第三方市场合作。[2]

总体而言，在经过一段时间的观望后，澳大利亚政府开始于2013—2017年尝试对接"一带一路"倡议，期望寻求有限合作。但随着澳方自2017年年底开始采取一系列负面的对华政策行动，中澳关系急转直下，尤其在美国对华战略不断转向的大背景下，澳大利亚似乎急于通过否定和拒绝"一带一路"倡议的现实与可能来巩固与美国的同盟关系。

2017年3月，在李克强总理成功访澳、两国于经贸等问题上达成共识的热烈氛围中，备受瞩目的中澳"一带一路"合作谅解备忘录却并未签订。由于担心澳美关系受到影响，澳大利亚拒绝正式对接堪培拉50亿澳元国家基础设施基金与中国的新丝绸之路战略。[3] 2018年1月，时任澳大利亚国际发展与太平洋事务部长的孔切塔·菲拉万蒂-维尔斯（Concetta Fierravanti-Wells）指责中国在太平洋岛国的基础设施项目不具成效，还附加了不利的金融条款。[4] 同年7月，中国驻澳大利亚大使成竞业在澳大利亚北方领地地区

---

[1] 左永刚、孙华：《中澳迈向"自贸繁荣"新时代 中国建筑获基建大单》，载中国一带一路网，https://www.yidaiyilu.gov.cn/p/10223.html，最后访问日期：2023年8月22日。

[2] 《中国同澳大利亚的关系》，载中华人民共和国外交部网站，https://www.mfa.gov.cn/web/gjhdq_676201/gj_676203/dyz_681240/1206_681242/sbgx_681246/#，最后访问日期：2023年8月22日。

[3] Jamie Smyth, "Australia rejects China push on Silk Road strategy", http://www.atimes.com/article/aust-ralia-rejects-one-belt-one-road-deal/, June 3, 2023.

[4] 《澳大利亚政客应多些自省意识（钟声）》，载人民网，http://world.people.com.cn/n1/2018/0112/c1002-29760049.html，最后访问日期：2024年9月10日。

首府达尔文参加活动时发表演讲，号召澳大利亚同中国签署"一带一路"倡议合作备忘录，但澳大利亚外交部却表现出对倡议的顾虑。[1] 2018 年 6 月，澳大利亚外长毕晓普在接受媒体采访时表示，澳大利亚担心"一带一路"会给南太平洋岛国带来沉重的债务负担，并直言"一带一路"是中国在地区扩大政治和战略影响的工具。[2] 2018 年 10 月，工党执政的维多利亚州政府与中国签署了"一带一路"合作谅解备忘录，这是两国"一带一路"合作中具有里程碑意义的成果。但维多利亚州政府及其州长却在随后不断遭到澳大利亚联邦政府的质疑。时任内政部长彼得·达顿（Peter Dutton）在接受采访时施压称："维多利亚需要解释为什么维州是本国唯一一个签署此协议的州。"[3] 2020 年 12 月，澳大利亚推出针对性明显的新《对外关系法》，特别规定所有州政府与外国签订协议前，都必须事先得到联邦外交部长的同意；同时赋予了联邦政府否决州政府等各级政府、机构与外国签订协议的权力。[4] 自 2021 年 1 月 1 日起，澳大利亚开始实施新修订的《外国投资法》，设立国家安全审查制度，对涉及国家安全用地或国家安全相关业务的投资项目实施严格审查。2021 年 12 月，澳大利亚修订了《关键基础设施安全法》，大幅扩大关键基础设施范围，增加强制经营实体报告网络安全事件义务和信息提供机制。[5] 而就在 2021 年 4 月，澳大利亚联邦政府正式宣布废除维多利亚州与中国签署的"一带一路"合作谅解备忘录及框架协议。澳大利亚外长佩恩在相关声明中称，这一协议不符合澳大利亚的外交政策和国家利益，这也是澳大利亚联邦政府第一次启用《对外关系法》授予的否决权。[6]

2. 发展机遇与政策修正下的前景期待

澳大利亚在面对"一带一路"倡议时的矛盾摇摆可见一斑：既不愿放弃

---

[1] "Chinese Ambassador Calls for Australia to Join Belt and Road Initiative", Ecns, http://www.ecns.cn/ne-ws/pol itics/2018-07-11/detail-ifyvzyvz7260366. shtml, April 5, 2022.

[2] David Wroe, "Australia Will Compete with China to Save Pacific Sovereignty, Says Bishop", https://www.smh.com.au/politics/federal/australia-will-compete-with-china-to-save-pacific-sovereignty-says-bishop-20180617-p4zm1h.html, December 27, 2022.

[3] 《澳联邦政府指控维州"擅自签署一带一路"，州长出面反驳》，载观察者网站，https://www.guancha.cn/internation/2020_05_27_551996.shtml，最后访问日期：2024 年 12 月 10 日。

[4] "Australia Puts China's Belt & Road Initiative (BRI) In A Limbo With New Legislation", The Australian Times, https://eurasiantimes.com/australia-puts-chinas-belt-road-initiative-bri-in-a-limbo-with-new-legislation/, April 5, 2022.

[5] 《对外投资合作国别（地区）指南——澳大利亚（2023 年版）》，载中华人民共和国商务部网站，http://www.mofcom.gov.cn/dl/gbdqzn/upload/aodaliya.pdf，最后访问日期：2024 年 9 月 10 日。

[6] 《澳大利亚外长宣布撕毁"一带一路"协议》，载观察者网，https://www.guancha.cn/intern-tion/2021_04_22_588372.shtml，最后访问日期：2022 年 3 月 21 日。

"一带一路"所带来的重要发展契机，亦无法完全无视澳国内对华战略疑虑的呼声，更忧心在美国心目中伙伴价值的丧失，至今澳大利亚也仍置身大洋洲的12个"一带一路"共建国之外。但需要明确的是，一方面，尽管澳大利亚不断释放消极信号，中国仍然希望改善并推动中澳关系向前发展，并在"一带一路"等合作倡议上积极争取澳大利亚的加入；另一方面，即使是在2017年后的明确回撤，澳大利亚政府也从未在政策层面彻底断绝"一带一路"的接触通道，而是在低频谨慎的行动中留有余地。

2018年8月，澳大利亚总理特恩布尔在新南威尔士大学发表对华政策讲话时表示赞赏中国改革开放取得的非凡成功，积极评价华侨、华人对澳社会所作贡献，期待同中方加强"一带一路"等领域的合作，推进澳中全面战略伙伴关系。同年10月，接任澳大利亚总理的莫里森在接受采访时虽未明确提及"一带一路"，但也表示"澳大利亚期待与中国在符合国际标准的管理水平和透明度基础上，加强在区域投资和基础设施发展方面的合作"[1]。2018年11月，中澳举行第六轮总理年度会晤。在两国关系出现曲折后的"转折点上"的这次会晤中，澳大利亚总理表示"欢迎中国在全球和地区问题上发挥的积极作用"，认可"中国的繁荣在本地区有积极的溢出效应"，澳大利亚"愿同中方推进全面战略伙伴关系，继续欢迎来自中国的投资，进一步加强在经贸、创新、矿业、旅游、能源等领域合作，不断扩大人文交流，并就气候变化等全球性挑战同中国加强沟通与合作"[2]。2019年4月，澳外交贸易部常务副部长孙芳安（Frances Adamson）在参加第二届"一带一路"国际合作高峰论坛期间再次强调，"正如莫里森总理所说，澳方欢迎'一带一路'倡议为满足本地区基础设施需求作出贡献"；澳大利亚参加本次论坛"显示其对加入'一带一路'倡议已经做好准备"，希望"在符合国际治理、透明度和债务可持续性标准的项目上"加强与中国的接触。[3] 2022年12月，中澳举行第六轮外交与战略对话，双方同意启动或重启包括双边关系、经贸问题、领事事务、气

---

[1] Li Xin, Ke Dawei, "Exclusive: Australia's Prime Minister Says China Not Targeted by Nnvestmentrestrictions", https://www.caixinglobal.com/2018-10-09/exclusive-australias-prime-minister-says-china-not-tar-geted-by-investment-restrictions-101333112.html, August 25, 2023.

[2] 《李克强同澳大利亚总理莫里森举行第六轮中澳总理年度会晤》，载中华人民共和国外交部网站，https://www.mfa.gov.cn/web/gjhdq_676201/gj_676203/dyz_681240/1206_681242/xgxw_681248/201811/t20181119_9374575.shtml，最后访问日期：2023年8月23日。

[3] "Remarks at Australia-China Reception", Secretary Frances Adamson, https://china.embassy.gov.au/bjng/Speech190425.html#:~:text=Secretary%20Frances%20Adamson%20Remarks%20at%20Australia-China%20Rec-eption%20Ambassador%20E2%80%99s, so%20many%20good%20friends%20and%20colleagues%20here%20tonig-ht, August 23, 2023.

候变化、防务、地区和国际问题在内的多领域对话沟通,支持包括1.5轨高级别对话、中澳工商界首席执行官圆桌会和两国商业团组互访在内的两国人文交流。[1] 2023年9月,包括澳大利亚前外长、前贸易部长在内的澳政府、工商界、学术界及媒体和艺术界的高级代表赴北京参加中澳高级别对话第七次会议。澳大利亚外长黄英贤(Penny Wong)肯定了这一"自2020年年初以来的首次对话","标志着两国在加强双边接触、稳定对华关系方面又迈出了一步"。澳方代表团团长、前贸易部长埃莫森等(Craig Emerson)则表示,"很高兴看到澳中关系在经历曲折后日趋成熟","澳方始终视中方为重要合作伙伴",双方"应重振多边机构中的合作,共促贸易投资自由化便利化"。[2]

应该看到,在刻意表现得强硬冷淡之下,由经济利益和发展机遇带动的对华交流一直存在。在联邦政府层面,无论官方表述为何,澳大利亚绝不希望被放弃分享中国经济发展可能带来的红利。在地方政府层面,无论联邦政府如何摇摆,澳大利亚地方政府及其商界对参与"一带一路"合作的热情都在联邦政府之上,包括新南威尔士州、维多利亚州、西澳大利亚州、南澳大利亚州、昆士兰州、塔斯马尼亚州和北方领地地区的各地方政府均对参与共建表达过明确意愿或已有"一带一路"项目运营或投产;即使维多利亚州签署的相关谅解备忘录在法律层面被迫中道而止,其签署备忘录后的优异数据与发展实效也已经作出了良好示范。[3] 在行业企业层面,澳大利亚的资源行业与商业服务公司对澳大利亚加入"一带一路"的反响尤为积极,多家咨询公司和律师事务所对澳大利亚加入后的相关问题和收益都给出了乐观反馈。在媒体和学界层面,有关"一带一路"的正面报道多引述澳大利亚商界信源,认为"一带一路"是该国经济发展的重要机会;经济利益同时也是澳大利亚主流学界评估对华外交决策的重要标准,并由此对"一带一路"倡议及与其相辅相成的亚投行筹建等作出了快速反应。可以认为,在当前的总体氛围与政策框架下,对于澳大利亚在"一带一路"倡议下的合作共建前景,仍可抱有期待。

---

[1] 《中澳外交与战略对话成果联合声明》,载中华人民共和国外交部网站,https://www.mfa.gov.cn/web/gjhdq_676201/gj_676203/dyz_681240/1206_681242/1207_681254/202212/t20221221_10993385.shtml,最后访问日期:2023年8月23日。

[2] 《王毅集体会见中澳高级别对话澳方代表团》,载中华人民共和国外交部网站,https://www.mfa.gov.cn/web/gjhdq_676201/gj_676203/dyz_681240/1206_681242/xgxw_681248/202309/t20230907_11139769.shtml,最后访问日期:2024年9月13日;Senator the Hon Penny Wong, "Australia-China high level dialogue", https://www.fore-ignminister.gov.au/minister/penny-wong/media-release/australia-china-high-level-dialogue, August 23, 2023.

[3] 岳圣淞:《澳新两国对"一带一路"倡议的认知比较与机制化建设》,载《辽宁大学学报(哲学社会科学版)》2021年第4期,第150页。

结　语

　　被太平洋四面合围、独踞一个大陆的澳大利亚，既踞海而心安，亦惧因海而孤悬。海洋是澳大利亚国土安全的天然屏障，也是其国土威胁的直接来源；是澳大利亚民生富足的第一倚仗，也是其生存竞争的第一战场；是澳大利亚远离外界纷扰的便利凭借，也是其焦虑孤立的地缘现实。澳大利亚对于其海洋立法的重视及其体系构建的庞杂完备需求一望可知。

　　澳大利亚有着极具特色的综合行政体系，联邦内阁下属的各部委下辖着跨界而互有关联的多个领域。海洋相关管理部门虽分属各部委之下，但仍已形成了从安全、资源、运输到科研、环境、文化的全局覆盖，以实现国内海洋法律体系下的权力分配与执行运转。值得注意的是，澳大利亚行政管理部门多与相关领域的非官方行业机构和专门性法人团体有着良好的体系协同与运作配合，这在海洋相关管理机构包括海上武装执法部门的职能运转和项目规划中也有突出体现。在政府直属的海上执法机构之外，澳大利亚有多个民间海上安全志愿者组织都极为活跃，并已经积累有相当的组织基础和专业声望。充分调动全民对国家的海洋文化认同和海洋使命承担，开发民间力量以辅助国家海洋行政管理，不失为澳大利亚海洋管理体系的特色经验。

　　无论是国内海洋立法还是国际海洋造法，澳大利亚都力图在各海洋相关规则体系的构建中或成为标准引领者或作为主要贡献方。一如，为支撑其在沿岸海域的传统国别海洋主张，在专门性立法中明确历史性水域的存在及其地位；为保障本国海洋渔业资源及产业的健康与可持续发展，在海洋安全相关立法中专章细化紧追权的行使；为迎合海洋能源开发利用的行业需求，从海底电缆管道至离岸能源作业各环节设施都予以额外的不断发展的保护性立法。如上各项，都成为澳大利亚国内海洋立法供给《公约》相应制度的国别贡献。又如，澳大利亚对南极固有利益的坚守及在南极秩序构建中地位的维持贯通如一。为此，从1933年宣示南极领土主权开始，澳大利亚海洋立法通过法律、规章、条例、公告等多种渊源将南极法律地位、资源养护、环境保护、海域通行、南极文化遗址保护等诸多问题涵盖其中，为澳大利亚在南极的可能权力行使提供法律支持。而在国际立法层面，澳大利亚一直是"南极条约体系"最具影响力的缔约国之一。在自誉为该条约体系效力的忠实维护者与执行者的同时，澳大利亚坚称对42%以上的南极大陆及其邻近海域享有主权。随着澳大利亚有关近南极圈海外领地的外大陆架划界案的通过，澳大

结　语

利亚在南极地区意图利用规则、引导规则以确保本国南极利益的试验性做法进一步引发对南极条约秩序与规则重塑走向的关注和担忧。再如，澳大利亚始终致力于树立和维系其在国际海洋环境保护中的先行者与力行者形象。除几乎在所有海洋职能部门都引入环境监测与评价模块外，澳大利亚也在以国际海事组织为代表的国际机构框架下积极参与包括海洋减排措施在内的各项新兴规则的纳入或构建，并为保障海洋环境相关国际条约下法律义务的履行，颁布了以"海洋保护法"为主题的系列国内立法。与此同时，澳大利亚海洋各专门性立法通过后续法律及各类次级规范不断更新修正，也极具动态地反映着澳大利亚由国际立法背书的最有利权益伸张及与周边国家间海洋谈判的最新成果。

在与周边国家的海洋争端解决中，澳大利亚表现出和平解决争端的较大诚意和灵活利用多重途径的良好成果。与葡萄牙、印度尼西亚、东帝汶之间围绕帝汶海的海洋划界争端，尤其成为澳大利亚争端解决立场与策略的集中试练。澳大利亚与上述三国间分别在不同历史阶段，交替利用政治谈判、国际法院裁判、《帝汶海条约》下仲裁、《公约》附件5下调解等多种机制尝试推动争端解决进程，并最终在《公约》生效后的第一例强制调解程序的基础上完成了与东帝汶间新一轮双边条约的签署，在帝汶海海洋划界及"巨日升"区域开发等问题上达成国家间和解。与此同时，面对本国关切的特殊渔业资源及海洋生物多样性保护诉求，国际法院、国际海洋法法庭、《公约》附件7下仲裁庭也都成为澳大利亚把握主动、先声夺人、争取后续司法收益的优先选项。无论是与周边国家划界谈判的系列成果，还是强制或非强制法律解决手段的积极实践，澳大利亚都为《公约》下争端解决机制的适用与发展提供了素材填充与示范反馈，也在一定程度上有益于本国遵守"规则下秩序"的口碑经营和外交底气。

南海问题与对中国海洋战略的戒备，已经成为裹挟包括"一带一路"倡议在内的中澳经济合作主题的重要政治因素。一方面，确保与美国安全同盟的稳定，始终是澳大利亚国家安全利益的第一要务。作为将国家安全利益系于澳美同盟的现有国际秩序受益者，澳大利亚要在安全上与美国保持一致，即需要在亚太秩序和海洋问题立场上与美国进退一体。另一方面，对于沿"海上丝绸之路"铺陈而来的合作共建倡议，作为四面环海的澳洲"孤岛"，澳大利亚对中国的海洋战略极为敏感，对南太平洋上岛国的利益格局变动高度焦虑。无论是经济还是安全，澳大利亚对中澳双边关系的利益权衡和取舍都绕不开南海问题评判和"印太战略"谋划。在选边困境之下，除国内政党政治生态的影响外，南海问题、地区领导力衰退以及美国主导的"印太战略"行进，都会成为笼罩中澳合作共建前路的阴云。如何在海洋命运共同体下寻求两国有关海洋战略安全、海洋有效治理、海洋和谐秩序的认知交会和惠益共识，将是中澳未来关系持续向好的探索重心。

参考文献

一、中文文献

1. 高京：《澳大利亚》，世界知识出版社1997年版。
2. 苏浩：《从哑铃到橄榄：亚太合作安全模式研究》，世界知识出版社2003年版。
3. 沈永兴、张秋生、高国荣编著：《列国志·澳大利亚》，社会科学文献出版社2010年版。
4. 薛桂芳：《澳大利亚海洋战略研究》，时事出版社2016年版。
5. 杜贵超、仓辉、胡双全等：《澳大利亚油气资源潜力及油气合作前景》，载《海峡科技与产业》2016年第2期。
6. 卓振伟：《澳大利亚与环印度洋联盟的制度变迁》，载《太平洋学报》2018年第12期。
7. 时宏远：《印度—澳大利亚海洋合作：动力与制约》，载《南亚研究季刊》2020年第1期。
8. 周乐萍：《澳大利亚海洋经济发展特性及启示》，载《海洋开发与管理》2021年第9期。
9. 岳圣淞：《澳新两国对"一带一路"倡议的认知比较与机制化建设》，载《辽宁大学学报（哲学社会科学版）》2021年第4期。
10. 王玥：《印太语境下澳大利亚与印度尼西亚的海洋安全合作》，载《印度洋经济体研究》2022年第4期。

二、外文文献

1. Smith, Madeleine, "Australian claims to the Timor sea's petroleum resources: Clever, cunning, or criminal?", *Monash University Law Review*, Vol. 37, 2012.
2. David Brewster, "The India-Australia Security and Defence Relationship: Developments, Constraints and Prospects", *Security Challenges*, Vol. 10, 2014.

三、数据库和网站

(一) 中文数据库和网站

1. 中华人民共和国中央人民政府网站，https：//www. gov. cn。
2. 中华人民共和国外交部网站，https：//www. mfa. gov. cn。
3. 中华人民共和国商务部网站，http：//www. mofcom. gov. cn。
4. 中华人民共和国商务部全球法规网站，http：//policy. mofcom. gov. cn。
5. 中华人民共和国人民政协网，https：//www. rmzxb. com. cn。
6. 中国一带一路网，https：//www. yidaiyilu. gov. cn。
7. 央广网，http：//china. cnr. cn。
8. 新华网，http：//www. news. cn。
9. 网易网，https：//www. 163. com。
10. 环球网，https：//world. huanqiu. com。
11. 观察者网，https：//www. guancha. cn。
12. 新浪网，http：//news. sina. com. cn。
13. 中国军网，http：//photo. chinamil. com. cn。
14. 青岛海洋国家实验室网站，http：//www. qnlm. ac/page? a = 14&b = 1&c = 248&p = detail。
15. 中国船东网，http：//csoa. cn。
16. 中国首都网，http：//mil. qianlong. com。
17. 中国南海网，http：//nanhai. haiwainet. cn。
18. 科普中国网，https：//www. kepuchina. cn。
19. 大河网，http：//newpaper. dahe. cn。

(二) 外文数据库和网站

1. The Australian Department of Foreign Affairs and Trade，https：//www. dfat. gov. au。
2. Australian Government，https：//www. australia. gov. au/。
3. Geoscience Australia，https：//ecat. ga. gov. au。
4. National Geographic，https：//www. nationalgeographic. com。
5. Australian Institute of Aboriginal and Torres Strait Islander Studies，https：//aiatsis. gov. au。
6. The Australian Institute of Marine Science，https：//www. aims. gov. au。
7. The Australian Department of Infrastructure，https：//www. infrastructure. gov. au。
8. Parliament of Australia，https：//www. aph. gov. au。

9. Australian Maritime Safety Authority, https://www.amsa.gov.au.

10. Australian National Maritime Museum, https://www.sea.museum.

11. The Australian Department of Agriculture, Fisheries and Forestry, https://www.agriculture.gov.au.

12. Australian Fisheries Management Authority, https://www.afma.gov.au.

13. Australian Minister for Trade and Tourism, https://www.trademinister.gov.au.

14. DCCEEW, https://www.dcceew.gov.au.

15. The Australian Bureau of Meteorology, http://www.bom.gov.au.

16. The Great Barrier Reef Marine Park Authority, https://www.gbrmpa.gov.au.

17. Australian Antarctic Program, https://www.antarctica.gov.au.

18. Sydney Harbour Federation Trust, https://www.harbourtrust.gov.au.

19. The Australian Department of Industry, Science and Resources, https://www.industry.gov.au.

20. NOPSEMA, https://www.nopsema.gov.au.

21. The Australian Department of Employment and Workplace Relations, https://www.dewr.gov.au.

22. Australian Seafarers Safety, Rehabilitation and Compensation Authority, https://www.seacare.gov.au.

23. Royal Australian Navy, https://www.navy.gov.au.

24. The Australian Department of Home Affairs, https://www.homeaffairs.gov.au.

25. The Australian Border Force, https://www.abf.gov.au.

26. Liqui Search, https://www.liquisearch.com.

27. Parliament of New South Wales, https://www.parliament.nsw.gov.au.

28. Australian Volunteer Coast Guard, https://coastguard.com.au.

29. Barnes, Thompson & Brown, https://legal-translations.com.au.

30. Australia Federal Register of Legislation, https://www.legislation.gov.au.

31. Australasian Legal Information Institute, http://www.austlii.edu.au.

32. Australian Defence, https://www.defence.gov.au.

33. The National Museum of Australia, https://www.nma.gov.au.

34. Australia Government DOD, https://news.defence.gov.au.

35. Australian Defence Ministers, https://www.minister.defence.gov.au.

36. Australian Embassy (China), https://china.embassy.gov.au.

37. Australian Embassy Tokyo, https://japan.embassy.gov.au.

38. Australian Minister for Foreign Affairs, https://www.foreignminister.gov.au.

39. Australian High Commission (New Zealand), https://newzealand.embassy.gov.au.

40. Australian High Commission (UK), http://uk.embassy.gov.au.

41. UNTC, https://treaties.un.org.

42. UN Office of Legal Affairs, https://legal.un.org.

43. UNEP Law and Environment Assistance Platform, https://leap.unep.org.

44. International Maritime Organization, https://www.imo.org.

45. Indian Ocean Rim Association, https://www.iora.int.

46. IHO, https://iho.int.

47. World Bank, https://databank.worldbank.org.

48. FAO, http://www.fao.org.

49. Centre for International Law, https://cil.nus.edu.sg.

50. ICJ, https://www.icj-cij.org.

51. ITLOS, https://www.itlos.org.

52. PCA, https://pca-cpa.org/.

53. DOI Foundation, https://doi.org.

54. U.S. Department of State, https://www.state.gov.

55. U.S. Department of Defense, https://www.defense.gov.

56. The White House, https://www.whitehouse.gov.

57. USNI News, https://news.usni.org.

58. Ministry of Foreign Affairs of Japan, http://www.mofa.go.jp.

59. US Navy, https://www.navy.mil.

60. Young Diplomats, https://www.young-diplomats.com.

61. Presidential Communications Office, http://pco.gov.ph.

62. The International Institute for Strategic Studies, https://www.iiss.org.

63. U.S. Energy Information Administration (EIA), https://www.eia.gov.

64. OilPrice.com, https://oilprice.com.

65. Incorrys, https://incorrys.com.

66. Woodside Energy, https://www.woodside.com.

67. NWSG, http://www.nwsg.com.au.

68. Chevron Australia, https://australia.chevron.com.

69. Chevron, https://www.chevron.com.

70. NS Energy, https://www.nsenergybusiness.com.

71. Total Energies, https://totalenergies.com.

72. Frontiers, https://www.frontiersin.org.

73. National Marine Science Committee, https://www.marinescience.net.au.

74. SBS Filipino, https://www.sbs.com.au.

75. Secretariat of the Pacific Regional Environment Programme, https://www.sprep.org.

76. Obama White House Archives, https://obamawhitehouse.archives.gov.

77. Global Defense Corp, https://www.globaldefensecorp.com.

78. The Manila Times, https://www.manilatimes.net.

79. ABC, http://www.abc.net.au.

80. Lowy Institute, https://www.lowyinstitute.org.

81. Asia Times, http://www.atimes.com.

82. Ecns, http://www.ecns.cn.

83. The Sydney Morning Herald, https://www.smh.com.au.

84. The Australian Times, https://eurasiantimes.com.

85. Caixin, https://www.caixinglobal.com.

附 录

附录1　1973年《海洋与水下土地法》[1]

Seas and Submerged Lands Act 1973

An Act relating to Sovereignty in respect of certain Waters of the Sea and in respect of the Airspace over, and the Sea-bed and Subsoil beneath, those Waters and to Sovereign Rights in respect of the Continental Shelf and the Exclusive Economic Zone and to certain rights of control in respect of the Contiguous Zone.

Preamble

WHEREAS a belt of sea adjacent to the coast of Australia, known as the territorial sea, and the airspace over the territorial sea and the bed and subsoil of the territorial sea, are within the sovereignty of Australia:

AND WHEREAS Australia as a coastal state has:

(a) sovereign rights in respect of the waters, the sea-bed and the subsoil that constitute the exclusive economic zone of Australia for the purposes of:

(i) exploring the zone; and

(ii) exploiting, conserving and managing the natural resources of the zone; and

(b) sovereign rights with regard to other activities for the economic exploitation and exploration of the exclusive economic zone of Australia, such as the production of energy from water, currents and winds; and

(c) jurisdiction in accordance with international law in relation to:

(i) the establishment and use of artificial islands, installations and structures in the exclusive economic zone; and

(ii) marine scientific research in the exclusive economic zone; and

(iii) the protection and preservation of the marine environment in the exclusive economic zone; and

---

[1] "Seas and Submerged Lands Act 1973", Australia Federal Register of Legislation, https://www.legislation.gov.au/Details/C2019C00259, December 3, 2024.

(d) other rights and duties in relation to the exclusive economic zone provided for in the United Nations Convention on the Law of the Sea;

AND WHEREAS Australia as a coastal state has sovereign rights in respect of the continental shelf (that is to say, the sea-bed and subsoil of certain submarine areas adjacent to its coast but outside the area of the territorial sea) for the purpose of exploring it and exploiting its natural resources;

AND WHEREAS Australia as a coastal state has the right under international law to exercise control within a contiguous zone to:

(a) prevent infringements of customs, fiscal, immigration or sanitary laws within Australia or the territorial sea of Australia;

(b) to punish infringements of those laws;

BE IT THEREFORE ENACTED by the Queen, the Senate and the House of Representatives of Australia, as follows:

Part I—Preliminary

1 Short title

This Act may be cited as the *Seas and Submerged Lands Act* 1973.

2 Commencement

This Act shall come into operation on the day on which it receives the Royal Assent.

3 Interpretation

(1) In this Act, unless the contrary intention appears:

Australia includes the Territories to which this Act extends.

contiguous zone has the same meaning as in Article 33 of the Convention.

continental shelf has the same meaning as in paragraph 1 of Article 76 of the Convention.

exclusive economic zone has the same meaning as in Articles 55 and 57 of the Convention.

Greater Sunrise special regime area means the area described in clause 1 of Schedule 2.

territorial sea has the same meaning as in Articles 3 and 4 of the Convention.

the Convention means the United Nations Convention on the Law of the Sea done at Montego Bay on 10 December 1982 (Parts II, V and VI of which are set out in Schedule 1).

Timor Sea Maritime Boundaries Treaty means the Treaty between Australia and the Democratic Republic of Timor-Leste Establishing their Maritime Boundaries in the Timor Sea done at New York on 6 March 2018, as in force from time to time.

Note: The Timor Sea Maritime Boundaries Treaty could in 2019 be viewed in the Australian Treaties Library on the AustLII website (http://www.austlii.edu.au).

(2) In this Act, including section 6, a reference to the territorial sea of Australia is a

reference to that territorial sea so far as it extends from time to time.

(2A) In this Act, including section 10A, a reference to the exclusive economic zone of Australia is a reference to that zone so far as it extends from time to time.

(3) In this Act, including section 11, a reference to the continental shelf of Australia is a reference to that continental shelf so far as it extends from time to time.

Note: Division 2AA of Part 2 affects the operation of laws in the part of the continental shelf of Australia in the Greater Sunrise special regime area.

(3A) In this Act, including section 13A, a reference to the contiguous zone of Australia is a reference to that zone so far as it extends from time to time.

(4) Where a Proclamation is in force under section 7, the territorial sea of Australia shall, for all purposes of this Act, be taken to extend to the limits declared by that Proclamation.

(4A) If a Proclamation is in force under section 10B, the exclusive economic zone of Australia is taken, for all purposes of this Act, to extend to the limits declared by that Proclamation.

(5) Where a Proclamation is in force under section 12, the continental shelf of Australia shall, for all purposes of this Act, be taken to extend to the limits declared by that Proclamation.

(5A) If a Proclamation is in force under section 13B, the contiguous zone of Australia is taken, for all purposes of this Act, to extend to the limits declared by that Proclamation.

4 Extension to Territories

This Act extends to all the Territories.

Part II—Sovereignty, sovereign rights and rights of control

Division 1—The territorial sea

5 Interpretation

In this Division, *the territorial sea* means the territorial sea of Australia.

6 Sovereignty in respect of territorial sea

It is by this Act declared and enacted that the sovereignty in respect of the territorial sea, and in respect of the airspace over it and in respect of its bed and subsoil, is vested in and exercisable by the Crown in right of the Commonwealth.

7 Limits of territorial sea

(1) The Governor-General may, from time to time, by Proclamation, declare, not inconsistently with Section 2 of Part II of the Convention, the limits of the whole or of any part of the territorial sea.

(2) For the purposes of such a Proclamation, the Governor-General may, in particular, determine either or both of the following:

(a) the breadth of the territorial sea;

(b) the baseline from which the breadth of the territorial sea, or of any part of the territorial sea, is to be measured.

8 Declaration of historic bays and historic waters

Where the Governor-General is satisfied:

(a) that a bay is an historic bay, he or she may, by Proclamation, declare that bay to be an historic bay and shall, by the same or another Proclamation, define the sea-ward limits of that bay; or

(b) that waters are historic waters, he or she may, by Proclamation, declare those waters to be historic waters and shall, by the same or another Proclamation, define the limits of those waters.

9 Charts of limits of territorial sea

(1) The Minister may cause to be prepared and issued such charts as he or she thinks fit showing any matter relating to the limits of the territorial sea.

(2) In particular, the Minister may cause to be prepared and issued large-scale charts showing the low-water line along the coast and may cause to be shown on such a chart any other matter referred to in subsection (1).

(3) The mere production of a copy of a paper purporting to be certified by the Minister to be a true copy of a chart prepared under this section is prima facie evidence of any matter shown on the chart relating to the limits of the territorial sea.

10 Sovereignty in respect of internal waters

It is by this Act declared and enacted that the sovereignty in respect of the internal waters of Australia (that is to say, any waters of the sea on the landward side of the baseline of the territorial sea) so far as they extend from time to time, and in respect of the airspace over those waters and in respect of the sea-bed and subsoil beneath those waters, is vested in and exercisable by the Crown in right of the Commonwealth.

Division 1A—The exclusive economic zone

10A Sovereign rights in respect of exclusive economic zone

It is declared and enacted that the rights and jurisdiction of Australia in its exclusive economic zone are vested in and exercisable by the Crown in right of the Commonwealth.

10B Limits of exclusive economic zone

The Governor-General may, from time to time, by Proclamation declare, not inconsistently with:

(a) Article 55 or 57 of the Convention; or

(b) any relevant international agreement to which Australia is a party;

the limits of the whole or of any part of the exclusive economic zone of Australia.

10C Charts of limits of exclusive economic zone

(1) The Minister may cause to be prepared such charts as he or she thinks fit showing any matter relating to the limits of the exclusive economic zone of Australia.

(2) The mere production of a copy of a paper purporting to be certified by the Minister to be a true copy of such a chart is prima facie evidence of any matter shown on the chart relating to the limits of the exclusive economic zone of Australia.

Division 2—The continental shelf

11 Sovereign rights in respect of continental shelf

It is by this Act declared and enacted that the sovereign rights of Australia as a coastal State in respect of the continental shelf of Australia, for the purpose of exploring it and exploiting its natural resources, are vested in and exercisable by the Crown in right of the Commonwealth.

12 Limits of continental shelf

The Governor-General may, from time to time by Proclamation, declare, not inconsistently with Article 76 of the Convention or any relevant international agreement to which Australia is a party, the limits of the whole or any part of the continental shelf of Australia.

13 Charts of limits of continental shelf

(1) The Minister may cause to be prepared and issued such charts as he or she thinks fit showing any matter relating to the limits of the continental shelf of Australia.

(2) The mere production of a copy of a paper purporting to be certified by the Minister to be a true copy of a chart prepared under this section is prima facie evidence of any matter shown on the chart relating to the limits of the continental shelf of Australia.

Division 2AA—Greater Sunrise special regime area

13AA Joint exercise of rights in Greater Sunrise special regime area

Within the Greater Sunrise special regime area, Australia is to exercise its rights as a coastal state pursuant to Article 77 of the Convention jointly with Timor-Leste.

Note: Under section 780M of the *Offshore Petroleum and Greenhouse Gas Storage Act 2006*, Australia's rights may be exercised by the Designated Authority, the Governance Board or the Dispute Resolution Committee provided for by the Timor Sea Maritime Boundaries Treaty.

13AB Operation of Commonwealth law in relation to Greater Sunrise special regime area

(1) A law of the Commonwealth, a State or a Territory does not apply in relation to an act, omission, matter or thing directly or indirectly connected with the exploration of, or exploitation of the natural resources of, the continental shelf in the Greater Sunrise special regime area.

(2) Subsection (1) is subject to a contrary intention.

13AC Cessation of effect of this Division

(1) This Division ceases to have effect at the start of the day after the Greater Sunrise Special Regime, within the meaning of the Timor Sea Maritime Boundaries Treaty, ceases to be in force under the treaty.

(2) The Minister must announce, by notifiable instrument, the day that regime ceases to be in force under that treaty.

Division 2A—The contiguous zone

13A Rights of control in respect of contiguous zone

It is declared and enacted that Australia has a contiguous zone.

Note: The rights of control that Australia, as a coastal state, has in respect of the contiguous zone of Australia are exercisable in accordance with applicable Commonwealth, State and Territory laws.

13B Limits of contiguous zone

The Governor-General may, from time to time, by Proclamation declare, not inconsistently with:

(a) Section 4 of Part II of the Convention; or

(b) any relevant international agreement to which Australia is a party;

the limits of the whole or of any part of the contiguous zone of Australia.

13C Charts of limits of contiguous zone

(1) The Minister may cause to be prepared such charts as he or she thinks fit showing any matter relating to the limits of the contiguous zone of Australia.

(2) The mere production of a copy of a paper purporting to be certified by the Minister to be a true copy of such a chart is prima facie evidence of any matter shown on the chart relating to the limits of the contiguous zone of Australia.

Division 3—Savings

14 Part II does not affect waters etc. within State limits

Nothing in this Part affects sovereignty or sovereign rights in respect of any waters of the sea that are waters of or within any bay, gulf, estuary, river, creek, inlet, port or harbour and:

(a) were, on 1st January, 1901, within the limits of a State; and

(b) remain within the limits of the State;

or in respect of the airspace over, or in respect of the sea-bed or subsoil beneath, any such waters.

15 Certain property not vested in Commonwealth

Nothing in this Part shall be taken to vest in the Crown in right of the Commonwealth any wharf, jetty, pier, breakwater, building, platform, pipeline, lighthouse, beacon, navigational aid, buoy, cable or other structure or works.

16 Saving of other laws

(1) The preceding provisions of this Part:

(a) do not limit or exclude the operation of any law of the Commonwealth or of a Territory, other than the Northern Territory, in force at the date of commencement of this Act or coming into force after that date; and

(b) do not limit or exclude the operation of any law of a State or of the Northern Territory in force at the date of commencement of this Act or coming into force after that date, except in so far as the law is expressed to vest or make exercisable any sovereignty or sovereign rights otherwise than as provided by the preceding provisions of this Part.

(2) A law of a State or of the Northern Territory shall not be taken to be within the words of exception in paragraph (b) of

subsection (1):

(a) by reason that the law makes provision with respect to, or touching or concerning, any sea-bed or subsoil that is declared by Division 1 to be within the sovereign of the Crown in right of the Commonwealth, or the living or non-living resources of any such sea-bed or subsoil, if proprietary rights in respect of that sea-bed or subsoil have become vested in the Crown in right of the State or of the Northern Territory, as the case may be, by or under a law of the Commonwealth; or

(b) by reason that the law makes provision with respect to, or touching or concerning, any sea-bed or subsoil referred to in Division 1 or Division 2 but in respect of which

paragraph (a) does not apply, or the living or non-living resources of any such sea-bed or subsoil, if the law is otherwise within powers with respect to particular matters that are conferred on the legislature of the State or of the Northern Territory, as the case may be, by the *Coastal Waters (State Powers) Act* 1980 or the *Coastal Waters (Northern Territory Powers) Act* 1980.

Schedule 1—Parts II, V and VI of the United Nations Convention on the Law of the Sea (omitted)

Schedule 2—Greater Sunrise special regime area

Note: See the definition of *Greater Sunrise special regime area* in subsection 3 (1).

1 Greater Sunrise special regime area

(1) The ***Greater Sunrise special regime area*** is the area of the continental shelf contained within the rhumb lines connecting the points described in the following table.

\multicolumn{4}{c}{Corners of boundary of Greater Sunrise special regime area}
Item	Point	Latitude of point	Longitude of point
1	GS-1	09°49′54.88″S	127°55′04.35″E
2	GS-2	09°49′54.88″S	128°20′04.34″E
3	GS-3	09°39′54.88″S	128°20′04.34″E
4	GS-4	09°39′54.88″S	128°25′04.34″E
5	GS-5	09°29′54.88″S	128°25′04.34″E
6	GS-6	09°29′54.88″S	128°20′04.34″E
7	GS-7	09°24′54.88″S	128°20′04.34″E
8	GS-8	09°24′54.88″S	128°00′04.34″E
9	GS-9	09°29′54.88″S	127°53′24.35″E
10	GS-10	09°29′54.88″S	127°52′34.35″E
11	GS-11	09°34′54.88″S	127°52′34.35″E
12	GS-12	09°34′54.88″S	127°50′04.35″E
13	GS-13	09°37′24.88″S	127°50′04.35″E
14	GS-14	09°37′24.89″S	127°45′04.35″E
15	GS-15	09°44′54.88″S	127°45′04.35″E
16	GS-16	09°44′54.88″S	127°50′04.35″E
17	GS-17	09°47′24.88″S	127°50′04.35″E
18	GS-18	09°47′24.88″S	127°55′04.35″E

(2) The position on the surface of the Earth of the Greater Sunrise special regime area is to be determined by reference to the Geocentric Datum of Australia as defined in Gazette No. 35 of 6 September 1995 (GDA94 geocentric data set).

2 Illustrative map of the Greater Sunrise special regime area (omitted)

The following map illustrates the Greater Sunrise special regime area and its location relative to Australia and Timor-Leste.

Note: The lines on the map that connect points TA-13, TA-12 and TA-11 reflect Article 2 of the Timor Sea Maritime Boundaries Treaty.

附录 2 《海洋与水下土地（领海基线）2016 年公告》[1]

Seas and Submerged Lands (Territorial Sea Baseline) Proclamation 2016

1 Name

This is the *Seas and Submerged Lands (Territorial Sea Baseline) Proclamation* 2016.

2 Commencement

(1) Each provision of this instrument specified in column 1 of the table commences, or is taken to have commenced, in accordance with column 2 of the table. Any other statement in column 2 has effect according to its terms.

Commencement information		
Column 1	Column 2	Column 3
Provisions	Commencement	Date/Details
1. The whole of this instrument	The day after this instrument is registered.	12 March 2016

Note: This table relates only to the provisions of this instrument as originally made. It will not be amended to deal with any later amendments of this instrument.

(2) Any information in column 3 of the table is not part of this instrument. Information may be inserted in this column, or information in it may be edited, in any published version of this instrument.

3 Authority

This instrument is made under section 7 of the *Seas and Submerged Lands Act* 1973.

4 Schedules

Each instrument that is specified in a Schedule to this instrument is amended or repealed as set out in the applicable items in the Schedule concerned, and any other item in a Schedule to this instrument has effect according to its terms.

5 Definitions

Note: A number of expressions used in this instrument are defined in the Act, including the following:

(a) the Convention;

(b) territorial sea.

---

[1] "Seas and Submerged Lands (Territorial Sea Baseline) Proclamation 2016", Australia Federal Register of Legislation, https://www.legislation.gov.au/Details/F2016L00302, December 3, 2024.

(1) In this instrument:

Act means the *Seas and Submerged Lands Act* 1973.

area of the indentation means the area lying between the low-water mark around the shore of the indentation and a line joining the low-water marks of its natural entrance points, and includes the area of any island within the indentation as if it were part of the water area.

baseline of the mainland, in relation to a State or the Northern Territory, means:

(a) for a State (other than Tasmania) or the Northern Territory—the line determined in accordance with sections 7, 10, 11 and 12; or

(b) for Tasmania—the line determined in accordance with sections 8, 10, 11 and 12.

bay has the meaning given by section 6.

Geocentric Datum of Australia means the datum described in Schedule 1.

historic bay means a bay that is declared by an instrument under paragraph 8 (a) of the Act to be an historic bay.

low-tide elevation has the same meaning as in Article 13 of the Convention.

low-water means lowest astronomical tide.

mile means an international nautical mile, being 1 852 metres.

straight line means a geodesic line.

(2) For the purposes of this instrument, the outermost permanent harbour works (other than offshore installations and artificial islands) which form an integral part of a harbour system are regarded as forming part of the coast.

(3) For the purposes of paragraphs 7 (d), 8 (d) and 9 (d), the low-water line of a low-tide elevation must not be taken into account unless a lighthouse or similar installation that is permanently above sea level has been built on the low-tide elevation.

(4) For the purposes of this instrument, the position on the surface of the Earth of a point, line or area is to be determined by reference to:

(a) if the position is to be determined by reference to any of the points of latitude and longitude specified in items 4012 to 4039 of Part 4 of Schedule 2—the International Terrestrial Reference Frame 2000, as defined by the International Earth Rotation Service at epoch 1 January 2000; or

(b) otherwise—the Geocentric Datum of Australia.

6 Bays

(1) Subject to subsection (2), an indentation is a bay if the distance between the low-water marks of the natural entrance points of the indentation does not exceed 24 miles.

(2) An indentation is not a bay if:

(a) for an indentation that has one mouth—the area of the indentation is less than that of the semi-circle whose diameter is a line drawn across the mouth of the indentation; and

(b) for an indentation that, because of the presence of islands, has more than one mouth—the area of the indentation is less than that of the semi-circle drawn on a line as long as the sum total of the lengths of the lines across the different mouths.

7 Baseline—mainland of Australia

Subject to sections 10, 11 and 12, the baseline from which the breadth of the part of the territorial sea adjacent to the mainland of Australia is to be measured is the line constituted by the following:

(a) the low-water line along the coast, except where that low-water line is landward of a line mentioned in paragraph (b), (c), (d) or (e);

(b) for each river that flows directly into the sea on the coast—the straight line drawn across the mouth of the river between points on the low-water lines of its banks, except where that line is landward of a line mentioned in paragraph (c) or (d);

(c) for each bay (other than an historic bay) on the coast—the straight line drawn between the low-water marks of the natural entrance points of the bay, except where that line is landward of, or identical with, a line mentioned in paragraph (d);

(d) the straight lines joining each of the points on the low-water line of the coast that are on, or closest to, the points of latitude and longitude specified in an item in Part 1 of Schedule 2;

(e) for each historic bay specified in column 1 of an item in Part 2 of Schedule 2:

(i) if 2 points of latitude and longitude are specified in column 2 of the item—the straight line joining each of the points on the low-water line of the coast that are on, or closest to, those points; and

(ii) if more than 2 points of latitude and longitude are specified in column 2 of the item— the line constituted by each of the straight lines joining, respectively, each of the points on the low-water line of the coast that are on, or closest to, 2 points specified opposite each other in that column of that item.

8 Baseline—mainland of Tasmania

Subject to sections 10, 11 and 12, the baseline from which the breadth of the part of the territorial sea adjacent to the mainland of Tasmania is to be measured is the line constituted by the following:

(a) the low-water line along the coast, except where that low-water line is landward of a line mentioned in paragraph (b), (c) or (d);

(b) for each river that flows directly into the sea on the coast—the straight line drawn across the mouth of the river between points on the low-water lines of its banks, except where that line is landward of a line mentioned in paragraph (c) or (d);

(c) for each bay on the coast—the straight line drawn between the low-water marks of the natural entrance points of the bay, except where that line is landward of, or identical with, a line mentioned in paragraph (d);

(d) the straight lines joining each of the points on the low-water line of the coast that are on, or closest to, the points of latitude and longitude specified in an item in Part 3 of Schedule 2.

9 Baseline—islands off the coast of the States or the Northern Territory

Subject to sections 10, 11 and 12, the baseline from which the breadth of the part of the territorial sea adjacent to an island, or a group of islands, located within a State or the Northern Territory, and seaward of the baseline of the mainland of that State or Territory, is to be measured is the line constituted by the following:

(a) the low-water line along the coast of the island, or along the coast of each island included in the group of islands, except where that low-water line is landward of a line mentioned in paragraph (b), (c) or (d);

(b) for each river that flows directly into the sea on the coast of the island, or on the coast of an island included in the group of islands—the straight line drawn across the mouth of the river between points on the low-water lines of its banks, except where the line is landward of a line mentioned in paragraph (c) or (d);

(c) for each bay on the coast of the island, or on the coast of an island included in the group of islands—the straight line drawn between the respective low-water marks of the natural entrance points of the bay, except where the line is landward of, or identical with, a line mentioned in paragraph (d);

(d) the straight lines joining each of the points on the low-water line of the coast of the island, or on the low-water line of the coast of an island included in the group of islands, that are on, or closest to, the points of latitude and longitude specified in an item in Part 4 of Schedule 2.

Note: See also section 13.

10 Low-tide elevations

The baseline from which the breadth of the part of the territorial sea adjacent to a low-tide elevation, situated wholly or partly at a distance not exceeding the breadth of the territorial sea from the mainland or an island, is to be measured is the low-water line on the low-tide elevation.

Note: See also section 13.

11 Low-water line of naturally formed area

(1) If the low-water line of a naturally formed area of land which is above water at hightide would intersect a straight baseline drawn in accordance with this instrument, the part of the straight baseline that would be between the points of intersection of the low-water line and that baseline is to be substituted with the line that would be the baseline between those points if the seaward part of the area of land were part of the coast of the mainland of the State or Territory within which the naturally formed area of land is located.

(2) For subsection (1):

(a) if the low-water line and baseline intersect at more than 2 points, the points of intersection of the low-water line of an area of land and a straight baseline are taken to be the 2 outermost points of intersection; and

(b) the seaward part of the area of land is the part, or parts, of the area of land on the seaward side of the straight baseline.

Note: See also section 13.

12 Low-water line of island

(1) If straight lines mentioned in paragraph 7 (d), 7 (e), 8 (d) or 9 (d) join different points on the low-water line of the same island, the baseline from which the breadth of the part of the territorial sea adjacent to that island, or the group of islands in which that island is included, between those points is to be measured is the line that would be the baseline if the seaward part of the coast of the island between those points were part of the coast of the mainland of the State or Territory within which the island is located.

(2) For subsection (1), the seaward part of the coast of an island between 2 points is the part of the coast of the island between those points that includes the most seaward part of the island.

Note: See also section 13.

13 Excluded islands and excluded group of islands

(1) For the purposes of sections 9, 10, 11 and 12, an island does not include:

(a) each of the following islands located within Queensland:

(i) Pearce Cay;

(ii) Turnagain Island;

(iii) Turu Cay; and

(b) an island included in a group of islands mentioned in subsection (2).

(2) For the purposes of sections 9, 10, 11 and 12, a group of islands does not include each of the following groups of islands located within Queensland:

(a) the group of islands known as Aubusi, Boigu and Moimi;

(b) the group of islands known as Dauan, Kaumag and Saibai;

(c) the group of islands known as Anchor Cay and East Cay;

(d) the group of islands known as Black Rocks and Bramble Cay;

(e) the group of islands known as Deliverance Island and Kerr Islet.

Schedule 1—Geocentric Datum of Australia (omitted)

Schedule 2—Straight baseline pointsunder Article 7 of the Convention

Note: See sections 7, 8 and 9.

Part 1—Coast of the mainland of Australia

Coast of the mainland of Australia	
Item	Description
1001	From 32°44′27.0″S 152°11′09.5″E to 32°44′23.9″S 152°11′30.6″E
1002	From 32°44′23.9″S 152°11′41.1″E to 32°44′24.3″S 152°11′56.5″E

续表

| \multicolumn{2}{c}{Coast of the mainland of Australia} ||
Item	Description
1003	From 32°44′24.4″S 152°11′58.2″E to 32°44′31.5″S 152°12′18.3″E
1004	From 32°44′31.8″S 152°12′19.6″E to 32°44′32.2″S 152°12′20.9″E
1005	From 32°44′32.5″S 152°12′21.6″E to 32°44′33.5″S 152°12′22.4″E
1006	From 32°44′33.7″S 152°12′22.6″E to 32°44′40.1″S 152°12′27.0″E
1007	From 32°44′41.0″S 152°12′27.1″E to 32°44′51.4″S 152°12′21.7″E
1008	From 32°44′53.1″S 152°12′21.0″E to 32°44′59.9″S 152°12′18.1″E
1009	From 32°45′00.9″S 152°12′16.7″E to 32°45′01.3″S 152°12′15.0″E
1010	From 32°45′02.0″S 152°12′12.7″E to 32°45′13.2″S 152°11′18.6″E
1011	From 32°45′13.2″S 152°11′18.6″E to 32°45′22.9″S 152°10′46.4″E
1012	From 32°45′22.9″S 152°10′46.4″E to 32°45′45.4″S 152°10′24.0″E
1013	From 32°45′46.5″S 152°10′21.4″E to 32°45′55.2″S 152°09′42.0″E
1014	From 32°45′55.2″S 152°09′42.0″E to 32°46′05.5″S 152°09′11.7″E
1015	From 32°46′06.3″S 152°09′06.8″E to 32°46′07.2″S 152°08′42.7″E
1016	From 32°46′07.2″S 152°08′42.7″E to 32°47′05.1″S 152°07′28.1″E
1017	From 36°43′31.9″S 149°59′30.2″E to 36°43′47.6″S 149°59′27.4″E
1018	From 36°43′49.4″S 149°59′26.9″E to 36°45′14.2″S 149°59′02.3″E
1019	From 36°45′14.2″S 149°59′02.3″E to 36°45′24.0″S 149°58′58.2″E
1020	From 36°45′25.4″S 149°58′57.8″E to 36°46′04.4″S 149°58′44.7″E
1021	From 36°46′04.4″S 149°58′44.7″E to 36°46′42.6″S 149°58′24.9″E
1022	From 36°46′44.8″S 149°58′23.4″E to 36°47′08.7″S 149°58′11.8″E
1023	From 36°47′13.1″S 149°58′09.8″E to 36°47′27.8″S 149°57′46.3″E
1024	From 36°47′28.6″S 149°57′45.8″E to 36°47′28.6″S 149°57′44.4″E
1025	From 39°08′12.3″S 146°22′25.7″E to 39°08′23.9″S 146°22′05.2″E
1026	From 39°08′24.9″S 146°22′01.1″E to 39°09′29.6″S 146°18′52.3″E
1027	From 39°09′30.9″S 146°18′41.9″E to 39°09′32.2″S 146°17′42.1″E
1028	From 39°09′30.1″S 146°17′33.2″E to 39°07′03.9″S 146°14′13.7″E
1029	From 39°06′53.4″S 146°14′02.0″E to 39°05′07.5″S 146°13′30.7″E
1030	From 39°04′16.8″S 146°13′19.8″E to 39°01′20.4″S 146°14′11.1″E
1031	From 39°01′16.4″S 146°14′12.6″E to 38°59′41.7″S 146°14′47.4″E
1032	From 38°59′39.8″S 146°14′48.8″E to 38°59′37.8″S 146°14′54.0″E
1033	From 35°38′35.0″S 138°31′23.1″E to 35°45′32.6″S 138°18′13.2″E

续表

\multicolumn{2}{c}{Coast of the mainland of Australia}
Item	Description
1034	From 35°45′32.6″S 138°18′13.2″E to 35°46′33.9″S 138°17′35.8″E
1035	From 35°46′41.6″S 138°17′30.7″E to 35°46′57.7″S 138°17′24.2″E
1036	From 35°47′07.0″S 138°17′16.1″E to 35°50′38.3″S 138°08′03.0″E
1037	From 35°53′11.3″S 136°32′03.8″E to 34°57′06.2″S 135°37′29.7″E
1038	From 34°56′57.9″S 135°37′29.5″E to 34°56′48.3″S 135°37′27.1″E
1039	From 32°54′22.8″S 134°03′32.7″E to 32°43′30.7″S 133°57′50.3″E
1040	From 32°43′30.7″S 133°57′50.3″E to 32°35′19.6″S 133°16′52.8″E
1041	From 32°34′59.3″S 133°16′36.0″E to 32°33′55.3″S 133°16′31.3″E
1042	From 32°33′55.3″S 133°16′31.3″E to 32°30′49.4″S 133°15′04.9″E
1043	From 32°30′20.7″S 133°14′55.8″E to 32°13′27.9″S 133°06′38.3″E
1044	From 32°13′27.9″S 133°06′38.3″E to 32°08′40.6″S 132°59′25.0″E
1045	From 32°08′35.4″S 132°59′21.9″E to 32°07′34.0″S 132°58′49.0″E
1046	From 32°07′34.0″S 132°58′49.0″E to 32°01′48.3″S 132°28′23.6″E
1047	From 33°58′47.4″S 123°17′15.3″E to 34°00′53.9″S 123°17′38.5″E
1048	From 34°01′27.4″S 123°17′29.6″E to 34°03′07.4″S 123°15′36.5″E
1049	From 34°03′11.1″S 123°15′32.4″E to 34°04′17.2″S 123°14′15.7″E
1050	From 34°04′17.2″S 123°14′15.7″E to 34°06′23.8″S 123°12′57.0″E
1051	From 34°07′09.0″S 123°12′26.3″E to 34°09′57.0″S 123°08′51.4″E
1052	From 34°09′53.4″S 123°08′06.7″E to 34°07′48.6″S 122°50′49.8″E
1053	From 34°07′48.6″S 122°50′49.8″E to 34°11′51.3″S 122°29′49.7″E
1054	From 34°11′51.3″S 122°29′49.7″E to 34°12′36.3″S 122°20′56.2″E
1055	From 34°12′36.4″S 122°20′55.1″E to 34°13′27.5″S 122°08′58.6″E
1056	From 34°13′27.8″S 122°08′55.1″E to 34°13′53.7″S 122°03′59.5″E
1057	From 34°13′53.8″S 122°03′55.7″E to 34°10′46.7″S 121°56′38.6″E
1058	From 34°10′46.5″S 121°56′38.1″E to 34°02′35.8″S 121°36′14.2″E
1059	From 34°02′35.2″S 121°36′13.9″E to 33°52′22.3″S 121°20′44.0″E
1060	From 33°52′22.3″S 121°20′44.0″E to 33°51′03.3″S 121°16′05.6″E
1061	From 32°22′15.1″S 115°42′50.8″E to 32°21′17.0″S 115°41′21.7″E
1062	From 32°21′08.8″S 115°41′17.5″E to 32°19′50.0″S 115°41′29.8″E
1063	From 32°19′50.0″S 115°41′29.8″E to 32°19′22.8″S 115°41′26.5″E
1064	From 32°19′15.3″S 115°41′26.3″E to 32°18′10.6″S 115°41′14.3″E

续表

Item	Coast of the mainland of Australia
	Description
1065	From 32°18′05.1″S 115°41′14.3″E to 32°16′16.3″S 115°41′08.9″E
1066	From 32°15′52.2″S 115°41′09.0″E to 32°14′39.5″S 115°40′50.7″E
1067	From 32°09′21.9″S 115°39′38.9″E to 32°07′14.9″S 115°39′28.3″E
1068	From 32°07′14.9″S 115°39′28.3″E to 32°03′58.9″S 115°38′07.0″E
1069	From 32°03′58.9″S 115°38′07.0″E to 32°01′38.8″S 115°31′44.1″E
1070	From 31°59′13.2″S 115°32′19.5″E to 31°56′19.6″S 115°45′13.0″E
1071	From 26°08′35.1″S 113°09′32.7″E to 26°07′22.7″S 113°10′51.5″E
1072	From 25°28′46.3″S 112°58′15.6″E to 25°16′27.4″S 113°04′27.4″E
1073	From 24°59′31.5″S 113°07′00.8″E to 24°59′11.2″S 113°07′05.2″E
1074	From 24°45′26.9″S 113°09′14.8″E to 24°45′00.7″S 113°09′36.1″E
1075	From 24°44′53.5″S 113°09′39.8″E to 24°29′20.1″S 113°24′28.0″E
1076	From 21°46′53.3″S 114°09′44.1″E to 21°43′03.6″S 114°18′01.3″E
1077	From 21°39′27.3″S 114°20′56.6″E to 21°38′59.8″S 114°21′23.0″E
1078	From 21°37′19.5″S 114°23′33.6″E to 21°35′52.2″S 114°30′10.7″E
1079	From 21°35′50.5″S 114°30′28.5″E to 21°31′33.6″S 114°45′24.9″E
1080	From 21°31′06.7″S 114°45′52.2″E to 21°15′42.7″S 115°01′24.8″E
1081	From 21°15′42.7″S 115°01′24.8″E to 20°58′19.9″S 115°19′25.1″E
1082	From 20°56′49.4″S 115°18′28.2″E to 20°56′22.1″S 115°18′34.8″E
1083	From 20°53′45.8″S 115°19′01.5″E to 20°53′32.6″S 115°19′00.5″E
1084	From 20°39′58.9″S 115°25′57.8″E to 20°26′00.6″S 115°30′01.8″E
1085	From 20°26′00.6″S 115°30′01.8″E to 20°21′50.7″S 115°30′45.7″E
1086	From 20°22′01.3″S 115°32′21.8″E to 20°22′37.4″S 115°33′32.3″E
1087	From 20°24′10.6″S 115°35′09.5″E to 20°28′35.5″S 116°32′18.6″E
1088	From 20°28′35.5″S 116°32′18.6″E to 20°26′24.6″S 116°36′47.4″E
1089	From 20°26′18.4″S 116°37′07.1″E to 20°21′12.3″S 116°49′55.5″E
1090	From 20°25′16.2″S 116°57′37.5″E to 20°25′46.3″S 117°04′09.7″E
1091	From 20°26′17.8″S 117°06′12.9″E to 20°32′49.0″S 117°10′36.3″E
1092	From 20°32′57.2″S 117°10′43.9″E to 20°34′32.9″S 117°12′10.8″E
1093	From 20°34′33.2″S 117°12′11.1″E to 20°37′36.8″S 117°12′13.0″E
1094	From 16°23′58.1″S 122°55′24.4″E to 16°23′18.0″S 122°55′04.1″E
1095	From 16°23′02.3″S 122°55′25.1″E to 16°16′32.7″S 123°03′25.9″E

续表

	Coast of the mainland of Australia
Item	Description
1096	From 16°16′24.7″S 123°03′36.3″E to 16°02′27.6″S 123°16′13.9″E
1097	From 16°01′55.8″S 123°18′41.0″E to 15°52′26.9″S 123°37′58.8″E
1098	From 15°51′42.3″S 123°38′24.4″E to 15°50′52.4″S 123°40′19.7″E
1099	From 15°50′52.4″S 123°40′19.7″E to 15°20′14.4″S 124°10′58.5″E
1100	From 15°20′14.4″S 124°10′58.5″E to 15°12′43.1″S 124°15′31.6″E
1101	From 15°12′36.4″S 124°15′34.4″E to 15°03′33.7″S 124°19′08.9″E
1102	From 15°02′43.4″S 124°19′34.8″E to 14°59′08.7″S 124°32′03.7″E
1103	From 14°59′08.7″S 124°32′03.7″E to 14°51′37.6″S 124°42′28.4″E
1104	From 14°51′37.6″S 124°42′28.4″E to 14°30′36.9″S 124°55′09.1″E
1105	From 14°30′34.6″S 124°55′10.3″E to 14°24′16.6″S 124°57′17.3″E
1106	From 14°22′59.5″S 124°58′24.4″E to 14°16′57.8″S 125°13′18.0″E
1107	From 14°16′57.8″S 125°13′18.0″E to 14°14′22.5″S 125°19′11.7″E
1108	From 14°14′22.5″S 125°19′11.7″E to 14°05′56.0″S 125°33′14.8″E
1109	From 14°05′56.0″S 125°33′14.8″E to 13°55′51.9″S 125°37′08.6″E
1110	From 13°55′02.6″S 125°37′35.8″E to 13°47′45.3″S 125°48′19.8″E
1111	From 13°47′45.3″S 125°48′19.8″E to 13°44′23.5″S 126°08′29.1″E
1112	From 13°44′18.6″S 126°09′23.1″E to 13°44′38.8″S 126°20′53.5″E
1113	From 13°45′00.5″S 126°22′38.7″E to 13°43′48.3″S 126°46′32.8″E
1114	From 14°50′43.9″S 129°02′30.8″E to 14°25′51.3″S 129°20′55.1″E
1115	From 12°38′51.8″S 130°19′47.6″E to 11°49′32.8″S 130°02′54.9″E
1116	From 11°20′20.7″S 130°14′45.8″E to 11°06′04.1″S 130°18′55.3″E
1117	From 11°11′14.2″S 131°16′51.2″E to 11°09′21.8″S 131°51′49.8″E
1118	From 11°09′21.8″S 131°51′49.8″E to 11°07′11.9″S 131°58′10.2″E
1119	From 11°07′17.2″S 132°08′14.3″E to 11°06′39.6″S 132°11′23.7″E
1120	From 11°06′39.8″S 132°11′26.3″E to 11°05′52.0″S 132°17′12.6″E
1121	From 11°05′49.7″S 132°17′31.7″E to 11°01′11.3″S 132°27′23.0″E
1122	From 10°57′57.6″S 132°35′39.0″E to 10°57′53.5″S 132°49′14.8″E
1123	From 10°57′56.6″S 132°49′57.2″E to 11°01′51.1″S 132°58′18.3″E
1124	From 11°05′29.1″S 132°59′59.8″E to 11°10′03.3″S 132°55′41.6″E
1125	From 11°10′09.4″S 132°55′39.7″E to 11°19′54.2″S 132°55′05.5″E
1126	From 11°56′50.2″S 134°44′54.8″E to 11°54′20.9″S 135°01′47.1″E

续表

\multicolumn{2}{c}{Coast of the mainland of Australia}
Item	Description
1127	From 11°55′06.1″S 135°07′22.6″E to 11°54′47.5″S 135°07′54.5″E
1128	From 11°54′18.0″S 135°09′14.7″E to 11°56′54.7″S 135°35′36.8″E
1129	From 11°44′35.6″S 135°52′18.8″E to 11°41′35.7″S 135°56′24.9″E
1130	From 11°37′53.3″S 136°01′22.0″E to 11°37′20.0″S 136°01′34.2″E
1131	From 11°36′02.7″S 136°03′26.8″E to 11°35′01.0″S 136°04′07.7″E
1132	From 11°34′14.9″S 136°05′32.3″E to 11°33′35.7″S 136°06′11.2″E
1133	From 11°32′26.6″S 136°07′24.8″E to 11°28′24.1″S 136°25′42.7″E
1134	From 11°28′22.8″S 136°25′46.0″E to 11°24′52.0″S 136°28′56.1″E
1135	From 11°24′47.2″S 136°28′59.4″E to 11°23′33.9″S 136°29′47.6″E
1136	From 11°02′20.1″S 136°43′28.9″E to 11°01′56.2″S 136°43′44.1″E
1137	From 11°01′35.0″S 136°43′50.6″E to 11°00′18.6″S 136°44′04.7″E
1138	From 11°00′21.4″S 136°45′48.4″E to 11°01′24.3″S 136°46′02.1″E
1139	From 11°01′26.0″S 136°46′02.2″E to 11°01′39.6″S 136°46′01.7″E
1140	From 11°02′08.9″S 136°46′01.7″E to 11°39′13.8″S 136°50′18.1″E
1141	From 11°39′13.8″S 136°50′18.1″E to 12°01′50.7″S 136°53′03.3″E
1142	From 12°01′50.7″S 136°53′03.3″E to 12°20′31.0″S 136°58′45.6″E
1143	From 12°30′20.8″S 136°48′20.1″E to 12°30′26.1″S 136°48′26.3″E
1144	From 12°30′34.8″S 136°48′31.2″E to 12°30′51.3″S 136°48′44.8″E
1145	From 12°30′59.5″S 136°48′46.3″E to 12°34′54.3″S 136°46′42.0″E
1146	From 12°35′06.6″S 136°46′24.3″E to 12°35′11.3″S 136°46′17.5″E
1147	From 12°35′25.2″S 136°46′01.4″E to 12°43′02.6″S 136°43′59.0″E
1148	From 12°43′06.6″S 136°43′58.3″E to 12°44′42.4″S 136°43′33.0″E
1149	From 12°44′42.4″S 136°43′33.0″E to 12°46′43.8″S 136°43′27.2″E
1150	From 12°46′43.8″S 136°43′27.2″E to 12°52′56.2″S 136°43′53.0″E
1151	From 12°53′17.9″S 136°43′51.9″E to 13°00′15.8″S 136°40′08.2″E
1152	From 13°00′15.8″S 136°40′08.2″E to 13°37′28.4″S 136°57′39.1″E
1153	From 13°37′37.7″S 136°57′47.2″E to 13°37′38.7″S 136°57′48.2″E
1154	From 13°37′42.0″S 136°57′49.2″E to 13°48′21.8″S 136°55′31.3″E
1155	From 13°48′21.8″S 136°55′31.3″E to 14°10′14.2″S 136°59′06.9″E
1156	From 14°10′18.3″S 136°59′07.4″E to 14°13′02.7″S 136°58′52.4″E
1157	From 14°13′06.6″S 136°58′52.3″E to 14°15′25.4″S 136°59′07.3″E

Coast of the mainland of Australia	
Item	Description
1158	From 14°15′44.9″S 136°59′05.6″E to 14°18′04.5″S 136°57′53.6″E
1159	From 14°18′04.5″S 136°57′53.6″E to 14°20′56.0″S 136°57′15.6″E
1160	From 14°21′10.8″S 136°56′55.3″E to 14°21′06.3″S 136°56′35.4″E
1161	From 14°21′12.2″S 136°55′40.0″E to 14°20′53.6″S 136°50′10.7″E
1162	From 14°20′53.5″S 136°50′10.5″E to 14°18′46.7″S 136°39′39.3″E
1163	From 14°18′28.7″S 136°39′24.2″E to 14°17′49.5″S 136°38′56.1″E
1164	From 14°14′46.9″S 136°19′32.1″E to 14°11′46.8″S 135°53′50.2″E
1165	From 15°24′03.4″S 136°15′25.9″E to 15°29′36.3″S 136°34′45.2″E
1166	From 15°29′36.3″S 136°34′45.2″E to 15°30′12.7″S 136°52′10.2″E
1167	From 15°29′55.7″S 136°53′19.2″E to 15°29′31.5″S 136°55′09.4″E
1168	From 15°29′32.9″S 136°55′16.0″E to 15°29′56.7″S 136°57′14.4″E
1169	From 15°29′56.9″S 136°57′28.9″E to 15°36′59.2″S 137°05′46.4″E
1170	From 15°37′12.1″S 137°05′47.3″E to 15°44′51.4″S 137°06′26.0″E
1171	From 15°45′15.5″S 137°06′25.4″E to 15°46′12.4″S 137°06′29.9″E
1172	From 15°51′11.0″S 137°04′44.4″E to 15°51′21.2″S 137°04′31.8″E
1173	From 15°52′00.3″S 137°04′10.3″E to 15°57′58.7″S 137°09′38.6″E
1174	From 16°53′03.9″S 139°00′58.2″E to 16°52′44.6″S 139°02′26.7″E
1175	From 16°51′27.0″S 139°02′58.4″E to 16°48′41.6″S 139°05′27.6″E
1176	From 16°48′37.4″S 139°05′31.5″E to 16°45′08.8″S 139°08′15.0″E
1177	From 16°40′34.5″S 139°09′34.0″E to 16°39′57.0″S 139°09′36.4″E
1178	From 16°30′17.4″S 139°14′27.8″E to 16°13′52.0″S 139°15′02.2″E
1179	From 16°13′44.8″S 139°15′14.4″E to 16°23′21.1″S 139°33′05.0″E
1180	From 16°27′02.8″S 139°40′37.0″E to 16°26′42.6″S 139°43′33.1″E
1181	From 16°26′42.6″S 139°43′33.1″E to 16°26′24.6″S 139°46′12.1″E
1182	From 16°26′26.6″S 139°46′25.1″E to 16°29′25.0″S 139°48′52.7″E
1183	From 16°29′46.0″S 139°49′05.4″E to 16°38′36.6″S 139°53′57.6″E
1184	From 16°38′43.1″S 139°53′57.4″E to 16°39′12.4″S 139°53′47.5″E
1185	From 16°39′36.8″S 139°53′34.1″E to 16°42′24.9″S 139°50′37.8″E
1186	From 16°42′36.2″S 139°50′30.2″E to 17°04′29.0″S 139°38′23.0″E
1187	From 17°08′36.7″S 139°37′01.2″E to 17°24′34.4″S 139°30′07.5″E
1188	From 11°04′09.7″S 142°07′46.7″E to 10°59′49.7″S 142°06′10.5″E

续表

	Coast of the mainland of Australia
Item	Description
1189	From 10°58′40.0″S 142°05′16.2″E to 10°53′11.1″S 142°01′24.5″E
1190	From 10°52′53.7″S 142°01′26.2″E to 10°51′06.6″S 142°01′15.9″E
1191	From 10°50′59.5″S 142°01′14.7″E to 10°36′26.4″S 141°54′34.3″E
1192	From 10°36′14.5″S 141°54′29.0″E to 10°21′23.1″S 142°02′33.3″E
1193	From 10°21′23.1″S 142°02′33.3″E to 10°15′30.8″S 142°02′14.5″E
1194	From 10°15′27.9″S 142°02′14.4″E to 10°15′01.8″S 142°02′13.0″E
1195	From 10°14′59.9″S 142°02′12.3″E to 10°13′08.9″S 142°03′05.3″E
1196	From 10°12′58.6″S 142°03′06.9″E to 10°07′19.6″S 142°03′06.0″E
1197	From 10°07′19.6″S 142°03′06.0″E to 10°02′41.1″S 142°03′34.5″E
1198	From 10°02′32.6″S 142°03′39.8″E to 09°57′53.2″S 142°04′40.0″E
1199	From 09°57′51.4″S 142°04′42.2″E to 09°56′54.0″S 142°05′00.5″E
1200	From 09°55′52.3″S 142°10′09.6″E to 09°56′08.9″S 142°10′41.9″E
1201	From 09°56′09.7″S 142°10′44.7″E to 09°56′31.3″S 142°12′10.7″E
1202	From 09°56′53.4″S 142°12′48.6″E to 09°58′29.4″S 142°14′14.2″E
1203	From 09°58′38.1″S 142°14′26.0″E to 10°04′45.7″S 142°19′37.7″E
1204	From 10°04′54.5″S 142°19′47.9″E to 10°09′12.1″S 142°30′14.6″E
1205	From 10°09′45.9″S 142°31′02.0″E to 10°10′46.9″S 142°31′17.0″E
1206	From 10°10′52.7″S 142°31′16.6″E to 10°11′09.5″S 142°31′19.5″E
1207	From 10°11′51.8″S 142°31′03.2″E to 10°14′46.3″S 142°29′36.0″E
1208	From 10°15′39.4″S 142°29′10.4″E to 10°27′44.9″S 142°27′04.7″E
1209	From 10°27′44.9″S 142°27′04.7″E to 10°35′46.3″S 142°38′34.5″E
1210	From 10°35′48.2″S 142°38′37.7″E to 10°39′17.5″S 142°45′16.1″E
1211	From 10°39′42.4″S 142°45′42.6″E to 10°42′46.4″S 142°46′29.9″E
1212	From 10°43′37.3″S 142°46′46.7″E to 10°50′14.4″S 142°47′01.2″E
1213	From 10°50′14.4″S 142°47′01.2″E to 11°00′07.7″S 142°59′25.1″E
1214	From 11°00′32.8″S 142°59′50.1″E to 11°09′13.9″S 143°04′45.5″E
1215	From 11°11′29.5″S 143°07′21.4″E to 11°23′48.2″S 143°04′59.7″E
1216	From 11°23′48.2″S 143°04′59.7″E to 11°42′01.5″S 143°11′44.3″E
1217	From 11°42′01.5″S 143°11′44.3″E to 11°49′01.3″S 143°29′17.4″E
1218	From 11°49′55.0″S 143°29′48.6″E to 11°55′59.5″S 143°29′25.8″E
1219	From 11°56′03.8″S 143°29′25.6″E to 12°17′42.1″S 143°25′11.8″E

续表

	Coast of the mainland of Australia
Item	Description
1220	From 12°17′42.1″S 143°25′11.8″E to 12°24′09.4″S 143°29′22.4″E
1221	From 12°24′21.2″S 143°29′23.9″E to 12°48′36.0″S 143°36′45.0″E
1222	From 12°48′41.0″S 143°36′44.9″E to 12°53′11.6″S 143°36′21.0″E
1223	From 12°53′11.6″S 143°36′21.0″E to 12°59′02.2″S 143°37′01.5″E
1224	From 12°59′32.9″S 143°37′04.7″E to 13°01′55.1″S 143°38′24.4″E
1225	From 13°02′09.7″S 143°38′27.3″E to 13°18′29.3″S 143°40′25.4″E
1226	From 13°18′29.3″S 143°40′25.4″E to 13°27′54.8″S 143°45′35.3″E
1227	From 13°27′54.8″S 143°45′35.3″E to 13°38′21.8″S 143°56′02.3″E
1228	From 13°38′24.8″S 143°56′06.6″E to 13°46′53.3″S 144°00′12.2″E
1229	From 13°46′53.3″S 144°00′12.2″E to 14°02′53.1″S 144°15′32.9″E
1230	From 14°03′05.4″S 144°16′09.9″E to 14°05′04.4″S 144°20′04.5″E
1231	From 14°05′08.4″S 144°20′21.1″E to 14°06′39.5″S 144°31′30.8″E
1232	From 14°06′59.3″S 144°31′57.4″E to 14°18′32.0″S 144°51′50.1″E
1233	From 14°18′42.8″S 144°52′06.3″E to 14°23′55.1″S 144°58′50.9″E
1234	From 14°24′05.7″S 144°59′08.5″E to 14°38′41.0″S 145°27′14.9″E
1235	From 14°40′14.7″S 145°28′42.3″E to 14°44′46.8″S 145°31′00.0″E
1236	From 14°44′50.3″S 145°31′01.0″E to 14°49′18.6″S 145°33′18.2″E
1237	From 14°49′28.5″S 145°33′15.7″E to 15°01′30.2″S 145°26′57.5″E
1238	From 15°01′30.2″S 145°26′57.5″E to 15°06′49.0″S 145°25′46.2″E
1239	From 15°07′14.1″S 145°25′39.8″E to 15°16′29.2″S 145°21′27.0″E
1240	From 17°38′55.0″S 146°08′57.1″E to 17°39′08.2″S 146°09′25.4″E
1241	From 17°39′23.1″S 146°09′38.0″E to 17°40′27.7″S 146°10′48.8″E
1242	From 17°40′40.8″S 146°10′55.2″E to 17°44′17.0″S 146°09′49.8″E
1243	From 17°44′17.0″S 146°09′49.8″E to 17°58′03.0″S 146°10′50.5″E
1244	From 17°58′06.6″S 146°10′51.2″E to 18°02′14.4″S 146°12′06.8″E
1245	From 18°02′14.4″S 146°12′06.8″E to 18°09′14.6″S 146°18′20.7″E
1246	From 18°09′27.2″S 146°18′29.3″E to 18°14′07.2″S 146°19′38.1″E
1247	From 18°14′07.8″S 146°19′38.5″E to 18°25′06.2″S 146°21′26.7″E
1248	From 18°25′08.5″S 146°21′27.6″E to 18°32′16.2″S 146°29′43.7″E
1249	From 18°32′34.2″S 146°30′08.3″E to 18°44′15.8″S 146°41′06.9″E
1250	From 18°44′34.9″S 146°41′23.0″E to 18°46′18.1″S 146°43′03.7″E

续表

\multicolumn{2}{c}{Coast of the mainland of Australia}	
Item	Description
1251	From 18°46′20.3″S 146°43′06.4″E to 19°06′30.2″S 146°52′52.6″E
1252	From 19°06′30.2″S 146°52′52.6″E to 19°10′53.3″S 147°00′49.1″E
1253	From 19°57′14.8″S 148°13′24.1″E to 19°58′18.7″S 148°26′53.0″E
1254	From 19°58′21.7″S 148°27′23.4″E to 19°59′18.9″S 148°33′36.2″E
1255	From 19°59′19.0″S 148°33′36.7″E to 20°00′49.1″S 148°37′31.7″E
1256	From 20°00′49.1″S 148°37′31.7″E to 20°02′11.4″S 148°52′53.9″E
1257	From 20°02′14.6″S 148°53′13.6″E to 20°03′34.7″S 148°57′54.9″E
1258	From 20°03′34.9″S 148°57′55.7″E to 20°14′25.7″S 149°10′27.6″E
1259	From 20°14′34.8″S 149°10′31.7″E to 20°15′10.5″S 149°11′07.4″E
1260	From 20°15′14.2″S 149°11′08.5″E to 20°28′49.5″S 149°08′02.6″E
1261	From 20°28′49.5″S 149°08′02.6″E to 20°36′03.3″S 149°11′15.3″E
1262	From 20°36′03.3″S 149°11′15.3″E to 20°43′37.5″S 149°28′00.8″E
1263	From 20°43′37.5″S 149°28′00.8″E to 20°45′38.9″S 149°37′23.3″E
1264	From 20°46′23.1″S 149°37′39.6″E to 20°56′37.8″S 149°44′27.6″E
1265	From 20°56′37.8″S 149°44′27.6″E to 20°59′14.6″S 149°48′07.3″E
1266	From 20°59′14.6″S 149°48′07.3″E to 21°00′03.0″S 149°53′41.4″E
1267	From 21°00′03.4″S 149°53′43.2″E to 21°00′08.1″S 149°53′52.5″E
1268	From 21°01′24.8″S 149°54′57.2″E to 21°06′28.0″S 149°58′00.0″E
1269	From 21°06′28.0″S 149°58′00.0″E to 21°27′59.6″S 150°18′33.3″E
1270	From 21°28′08.0″S 150°18′38.6″E to 21°40′22.4″S 150°21′24.7″E
1271	From 21°40′22.4″S 150°21′24.7″E to 21°45′45.8″S 150°26′28.0″E
1272	From 21°45′45.8″S 150°26′28.0″E to 21°56′15.1″S 150°41′31.0″E
1273	From 21°56′15.1″S 150°41′31.0″E to 21°57′02.6″S 150°42′08.5″E
1274	From 21°57′02.6″S 150°42′08.5″E to 21°57′07.3″S 150°42′10.6″E
1275	From 21°57′14.0″S 150°42′09.0″E to 22°05′24.5″S 150°40′37.0″E
1276	From 22°05′24.5″S 150°40′37.0″E to 22°20′12.0″S 150°43′18.3″E
1277	From 22°20′12.0″S 150°43′18.3″E to 22°24′40.5″S 150°44′58.2″E
1278	From 22°24′40.5″S 150°44′58.2″E to 22°26′50.9″S 150°45′54.3″E
1279	From 22°26′54.1″S 150°45′56.6″E to 22°28′36.8″S 150°46′26.9″E
1280	From 22°28′36.8″S 150°46′26.9″E to 22°39′14.9″S 150°57′41.7″E
1281	From 22°39′16.6″S 150°57′43.2″E to 22°43′32.7″S 150°59′28.8″E

续表

	Coast of the mainland of Australia
Item	Description
1282	From 22°44′05.2″S 150°59′53.5″E to 23°09′13.9″S 151°05′10.6″E
1283	From 23°09′13.9″S 151°05′10.6″E to 23°11′52.1″S 151°06′08.7″E
1284	From 23°11′52.1″S 151°06′08.7″E to 23°24′31.3″S 151°11′05.6″E
1285	From 23°24′31.3″S 151°11′05.6″E to 23°28′54.9″S 151°14′01.6″E
1286	From 23°29′14.1″S 151°14′18.8″E to 23°31′43.9″S 151°16′33.3″E
1287	From 23°31′55.2″S 151°16′41.8″E to 23°45′11.6″S 151°20′06.6″E
1288	From 23°48′18.5″S 151°22′06.6″E to 23°48′48.6″S 151°23′16.3″E
1289	From 23°48′50.8″S 151°23′19.7″E to 23°57′05.2″S 151°29′26.3″E
1290	From 23°57′05.2″S 151°29′26.3″E to 23°58′24.5″S 151°37′33.9″E
1291	From 23°58′24.5″S 151°37′33.9″E to 23°58′34.0″S 151°46′31.2″E
1292	From 23°58′35.4″S 151°46′34.3″E to 24°08′52.3″S 151°53′08.8″E
1293	From 24°45′10.7″S 152°24′26.0″E to 24°41′53.6″S 153°14′50.4″E
1294	From 25°47′37.4″S 153°04′38.3″E to 25°48′38.1″S 153°04′22.4″E
1295	From 26°48′06.4″S 153°09′07.0″E to 27°01′39.3″S 153°28′05.3″E
1296	From 27°01′42.8″S 153°28′07.2″E to 27°23′27.8″S 153°33′11.3″E
1297	From 27°23′28.6″S 153°33′11.4″E to 27°25′06.8″S 153°33′19.4″E
1298	From 27°25′07.4″S 153°33′19.3″E to 27°26′11.1″S 153°32′48.2″E
1299	From 27°43′36.5″S 153°27′10.3″E to 27°44′39.1″S 153°26′48.1″E
1300	From 27°55′58.5″S 153°25′52.1″E to 27°56′06.0″S 153°26′00.0″E

Part 2—Historic bays

	Historic bays	
	Column 1	Column 2
Item	Historic bay	Description
2001	Anxious Bay	From 33°11′58.9″S 134°19′43.1″E to 33°35′35.9″S 134°45′08.0″E From 33°35′45.2″S 134°46′00.3″E to 33°35′53.9″S 134°46′35.0″E From 33°36′37.9″S 134°48′25.0″E to 33°37′22.9″S 134°49′45.0″E
2002	Encounter Bay	From 35°35′42.6″S 138°36′09.4″E to 35°35′42.8″S 138°57′29.0″E
2003	Lacepede Bay	From 36°35′47.4″S 139°50′02.8″E to 36°56′32.5″S 139°40′30.4″E
2004	Rivoli Bay	From 37°29′59.1″S 140°00′53.4″E to 37°33′54.9″S 140°06′24.4″E From 37°29′46.8″S 140°00′43.0″E to 37°29′51.8″S 140°00′46.0″E

Part 3—Coast of the mainland of Tasmania

	Coast of the mainland of Tasmania
Item	Description
3001	From 41°51′12.9″S 148°16′39.8″E to 41°51′22.2″S 148°17′24.0″E
3002	From 41°51′23.4″S 148°17′28.3″E to 41°52′12.4″S 148°18′56.3″E
3003	From 41°52′12.9″S 148°18′57.1″E to 41°52′35.7″S 148°18′58.3″E
3004	From 41°52′37.0″S 148°18′58.1″E to 41°53′18.8″S 148°18′36.4″E
3005	From 41°53′19.7″S 148°18′35.7″E to 41°53′40.5″S 148°18′33.0″E
3006	From 42°13′21.3″S 148°20′48.6″E to 42°20′27.0″S 148°20′45.3″E
3007	From 42°20′30.9″S 148°20′44.7″E to 42°38′58.6″S 148°10′09.1″E
3008	From 42°38′58.6″S 148°10′09.1″E to 43°07′21.7″S 148°03′25.1″E
3009	From 43°07′22.0″S 148°03′25.0″E to 43°13′18.0″S 148°00′41.5″E
3010	From 43°13′18.0″S 148°00′41.5″E to 43°14′10.1″S 148°00′34.1″E
3011	From 43°14′37.6″S 148°00′26.2″E to 43°14′45.8″S 148°00′19.2″E
3012	From 43°14′46.0″S 148°00′18.7″E to 43°31′58.0″S 147°17′59.5″E
3013	From 43°31′58.6″S 147°17′57.5″E to 43°38′18.8″S 146°52′16.2″E
3014	From 43°38′34.4″S 146°49′32.5″E to 43°39′50.4″S 146°15′40.3″E
3015	From 43°39′50.4″S 146°15′38.9″E to 43°39′49.9″S 146°14′57.0″E
3016	From 43°39′48.9″S 146°14′51.7″E to 43°39′44.8″S 146°14′35.3″E
3017	From 43°39′44.6″S 146°14′34.9″E to 43°34′20.6″S 146°01′50.4″E
3018	From 43°29′16.3″S 146°01′38.3″E to 43°29′01.2″S 146°01′32.9″E
3019	From 43°29′01.2″S 146°01′32.9″E to 43°28′10.2″S 146°00′30.1″E
3020	From 43°28′00.7″S 146°00′22.6″E to 43°27′59.7″S 146°00′22.0″E
3021	From 43°27′57.9″S 146°00′20.6″E to 43°26′02.9″S 145°59′50.8″E
3022	From 43°26′02.9″S 145°59′50.8″E to 43°25′41.9″S 145°58′01.8″E
3023	From 43°25′41.1″S 145°57′59.6″E to 43°25′41.1″S 145°57′58.7″E
3024	From 43°25′41.1″S 145°57′57.6″E to 43°25′17.6″S 145°55′58.6″E
3025	From 43°25′17.6″S 145°55′58.3″E to 43°25′12.2″S 145°55′21.1″E
3026	From 43°25′12.1″S 145°55′20.2″E to 43°25′09.7″S 145°55′14.8″E
3027	From 43°25′04.4″S 145°55′13.3″E to 43°22′56.0″S 145°55′09.2″E
3028	From 43°22′54.2″S 145°55′08.6″E to 43°19′21.4″S 145°52′14.0″E
3029	From 40°50′09.7″S 144°42′39.6″E to 40°50′00.3″S 144°42′19.0″E
3030	From 40°49′59.1″S 144°42′17.6″E to 40°49′39.0″S 144°41′59.7″E

续表

\multicolumn{2}{c}{Coast of the mainland of Tasmania}	
Item	Description
3031	From 40°49′36.8″S 144°41′59.2″E to 40°49′17.4″S 144°41′50.9″E
3032	From 40°49′14.9″S 144°41′50.6″E to 40°48′46.0″S 144°41′43.3″E
3033	From 40°48′43.3″S 144°41′43.4″E to 40°48′14.3″S 144°41′46.2″E
3034	From 40°48′13.8″S 144°41′46.3″E to 40°48′06.3″S 144°41′48.1″E
3035	From 40°48′06.3″S 144°41′48.1″E to 40°48′00.6″S 144°41′48.8″E
3036	From 40°47′59.9″S 144°41′49.9″E to 40°47′52.3″S 144°42′07.0″E
3037	From 40°44′06.9″S 144°41′03.2″E to 40°43′32.3″S 144°40′39.8″E
3038	From 40°43′27.6″S 144°40′36.7″E to 40°43′05.3″S 144°40′31.6″E
3039	From 40°43′03.9″S 144°40′31.1″E to 40°40′16.0″S 144°40′10.1″E
3040	From 40°40′14.8″S 144°40′10.2″E to 40°37′33.8″S 144°40′41.5″E
3041	From 40°37′33.1″S 144°40′41.7″E to 40°36′29.2″S 144°40′57.7″E
3042	From 40°36′29.2″S 144°40′57.7″E to 40°35′00.8″S 144°40′45.1″E
3043	From 40°34′59.5″S 144°40′45.2″E to 40°33′55.0″S 144°40′39.3″E
3044	From 40°33′53.5″S 144°40′38.8″E to 40°33′45.5″S 144°40′42.4″E
3045	From 40°33′45.4″S 144°40′42.5″E to 40°30′21.1″S 144°42′14.2″E
3046	From 40°30′21.1″S 144°42′14.2″E to 40°30′15.8″S 144°42′13.4″E
3047	From 40°30′14.7″S 144°42′13.1″E to 40°29′36.8″S 144°42′07.5″E
3048	From 40°29′36.4″S 144°42′07.7″E to 40°29′09.2″S 144°42′29.1″E
3049	From 40°23′57.7″S 144°47′05.8″E to 40°23′19.0″S 144°53′04.4″E
3050	From 40°25′35.2″S 144°58′14.0″E to 40°42′37.4″S 145°16′27.2″E

Part 4—Islands off the coasts of the States and the Northern Territory

\multicolumn{2}{c}{Islands off the coasts of the States and the Northern Territory}	
Item	Description
4001	From 40°12′34.1″S 148°20′03.7″E to 40°17′30.6″S 148°20′00.5″E
4002	From 40°29′22.3″S 148°23′52.8″E to 40°31′07.9″S 148°20′58.9″E
4003	From 40°31′22.3″S 148°20′48.8″E to 40°33′44.6″S 148°14′50.1″E
4004	From 40°33′44.6″S 148°14′50.1″E to 40°35′25.1″S 148°11′56.4″E
4005	From 40°33′55.0″S 148°06′47.6″E to 40°33′24.3″S 148°05′53.3″E
4006	From 40°33′22.6″S 148°05′49.6″E to 40°29′49.0″S 148°01′08.2″E

续表

\multicolumn{2}{c}{Islands off the coasts of the States and the Northern Territory}
Item	Description
4007	From 40°29′48.2″S 148°01′07.0″E to 40°22′48.3″S 147°53′31.0″E
4008	From 40°22′48.3″S 147°53′31.0″E to 40°18′57.1″S 147°48′07.6″E
4009	From 40°17′52.1″S 147°47′05.4″E to 40°17′47.8″S 147°47′00.0″E
4010	From 40°17′37.9″S 147°46′49.5″E to 40°07′48.0″S 147°43′11.2″E
4011	From 40°07′46.5″S 147°43′11.4″E to 40°06′13.3″S 147°43′32.4″E
4012	From 40°05′29.3″S 147°43′21.8″E to 39°52′28.5″S 147°44′50.2″E
4013	From 54°46′40.4″S 158°50′14.9″E to 54°46′49.6″S 158°48′57.1″E
4014	From 54°46′49.7″S 158°48′54.7″E to 54°46′50.9″S 158°48′13.2″E
4015	From 54°46′51.9″S 158°48′04.0″E to 54°46′29.3″S 158°46′30.5″E
4016	From 54°46′28.3″S 158°46′27.9″E to 54°45′59.2″S 158°46′30.7″E
4017	From 54°45′59.2″S 158°46′30.7″E to 54°45′30.0″S 158°46′31.8″E
4018	From 54°45′29.3″S 158°46′32.0″E to 54°44′33.1″S 158°46′58.0″E
4019	From 54°44′32.4″S 158°46′58.3″E to 54°43′49.9″S 158°47′21.5″E
4020	From 54°43′49.9″S 158°47′21.5″E to 54°41′19.8″S 158°47′53.7″E
4021	From 54°41′13.2″S 158°47′55.6″E to 54°38′15.1″S 158°48′51.7″E
4022	From 54°38′11.6″S 158°48′52.6″E to 54°36′25.0″S 158°49′11.9″E
4023	From 54°36′22.7″S 158°49′13.6″E to 54°35′28.8″S 158°49′50.4″E
4024	From 54°35′28.8″S 158°49′50.4″E to 54°35′03.0″S 158°50′06.2″E
4025	From 54°35′02.3″S 158°50′06.6″E to 54°34′16.7″S 158°50′34.8″E
4026	From 54°34′16.7″S 158°50′34.8″E to 54°31′51.8″S 158°50′49.8″E
4027	From 54°31′48.3″S 158°50′51.4″E to 54°31′10.6″S 158°51′04.4″E
4028	From 54°31′04.7″S 158°51′08.7″E to 54°30′56.3″S 158°51′16.1″E
4029	From 54°30′51.3″S 158°51′20.5″E to 54°29′47.2″S 158°52′30.8″E
4030	From 54°29′46.4″S 158°54′29.5″E to 54°29′50.7″S 158°55′44.4″E
4031	From 54°29′50.7″S 158°55′44.4″E to 54°29′13.3″S 158°55′53.9″E
4032	From 54°29′13.0″S 158°55′53.9″E to 54°28′38.8″S 158°55′50.2″E
4033	From 54°28′36.9″S 158°55′51.9″E to 54°28′11.5″S 158°56′08.1″E
4034	From 54°28′11.6″S 158°56′10.3″E to 54°28′17.9″S 158°56′23.7″E
4035	From 54°28′18.6″S 158°56′24.9″E to 54°28′22.2″S 158°56′27.0″E
4036	From 54°28′23.0″S 158°56′27.9″E to 54°29′27.5″S 158°57′09.7″E
4037	From 54°29′29.3″S 158°57′09.8″E to 54°29′56.7″S 158°56′46.9″E

续表

\multicolumn{2}{c}{Islands off the coasts of the States and the Northern Territory}
Item	Description
4038	From 54°29′56.7″S 158°56′46.9″E to 54°30′01.8″S 158°56′42.7″E
4039	From 54°30′01.6″S 158°56′42.2″E to 54°29′59.9″S 158°56′36.0″E
4040	From 28°52′36.2″S 113°48′33.8″E to 28°47′36.8″S 113°44′33.8″E
4041	From 28°43′43.2″S 113°42′19.8″E to 28°28′44.7″S 113°39′38.4″E
4042	From 28°28′44.7″S 113°39′38.4″E to 28°20′20.3″S 113°35′26.4″E
4043	From 28°17′52.3″S 113°36′26.6″E to 28°25′33.2″S 113°44′46.4″E
4044	From 28°25′33.2″S 113°44′46.4″E to 28°27′26.7″S 113°48′41.8″E
4045	From 28°27′46.1″S 113°49′01.2″E to 28°37′38.7″S 113°53′14.0″E
4046	From 28°37′38.7″S 113°53′14.0″E to 28°47′55.9″S 114°02′31.8″E
4047	From 28°48′05.2″S 114°02′33.8″E to 28°53′39.8″S 114°00′42.1″E

Schedule 3—Repeals（omitted）

附录3 《海洋与水下土地2005年1号修订公告》[1]

Seas and Submerged Lands Amendment Proclamation 2005（No. 1）

1 Name of Proclamation

This Proclamation is the *Seas and Submerged Lands Amendment Proclamation* 2005 (*No.* 1).

2 Commencement

This Proclamation commences on the day the Treaty between the Government of Australia and the Government of New Zealand Establishing Certain Exclusive Economic Zone Boundaries and Continental Shelf Boundaries, done at Adelaide on 25 July 2004, enters into force.

3 Revocation of previous Amendment Proclamation

The *Seas and Submerged Lands Amendment Proclamation* 2004 (*No.* 1) made on 16 December 2004 is revoked.

4 Amendment of Proclamation

Schedule 1 amendsthe Proclamation made under section 10B of the *Seas and Submerged Lands Act* 1973 on 26 July 1994 and published in the *Gazette* on 29 July 1994.

Schedule 1　　Amendments

（section 4）

[1] **Paragraph（c）**

omit everything before subparagraph（c）（i）, insert

（c）for the purposes of items 1, 4（other than paragraph（a））and 7 in the Schedule:

[2] **Sub-subparagraph（d）（ii）（B）**

omit

　　spheroid.

insert

　　spheroid; and

---

[1] "Seas and Submerged Lands Amendment Proclamation 2005（No. 1）", Australia Federal Register of Legislation, https：//www. legislation. gov. au/Details/F2005L01989, December 3, 2024.

[3] **After paragraph (d)**

insert

(e) for the purposes of items 5, 6 and 8 in the Schedule, all geographic coordinates are expressed in terms of the International Terrestrial Reference Frame 2000, as defined by the International Earth Rotation Service at epoch 1 January 2000.

[4] **Schedule, item 5**

substitute

5 Norfolk Island/New Zealand

The line:

(a) commencing at the point of latitude 30° 53′ 11.23″ south, longitude 171° 13′ 28.85″ east; and

(b) then running south-westerly along the geodesic to the point of latitude 31° 16′ 01.68″ south, longitude 170° 37′ 06.34″ east; and

(c) then south-westerly along the geodesic to the point of latitude 31° 19′ 31.67″ south, longitude 170° 31′ 15.10″ east; and

(d) then south-westerly along the geodesic to the point of latitude 31° 40′ 26.30″ south, longitude 169° 56′ 12.27″ east; and

(e) then south-westerly along the geodesic to the point of latitude 31° 47′ 23.99″ south, longitude 169° 44′ 25.06″ east; and

(f) then south-westerly along the geodesic to the point of latitude 32° 04′ 50.57″ south, longitude 169° 14′ 37.00″ east; and

(g) then south-westerly along the geodesic to the point of latitude 32° 06′ 52.74″ south, longitude 169° 11′ 06.79″ east; and

(h) then south-westerly along the geodesic to the point of latitude 32° 25′ 18.55″ south, longitude 168° 39′ 03.72″ east; and

(i) then clockwise westerly along the geodesic arc of radius 200 nautical miles concave to Norfolk Island to the point of latitude 32° 22′ 18.95″ south, longitude 166° 58′ 54.37″ east; and

(j) then clockwise westerly along the geodesic arc of radius 200 nautical miles concave to Norfolk Island to the point of latitude 32° 09′ 22.23″ south, longitude 166° 17′ 34.30″ east; and

(k) then clockwise north-westerly along the geodesic arc of radius 200 nautical miles concave to Norfolk Island to the point of latitude 31° 53′ 49.17″ south, longitude 165° 46′ 20.73″ east; and

(l) then clockwise north-westerly along the geodesic arc of radius 200 nautical miles concave to Norfolk Island to the point of latitude 31° 30′ south, longitude 165° 13′ 27.08″ east.

[5] **Schedule, item 6**

substitute

6 Macquarie Island

The line:

(a) commencing at the point of latitude 51° 04′ 48.96″ south, longitude 158° 01′ 25.98″ east; and

(b) then running clockwise easterly along the geodesic arc of radius 200 nautical miles concave to Macquarie Island to the point of latitude 51° 01′ 38.44″ south, longitude 158° 59′ 53.57″ east; and

(c) then clockwise easterly along the geodesic arc of radius 200 nautical miles concave to Macquarie Island to the point of latitude 51° 10′ 36.30″ south, longitude 160° 37′ 30.11″ east; and

(d) then south-easterly along the geodesic to the point of latitude 51° 26′ 17.80″ south, longitude 160° 57′ 46.87″ east; and

(e) then south-easterly along the geodesic to the point of latitude 52° 11′ 26.54″ south, longitude 161° 57′ 11.15″ east; and

(f) then south-easterly along the geodesic to the point of latitude 52° 15′ 53.24″ south, longitude 162° 03′ 07.43″ east; and

(g) then south-easterly along the geodesic to the point of latitude 52° 27′ 43.12″ south, longitude 162° 18′ 59.49″ east; and

(h) then south-easterly along the geodesic to the point of latitude 52° 40′ 46.86″ south, longitude 162° 36′ 30.28″ east; and

(i) then south-easterly along the geodesic to the point of latitude 52° 46′ 50.62″ south, longitude 162° 44′ 42.77″ east; and

(j) then south-easterly along the geodesic to the point of latitude 52° 47′ 42.61″ south, longitude 162° 45′ 53.41″ east; and

(k) then south-easterly along the geodesic to the point of latitude 53° 42′ 58.16″ south, longitude 164° 03′ 13.39″ east; and

(l) then south-easterly along the geodesic to the point of latitude 53° 50′ 59.84″ south, longitude 164° 14′ 42.04″ east; and

(m) then south-easterly along the geodesic to the point of latitude 54° 13′ 58.99″ south, longitude 164° 26′ 41.46″ east; and

(n) then south-easterly along the geodesic to the point of latitude 54° 40′ 13.65″ south, longitude 164° 40′ 40.22″ east; and

(o) then south-easterly along the geodesic to the point of latitude 54° 41′ 43.03″ south, longitude 164° 41′ 28.44″ east; and

附录3 《海洋与水下土地2005年1号修订公告》

(p) then clockwise south-westerly along the geodesic arc of radius 200 nautical miles concave to Macquarie Island to the point of latitude 54° 56′ 14.18″ south, longitude 164° 39′ 00.39″ east; and

(q) then clockwise south-westerly along the geodesic arc of radius 200 nautical miles concave to Macquarie Island to the point of latitude 55° 00′ 11.94″ south, longitude 164° 38′ 17.35″ east; and

(r) then clockwise south-westerly along the geodesic arc of radius 200 nautical miles concave to Macquarie Island to the point of latitude 55° 10′ 06.11″ south, longitude 164° 36′ 21.26″ east; and

(s) then clockwise south-westerly along the geodesic arc of radius 200 nautical miles concave to Macquarie Island to the point of latitude 55° 14′ 12.61″ south, longitude 164° 35′ 21.12″ east; and

(t) then clockwise south-westerly along the geodesic arc of radius 200 nautical miles concave to Macquarie Island to the point of latitude 55° 42′ 50.10″ south, longitude 164° 26′ 46.41″ east; and

(u) then clockwise south-westerly along the geodesic arc of radius 200 nautical miles concave to Macquarie Island to the point of latitude 55° 52′ 23.70″ south, longitude 164° 23′ 57.71″ east; and

(v) then clockwise south-westerly along the geodesic arc of radius 200 nautical miles concave to Macquarie Island to the point of latitude 56° 38′ 56.15″ south, longitude 163° 56′ 44.86″ east; and

(w) then clockwise south-westerly along the geodesic arc of radius 200 nautical miles concave to Macquarie Island to the point of latitude 56° 52′ 19.72″ south, longitude 163° 44′ 04.71″ east; and

(x) then clockwise south-westerly along the geodesic arc of radius 200 nautical miles concave to Macquarie Island to the point of latitude 57° 09′ 53.30″ south, longitude 163° 23′ 17.53″ east.

[6] **Schedule, after item 7**

insert

8 Lord Howe Island

The line:

(a) commencing at the point of latitude 32° 30′ south, longitude 163° 06′ 58.81″ east; and

(b) then running clockwise southerly along the geodesic arc of radius 200 nautical miles concave to Lord Howe Island to the point of latitude 33° 52′ 40.25″ south, longitude 162° 21′ 59.44″ east.

附录 4 《海洋与水下土地（大陆架界限）2012 年公告》[1]

Seas and Submerged Lands (Limits of Continental Shelf) Proclamation 2012

1 Name of Proclamation

This Proclamation is the *Seas and Submerged Lands (Limits of Continental Shelf) Proclamation* 2012.

2 Commencement

This Proclamation commences on the day after it is registered.

3 Repeal

The *Seas and Submerged Lands (Limits of Continental Shelf in the Tasman Sea and South Pacific Ocean) Proclamation* 2005 (Federal Register of Legislative Instruments No. F2005L01990) is repealed.

4 Continental shelf—mainland Australia (including Tasmania, other than Macquarie Island), Lord Howe Island and Norfolk Island

The outer limit of certain parts of Australia's continental shelf adjacent to the coast of the mainland of Australia (including Tasmania, other than Macquarie Island) and adjacent to the coasts of Lord Howe Island and Norfolk Island is the line specified in Part 1 of Schedule 1.

Note 1 The line is not continuous and is broken in several places as set out in Part 1 of Schedule 1. See the map in Schedule 6 for a general illustration of the line specified in Part 1 of Schedule 1.

Note 2 For information about Part 2 of Schedule 1, see subsection 9 (2).

5 Continental shelf—Macquarie Island

The outer limit of Australia's continental shelf adjacent to the coast of Macquarie Island is the line specified in Schedule 2.

Note See the map in Schedule 6 for a general illustration of the line specified in Schedule 2.

6 Continental shelf—Heard Island and McDonald Islands

The outer limit of Australia's continental shelf adjacent to the coasts of Heard Island and McDonald Islands is the line specified in Part 1 of Schedule 3.

Note 1 See the map in Schedule 6 for a general illustration of the line specified in Part

---

[1] "Seas and Submerged Lands (Limits of Continental Shelf) Proclamation 2012", Australia Federal Register of Legislation, https://www.legislation.gov.au/Details/F2012L01081, December 3, 2024.

1 of Schedule 3.

Note 2 For information about Part 2 of Schedule 3, see subsection 9 (2).

7 Continental shelf—Cocos (Keeling) Islands

The outer limit of Australia's continental shelf adjacent to the coast of Cocos (Keeling) Islands is the line specified in Schedule 4.

Note See the map in Schedule 6 for a general illustration of the line specified in Schedule 4.

8 Continental shelf—Christmas Island

The outer limit of certain parts of Australia's continental shelf adjacent to the coast of Christmas Island is the line specified in Schedule 5.

Note See the map in Schedule 6 for a general illustration of the line specified in Schedule 5.

9 Operation of Schedules 1 to 5

(1) In Schedules 1 to 5:

(a) lines are specified by reference to points; and

(b) the columns of an item in a table in which a point is specified set out information about the point; and

(c) the information about the point:

(i) includes the point identifier shown in the first column of an item in the table (the point identifier is sometimes used in this Proclamation to refer to the point); and

(ii) may also include a treaty point reference, which is a reference to how the point is referred to in the relevant treaty for a point mentioned in section 10; and

(iii) also includes geographic coordinates for the point (for more about geographic coordinates, see section 11); and

(d) the geographic coordinates for a point determine the location of the point for this Proclamation.

Note For some points mentioned in Schedule 1, the information may include more than one treaty (and more than one treaty point reference).

(2) In Schedules 1 and 3:

(a) the geographic coordinates for a point (and the datum by reference to which they are determined) shown in Part 1 of each Schedule determine the location of the point for this Proclamation; and

(b) the geographic coordinates shown in Part 2 of each Schedule:

(i) represent the authoritative conversion for some of the points mentioned in Part 1 of each Schedule into the International Terrestrial Reference Frame 2000 (ITRF2000), as defined by the International Earth Rotation and Reference Systems Service at epoch 1 January

2000 in *IERS Technical Note No. 31*; and

　　(ⅱ) are included for the information of readers; and

　　(ⅲ) do not determine the location of those points for this Proclamation; and

　　(ⅳ) are included to clarify the relationship between certain historical datums and ITRF 2000, so that a connection with future datums can be maintained.

10 Relevant treaties

The relevant treaty for a point is as follows:

　　(a) for points AUS-CS-1 to AUS-CS-20 in Schedule 1—*Treaty between Australia and the Independent State of Papua New Guinea concerning Sovereignty and Maritime Boundaries in the area between the two Countries, including the area known as Torres Strait, and Related Matters*, Australian Treaty Series 1985 No. 4;

　　(b) for points AUS-CS-101 and AUS-CS-102 in Schedule 1—*Agreement between the Government of Australia and the Government of Solomon Islands establishing Certain Sea and Seabed Boundaries*, Australian Treaty Series 1989 No. 12;

　　(c) for points AUS-CS-102 to AUS-CS-123 in Schedule 1 and points HMI-CS-1 to HMI-CS-7 in Schedule 3—*Agreement on Maritime Delimitation between the Government of Australia and the Government of the French Republic*, Australian Treaty Series 1983 No. 3;

　　(d) for points AUS-CS-124 to AUS-CS-150 in Schedule 1 and points MAC-CS-1 to MAC-CS-24 in Schedule 2—*Treaty between the Government of Australia and the Government of New Zealand establishing Certain Exclusive Economic Zone Boundaries and Continental Shelf Boundaries*, Australian Treaty Series 2006 No. 4.

　　Note 1 For some points mentioned in Schedule 1, more than one treaty is relevant (and more than one treaty point reference is mentioned for the point).

　　Note 2 No treaty is relevant for Schedule 4 [which relates to Cocos (Keeling) Islands] or Schedule 5 (which relates to Christmas Island).

　　Note 3 In 2012, the text of a treaty in the Australian Treaty Series was accessible through the Australian Treaties Library on the AustLII website (www. austlii. edu. au).

11 Geographic coordinates

　　(1) The following table shows the abbreviation used in this Proclamation for each datum mentioned in the table.

Item	Abbreviation	Datum
1	AGD66	Australian Geodetic Datum 1966
2	ITRF2000	International Terrestrial Reference Frame 2000, as defined by International Earth Rotation and Reference Systems Service at epoch 1 January 2000 in *IERS Technical Note No.* 31

附录 4 《海洋与水下土地（大陆架界限）2012 年公告》

续表

Item	Abbreviation	Datum
3	WGS72	World Geodetic System 1972
4	WGS84	World Geodetic System 1984

(2) For this Proclamation, a geographic coordinate is determined by reference to the datum mentioned in Schedules 1 to 5 for the coordinate.

(3) For this Proclamation, the datums mentioned in subsection (4) are taken to be equivalent.

Note See *US National Imagery and Mapping Agency, Technical Report—NIMA TR*8350.2 *Third Edition* (*including amendments to* 23 *June* 2004) —*Department of Defense World Geodetic System* 1984—*Its Definition and Relationships with Local Geodetic Systems*, in particular Chapters 2.2.1 and 7.

(4) The datums are:

(a) WGS84; and

(b) ITRF2000.

Schedule 1　Outer limit of parts of continental shelf adjacent to coasts of mainland Australia (including Tasmania, other than Macquarie Island), Lord Howe Island and Norfolk Island (omitted)

Schedule 2　Outer limit of continental shelf adjacent to coast of Macquarie Island (omitted)

Schedule 3　Outer limit of continental shelf adjacent to coasts of Heard Island and McDonald Islands (omitted)

Schedule 4　Outer limit of continental shelf adjacent to coast of Cocos (Keeling) Islands (omitted)

Schedule 5　Outer limit of parts of continental shelf adjacent to coast of Christmas Island (omitted)

Schedule 6　Map (omitted)

附录5　《海洋与水下土地（历史性海湾）2016年公告》[1]

Seas and Submerged Lands (Historic Bays) Proclamation 2016

1 Name

This is the *Seas and Submerged Lands (Historic Bays) Proclamation* 2016.

2 Commencement

(1) Each provision of this instrument specified in column 1 of the table commences, or is taken to have commenced, in accordance with column 2 of the table. Any other statement in column 2 has effect according to its terms.

Commencement information		
Column 1	Column 2	Column 3
Provisions	Commencement	Date/Details
1. The whole of this instrument	The day after this instrument is registered.	12 March 2016

Note: This table relates only to the provisions of this instrument as originally made. It will not be amended to deal with any later amendments of this instrument.

(2) Any information in column 3 of the table is not part of this instrument. Information may be inserted in this column, or information in it may be edited, in any published version of this instrument.

3 Authority

This instrument is made under paragraph 8 (a) of the *Seas and Submerged Lands Act* 1973.

4 Schedules

Each instrument that is specified in a Schedule to this instrument is amended or repealed as set out in the applicable items in the Schedule concerned, and any other item in a Schedule to this instrument has effect according to its terms.

5 Definitions

(1) In this instrument:

Act means the *Seas and Submerged Lands Act* 1973.

Geocentric Datum of Australia means the datum described in Schedule 1.

---

[1] "Seas and Submerged Lands (Historic Bays) Proclamation 2016", Australia Federal Register of Legislation, https://www.legislation.gov.au/Details/F2006L00526, December 3, 2024.

low-water means lowest astronomical tide.

straight line means a geodesic line.

(2) For the purposes of this instrument, the position on the surface of the Earth of a point, line or area is to be determined by reference to the Geocentric Datum of Australia.

6 Declaration of historic bays

For paragraph 8 (a) of the Act, each of the following bays is declared to be an historic bay:

(a) Anxious Bay;

(b) Encounter Bay;

(c) Lacepede Bay;

(d) Rivoli Bay.

7 Sea-ward limits—Anxious Bay

(1) Subject to section 11, the sea-ward limits of Anxious Bay are defined by each of the straight lines constituted by joining the 2 points on the low-water line of the coast that are on, or closest to, 2 points of latitude and longitude specified in the same paragraph in subsection (2).

(2) For subsection (1), the points of latitude and longitude are:

(a) from 33°11′58.9″S 134°19′43.1″E to 33°35′35.9″S 134°45′08.0″E; and (b) from 33°35′45.2″S 134°46′00.3″E to 33°35′53.9″S 134°46′35.0″E; and (c) from 33°36′37.9″S 134°48′25.0″E to 33°37′22.9″S 134°49′45.0″E.

8 Sea-ward limits—Encounter Bay

(1) Subject to section 11, the sea-ward limits of Encounter Bay are defined by the straight line constituted by joining the 2 points on the low-water line of the coast that are on, or closest to, the points of latitude and longitude specified in subsection (2).

(2) For subsection (1), the points of latitude and longitude are from 35°35′42.6″S 138°36′09.4″E to 35°35′42.8″S 138°57′29.0″E.

9 Sea-ward limits—Lacepede Bay

(1) Subject to section 11, the sea-ward limits of Lacepede Bay are defined by the straight line constituted by joining the 2 points on the low-water line of the coast that are on, or closest to, the points of latitude and longitude specified in subsection (2).

(2) For subsection (1), the points of latitude and longitude are from 36°35′47.4″S 139°50′02.8″E to 36°56′32.5″S 139°40′30.4″E.

10 Sea-ward limits—Rivoli Bay

(1) Subject to section 11, the sea-ward limits of Rivoli Bay are defined by each of the straight lines constituted by joining the 2 points on the low-water line of the coast that are on, or closest to, 2 points of latitude and longitude specified in the same paragraph in subsection (2).

(2) For subsection (1), the points of latitude and longitude are:

(a) from 37°29′59.1″S 140°00′53.4″E to 37°33′54.9″S 140°06′24.4″E; and (b) from

37°29′46.8″S 140°00′43.0″E to 37°29′51.8″S 140°00′46.0″E.

11 Low-water line of the same island

(1) If straight lines mentioned in section 7, 8, 9 or 10 join 2 different points on the low-water line of the same island, the sea-ward limits of the historic bay between those points are defined by the line constituted by a line following the low-water line of the sea-ward part of the coast of the island between those points.

(2) For subsection (1), the sea-ward part of the coast of an island is the part of the coast of the island that includes the most sea-ward point of the island.

Schedule 1—Geocentric Datum of Australia

Note: See the definition of *Geocentric Datum of Australia* in subsection 5 (1).

1 Reference ellipsoid

Geodetic Reference System 1980 ellipsoid with a semi-major axis of 6 378 137 metres and an inverse flattening of 298.257 222 101.

2 Reference frame

The Geocentric Datum of Australia is realised by the coordinates of the following Australian Fiducial Network geodetic stations referred to the Geodetic Reference System 1980 ellipsoid determined within the International Earth Rotation Service Terrestrial Reference Frame 1992 at the epoch of 1994.0.

		Reference frame		
Item	Geodetic station	South latitude	East longitude	Ellipsoidal height (metres)
1	AU 012 Alice Springs	23°40′12.44592″	133°53′07.84757″	603.358
2	AU 013 Karratha	20°58′53.17004″	117°05′49.87255″	109.246
3	AU 014 Darwin	12°50′37.35839″	131°07′57.84838″	125.197
4	AU 015 Townsville	19°20′50.42839″	146°46′30.79057″	587.077
5	AU 016 Hobart	42°48′16.98506″	147°26′19.43548″	41.126
6	AU 017 Tidbinbilla	35°23′57.15627″	148°58′47.98425″	665.440
7	AU 019 Ceduna	31°52′00.01664″	133°48′35.37527″	144.802
8	AU 029 Yaragadee	29°02′47.61687″	115°20′49.10049″	241.291

Schedule 2—Repeals (omitted)

附录6　1933年《澳大利亚南极领地接纳法》[1]

Australian Antarctic Territory Acceptance Act 1933

An Act to provide for the acceptance of certain territory in the Antarctic Seas as a Territory under the authority of the Commonwealth

1 Short title [see Note 1]

This Act may be cited as the*Australian Antarctic Territory Acceptance Act* 1933.

2 Acceptance of the Territory [see Note 2]

That part of the territory in the Antarctic seas which comprises all the islands and territories, other than Adelie Land, situated south of the 60th degree south latitude and lying between the 160th degree east longitude and the 45th degree east longitude, is hereby declared to be accepted by the Commonwealth as a Territory under the authority of the Commonwealth, by the name of the Australian Antarctic Territory.

---

[1] "Australian Antarctic Territory Acceptance Act 1933", Australia Federal Register of Legislation, https://www.legislation.gov.au/Details/C2004C00416, December 3, 2024.

附录7　1954年《澳大利亚南极领地法》[1]

Australian Antarctic Territory Act 1954

An Act to provide for the Government of the Australian Antarctic Territory

Preamble

WHEREAS the Australian Antarctic Territory was, by the Australian *Antarctic Territory Acceptance Act* 1933, accepted by the Commonwealth as a Territory under the authority of the Commonwealth:

AND WHEREAS the Australian Antarctic Territory has been governed by the Commonwealth under the provisions of that Act:

AND WHEREAS it is desirable to make other provision for the government of the Australian Antarctic Territory:

BE IT THEREFORE ENACTED by the Queen's Most Excellent Majesty, the Senate, and the House of Representatives of the Commonwealth of Australia, as follows:

1 Short title [*see* Note 1]

This Act may be cited as the*Australian Antarctic Territory Act* 1954.

2 Commencement [*see* Note 1]

This Act shall come into operation on the day on which it receives the Royal Assent.

4 Definitions

In this Act, unless the contrary intention appears:

Act does not include an enactment.

criminal laws means any laws (whether written, unwritten, substantive or procedural) relating to offences, whether indictable or not, including laws about:

(a) the investigation of offences; and

(b) the punishment of offenders, including the penalties or loss of benefits to which offenders are liable; and

(c) the forfeiture and confiscation of the proceeds of crime;

and any laws providing for the interpretation of such laws.

---

[1] "Australian Antarctic Territory Act 1954", Australia Federal Register of Legislation, https://www.legisla-tion.gov.au/Details/C2012C00725, December 3, 2024.

enactment has the same meaning as in the *Australian Capital Territory (Self-Government) Act* 1988.

Ordinance means an Ordinance made under this Act.

the Territory means the Australian Antarctic Territory which was accepted by the Commonwealth by the *Australian Antarctic Territory Acceptance Act* 1933, that is to say, that part of the territory in the Antarctic seas which comprises all the islands and territories, other than Adelie Land, situated south of the sixtieth degree south latitude and lying between the one hundred and sixtieth degree east longitude and the forty-fifth degree east longitude.

5 Existing laws to cease to be in force

The laws in force in the Territory immediately before the commencement of this Act (not being laws of the Commonwealth in force in the Territory) shall, upon the commencement of this Act, cease to be in force.

6 Laws of Australian Capital Territory to be in force

(1) Subject to this Act, the laws (other than the criminal laws) in force from time to time in the Australian Capital Territory (including the principles and rules of common law and equity so in force) are, by virtue of this section, so far as they are applicable to the Territory and are not inconsistent with an Ordinance, in force in the Territory as if the Territory formed part of the Australian Capital Territory.

(2) Subject to this Act, the criminal laws in force from time to time in the Jervis Bay Territory are, by virtue of this section (so far as they are applicable to the Territory and are not inconsistent with an Ordinance) in force in the Territory as if the Territory formed part of the Jervis Bay Territory.

(2A) Chapter 2 of the *Criminal Code* does not apply in relation to, or in relation to matters arising under, a law in force in the Territory under subsection (1) or (2).

(3) Subsection (1) does not extend to a law in force in the Australian Capital Territory, if that law is an Act or a provision of an Act other than:

(a) section 6 of the *Seat of Government Acceptance Act* 1909; and

(b) sections 3, 4 and 12C of the *Seat of Government (Administration) Act* 1910 and the Schedule to that Act.

(4) Subsection (2) does not extend to a criminal law in force in the Jervis Bay Territory if that law is an Act or a provision of an Act.

7 Powers and functions under applied laws

(1) Subject to subsection (2), where a power or function is vested in a person or authority (other than a court) by a law in force in the Territory under section 6, the power or function is, in relation to the Territory, vested in, and may be exercised or performed by, that person or authority.

(2) The Governor-General may direct that a power or function of the kind mentioned in subsection (1) be vested in a different specified person or authority and, where such a direction is in force:

(a) subsection (1) does not apply to the relevant power or function; and

(b) the power or function is vested in, and may be exercised or performed by, the specified person or authority.

8 Application of Commonwealth Acts

(1) An Act or a provision of an Act (whether passed before or after the commencement of this Act) is not, except as otherwise provided by that Act or by another Act, in force as such in the Territory, unless expressed to extend to the Territory.

(2) An Ordinance shall not be made so as to affect the application of its own force in, or in relation to, the Territory of an Act or a provision of an Act.

9 Ordinance may amend or repeal adopted laws

A law in force in the Territory by virtue of section six of this Act may be amended or repealed by an Ordinance or by a law made under an Ordinance.

10 A. C. T. courts to have jurisdiction in the Territory

(1) The courts of the Australian Capital Territory have jurisdiction in and in relation to the Territory.

(2) The *Australian Capital Territory Supreme Court Act* 1933 and the practice and procedure of each court of the Australian Capital Territory in force from time to time apply in the Territory as if:

(a) where the court is exercising its jurisdiction in relation to criminal laws in force in the Territory under section 6—the Territory formed part of the Jervis Bay Territory; and

(b) in any other case—the Territory formed part of the Australian Capital Territory.

(3) For the purposes of subsection (2), a reference in the *Australian Capital Territory Supreme Court Act* 1933 to an Ordinance or enactment is a reference to an Ordinance or enactment, as the case may be, in force under this Act.

11 Ordinances

(1) The Governor-General may make Ordinances for the peace, order and good government of the Territory.

(2) Notice of the making of an Ordinance shall be published in the *Gazette*, and an Ordinance shall, unless the contrary intention appears in the Ordinance, come into operation on the date of publication of the notice.

12 Tabling of Ordinances in Parliament

(1) An Ordinance shall be laid before each House of the Parliament within fifteen sitting days of that House after the making of the Ordinance, and, if it is not so laid before

each House of the Parliament, ceases to have effect.

(2) If either House of the Parliament, in pursuance of a motion of which notice has been given within fifteen sitting days after an Ordinance has been laid before that House, passes a resolution disallowing the Ordinance or a part of the Ordinance, the Ordinance or part so disallowed thereupon ceases to have effect.

(3) If, at the expiration of fifteen sitting days after notice of a motion to disallow an Ordinance or part of an Ordinance has been given in a House of the Parliament, being notice given within fifteen sitting days after the Ordinance has been laid before that House:

(a) the notice has not been withdrawn and the motion has not been called on; or

(b) the motion has been called on, moved and seconded and has not been withdrawn or otherwise disposed of;

the Ordinance or part, as the case may be, specified in the motion shall thereupon be deemed to have been disallowed.

(3A) If, before the expiration of fifteen sitting days after notice of a motion to disallow an Ordinance or part of an Ordinance has been given in a House of the Parliament:

(a) the House of Representatives is dissolved or expires, or the Parliament is prorogued; and

(b) at the time of the dissolution, expiry or prorogation, as the case may be:

(i) the notice has not been withdrawn and the motion has not been called on; or

(ii) the motion has been called on, moved and seconded and has not been withdrawn or otherwise disposed of;

the Ordinance shall, for the purposes of the last two preceding subsections, be deemed to have been laid before that first-mentioned House on the first sitting day of that first-mentioned House after the dissolution, expiry or prorogation, as the case may be.

(4) Where an Ordinance is disallowed, or is deemed to have been disallowed, under this section or ceases to have effect by virtue of the operation of subsection (1), the disallowance of the Ordinance or the operation of subsection (1) in relation to the Ordinance, as the case may be, has the same effect as a repeal of the Ordinance.

(4A) Where:

(a) an Ordinance (in this subsection referred to as the **relevant Ordinance**) is disallowed, or is deemed to have been disallowed, under this section or ceased to have effect by virtue of the operation of subsection (1); and

(b) the relevant Ordinance repealed, in whole or in part, another Ordinance or any other law that was in force immediately before the relevant Ordinance came into operation;

the disallowance of the relevant Ordinance or the operation of subsection (1) in relation to the relevant Ordinance, as the case may be, has the effect of reviving that other Ordinance or law, as the case may be, from and including the date of the disallowance or the date on which the relevant Ordinance ceased to have effect by virtue of that operation of subsection (1), as the case may be, as if the relevant Ordinance had not been made.

(4B) A reference in subsection (4) or (4A) to an Ordinance shall be read as including a reference to a part of an Ordinance, and a reference in subsection (4A) to a law has a corresponding meaning.

12A Ordinance not to be re-made while required to be tabled

(1) Where an Ordinance (in this section called the *original Ordinance*) has been made, no Ordinance containing a provision being the same in substance as a provision of the original Ordinance shall be made during the period defined by subsection (2) unless both Houses of the Parliament by resolution approve the making of an Ordinance containing a provision the same in substance as that provision of the original Ordinance.

(2) The period referred to in subsection (1) is the period starting on the day on which the original Ordinance was made and ending at the end of 7 days after:

(a) if the original Ordinance has been laid, in accordance with subsection 12 (1), before both Houses of the Parliament on the same day—that day;

(b) if the original Ordinance has been so laid before both Houses on different days— the later of those days; or

(c) if the original Ordinance has not been so laid before both Houses— the last day on which subsection 12 (1) could have been complied with.

(3) If a provision of an Ordinance is made in contravention of this section, the provision has no effect.

12B Ordinance not to be re-made while subject to disallowance

(1) Where notice of a motion to disallow an Ordinance has been given in a House of the Parliament within 15 sitting days after the Ordinance has been laid before that House, no Ordinance containing a provision being the same in substance as a provision of the first-mentioned Ordinance shall be made unless:

(a) the notice has been withdrawn;

(b) the Ordinance is deemed to have been disallowed under subsection 12 (3);

(c) the motion has been withdrawn or otherwise disposed of; or

(d) subsection 12 (3A) has applied in relation to the Ordinance.

(2) Where:

(a) because of subsection 12 (3A), an Ordinance is deemed to have been laid before a House of the Parliament on a particular day; and

(b) notice of a motion to disallow the Ordinance has been given in that House within 15 sitting days after that day;

no Ordinance containing a provision being the same in substance as a provision of the first-mentioned Ordinance shall be made unless:

(c) the notice has been withdrawn;

(d) the Ordinance is deemed to have been disallowed under subsection 12 (3);

(e) the motion has been withdrawn or otherwise disposed of; or

(f) subsection 12 (3A) has applied again in relation to the Ordinance.

(3) If a provision of an Ordinance is made in contravention of this section, the provision has no effect.

(4) This section does not limit the operation of section 12A or 12C.

(5) In this section:

Ordinance includes a part of an Ordinance.

12C Disallowed Ordinance not to be re-made unless resolution rescinded or House approves

If an Ordinance or a part of an Ordinance is disallowed, or is deemed to have been disallowed, under section 12, and an Ordinance containing a provision being the same in substance as a provision so disallowed, or deemed to have been disallowed, is made within 6 months after the date of the disallowance, that provision has no effect, unless:

(a) in the case of an Ordinance, or a part of an Ordinance, disallowed by resolution—the resolution has been rescinded by the House of the Parliament by which it was passed; or

(b) in the case of an Ordinance, or a part of an Ordinance, deemed to have been disallowed—the House of the Parliament in which notice of the motion to disallow the Ordinance or part was given has approved, by resolution, the making of a provision the same in substance as the provision deemed to have been disallowed.

12D Regulations, rules and by-laws

(1) All regulations made under an Ordinance shall be laid before each House of the Parliament within 15 sitting days of that House after the day on which the regulations are made and, if they are not so laid before each House of the Parliament, have no effect.

(2) Subsections 12 (2) to (4B), inclusive, and sections 12A, 12B and 12C apply in relation to regulations laid before a House of the Parliament as if, in those provisions, references to an Ordinance were references to regulations and references to a provision of an Ordinance were references to a regulation.

(3) In this section, ***regulations*** includes rules and by-laws.

13 Grant of pardon, remission etc

(1) The Governor-General, acting with the advice of the Minister, by warrant under the Governor-General's hand, may grant to a person convicted by a court exercising criminal

jurisdiction in the Territory a pardon, either free or conditional, or a remission or commutation of sentence, or a respite, for such period as the Governor-General thinks fit, of the execution of sentence, and may remit any fine, penalty or forfeiture imposed or incurred under a law in force in the Territory.

(2) Where an offence has been committed in the Territory, or where an offence has been committed outside the Territory for which the offender may be tried in the Territory, the Governor-General, acting with the advice of the Minister, by warrant under the Governor-General's hand, may grant a pardon to any accomplice who gives evidence that leads to the conviction of the principal offender or any of the principal offenders.

附录8 2018年《澳大利亚与东帝汶民主共和国确立在帝汶海海洋边界的条约》[1]

Treaty Between Australia and the Democratic Republic of
Timor-Leste Establishing Their Maritime Boundaries in the Timor Sea

THE GOVERNMENT OF AUSTRALIA (Australia) and THE GOVERNMENT OF THE DEMOCRATIC REPUBLIC OF TIMOR-LESTE (Timor-Leste) (hereinafter referred to as the Parties);

HAVING REGARD to the United Nations Convention on the Law of the Sea, done at Montego Bay on 10 December 1982 (the Convention);

TAKING INTO PARTICULAR ACCOUNT Articles 74 (1) and 83 (1) of the Convention, regarding the delimitation of the exclusive economic zone and the continental shelf;

WISHING to delimit the maritime areas between Australia and Timor-Leste in the Timor Sea;

WISHING ALSO in this context to establish a special regime for the Greater Sunrise Fields for the benefit of both Parties;

REAFFIRMING the importance of developing and managing the living and non-living resources of the Timor Sea in an economically and environmentally sustainable manner, and the importance of promoting investment and long-term development in Australia and Timor-Leste;

HAVING REACHED, with the assistance of the Conciliation Commission established under Article 298 and Annex V of the Convention, an overall negotiated solution to the dispute between the Parties concerning the delimitation of their permanent maritime boundaries;

RECOGNISING that there exists an inextricable link between the delimitation of the maritime boundaries and the establishment of the special regime for the Greater Sunrise Fields and that both elements are integral to the agreement of the Parties to this Treaty;

CONSCIOUS of the importance of promoting Timor-Leste's economic development;

REAFFIRMING that benefits will flow to both Australia and Timor-Leste from the establishment of a stable long-term basis for Petroleum Activities in the area of seabed between

---

[1] "Treaty between Australia and the Democratic Republic of Timor-Leste Establishing Their Maritime Boundaries in the Timor Sea", The Australian Department of Foreign Affairs and Trade, https://www.dfat.gov.au/sites/default/files/treaty-maritime-arrangements-australia-timor-leste.pdf, December 3, 2024.

Australia and Timor-Leste;

RESOLVING as good neighbours and in a spirit of co-operation and friendship, to settle finally their maritime boundaries in the Timor Sea in order to achieve an equitable solution;

ACKNOWLEDGING that the settlement contained in this Treaty is based on a mutual accommodation between the Parties without prejudice to their respective legal positions;

AFFIRMING the compatibility of this Treaty with the Convention;

AFFIRMING that nothing in this Treaty shall be interpreted as prejudicing the rights of third States with regard to delimitation of the exclusive economic zone and the continental shelf in the Timor Sea;

HAVE AGREED as follows:

Article 1: Definitions

1. For the purposes of this Treaty, including its Annexes:

(a) "1972 Seabed Treaty Boundary" means the boundary established by Articles 1 and 2 of the Agreement between the Government of the Commonwealth of Australia and the Government of the Republic of Indonesia Establishing Certain Seabed Boundaries in the Area of the Timor and Arafura Seas, supplementary to the Agreement of 18 May 1971 (Jakarta, 9 October 1972);

(b) "Bayu-Undan Pipeline" means the export pipeline which transports gas produced from the Bayu-Undan Gas Field to the Darwin liquefied natural gas processing facility at Wickham Point;

(c) "Bayu-Undan Gas Field" means the field which, at the time of signing of this Treaty, is subject to the Production Sharing Contracts JPDA 03-12 and JPDA 03-13;

(d) "Buffalo Oil Field" means the field known as Buffalo which, at the time of the signing of this Treaty, lies in the WA-523-P exploration permit area;

(e) "Commercial Depletion" means the date by which the relevant authority confirms that the contractor or titleholder has fulfilled all of its production and decommissioning obligations under the relevant development or decommissioning plan, contract or licence and that the relevant contract or licence has terminated or otherwise expired;

(f) "Development Concept" means the basic terms on which the Greater Sunrise Fields are to be developed;

(g) "Development Plan" means the development, exploitation and management plan for the Petroleum in the Greater Sunrise Fields consistent with Good Oilfield Practice, including, but not limited to, details of the sub-surface evaluation and facilities, production facilities, the production profile for the expected life of the project, the expected life of the

附录8 2018年《澳大利亚与东帝汶民主共和国确立在帝汶海海洋边界的条约》

fields, the estimated capital and non-capital expenditure covering the feasibility, fabrication, installation and pre-production stages of the project, which is approved and assessed in accordance with the criteria established in Article 9 (3) of Annex B of this Treaty;

(h) "Good Oilfield Practice" means such practices and procedures employed in the petroleum industry worldwide by prudent and diligent operators under conditions and circumstances similar to those experienced in connection with the relevant aspects of Petroleum operations, having regard to relevant factors including:

(i) conservation of Petroleum, which includes the utilisation of methods and processes to maximise the recovery of hydrocarbons in a technically and economically efficient manner, and to minimise losses at the surface;

(ii) operational safety, which entails the use of methods and processes aimed at preventing major accident events and occupational health and safety incidents; and

(iii) environmental protection, which calls for the adoption of methods and processes that minimise the impact of the Petroleum operations on the environment;

(i) "Greater Sunrise Contractor" means all those individuals or bodies corporate holding from time to time a permit, lease, licence or contract in respect of an area within the Special Regime Area under which exploitation, including any appraisal activities related to that exploitation, and production of Petroleum may be carried out;

(j) "Greater Sunrise Fields" means that part of the rock formation known as the Plover Formation (Upper and Lower) that underlies the Special Regime Area and contains the Sunrise and Troubadour deposits of Petroleum, together with any extension of those deposits that is in direct hydrocarbon fluid communication with either deposit;

(k) "Greater Sunrise Production Sharing Contract" means the contract entered into in accordance with Article 4 of Annex B of this Treaty, between the Designated Authority and the Greater Sunrise Contractor for the development of, and production from, the Greater Sunrise Fields and replacing Production Sharing Contracts JPDA 03-19 and JPDA 03-20 and Retention Leases NT/RL2 and NT/RL4;

(l) "International Unitisation Agreement" means the Agreement between the Government of Australia and the Government of the Democratic Republic of Timor-Leste relating to the Unitisation of the Sunrise and Troubadour Fields (Dili, 6 March 2003);

(m) "Kitan Oil Field" means the field which, at the time of signing this Treaty, is subject to the Production Sharing Contract JPDA 06-105;

(n) "Laminaria and Corallina Fields" means the fields known as Laminaria and Corallina which, at the time of the signing of this Treaty, lie partly in the AC/L5 and WA-18-L production licence areas;

(o) "Petroleum" means:

(i) any naturally occurring hydrocarbon, whether in a gaseous, liquid or solid state;

(ii) any naturally occurring mixture of hydrocarbons, whether in a gaseous, liquid or solid state; or

(iii) any naturally occurring mixture of one or more hydrocarbons, whether in a gaseous, liquid or solid state, as well as other gaseous substances produced in association with such hydrocarbons, including, but not limited to, helium, nitrogen, hydrogen sulphide and carbon dioxide; and

includes any Petroleum as defined by sub-paragraph (i), (ii) or (iii) that has been returned to a natural reservoir;

(p) "Petroleum Activities" means all activities undertaken to produce Petroleum, authorised or contemplated under a contract, permit or licence, and includes exploration, development, initial processing, production, transportation and marketing, as well as the planning and preparation for such activities;

(q) "Pipeline" means any pipeline by which Petroleum is discharged from the Special Regime Area;

(r) "Production Sharing Contract" means a contract between the Designated Authority, whether as established under this Treaty or as established under the Timor Sea Treaty, and a limited liability corporation or entity with limited liability under which production from a specified area is shared between the parties to the contract;

(s) "Retention Leases" means the retention leases granted by Australia pursuant to the *Offshore Petroleum and Greenhouse Gas Storage Act* 2006 (Cth) to individuals or bodies corporate, as renewed from time to time, referred to as Retention Lease NT/RL2 and Retention Lease NT/RL4;

(t) "Special Regime Area" means the area of the continental shelf described in Annex C of this Treaty;

(u) "Special Regime Installation" means any installation, structure or facility located within the Special Regime Area for the purposes of engaging in or conducting Petroleum Activities;

(v) "Timor Sea Treaty" means the Timor Sea Treaty between the Government of East Timor and the Government of Australia (Dili, 20 May 2002); and

(w) "Valuation Point" means the point of the first commercial sale of Petroleum produced from the Special Regime Area which shall occur no later than the earlier of:

(i) the point where the Petroleum enters a pipeline; and

(ii) the marketable petroleum commodity point for the Petroleum.

2. Unless otherwise expressly provided, terms in this Treaty are to be given the same meaning as in the Convention.

附录8 2018年《澳大利亚与东帝汶民主共和国确立在帝汶海海洋边界的条约》

Article 2: Continental Shelf Boundary

1. Subject to Article 3 of this Treaty, the continental shelf boundary between the Parties in the Timor Sea comprises the geodesic lines connecting the following points:

Point	Latitude	Longitude
TA-1	10° 27′ 54.91″S	126° 00′ 04.40″E
TA-2	11° 24′ 00.61″S	126° 18′ 22.48″E
TA-3	11° 21′ 00.00″S	126° 28′ 00.00″E
TA-4	11° 20′ 00.00″S	126° 31′ 00.00″E
TA-5	11° 20′ 02.90″S	126° 31′ 58.40″E
TA-6	11° 04′ 37.65″S	127° 39′ 32.81″E
TA-7	10° 55′ 20.88″S	127° 47′ 08.37″E
TA-8	10° 53′ 36.88″S	127° 48′ 49.37″E
TA-9	10° 43′ 37.88″S	127° 59′ 20.36″E
TA-10	10° 29′ 11.87″S	128° 12′ 28.36″E
TA-11	09° 42′ 21.49″S	128° 28′ 35.97″E
TA-12	09° 37′ 57.54″S	128° 30′ 07.24″E
TA-13	09° 27′ 54.88″S	127° 56′ 04.35″E

2. The line connecting points TA-1 and TA-2, and the lines connecting points TA-11, TA-12, and TA-13 are "Provisional", which for the purposes of this Treaty means that they are subject to adjustment in accordance with Article 3 of this Treaty.

3. For the purposes of this Treaty, all coordinates are determined by reference to the World Geodetic System 1984. For the purposes of this Treaty, the World Geodetic System 1984 shall be deemed equivalent to the Geodetic Datum of Australia 1994.

Article 3: Adjustment of the Continental Shelf Boundary

1. Should Timor-Leste and Indonesia agree an endpoint to their continental shelf boundary west of point A17 or east of point A16 on the 1972 Seabed Treaty Boundary, the continental shelf boundary between Australia and Timor-Leste shall be adjusted in accordance with paragraphs 2, 3 and 4 of this Article.

2. On the later of:

(a) the Commercial Depletion of the Laminaria and Corallina Fields; and

(b) the entry into force of an agreement between Timor-Leste and Indonesia delimiting the continental shelf boundary between those two States, the continental shelf boundary between Australia and Timor-Leste shall, unless paragraph 3 of this Article applies, be adjusted so that it proceeds in a geodesic line from point TA-2, as defined in Article 2 (1) of this Treaty, to a point between points A17 and A18 on the 1972 Seabed Treaty Boundary at which the continental shelf boundary agreed between Timor-Leste and Indonesia meets the 1972 Seabed Treaty Boundary.

3. In the event that the continental shelf boundary agreed between Timor-Leste and Indonesia meets the 1972 Seabed Treaty Boundary at a point to the west of point A18 on the 1972 Seabed Treaty Boundary, the continental shelf boundary shall be adjusted so that it proceeds in a geodesic line from point TA-2, as defined in Article 2 (1) of this Treaty, to point A18.

4. On the later of:

(a) the Commercial Depletion of the Greater Sunrise Fields; and

(b) the entry into force of an agreement between Timor-Leste and Indonesia delimiting the continental shelf boundary between those two States, the continental shelf boundary between Australia and Timor-Leste shall be adjusted so that it proceeds in a geodesic line from point TA-11, as defined in Article 2 (1) of this Treaty, to the point at which the continental shelf boundary agreed between Timor-Leste and Indonesia meets the 1972 Seabed Treaty Boundary.

Article 4: Exclusive Economic Zone Boundary

1. The exclusive economic zone boundary between the Parties in the Timor Sea comprises the geodesic lines connecting the following points:

Point	Latitude	Longitude
TA-5	11° 20′ 02.90″S	126° 31′ 58.40″E
TA-6	11° 04′ 37.65″S	127° 39′ 32.81″E
TA-7	10° 55′ 20.88″S	127° 47′ 08.37″E
TA-8	10° 53′ 36.88″S	127° 48′ 49.37″E
TA-9	10° 43′ 37.88″S	127° 59′ 20.36″E
TA-10	10° 29′ 11.87″S	128° 12′ 28.36″E

2. The Parties may agree to extend the exclusive economic zone boundary established by paragraph 1 of this Article, as necessary.

Article 5: Depiction of Maritime Boundaries

The maritime boundaries described in Articles 2 and 4 of this Treaty are depicted for illustrative purposes at Annex A of this Treaty.

Article 6: Without Prejudice

1. Nothing in this Treaty shall be interpreted as prejudicing negotiations with third States with regard to delimitation of the exclusive economic zone and the continental shelf in the Timor Sea.

2. In exercising their rights as coastal States, the Parties shall:

(a) provide due notice of activities conducted on the continental shelf and in the exclusive economic zone consistent with the terms of the Convention; and

(b) not infringe upon or unjustifiably interfere with the exercise of rights and freedoms of other States as provided for in the Convention.

Article 7: Greater Sunrise Special Regime

1. The Parties hereby establish the Greater Sunrise Special Regime as set out in Annex B of this Treaty for the Special Regime Area.

2. Within the Special Regime Area, the Parties shall jointly exercise their rights as coastal States pursuant to Article 77 of the Convention.

3. The governance and exercise of jurisdiction within the Special Regime Area is as set out in the Greater Sunrise Special Regime.

4. Except as provided in this Treaty, the rights and obligations of the Parties in the Special Regime Area are governed by the Convention.

5. When the Greater Sunrise Special Regime ceases to be in force, the Parties shall individually exercise their rights as coastal States pursuant to Article 77 of the Convention on the basis of the continental shelf boundary as delimited by this Treaty.

6. Except as provided in Article 3 of this Treaty, the entry into force of an agreement between Timor-Leste and Indonesia delimiting the continental shelf boundary between those two States shall have no effect on the Greater Sunrise Special Regime.

Article 8: Straddling Deposits

If any Petroleum deposit extends across the continental shelf boundary as defined in Articles 2 and 3 of this Treaty, the Parties shall work expeditiously and in good faith to reach agreement as to the manner in which that deposit is to be most effectively exploited and equitably shared.

Article 9: Previous Agreements

1. Upon the entry into force of this Treaty, the following agreements shall cease to be in force:

(a) the Timor Sea Treaty; and

(b) the International Unitisation Agreement.

2. This Treaty shall have no effect on rights or obligations arising under the agreements set out in paragraph 1 of this Article while they were in force.

Article 10: Compensation

The Parties agree that neither Party shall have a claim for compensation with respect to Petroleum Activities conducted in the Timor Sea as a result of:

(a) the cessation of the Joint Petroleum Development Area as established by Article 3 of the Timor Sea Treaty upon termination of that treaty;

(b) the establishment of the continental shelf boundary under this Treaty;

(c) an adjustment to the continental shelf boundary as a result of the application of Article 3 of this Treaty; or

(d) the cessation of the Greater Sunrise Special Regime.

Article 11: Permanence of the Treaty

1. The Parties agree that this Treaty shall not be subject to a unilateral right of denunciation, withdrawal or suspension.

2. This Treaty may be amended only by agreement between the Parties, and by express provision to that effect.

3. The Annexes to this Treaty form an integral part thereof.

4. All of the provisions of this Treaty are inextricably linked and form a single whole. The provisions of this Treaty are not separable in any circumstances, and each provision of this Treaty constitutes an essential basis of the Parties' agreement to be bound by this Treaty as a whole.

Article 12: Settlement of Disputes

1. Without prejudice to paragraph 3 of this Article, for a period of five years following the entry into force of this Treaty, any dispute regarding the interpretation or application of this Treaty which is not settled by negotiation within six months of either Party notifying the other Party of the existence of the dispute, may be submitted by the Parties jointly to one or more members of the Conciliation Commission.

2. Once the dispute has been submitted in accordance with paragraph 1 of this Article, the member or members of the Conciliation Commission shall hear the Parties, examine their claims and objections, and make proposals to the Parties with a view to reaching an amicable settlement.

3. Subject to paragraph 4 of this Article, any dispute concerning the interpretation or application of this Treaty, which cannot be settled by negotiation within six months of either Party notifying the other Party of the existence of the dispute, may be submitted by either Party to an arbitral tribunal in accordance with Annex E of this Treaty.

4. The Parties shall not submit to an arbitral tribunal under this Article any dispute concerning the interpretation or application of Article 2, 3, 4, 5, 7 or 11, Annex A or Annex D of this Treaty, or any dispute falling within the scope of Article 8 of Annex B, which shall be settled in accordance with the provisions of that Article.

Article 13: Entry into Force

This Treaty shall enter into force on the day on which Australia and Timor-Leste have notified each other in writing through diplomatic channels that their respective requirements for entry into force of this Treaty have been fulfilled.

Article 14: Registration

The Parties shall transmit this Treaty by joint letter to the Secretary-General of the United

附录8　2018年《澳大利亚与东帝汶民主共和国确立在帝汶海海洋边界的条约》

Nations for registration in accordance with the provisions of Article 102 of the Charter of the United Nations.

IN WITNESS WHEREOF, the undersigned, being duly authorised thereto by their respective Governments, have signed this Treaty.

DONE at New York, on this sixth day of March, two thousand and eighteen, in two counterparts in English and Portuguese. In the event of a discrepancy, the English language version shall prevail.

For the Government of Australia	For the Government of the Democratic Republic of Timor-Leste
The Hon Julie Bishop MP Minister for Foreign Affairs	His Excellency Hermenegildo Augusto Cabral Pereira Minister in the Office of the Prime Minister for the Delimitation of Borders and the Agent in the Conciliation
IN THE PRESENCE OF the Chair of the Conciliation Commission	
His Excellency Ambassador Peter Taksøe-Jensen	

Signed in the presence of the Secretary-General of the United Nations, His Excellency António Manuel de Oliveira Guterres.

ANNEX A: Depiction of Maritime Boundaries as Described in Articles 2 and 4 of the Treaty (Article 5) (omitted)

ANNEX B: Greater Sunrise Special Regime

Article 1: Objective of the Greater Sunrise Special Regime

The objective of the Greater Sunrise Special Regime is the joint development, exploitation and management of Petroleum in the Greater Sunrise Fields for the benefit of both Parties.

Article 2: Title to Petroleum and Revenue Sharing

1. Australia and Timor-Leste shall have title to all Petroleum produced in the Greater Sunrise Fields.

2. The Parties shall share upstream revenue, meaning revenue derived directly from the upstream exploitation of Petroleum produced in the Greater Sunrise Fields:

(a) in the ratio of 30 per cent to Australia and 70 per cent to Timor-Leste in the event that the Greater Sunrise Fields are developed by means of a Pipeline to Timor-Leste; or

(b) in the ratio of 20 per cent to Australia and 80 per cent to Timor-Leste in the event that the Greater Sunrise Fields are developed by means of a Pipeline to Australia.

3. For the purposes of this Annex, upstream revenue is limited to first tranche petroleum, profit petroleum and taxation in accordance with Article 3 of this Annex.

Article 3: Taxation

1. Subject to paragraph 3 of this Article, upstream revenue includes taxation by the Parties

as applicable in accordance with their respective laws. The Parties shall provide each other with a list of the applicable taxes.

2. The application of the Parties' taxation law shall be specified in the fiscal regime as agreed between the Parties and the Greater Sunrise Contractor, in accordance with obligations under Article 22 of the Timor Sea Treaty and Article 27 of the International Unitisation Agreement.

3. Taxation under paragraph 1 of this Article shall only apply in respect of Petroleum Activities and Special Regime Installations prior to the Valuation Point.

4. Timor-Leste taxation law shall apply to all other activities related to the development and exploitation of Petroleum in the Special Regime Area, unless otherwise provided for by the terms of this Treaty.

Article 4: Greater Sunrise Production Sharing Contract

As soon as practicable, the Designated Authority shall enter into the Greater Sunrise Production Sharing Contract under conditions equivalent to those in Production Sharing Contracts JPDA 03-19 and JPDA 03-20, and to the legal rights held under Retention Leases NT/RL2 and NT/RL4 in accordance with Article 22 of the Timor Sea Treaty and Article 27 of the International Unitisation Agreement.

Article 5: Regulatory Bodies

The Parties hereby establish a two-tiered regulatory structure for the regulation and administration of the Greater Sunrise Special Regime, consisting of a Designated Authority and a Governance Board.

Article 6: Designated Authority

1. The Designated Authority shall be responsible for carrying out the day-to-day regulation and management of Petroleum Activities in the Special Regime Area. In doing so, the Designated Authority acts on behalf of Australia and Timor-Leste and reports to the Governance Board.

2. The Designated Authority shall:

(a) be the Timor-Leste statutory authority as determined by the member of the Government of Timor-Leste responsible for the petroleum sector to act as the Designated Authority;

(b) regulate the Special Regime Area according to Good Oilfield Practice;

(c) be financed from fees collected under the applicable Petroleum Mining Code and the Greater Sunrise Production Sharing Contract; and

(d) subject to Articles 7 and 8 of this Annex, exercise its powers and functions, as set out in this Article, without interference by any other entity and in accordance with this Treaty.

3. The Designated Authority shall have the following powers and functions:

(a) day-to-day regulation and management of Petroleum Activities in the Special Regime Area in accordance with this Treaty and its functions as outlined in the applicable Petroleum Mining Code and any regulations thereunder, except with respect to Strategic Issues;

附录8 2018年《澳大利亚与东帝汶民主共和国确立在帝汶海海洋边界的条约》

(b) three times a year, meeting with and reporting to the Governance Board on:

(i) the exercise of its powers and functions, in accordance with the applicable regulatory framework;

(ii) progress on the preparation of the Development Plan and, once approved, progress against the Development Plan and schedule;

(iii) production and revenue data from the Greater Sunrise Fields;

(iv) updates on issues referred to the Dispute Resolution Committee, if any;

(v) the Greater Sunrise Contractor's compliance with regulatory standards, including its local content obligations as set out in this Treaty, the Development Plan and the Greater Sunrise Production Sharing Contract; and

(vi) safety, environmental and well-integrity management;

(c) pursuant to Article 9 of this Annex, powers and functions with respect to the Development Plan;

(d) entering into the Greater Sunrise Production Sharing Contract, subject to the approval of the Governance Board, in accordance with Articles 4 and 7 (3) (b) of this Annex;

(e) supervising, managing and agreeing on non-material amendments to the Greater Sunrise Production Sharing Contract;

(f) agreeing material amendments to the Greater Sunrise Production Sharing Contract as defined in that Contract or terminating the Greater Sunrise Production Sharing Contract, subject to approval of the Governance Board in accordance with Article 7 (3) (b) of this Annex;

(g) approving assignments, production plans, lifting agreements and other technical documents and agreements relating to the Greater Sunrise Production Sharing Contract;

(h) reporting annual income and expenditure, as these relate to the Special Regime Area, to the Governance Board;

(i) accessing, consolidating and disseminating, on an annual basis, all information pertaining to the Greater Sunrise Fields' reserves based on information provided by the Greater Sunrise Contractor or as otherwise audited by the Designated Authority;

(j) collecting revenues received from Petroleum Activities and Special Regime Installations prior to the Valuation Point on behalf of both Parties and distribution thereof;

(k) auditing and inspecting the Greater Sunrise Contractor's books and accounts;

(l) inspecting Special Regime Installations in the Special Regime Area;

(m) ensuring compliance by the Greater Sunrise Contractor with its local content obligations in accordance with this Treaty, the Development Plan and the Greater Sunrise Production Sharing Contract, including by giving directions and instructions as necessary;

(n) issuing regulations to protect the marine environment in the Special Regime Area and monitoring compliance with them, ensuring there is a contingency plan for combatting pollution from Petroleum Activities in the Special Regime Area, and investigating safety and environmental incidents in the Special Regime Area;

(o) issuing regulations and developing and adopting standards and procedures on occupational health and safety for persons employed on Special Regime Installations that are no less effective than those standards and procedures that would apply to persons employed on similar structures in Australia and Timor-Leste;

(p) requesting assistance from the appropriate authorities for search and rescue operations, security threats, air traffic services, anti-pollution prevention measures, and safety and environmental incidents, or the activation of emergency procedures, in accordance with international law;

(q) establishing safety zones to ensure the safety of navigation and Special Regime Installations, in accordance with the Convention;

(r) controlling movements into, within and out of the Special Regime Area of vessels, aircraft, structures, and other equipment employed in exploration for and exploitation of the Greater Sunrise Fields, consistent with Articles 17, 18 and 19 of this Annex;

(s) pursuant to Article 21 of this Annex, powers and functions with respect to the decommissioning plan, including entry into and oversight of financial arrangements for the decommissioning plan;

(t) oversight of the abandonment and decommissioning phase of the Greater Sunrise Fields;

(u) authorising the construction, operation and use of Special Regime Installations, subject to the provisions in this Annex; and

(v) any other powers or functions in respect of the Special Regime Area, including regulatory powers, conferred upon it by the Governance Board.

4. The Designated Authority shall refer all Strategic Issues as defined in Article 7 (3) of this Annex to the Governance Board and, in the event of a dispute between the Designated Authority and the Greater Sunrise Contractor as to whether an issue is a Strategic Issue, either the Designated Authority or the Greater Sunrise Contractor may refer that issue to the Governance Board.

5. Within 14 days of a Strategic Issue being referred to the Governance Board, the Designated Authority and the Greater Sunrise Contractor may provide any relevant information concerning the issue and the Designated Authority may provide any recommendations on the issue.

Article 7: Governance Board

1. The Governance Board shall be comprised of one representative appointed by Australia and two representatives appointed by Timor-Leste. The representatives on the Governance Board shall not have any direct financial or other commercial interest in the operation of the Greater Sunrise Special Regime that would create any reasonable perception of, or actual, conflict of in-

terest, and they shall disclose details of any material personal interest in connection with their position on the Governance Board.

2. The Governance Board shall have the following powers and functions:

(a) providing strategic oversight over the Greater Sunrise Special Regime;

(b) establishing and overseeing an assurance and audit framework for revenue verification and offshore petroleum regulation and administration. This shall include:

(i) issuing an annual 'Statement of Expectation' to frame the operation and management of the Greater Sunrise Special Regime to guide the work of the Designated Authority;

(ii) reporting requirements of the Designated Authority in accordance with Article 6 (3) (b) of this Annex; and

(iii) engaging an independent qualified firm to conduct an annual audit in accordance with international auditing standards so as to provide a high level of assurance over the completeness and accuracy of revenues payable from Petroleum Activities in the Special Regime Area including monthly reporting, incorporating an explanation for variances between forecast and actual revenue;

(c) making decisions on Strategic Issues referred to it under Article 6 (4) of this Annex, in accordance with paragraphs 5 and 6 of this Article;

(d) approving amendments to the Interim Petroleum Mining Code and any regulations thereunder;

(e) approving the final Petroleum Mining Code and any regulations thereunder, and any amendments thereto;

(f) other than as necessary for Strategic Issues, meet three times a year with the Designated Authority and receive reports under Article 6 (3) (b) of this Annex; and

(g) conferring any additional powers and functions on the Designated Authority.

3. Subject to paragraph 4 of this Article, the following is an exhaustive list of Strategic Issues:

(a) assessment and approval of a Development Plan pursuant to Article 9 (2) of this Annex and any material change to a Development Plan as defined in that Development Plan, pursuant to Article 9 (4) of this Annex;

(b) approval of the decision by the Designated Authority to enter into or terminate the Greater Sunrise Production Sharing Contract, or propose any material changes to that Contract as defined in that Contract;

(c) approval of, and any material change to, a decommissioning plan, in accordance with Article 21 of this Annex; and

(d) approval of the construction and operation of a Pipeline.

4. The Governance Board may add additional Strategic Issues to those listed in paragraph 3 of this Article.

5. In making a decision on a Strategic Issue, the Governance Board shall give due consideration to all recommendations and relevant information provided by the Designated Authority and relevant information provided by the Greater Sunrise Contractor.

6. All decisions of the Governance Board shall be made by Consensus, within 30 days or such other period as may be agreed with both the Designated Authority and the Greater Sunrise Contractor, and be final and binding on the Designated Authority and the Greater Sunrise Contractor. For the purposes of this Treaty "Consensus" means the absence of formal objection to a proposed decision.

7. If the Governance Board has exhausted every effort to reach Consensus on a Strategic Issue, either the Designated Authority or the Greater Sunrise Contractor may refer that issue to the Dispute Resolution Committee for resolution. Nothing in this paragraph limits the Governance Board's own right to refer any Strategic Issue to the Dispute Resolution Committee.

Article 8: Dispute Resolution Committee

1. The Dispute Resolution Committee shall:

(a) be an independent body with a mandate to hear any matters referred to it under Article 7 (7) or Article 9 (2) of this Annex or any matters as otherwise agreed by the Designated Authority and the Greater Sunrise Contractor;

(b) be comprised of:

(i) one member appointed from each of the Parties (Party Appointees); and

(ii) a third independent member, who will act as Chair, to be selected by the Party Appointees when a matter is referred to the Dispute Resolution Committee from a list of approved experts selected and maintained by Australia and Timor-Leste and refreshed every three years, and in case of disagreement, by the Secretary-General of the Permanent Court of Arbitration;

(c) establish its own procedures;

(d) make all decisions in writing and by Consensus, or where Consensus cannot be reached, by simple majority, within 60 days or as otherwise agreed with the referring party or parties;

(e) in making any decision, provide a reasonable opportunity for the Designated Authority and the Greater Sunrise Contractor to submit any relevant information and give due consideration to any information so provided; and

(f) have the power to request any information from the Designated Authority and/or the Greater Sunrise Contractor which it considers reasonably necessary to make its decision.

2. Members of the Dispute Resolution Committee shall not have any direct financial or other commercial interest in the operation of the Greater Sunrise Special Regime that would create any reasonable perception of, or actual, conflict of interest, and they shall disclose details of any material personal interest in connection with their position on the Dispute Resolution Committee. Serving

members of the Governance Board shall not be members of the Dispute Resolution Committee.

3. All decisions of the Dispute Resolution Committee shall be final and binding on the Designated Authority and the Greater Sunrise Contractor.

Article 9: Development Plan for the Greater Sunrise Fields

1. Production of Petroleum from the Greater Sunrise Fields shall not commence until a Development Plan, which has been submitted by the Greater Sunrise Contractor in accordance with the Greater Sunrise Production Sharing Contract and the process provided for in this Article, has been approved in accordance with this Article.

2. The process of assessing and approving a Development Plan for the Greater Sunrise Fields is as follows:

(a) the Development Plan shall be assessed against the criteria listed at paragraph 3 of this Article (Development Plan Criteria);

(b) the Greater Sunrise Contractor shall submit the Development Plan to both the Governance Board and the Designated Authority;

(c) the Designated Authority shall consider the Development Plan and shall provide its recommendations to the Governance Board as to whether it should be approved or rejected within 180 days of receipt, if practicable. During this period, the Designated Authority may exchange views and information with the Greater Sunrise Contractor regarding the Development Plan. Any amendments agreed between the Designated Authority and the Greater Sunrise Contractor may be included in the Development Plan prior to the Designated Authority's recommendation to the Governance Board;

(d) the Governance Board shall consider the Development Plan, the Designated Authority's recommendation and any other information submitted by the Designated Authority;

(e) if the Governance Board considers that the Development Plan is both in accordance with the approved Development Concept and meets the Development Plan Criteria, the Governance Board shall approve the Development Plan within 180 days of receipt, if practicable;

(f) if the Governance Board does not approve the Development Plan under paragraph 2 (e) of this Article, the Development Plan is rejected and the Governance Board shall specify its reasons for not approving it to the Greater Sunrise Contractor and Designated Authority. Any of these parties may, at their discretion, refer the matter to the Dispute Resolution Committee within 15 days of the Governance Board's decision;

(g) the Dispute Resolution Committee shall review the Development Plan, the Designated Authority's recommendation and any other information submitted pursuant to this Article. The Dispute Resolution Committee shall determine whether the Development Plan meets the Development Plan Criteria within 90 days of referral of the matter, or such other period as may be agreed with the Greater Sunrise Contractor;

(h) if the Dispute Resolution Committee determines that the Development Plan is in accordance with the approved Development Concept and meets the Development Plan Criteria, the Dispute Resolution Committee shall approve the Development Plan;

(i) if the Dispute Resolution Committee determines that the Development Plan either is not in accordance with the approved Development Concept, or does not meet the Development Plan Criteria, the Dispute Resolution Committee shall reject the Development Plan, specifying its reasons for doing so; and

(j) the Parties shall be bound by, and give effect to, the decision of the Governance Board or, if applicable, the Dispute Resolution Committee pursuant to this Article.

3. The criteria that shall apply to the assessment of any Development Plan under paragraph 2 of this Article are as follows:

(a) the Development Plan supports the development policy, objectives and needs of each of the Parties, while at the same time providing a fair return to the Greater Sunrise Contractor;

(b) the project is commercially viable;

(c) the Greater Sunrise Contractor is seeking to exploit the Greater Sunrise Fields to the best commercial advantage;

(d) the project is technically feasible;

(e) the Greater Sunrise Contractor has, or has access to, the financial and technical competence to carry out the development of the Greater Sunrise Fields;

(f) the Development Plan is consistent with Good Oilfield Practice and, in particular, documents the Greater Sunrise Contractor's quality, health, safety and environmental strategies;

(g) the Development Plan demonstrates clear, measurable and enforceable commitments to local content through a local content plan, in accordance with Article 14 of this Annex;

(h) the Greater Sunrise Contractor could reasonably be expected to carry out the Development Plan during the specified period;

(i) the Greater Sunrise Contractor has, as applicable, entered into binding, arms-length arrangements for the sale and/or processing of gas, including liquefied natural gas, from the Greater Sunrise Fields or has provided sufficient details of any such processing and/or sale agreements to be entered into by affiliates of the Greater Sunrise Contractor or other companies; and

(j) the Greater Sunrise Contractor has provided summaries of, or where applicable, the project execution plan and the petroleum production plan, including relevant engineering and cost specifications, in accordance with the applicable regulatory framework and Good Oilfield Practice.

4. The Greater Sunrise Contractor may at any time submit, and if at any time the Designated Authority so decides may be required to submit, proposals to bring up to date or otherwise amend a Development Plan. All amendments of, or additions to, any Development Plan require

prior approval of the Designated Authority, which in turn requires the approval of the Governance Board.

5. The Designated Authority shall require the Greater Sunrise Contractor not to change the status or function of any Special Regime Installation in any way except in accordance with an amendment to a Development Plan in accordance with paragraph 4 of this Article.

Article 10: Pipeline

1. A Pipeline which commences within the Special Regime Area and lands in the territory of Australia shall be under the exclusive jurisdiction of Australia. A Pipeline which commences within the Special Regime Area and lands in the territory of Timor-Leste shall be under the exclusive jurisdiction of Timor-Leste. The Party exercising exclusive jurisdiction has both rights and responsibilities in relation to the Pipeline.

2. The Party exercising exclusive jurisdiction under paragraph 1 of this Article shall cooperate with the Designated Authority in relation to the Pipeline to ensure the effective management and regulation of the Special Regime Area.

3. There shall be open access to the Pipeline. The open access arrangements shall be in accordance with good international regulatory practice. If Australia has exclusive jurisdiction over the pipeline, it shall consult with Timor-Leste over access to the Pipeline. If Timor-Leste has exclusive jurisdiction over the Pipeline, it shall consult with Australia over access to the Pipeline.

Article 11: Petroleum Mining Code

1. The Interim Petroleum Mining Code, including the interim regulations, as in force at the date of entry into force of this Treaty shall govern the development and exploitation of Petroleum from within the Greater Sunrise Fields, as well as the export of such Petroleum until such a time as a final Petroleum Mining Code is approved by the Governance Board.

2. The Governance Board shall coordinate with the Designated Authority, and shall endeavour to approve and issue a final Petroleum Mining Code within six months of the entry into force of this Treaty or, if such a date is not achieved, as soon as possible thereafter.

Article 12: Audit and Information Rights

1. For the purposes of transparency, the Greater Sunrise Contractor shall include in its agreements with the operators of the downstream facilities the necessary provisions to ensure that the Designated Authority has audit and information rights from the operators of downstream facilities, and from their respective affiliates, equivalent to those audit and information rights the Designated Authority has in respect to the Greater Sunrise Production Sharing Contract. In the event of a request by the Designated Authority, the Greater Sunrise Contractor shall consult with the operators of the downstream facilities with a view to providing access to metering facilities.

2. The rights mentioned in paragraph 1 of this Article are granted to ensure that the Desig-

nated Authority is able to verify the volume and value of natural gas.

Article 13: Applicable Law

Petroleum Activities in the Special Regime Area shall be governed by this Annex, the applicable Petroleum Mining Code and any regulations issued thereunder.

Article 14: Local Content

1. The Greater Sunrise Contractor shall set out its local content commitments during the development, operation and decommissioning of the Greater Sunrise Fields through a local content plan to be included as part of the Development Plan and the decommissioning plan.

2. The local content plan shall contain clear, measurable, binding and enforceable local content commitments, including to:

(a) improve Timor-Leste's workforce and skills development and promote employment opportunities and career progression for Timor-Leste nationals through capacity-building initiatives, training of Timor-Leste nationals and a preference for the employment of Timor-Leste nationals;

(b) improve Timor-Leste's supplier and capability development by seeking the procurement of goods and services (including engineering, fabrication and maintenance services) from Timor-Leste in the first instance; and

(c) improve and promote Timor-Leste's commercial and industrial capacity through the transfer of knowledge, technology and research capability.

3. The Greater Sunrise Contractor shall ensure that any subcontracts entered into for the supply of goods and services for the Special Regime Area give effect to its local content commitments.

4. Failure by the Greater Sunrise Contractor to meet its local content commitments shall be deemed as non-compliance and subject to the mechanisms and penalties referred to in the local content plan as agreed between the Designated Authority and the Greater Sunrise Contractor.

5. The Parties shall consult with a view to ensuring that the exercise of jurisdiction by either Party under Articles 17, 18 and 19 does not hinder the implementation of local content commitments referred to in this Article.

Article 15: Cooperation and Coordination

In the Special Regime Area, each Party shall, as appropriate, cooperate and coordinate with, and assist, the other Party, including in relation to:

(a) search and rescue operations with respect to Special Regime Installations; and

(b) surveillance activities with respect to Special Regime Installations.

Article 16: Exercise of Jurisdiction

1. In exercising jointly their rights as coastal States pursuant to Article 77 of the Convention, Australia and Timor-Leste exercise jurisdiction in accordance with the Convention with re-

spect to:

(a) customs and migration pursuant to Article 17 of this Annex;

(b) quarantine pursuant to Article 18 of this Annex;

(c) environmental protection, management and regulation;

(d) marine scientific research;

(e) air traffic services related to Special Regime Installations;

(f) security and establishment of safety zones around Special Regime Installations;

(g) health and safety;

(h) management of living resources; and

(i) criminal jurisdiction pursuant to Article 20 of this Annex.

2. The Parties agree to consult as necessary on the cooperative exercise of the jurisdictional competencies set out in paragraph 1 of this Article.

3. The Parties have agreed to delegate the exercise of certain jurisdictional and regulatory competencies to the Designated Authority, as specified in this Treaty.

Article 17: Customs and Migration

1. The Parties may apply their customs and migration laws to persons, equipment and goods entering their territory from, or leaving their territory for, the Special Regime Area and adopt arrangements to facilitate entry and departure.

2. Limited liability corporations or other limited liability entities shall ensure, unless otherwise authorised by Australia or Timor-Leste, that persons, equipment and goods do not enter Special Regime Installations without first entering Australia or Timor-Leste, and that their employees and the employees of their subcontractors are authorised by the Designated Authority to enter the Special Regime Area.

3. Australia and Timor-Leste may apply customs and migration controls to persons, equipment and goods entering the Special Regime Area without the authority of either country and may adopt arrangements to co-ordinate the exercise of such rights.

4. Goods and equipment shall not be subject to customs duties where they are:

(a) entering the Special Regime Area for purposes related to Petroleum Activities; or

(b) leaving or in transit through either Australia or Timor-Leste for the purpose of entering the Special Regime Area for purposes related to Petroleum Activities.

5. Goods and equipment leaving the Special Regime Area for the purpose of being permanently transferred to either Australia or Timor-Leste may be subject to customs duties of that country.

Article 18: Quarantine

1. The Parties may apply their quarantine laws to persons, equipment and goods entering their territory from, or leaving their territory for, the Special Regime Area and adopt arrange-

ments to facilitate entry and departure.

2. The Parties shall consult with a view to reaching agreement with each other before entering into a commercial arrangement with the Greater Sunrise Contractor with respect to quarantine.

Article 19: Vessels

1. Vessels of the nationality of Australia or Timor-Leste engaged in Petroleum Activities in the Special Regime Area shall be subject to the law of their nationality in relation to safety and operating standards and crewing regulations.

2. Vessels with the nationality of other countries engaged in Petroleum Activities in the Special Regime Area shall, in relation to safety and operating standards and crewing regulations, apply:

(a) the laws of Australia, if the vessels are operating from an Australian port; or

(b) the laws of Timor-Leste, if the vessels are operating from a Timor-Leste port.

3. Such vessels engaged in Petroleum Activities in the Special Regime Area that do not operate out of either Australia or Timor-Leste shall under the law of both Australia and Timor-Leste be subject to the relevant international safety and operating standards.

4. The Parties shall, promptly upon the entry into force of this Treaty and consistent with their laws, consult with a view to reaching the agreement required for swift recognition of any international seafarer certifications issued by the other Party, so as to allow their national seafarers to have access to employment opportunities aboard vessels operating in the Special Regime Area.

Article 20: Criminal Jurisdiction

1. A national or permanent resident of Australia or Timor-Leste shall be subject to the criminal law of that country in respect of acts or omissions occurring in the Special Regime Area connected with or arising out of Petroleum Activities, provided that a permanent resident of Australia or Timor-Leste who is a national of the other country shall be subject to the criminal law of that country.

2. Subject to paragraph 4 of this Article, a national of a third State, not being a national or permanent resident of either Australia or Timor-Leste, shall be subject to the criminal law of both Australia and Timor-Leste in respect of acts or omissions occurring in the Special Regime Area connected with or arising out of Petroleum Activities. Such a person shall not be subject to criminal proceedings under the law of either Australia or Timor-Leste if he or she has already been tried and discharged or acquitted by a competent tribunal or already undergone punishment for the same act or omission under the law of the other country or where the competent authorities of one country, in accordance with its law, have decided in the public interest to refrain from prosecuting the person for that act or omission.

3. In cases referred to in paragraph 2 of this Article, Australia and Timor-Leste shall, as and when necessary, consult each other to determine which criminal law is to be applied, taking into account the nationality of the victim and the interests of the country most affected by the al-

附录 8　2018 年《澳大利亚与东帝汶民主共和国确立在帝汶海海洋边界的条约》

leged offence.

4. The criminal law of the flag State shall apply in relation to acts or omissions on board vessels, including seismic or drill vessels in, or aircraft in flight over, the Special Regime Area.

5. Australia and Timor-Leste shall provide assistance to and co-operate with each other, including through agreements or arrangements as appropriate, for the purposes of enforcement of criminal law under this Article, including the obtaining of evidence and information.

6. Both Australia and Timor-Leste recognise the interest of the other country where a victim of an alleged offence is a national of that other country and shall keep that other country informed to the extent permitted by its law, of action being taken with regard to the alleged offence.

7. Australia and Timor-Leste may make arrangements permitting officials of one country to assist in the enforcement of the criminal law of the other country. Where such assistance involves the detention of a person who under paragraph 1 of this Article is subject to the jurisdiction of the other country that detention may only continue until it is practicable to hand the person over to the relevant officials of that other country.

Article 21: Decommissioning

1. The Greater Sunrise Contractor shall submit to the Designated Authority a preliminary decommissioning plan and, in so far as possible, preliminary decommissioning cost estimate as part of the Development Plan.

2. As soon as practicable, but in any case no later than seven years after commencement of production of Petroleum in the Special Regime Area, the Greater Sunrise Contractor shall be required to submit to the Designated Authority a decommissioning plan and total estimate of decommissioning costs for approval in accordance with Articles 6 (3) (s) and 7 (3) (c) of this Annex, which shall be updated in accordance with the Development Plan and the applicable Petroleum Mining Code.

3. The Designated Authority and the Greater Sunrise Contractor shall enter into an agreement on the holding of decommissioning cost reserves to meet the costs of fulfilling decommissioning obligations. This agreement shall be incorporated into the Greater Sunrise Production Sharing Contract. Any reserves remaining after decommissioning shall be divided between the Parties in the same ratio as their upstream revenue share pursuant to Article 2 of this Annex.

4. Following Commercial Depletion of the Greater Sunrise Fields, the Parties shall consult with a view to reaching agreement on arrangements as necessary with regard to access and monitoring of any remaining structures, including partially remaining structures, for the purposes of environmental protection and compliance with either Party's domestic laws or regulations.

Article 22: Special Regime Installations

1. The Greater Sunrise Contractor shall inform the Designated Authority of the exact position of every Special Regime Installation.

2. For the purposes of exploiting the Greater Sunrise Fields and subject to Articles 17 and 18 of this Annex and to the requirements of safety, neither Government shall hinder the free movement of personnel and materials between Special Regime Installations and landing facilities on those structures shall be freely available to vessels and aircraft of Australia and Timor-Leste.

Article 23: Duration of the Greater Sunrise Special Regime

1. The Greater Sunrise Special Regime shall cease to be in force following the Commercial Depletion of the Greater Sunrise Fields.

2. The Parties shall confirm their common understanding that the Greater Sunrise Fields have been commercially depleted and that the Greater Sunrise Special Regime has ceased to be in force by an exchange of notes through diplomatic channels.

ANNEX C: Special Regime Area

1. The Special Regime Area consists of the area of the continental shelf contained within the rhumb lines connecting the following points:

Point	Latitude	Longitude
GS-1	09° 49' 54.88"S	127° 55' 04.35"E
GS-2	09° 49' 54.88"S	128° 20' 04.34"E
GS-3	09° 39' 54.88"S	128° 20' 04.34"E
GS-4	09° 39' 54.88"S	128° 25' 04.34"E
GS-5	09° 29' 54.88"S	128° 25' 04.34"E
GS-6	09° 29' 54.88"S	128° 20' 04.34"E
GS-7	09° 24' 54.88"S	128° 20' 04.34"E
GS-8	09° 24' 54.88"S	128° 00' 04.34"E
GS-9	09° 29' 54.88"S	127° 53' 24.35"E
GS-10	09° 29' 54.88"S	127° 52' 34.35"E
GS-11	09° 34' 54.88"S	127° 52' 34.35"E
GS-12	09° 34' 54.88"S	127° 50' 04.35"E
GS-13	09° 37' 24.88"S	127° 50' 04.35"E
GS-14	09° 37' 24.89"S	127° 45' 04.35"E
GS-15	09° 44' 54.88"S	127° 45' 04.35"E
GS-16	09° 44' 54.88"S	127° 50' 04.35"E
GS-17	09° 47' 24.88"S	127° 50' 04.35"E
GS-18	09° 47' 24.88"S	127° 55' 04.35"E

2. The following is a depiction of the outline of the Special Regime Area and the Greater Sunrise Fields for illustrative purposes only: (omitted)

ANNEX D: Transitional Provisions (omitted)

ANNEX E: Arbitration (omitted)

附录9 澳大利亚缔结和加入的国际海洋法条约

（一）联合国海洋法公约及其相关条约

序号	条约名称	签署日期 （年/月/日）	批准日期 （年/月/日）
1	《大陆架公约》 Convention on the Continental Shelf	1958/10/30	1963/5/14
2	《领海及毗连区公约》 Convention on the Territorial Sea and the Contiguous Zone	1958/10/30	1963/5/14
3	《公海公约》 Convention on the High Seas	1958/10/30	1963/5/14
4	《捕鱼及养护公海生物资源公约》 Convention on Fishing and Conservation of the Living Resources of the High Seas	1958/10/30	1963/5/14
5	《关于强制解决争端之任择议定书》 Optional Protocol of Signature concerning the Compulsory Settlement of Disputes		1963/5/14
6	《联合国海洋法公约》 United Nations Convention on the Law of the Sea	1982/12/10	1994/10/5
7	《关于执行1982年12月10日〈联合国海洋法公约〉第十一部分的协定》 Agreement relating to the implementation of Part XI of the United Nations Convention on the Law of the Sea of 10 December 1982	1994/7/29	1994/10/5
8	《执行1982年12月10日〈联合国海洋法公约〉有关养护和管理跨界鱼类种群和高度洄游鱼类种群的规定的协定》 Agreement for the Implementation of the Provisions of the United Nations Convention on the Law of the Sea of 10 December 1982 relating to the Conservation and Management of Straddling Fish Stocks and Highly Migratory Fish Stocks	1995/12/4	1999/12/23
9	《国际海洋法法庭特权与豁免协定》 Agreement on the Privileges and Immunities of the International Tribunal for the Law of the Sea	1999/5/26	2001/5/11

（二）南极条约体系下相关公约

序号	条约名称	签署/批准/加入/接收日期（年/月/日）	对澳大利亚生效日期（年/月/日）
1	《南极条约》 Antarctic Treaty	1959/12/1	1961/6/23
2	《南极海豹保护公约》 Convention for the Conservation of Antarctic Seals	1972/10/5	1987/7/31
3	《南极海洋生物资源养护公约》 Convention on the Conservation of Antarctic Marine Living Resources	1980/9/11	1982/4/7
4	《关于环境保护的南极条约议定书》 Protocol on Environmental Protection to the Antarctic Treaty	1991/10/4	1998/4/14

（三）国际海事组织框架下的相关条约

类别	条约名称	签署/批准/加入/接收日期（年/月/日）	对澳大利亚生效日期（年/月/日）
	1948年《国际海事组织公约》 Convention on the Intergovernmental Maritime Consultative Organization	1948/3/6	1958/3/17
与海上航行安全有关的条约	1976年《国际海事卫星组织公约》 Convention on the International Maritime Satellite Organization	1979/3/10	1979/7/16
	1972《国际海上避碰规则公约》 Convention on the International Regulations for Preventing Collisions at Sea	1980/2/28	1980/2/29
	1972年《国际集装箱安全公约》 International Convention for Safe Containers	1980/2/22	1981/2/22
	1974年《国际海上人命安全公约》 International Convention for the Safety of Life at Sea	1983/8/17	1983/11/17
	1979年《国际海上搜寻和救助公约》 International Convention on Maritime Search and Rescue	1983/11/7	1985/6/22

附录9 澳大利亚缔结和加入的国际海洋法条约

续表

类别	条约名称	签署/批准/加入/接收日期（年/月/日）	对澳大利亚生效日期（年/月/日）
与海上航行安全有关的条约	1988年《制止危及海上航行安全非法行为公约》 Convention for the Suppression of Unlawful Acts against the Safety of Maritime Navigation	1993/2/19	1993/5/20
	1988年《制止危及大陆架固定平台安全非法行为议定书》 Protocol for the Suppression of Unlawful Acts against the Safety of Fixed Platforms Located on the Continental Shelf	1993/2/19	1993/5/20
	1988年《国际搜救卫星COSPAS-SARSAT系统计划协定》 The International COSPAS-SARSAT Programme Agreement		1991/6/22
	1989年《国际救助公约》 International Convention on Salvage	1997/1/8	1998/1/8
与防治海洋污染有关的条约	1969年《国际干预公海油污事故公约》 International Convention Relating to Intervention on the High Seas in Cases of Oil Pollution Casualties	1983/11/7	1984/2/5
	1972年《防止倾倒废物及其他物质污染海洋的公约》 Convention on The Prevention Of Marine Pollution By Dumping Of Wastes And Other Matter	1985/8/21	1985/9/20
	《关于1973年国际防止船舶造成污染公约的1978年的议定书》 International Convention for the Prevention of Pollution from Ships, 1973 as modified by the Protocol of 1978 relating thereto	1987/10/14	1988/7/1
	《经1978年议定书修订的〈1973年国际防止船舶造成污染公约〉的1997年议定书》 Protocol of 1997 to amend the International Convention for the Prevention of Pollution from Ships, 1973, as modified by the Protocol of 1978 relating thereto	2007/8/10	2007/11/10
	1990年《国际油污防备、反应和合作公约》 International Convention on Oil Pollution Preparedness, Response and Co-operation	1992/7/6	1995/5/13

续表

类别	条约名称	签署/批准/加入/接收日期（年/月/日）	对澳大利亚生效日期（年/月/日）
与防治海洋污染有关的条约	2000年《有毒有害物质污染事故防备、反应与合作议定书》 Protocol on Preparedness, Response And Co-operation To Pollution Incidents By Hazardous And Noxious Substances	2005/3/16	2007/6/14
	2001年《控制船舶有害防污底系统国际公约》 International Convention on the Control of Harmful Anti-fouling Systems on Ships	2007/1/9	2008/9/17
	2001年《国际燃油污染损害民事责任公约》 International Convention on Civil Liability for Bunker Oil Pollution Damage	2009/3/16	2009/6/16
与船舶及船员管理有关的条约	1966年《国际船舶载重线公约》 International Convention on Load Lines	1968/7/29	1968/10/29
	1969年《国际船舶吨位丈量公约》 International Convention on Tonnage Measurement of Ships	1982/5/21	1982/8/21
	1978年《海员培训、发证和值班标准国际公约》 International Convention on Standards of Training, Certification and Watchkeeping for Seafarers, 1978	1983/11/7	1984/4/28
	1965年《便利国际海上运输公约》 Convention on Facilitation of International Maritime Traffic	1986/4/28	1986/6/27
	2004年《国际船舶压载水和沉积物控制与管理公约》 International Convention For The Control And Management Of Ships' Ballast Water And Sediments	2005/5/27	2017/9/8